Thoughts Without Cigarettes

. . .

Thoughts Without Cigarettes

A MEMOIR

. . .

OSCAR HIJUELOS

GOTHAM BOOKS

GOTHAM BOOKS
Published by Penguin Group (USA) Inc.
375 Hudson Street, New York, New York 10014, U.S.A.
Penguin Group (Canada), 90 Eglinton Avenue East, Suite 700, Toronto,
Ontario M4P 2Y3, Canada (a division of Pearson Penguin Canada Inc.);
Penguin Books Ltd, 80 Strand, London WC2R 0RL,
England; Penguin Ireland, 25 St Stephen's Green, Dublin 2,
Ireland (a division of Penguin Books Ltd);
Penguin Group (Australia), 250 Camberwell Road, Camberwell,
Victoria 3124, Australia (a division of Pearson Australia Group Pty Ltd);
Penguin Books India Pvt Ltd, 11 Community Centre,
Panchsheel Park, New Delhi—110 017, India;
Penguin Group (NZ), 67 Apollo Drive, Rosedale, Auckland 0632,
New Zealand (a division of Pearson New Zealand Ltd);
Penguin Books (South Africa) (Pty) Ltd, 24 Sturdee Avenue,
Rosebank, Johannesburg 2196, South Africa

Penguin Books Ltd, Registered Offices: 80 Strand, London WC2R 0RL, England

Published by Gotham Books, a member of Penguin Group (USA) Inc.

First printing, June 2011
1 3 5 7 9 10 8 6 4 2

Copyright © 2011 by Cuban Ink, Inc.
All rights reserved

Gotham Books and the skyscraper logo are trademarks of Penguin Group (USA) Inc.

LIBRARY OF CONGRESS CATALOGING-IN-PUBLICATION DATA
has been applied for.

ISBN 978-1-592-40629-6

Photos throughout courtesy of the author.

Poem by Magdalena Torrens Hijuelos in the Introduction by Oscar Hijuelos (pp xix-xx), from
Burnt Sugar: Contemporary Cuban Poetry in English and Spanish, edited by Lori Marie Carlson
and Oscar Hijuelos and translated by Lori Marie Carlson. Introduction, Copyright 2006 by
Oscar Hijuelos. Reprinted with permission of Free Press, a Division of Simon and Schuster.

Printed in the United States of America
Set in Granjon • *Designed by Elke Sigal*

While the author has made every effort to provide accurate telephone numbers and Internet
addresses at the time of publication, neither the publisher nor the author assumes any
responsibility for errors, or for changes that occur after publication. Further, the publisher does
not have any control over and does not assume any responsibility for author or third-party Web
sites or their content.

This is a memoir. It reflects the author's present recollections of his experiences over
a period of years. Dialogue and events have been re-created from memory.

To my family and the folks
who have always looked out for me.

. . .

Contents

A Prelude of Sorts   *xiii*

PART ONE
The Way Some Things Worked Out

CHAPTER 1 · When I Was Still Cuban   *3*

CHAPTER 2 · A Few Notes on My Past   *53*

CHAPTER 3 · Some Moments of Freedom   *99*

CHAPTER 4 · Childhood Ends   *127*

PART TWO
What Happened Afterward

CHAPTER 5 · Getting By   *177*

CHAPTER 6 · My Two Selves   *193*

CHAPTER 7 · My Life on Madison Avenue   *235*

CHAPTER 8 · Our House in the Last World   *267*

CHAPTER 9 · Roma   *289*

CHAPTER 10 · Another Book   *323*

Acknowledgments   *369*

Thoughts Without Cigarettes

. . .

. . .

The year is 1985 and Professor John D Swsinhnder [*sic*] is getting into his rocket. 10, 9, 8, 7, 6, 5, 4, 3, 2, 1, blast off! He was drifting in space at a speed of ten thousand miles an hour. In a short time he was on the moon. He is going there to prove that the moon is made of green cheese. He picked up a rock and bit it.

He said, "If this is cheese than [*sic*] my teeth are not cracked." But they were.

In a minute not to lose he got in his rocket and went back to see his dentist. He did not prove that the moon was made of green cheese. But instead he proved never bite rock.

—from "A Trip to the Moon,"
Oscar Hijuelos, age ten

A Prelude of Sorts

. . .

Seems just like yesterday (an illusion) that I was sitting out front on my stoop on 118th Street, on an autumn day, in 1963 or so, feeling rather indignantly disposed and pissed off because my best friend from across the way, with a somewhat smug look in his eyes, kept blowing smoke into my face. He was thirteen, a year older than me, and had already been going through at least a carton of Winstons a week for as long as I could remember—cigarettes that his mother, the venerable Mrs. Muller-Thym, coming back from the A&P, gave, fair-mindedly, to each of her sons on Fridays. (Think he must have started smoking at the age of seven or eight.) We usually got along like pals, running through the backyards and basements together, or else hanging out in the book-laden clutter of his room, playing cards and chess or listening to jazz recordings by Art Blakey and Ahmed Jamal, while occasionally sneaking rum and whiskey from his father's stash of high-class booze down the hall, which we'd mix into glasses of Coca-Cola, without ice, and drink until the world went spinning and everything became beautiful in an exciting way. The guy was definitely head and shoulders smarter than just about anyone else in that neighborhood, including me, and generous to boot, for he was always giving away his cigarettes and candy and loose change on the street. But on that particular afternoon, he had gotten some kind of hair up his ass. With a smirk on his face, and walking right up to me, he had blown, slowly and with great self-satisfied deliberation, rings of that smoke at my mug. I don't know why he did this—perhaps because he, like so many of the other kids on that street, sometimes thought me passively disposed on account of the fact that my mother, never forgetting my childhood illness, had always kept a tight leash on me. Or because he just felt naughtily inclined or wanted to express some notion of superiority that day. But whatever he may have been thinking in those moments, I discovered that I had a fairly short fuse. So when I told him, "Come on, man, don't do that!" in the manner that kids in those days talked, and maybe, "But hey, I'm not messing with ya," and he kept blowing that smoke at me anyway, I yanked the cigarette out of his hand and put it out on his head.

Thankfully, its burning tip met with the thick matting of his slickened dark hair, but I can still remember the crisp sound it made, like air being quickly released from a bicycle tire, and, of course, that strangely repellent smell of singed organic matter, which foreshadowed, to my young Catholic mind, the possible punishments of hell. Perhaps I ended up chasing him around the block, but he was always too fast for me, or perhaps, I can't exactly remember, he ran down into a basement or the park, hiding out somewhere in the bushes along one of the terraced walkways that descended from Morningside Drive into East Harlem, on tracks of cracked, glass-strewn pavement. If so, he might have waited until sometime near dark, while I, out of sorts and craving a cigarette of my own, went home to yet another one of those evenings in our Cuban household that tended to leave me feeling restless and confused.

PART ONE

. . .

The Way Some Things Worked Out

CHAPTER 1

. . .

When I Was Still Cuban

Pretend it's sometime in 1955 or 1956 and that you are hanging over the roof's edge of my building, as I often did as a teenager, looking down at the street some six stories below. You would have seen, on certain mornings, my mother, Magdalena, formerly of Holguín, Cuba, and now a resident of the "United Stays," pacing back and forth fitfully before our stoop, waiting for a car. She would have been eye-catching, even lovely, with her striking dark features and pretty face, her expression, however, somewhat gaunt. Muttering to herself, she would have had the jitters, not only from her inherently high-strung nature but also because she'd probably spent the night sitting up with my pop worrying about their youngest son—me.

As green and white transit buses came forlornly chugging up the hill along Amsterdam from 125th Street, she would have stood there, perhaps with my older brother, José, by her side, watching the avenue for a car to turn onto the street, all the while dreading what the day might hold for her. Sometimes it would have rained or it would have been brutally cold. Sometimes it would be sunny, or snow would be falling so daintily everywhere around her. She might call out to a

· 3 ·

friend to come down from one of the buildings nearby, say my god-mother, Carmen, *mi madrina*, a red-haired *cubana*, with her flamenco dancer's face and intense dark eyes. Coming down in a bathrobe and slippers to reassure her, she'd tell my mother not to worry so much, it wasn't good for her after all—the kid would be fine. "*Ojalá*," my mother, her stomach in knots, would answer, though always shaking her head.

A car would finally pull over to the curb. The driver, a friend of my father's, or someone he had paid, would take her either to 125th Street and Lenox Avenue, where she might catch a train, or directly up to Greenwich, Connecticut, where I, her five-year-old son, lay languishing in a hospital. Through the Bronx and over to the highway north to Connecticut they would go and, coming to that placid town, the kind of place she'd never have visited otherwise, enter a different world. In the spring, she'd ride along the loveliest of shadow-dappled streets, the sunlight shimmering through the leafy boughs of elm and oak trees overhead, as if they were passing through a corridor like one of the roads out of Havana; and in the winter, snow, in plump drifts and brilliant, would have been everywhere, so Christmas-y and postcard-pretty. After following her directions, which she would have recited carefully to the driver from a piece of paper—torn out of a composition notebook page or from a brown grocery bag—they would have found the hospital along King Street, off in its own meadow and reached by a winding flagstone driveway, the Byram Woods looming as a lovely view just nearby.

Each time she'd have to bring someone along to help her out with the nurses and staff. My mother had to. For what English she knew, even after some thirteen years in this country, consisted of only a few phrases and words, and even those were pronounced with her strong Cuban accent and the trepidations of a woman who, until then, had rarely ventured out from the insular immigrant's bubble of our household. It's possible that one of the Zabalas sisters, three schoolteacherly *cubanas* living over on 111th Street, who all spoke good English, accompanied her. Or perhaps my brother or my godfather, Horacio, a bank teller, went along. Still, even with that help, just to navigate the hospital's bureaucracy must have been a misery for her—and not only because she had to depend on someone to translate her exchanges with the ward personnel but because of her fears about what she might be told. In those days, the disease I suffered from, nephritis, or *nee-free-tees*, as she'd pronounce it, which is now easily treatable with a broad spectrum of drugs, was then often fatal to children. That thought alone must have kept her awake on many nights, and particularly so during the first six months of my stay, when, as a safeguard against my catching other infections, I wasn't allowed to see anyone at all.

As an aside, I will tell you that for years I didn't even know the hospital's name: A kind of chronic disinformation has always been a part of my family's life, and if I have only recently learned that institution's name, it's because, in tandem with this writing, I happened to mention to my brother how strange it was that, for all the times I had asked my mother about just where I had stayed, she never seemed able to come up with a name except to say, "*fue allá en* Connecticut." He knew it, however, and it makes sense that this riddle, which would plague me for decades, would have a far less mysterious solution than I could have ever imagined: for that place turned out to be called, quite simply, the St. Luke's Convalescent Hospital.

A cousin, circa 1928, of its New York City namesake, where I had been taken first, the St. Luke's Convalescent Hospital consisted of a red-brick three-story structure with a white portico entranceway, and two adjacent, somewhat lower wings at either side. In the quaintness of its architecture, it suggested, from a distance, perhaps a plantation manor house. (This I know less from memory than from a postcard I recently saw of the place.) Somewhere inside the ward in which I stayed, with its locked doors and high windows, its smells of both medicine and Lysol, and its hums of pumping dialysis machines that gave off breathing sounds from down the hall, one found the visitors' room, whose main feature was a glass partition that had a speaking grille. A nurse would bring me in from the ward, where a dozen other beds both emptied and filled with children monthly, and there behind that visitors' room partition, eyes blinking, I would sit,

6 · *Thoughts Without Cigarettes*

while my mother, the nice-looking lady on the other side, no doubt tried to make friendly conversation with the five-year-old boy, her son, the delicate-looking little blond with the bloated limbs, who, as the months passed, seemed to remember her less and less.

Of course, she was my mother, I knew that—she kept telling me so—"*Soy tu mamá!*" But she also seemed a stranger, and all the more so whenever she started to speak Spanish, a language which, as time went by, sounded both familiar and oddly strange to me. I surely understood what she was saying (I always would); her words seemed to have something to do with our apartment on West 118th Street, *con tu papá y tu hermano*, and, yes, Cuba, that beautiful wonderland, so far away, of love and magic, which I had visited not so long before. Facing me, she'd raise the pitch of her voice, arch her eyebrows as if I would hear her better. She'd wipe a smear of lipstick onto a Kleenex from her black purse, muttering under her breath. I remember nodding at her words; I remember understanding my mother when she said, "*Mira aquí!*" ("Look what I have!") as she reached into her bag for a little ten-cent toy; and "*Sabes que eres mi hijo?*" ("Do you know that you're my son?") and things like "*Pero, por qué estás tan callado?*" ("Why are you so quiet?") and "*Y que té pasa?*" ("What's wrong with you?")

What happened to be wrong with me came down to the fact that I never answered my mother in the language she most wanted to hear, *el español.* I just couldn't remember the words, and this must have truly perplexed her, for I've been told that, before I went into the hospital, I spoke Spanish as cheerfully and capaciously as any four-year-old Cuban boy. I certainly didn't know much English before then. Maybe I'd picked up some from the neighbors in our building or from my brother, José, who, seven years older than I, attended the local Catholic grammar school and, like any kid, hung out on the streets; but, in our household, Spanish, as far as I can remember, was the rule.

On the weekends, before my life had changed, whenever our apartment filled with visitors, and my father's friends from all over the city came by to visit, it was Spanish they spoke. Oh, some like my sharp cousin Jimmy Halley, formerly of Holguín, Cuba, and a building manager in Queens, and *mi padrino*, Horacio, who worked for a Chase branch in Chinatown, knew English, as did my father from his job as a cook in the Men's Bar of the Biltmore Hotel. But I have no memories of hearing them speak it. I must have exchanged some words with our elderly, genteel across-the-hall neighbor, Mrs. Blair, or with our German superintendent, the jolly Mr. Hess, rotund and red cheeked, always sweeping with a broom in the halls. But since I spent most of my days as an infant with my mother, going just about everywhere with her—to the nearby Columbia University campus, by whose fountains we would sit, or down the hill to Morningside Drive and the circle that looked eastward over Harlem, where the other young mothers from that block sometimes gathered with their strollers and baby carriages—that language, Spanish, must have permeated me like honey, or wrapped around my soul like a blanket or, if you like, a mantilla, or, as my mother, of a poetic bent, might say, like the sunlight of a Cuban spring.

It was on Morningside Drive, incidentally, where the first pictures of me as an infant were taken: They show this thin and rather delicately featured child, with curling blond hair, in white booties and a dainty outfit, standing by a bench, a passably cute toddler, but not the sort one would have associated, at first glance, with the usual expectations of what the offspring of a Cuban couple should look like, which is to say, anything but a little towhead *americano*.

Now, if I turned out that way, it's because I owed my looks to a great-great-grandfather on my father's side who had been Irish; white as white could be, I had hazel eyes, and altogether an appearance that, given my parents' more "Spanish" looks, set me apart from them. My mother's antecedents, the Torrens y Barrancas and Olivers y Guap families, were light-skinned Catalans, and my *papi*, Pascual Hijuelos, a Gallego by ancestry, and blond as a child himself, tended toward a Spaniard's ruddiness that, in fact, was probably Celtic as well. But both of my parents had dark hair and dark eyes and were unmistakably Cuban in their manner, their speech, and, yes, in that great definer of identity, their body language and souls. My brother, José, fell somewhere in between: He was also fair skinned, his eyes were dark and intense, and his hair, of a brownish-red coloration, bespoke somewhat more Latino origins, though, while growing up and as a ringer in his late teens for that old-time actor John Garfield, he too would hear that he didn't particularly look or seem Cuban, at least not until he had occasion to speak Spanish. And while I've long since discovered that a few of my relatives attracted the same mistaken notion from strangers—"Are ya really Cuban?"—but were hardly bothered by it, *for they knew just who they were,* I'd find out that vaguely consoling fact years later, after it no longer seemed to matter and the damage to my ego had already been done.

In the hospital, my mother would sit back, across from me, muttering something to herself—no one being around to help her. Maybe in her moments alone, waiting, she prayed—a little black rosary inside her purse—though I bet that just as often as she asked God for guidance or gave thanks, she chastised him for doing such a lousy job. And why wouldn't she? Somewhere along the line, during this long period of separation from my family, when that partition between my mother and me became the story of our lives, I had absorbed English from the nurses, doctors, and children of my acquaintance with some kind of desperate ease. English in, Spanish out, or at least deeply submerged inside me—from my childhood onward, I have had long complicated dreams in which only Spanish is spoken.

· · ·

The kicker was that I'd gotten sick in Cuba, on a trip born, in part, of my mother's homesickness. Since coming to New York in 1943 as my father Pascual's young bride from Holguín, she'd returned only once, with my brother some six years before, in 1949 or so, and I suppose that, aside from missing her family, she wanted to show me, her second son, off to them. But it's also possible that by then, my mother and father needed a break from each other, for at that point, their marriage was already going through its share of tensions having to do with some lingering animosities between them that went back to an earlier time. (You must now see my father as he surely had been in the 1940s: a jaunty lady-killer, about six foot one, with a former *campesino*'s wide-eyed wonderment over life in the city, a smoothness in his manner, his wavy dark hair brilliant with lotion, and his face redolent of both cologne and cocky self-confidence, all of which amounted to a formula: Pascual + nightlife = my mother's loneliness and befuddlement.)

My father had originally come up to join two of his sisters who had left Cuba for New York in the early 1940s. My aunt Borja, five years younger than my father and married to a fellow named Eduardo Basulto, worked as a bilingual travel agent for Pan American airlines. She had studied English in either Holguín or Havana and had started with the airline just after they initiated their popular Cuba-bound routes from New York in 1939. I think she'd been transferred to New York as the result of a promotion, and what her husband did, I do not know—I've heard that he was a businessman, in what line of *negocios* I can't say—but it was his signature and name, Basulto, that adorned the lease to the first-floor apartment in which my brother and I would be raised. Now, how and why Eduardo Basulto ended up settling on a first-floor tenement flat in such a nondescript university neighborhood, way uptown from the bustle, where mostly working-class Irish and college folks lived, I can't say. Perhaps he'd gotten tipped off by a Cuban who lived around there, or perhaps, while looking through the want ads in a Spanish-language newspaper, like *El Diario*, had come upon a listing for a cheap apartment in a "quiet enclave" near a park and just a five-minute walk from the subway station on Broadway. Situated at 419 West 118th Street, in a building that had gone up around 1900, that apartment was a far cry from a typical *solar* in Cuba. Of a "railroad" configuration, it consisted of a living room that faced the street; an adjoining bedroom with French doors, the room's window opening to a darkish courtyard; a narrow kitchen, which with its leaking pipes had already seen better days; and a long dimly lit hallway that led to a bathroom and two smaller rooms in the back. Neither fancy nor completely crumbling (yet) and situated directly above a basement with rumbling boilers and noisome plumbing, as a more or less temporary place to live, it would do. Slowly my aunt and her husband filled it with furnishings. Some bric-a-brac and photographs from Cuba soon adorned the walls, and blue linoleum had been put in by the management company to cover the floors. Outside in the entryway foyer, the name *Basulto* in discreet lettering was printed on a slot over the mailbox and bell for apartment number 2, alongside such others as Blair and Walker and Hall.

Once they had settled in, my father's oldest sister, Maya, and her dapper husband, Pedro Tellería, joined them. It must have seemed a logical and familial thing for them to do; Pedro made his living as a musician, playing the double bass with one of Xavier Cugat's orchestras, and as it happened, during that early heyday of big-band Cuban music, often performed in some of the more fancy venues in the city. As for Maya, she too went to work, in Macy's as a salesclerk, and along the way, missing my father, with whom she was close, began to write him regularly, her letters encouraging him to come north for a visit—*de visita*—a notion that he, under his sister's sway (my mother would always say that she "dominated" him) took to heart.

By then, my father, raised on farms near Jiguaní in eastern Cuba, and a *campesino* to his bones, had begun his courtship of my mother in earnest; he'd met her in 1939, when she was working as a ticket girl in a movie house in Holguín. Perhaps he'd gone there to look for women or to take in a movie or two, though Jiguaní, a largish town in its own right, must have surely had its share of cinemas. Whatever the circumstances, an afternoon arrived when he found himself waiting in a line by the ticket seller's window of the Neptuno movie theater along one of the main drags of that city. Behind a glass or wire-meshed booth sat my mother, then twenty-six years of age and in her prime—with a good figure and of a fair height, about five foot five in low-heeled shoes, her hair dark, curled, and falling to her shoulders, her face so intelligent, whimsical, and filled with life, her lips pursed in a smile.

She must have given him a mirthful up-and-down—because he was already some kind of man, exuding a perfume-drenched sweat and virility that she would one day describe to me, laughing, as *"muy muy fuerte"* ("Oh so very powerful"). She must have liked something about him, perhaps the hopefulness that she saw in his eyes. Doubtless he was cordial and gentlemanly around her, didn't drink or smoke, though he would have shown the hard edges of a fellow brought up on a farm. Since she always took in the movies after her shift ended, she probably joined him inside the theater, and as he slipped in a few words during those stretches when that interior, filled with cigarette smoke and the cries of infants, grew cacophonous with conversation, he probably tried to talk her into going out somewhere, to a dance hall or for a stroll in one of Holguín's small parks or to dally in a café. Eventually there came the moment when she first heard him say his name: "*Soy* José-Pascual Hijuelos de Jiguaní," and she told him her own, "Magdalena de la Luz."

Possibly, as she sat across from him during a meal in one of the town's *placitas*, she noticed the way he chewed his food loudly, smacking his lips; and while this may have offended her always snooty sensibilities, for she had come from a good family that had fallen on hard times, there would have been something so engaging about his smile and the way he looked at her, as if she were the only one in the world, that she would have forgiven that crudeness. Somewhere along the line, after they'd been seeing each other for a while, they would have started fooling around in some manner and laughed at the stars the way young people, feeling immortal, do while strolling through the night, the velvet sky hanging over them. They would have made a hell of an impression in the local dance halls, and the more they saw each other, the more she would have felt confused by her growing feelings for this plainspoken fellow from Jiguaní. At the time, there was someone else hovering about the periphery of her life, a well-off lawyer who'd been after her lately. But perhaps he was dull as a button, a very proper sort, a gentleman, ever so obedient and respectful around women, the sort to insist upon a chaperone—in other words, a bore—while she, a live wire in those days, wanted someone a little more exciting even if he might be a little blunt in his manner, but not overly so, like the tall *campesino* who'd smelled of both the farm and cologne, and seemed, from the way he stared at her, to know something about women.

After a while, they began spending time in each other's family homes, so they might find out what they were getting into. Now, while my father grew up mainly in the countryside of Oriente province, with a bloodline going back to who knows when in Cuba—the 1820s, if not earlier, I've heard—my mother came from a family whose beginnings in Cuba were of far more recent vintage, the early 1890s. That's when my maternal grandfather, one Gerónimo Torrens, from whom I derived my middle name (yes, Jerome), first arrived in eastern Cuba from Barcelona as an officer with the Spanish army. In those contentious times—the Cubans had been struggling to gain independence from Spain on and off since the first wars of the 1830s—my grandfather oversaw the collecting of road and bridge tariffs from the local Cuban populace in and around the districts of Holguín. Though a photograph of him, taken in his later middle age, circa 1920 or so, conveys the image of a bald and prosperous, somewhat portly gentleman with a quite serious no-nonsense countenance, he had carried out his duties as a young officer rather casually, often looking the other way when it came to the Cubans, whose affable manner and patriotic fervor had won his sympathies. (My mother would always talk about the way he, a Catalan and therefore a separatist by inclination, never charged the Cubans for their passage through his toll roads and how he was well liked because of it.) He was certainly taken by the forested beauty of the region and by the friendly nature of its people, for by the time the Cuban republic finally came into being in 1902, he, like so many other Spaniards before him, decided to put down roots there.

From a prosperous family in Barcelona, owners of one of the most successful shoe factories in Cataluña, he established a thriving shoe business of his own in Holguín. Along the way, he brought my maternal grandmother, María, over from Mallorca to join him. Whether they had married in Spain or tied the bonds in Holguín, I can't say, but as an immigrant vested in that young nation's future, Gerónimo, a Cuban by choice, brought into the world three *holguinera* daughters—María (1910), Magdalena (1913), and Margarita, or Cheo (1915), whom he, prospering from a postwar boom, raised in a fine house by a park not far from Holguín's highest hill, Loma de la Cruz.

Which is to say that my mother, the same lady I'd sometimes see quietly muttering heaven knows what to herself as she went about washing the dishes, had grown up in the genteel and fairly comfortable existence of the Cuban upper middle class, with servants, cooks, and laundresses helping to run the household. They were well-off enough that she had journeyed as a young girl with her family to Spain, spending some months shuttling between Barcelona and Majorca, where on nearly every evening, they went to an opera or a ballet or a *zarzuela*; and when she and her family weren't out enjoying that cultured life, my mother spent time with her *abuelos*, whom she, with wonderment in her eyes, always remembered as kindly and refined—"*gente refinada*," as she'd put it—their life, as she had experienced it, but a glimpse of a world she would never see again. What she must have dreamed about on those transatlantic voyages to and from Spain as she'd stand by the railings of one of those ships, looking over the pitching grayness of the ocean, I can't say. But as an elegant little girl in a sunbonnet and prim blue dress, with a slightly petulant look on her face, she had an imagination that would have populated those bell-waves with sirens and mermaids—no wonder, then, that she'd speak in later years of once having sailed across the Atlantic during the times of Columbus, via the enchantments of past reincarnations.

But it was not as if she returned home to a house that was lacking in the arts. My *abuelo*, a member of the Masonic Society, who sang opera and wrote poetry that he'd publish in Spain and in local Cuban newspapers, did everything he could to re-create the same kind of salon society in his home. Inviting many local artists into his house for weekly gatherings, he, without an iota of the *campesino* in him and a most formal man, became locally famous for such cultural fetes, which my mother, as a girl, had been encouraged to perform in. Though she never elaborated on just how those afternoons unfolded, beyond saying that their visitors sang, acted, played instruments, and recited famous poems and speeches, she'd come away from that time with an aristocratic and somewhat artistic air, even a haughtiness that would develop all the more as she grew older—and, in fact, poorer, for in the midst of those glories came her family's decline, thanks to her father's ambitions and, perhaps, his overly patriotic soul.

He'd been a moderately wealthy and rather levelheaded business-man who in a moment of lapsed judgment placed both his trust and financial resources in the hands of one Gerardo Machado, a Liberal Party candidate for the presidency of Cuba, into whose coffers my grandfather's money, by way of a large loan, had flowed. He must have been elated over Machado's victory in 1925 and proud of the services he had rendered to his adopted country, until, having gotten into debt, he found it necessary to journey to Havana to address Machado about the urgently pressing matter of repayment, a notion to which Machado, in the tradition of a good man changed to the bad by power—as president he was to be known in Cuba as a "second Nero"—did not warm. Traveling frequently to Havana, my grandfather always came back to Holguín empty-handed, and his grief over that betrayal, as well as the financial ruin that accompanied it, accounted, in my mother's opinion—*"Ay pero, hijo, fue algo muy triste"*—for the stroke that took his life one evening. He was taking a shower and singing the bolero "Dónde Estás Corazón," when in mid-verse his voice, a fine baritone, simply stopped. My mother, opal eyed and lovely, had just turned fourteen.

Appropriately, his funeral was grand, a procession replete with a horse-drawn hearse, gloomy priests, men in dark tri-cornered hats beating drums solemnly, and hundreds of prayerful mourners winding from the street outside their house, where his body had lain in state overnight, to the church and then the *campo santo*. Lingering by his grave that day, my mother surely had her regrets, for, with the onset of adolescence, she had apparently become fond of tormenting him and, for that matter, quite a number of people with her untoward behaviors.

At school, despite winning prizes for writing essays and poetry and for singing the Cuban anthem, "La Bayamesa," better than anyone else, she often got in trouble with her teachers for a generally insolent attitude. She had been the plague of a hapless local haberdasher whose female manikins, in the fine array of their 1920s flapper dresses, displayed in a row outside his arcade shop, my mother regularly knocked over at dusk just because she felt like it (this, in the dreams of her later life, she'd always remember as if it had just happened, with fondness and in detail, down to the mole just below the shopkeeper's quivering, mustachioed lips.) She loved to repeat aloud to anyone who'd listen the randy verses she'd overhear on the streets; and when it rained, the sky bursting open, no matter the time of night, she couldn't help but run outside and spin in circles in the torrential downpours, ruining her clothes and getting drenched to the bone. Why she did so she never knew. She'd consort with local *brujas*—or witches—whose homes she treated like second schools, made friends with the lowliest children from the streets, and expressed, fitfully, a longing to hang around the local dance halls. Unlike her sisters, she had gotten some *cucarachas* in her head, and her *papá*, a strict Spaniard at heart, responded as he only could. Her mother, María, never laid a hand on her, but her father did, over and over again— "*Me pegaba, mucho, mucho,*" she'd later tell me—often with a strap or a belt, and most violently so during periods of his greatest distress.

But no matter how much he beat her, it only provoked her further. Though she loved her *papi* more than any man in the world, she, sticking her tongue out at him, often spoke to her father in a manner that no daughter ever should. Even after he'd fallen on hard times, and there came the point when he no longer had the spirit or will to punish her, she still couldn't help herself. My mother, a creature of habit, had become so accustomed to his beatings that when they stopped, her world turned upside down, and, seeing him brought so low, she'd practically beg her *papi* to beat her again, as if that would somehow bring back the better days of old.

Probably neighbors or some of her *papá*'s former employees helped them to vacate their fine house for a more humble dwelling, but that move, by horse-drawn carts, or *camión*, with most of their furnishings having been sold off, must have been a disheartening and frightening experience for them, if not a pure misery. Far from Spain, with no other family in Cuba to call upon for reassurance, they surely must have felt so alone—and scattered; no wonder her nerves took a turn for the worse. I don't know what skills *Abuela* María had, if any, or how she might have supported her young daughters, though I believe she may have become a seamstress. I do know that she was a woman of great piety, *"una santa,"* of a sweet and quiet disposition, and the sort who, never hurting a soul, didn't know quite what to do with her spirited daughter. Spicing up any gathering with her vivacious manner, my mother seems to have become in her own way something of a minor celebrity in the dance halls of Holguín, where, she'd one day tell me, she became known as a "queen of the rumba."

At carnival time, as throngs of partiers and musicians snaked through the streets, a battery of drummers beating out "La Chambe-lona" on their congas, she especially shined as a dancer, and among her nicknames, there was one, having to do with the movies, that apparently came about because of her high cheekbones and nearly luminescent eyes: the "Katie Hepburn" of Holguín. (While there are a few similarities between them, I have seen her in an early photograph, in which she, with a pageboy hairdo, slightly plumpish face, and a question-mark curl licking her ear, more easily resembled a silent film vamp like Theda Bara or Clara Bow, stars of her teenage years.) By the 1930s, as a pretty, light-skinned *cubanita* of a fierce intelligence and vivacious temperament, exuding an aristocratic air but also seem-ing accessible—*"Yo gozaba!"*—"I had my fun!"—she had no problem attracting the attentions of men, among them that boring but sturdy lawyer whom she'd turn away and of course, my father.

And my pop? Altogether, it's hard to imagine that he, born in 1915 into a long-established farming family, experienced anything like loneliness while growing up in a house with so many siblings around: the two eldest, María Teresa (or Maya, as she was called when I knew her) and my father's *hermano major*, Oscar, born in Jiguaní in 1903 and 1905 respectively, were followed in the next decade by Concepcion, Manuela, Isabel Regina, Graciela Antonia (or Chelo), Borja Angeles, and, in 1920, Olga del Carmen. (Cari-dad Luisa, the least fortunate of that family of otherwise long-lived females, who would have brought the number of Hijuelos-Gallego sisters to eight, was born in 1910 and died in 1912, probably of a fever.) Include my grandmother and grandfather, Regina Gallego and Leocadio Hijuelos; a retinue of household help (Negritos mainly, with shacks on a property consisting of hundreds of hectares of fruit, timber, and tobacco land); as well as countless relatives, both young and old, living nearby and often visiting their household (the Hijuelos-Gallego family tree, based in and around Jiguaní, included the surnames O'Connor, Diéguez, Peréz, Fonseca, García, Cabrera, and Lozano, among others)—he must have been constantly in the company of *someone*, with little privacy, if any. (However, remembering how he sometimes lived to be around people, I can't imagine his ever having wanted to be left alone.)

Ten years his senior and known as a great horseman, my *tio* Oscar ran the farms alongside my *abuelo* Leocadio, most of his days spent on a chestnut mare, keeping after their workers. (I've been told there were three properties. They sold timber, with pine, ebony, mahogany, and oak woods growing there in abundance.) As the older brother, he would have taught my father to ride at an early age and surely have helped him through the rituals of manhood, taking him to cockfights, perhaps to a bordello, and who knows where else; for the longest time, they were inseparable, going everywhere together and making quite an impression on the people of Jiguaní, who'd remember the older brother for his steely (macho) air of authority and the other for his friendliness. It's likely that, given the difference in their years, Oscar had loved his younger brother as deeply as he might a son. (Not so long ago, I met a black *cubano* in his late eighties, a retired New York City schoolteacher, who, remembering them from his teenage years in Jiguani, told me that they were always riding through town side by side on their horses, and that in their height—each was over six feet tall and broad shouldered—they made quite an impression as men to be reckoned with, but affably so: "They were good to one another, above all," this schoolteacher had told me.)

Physically, they were practically twins. Each possessed a longish face; broad ridged forehead; large, slightly hooked nose; and protuberant, fleshy ears. Quite fair in complexion, even ruddy, they had wavy dark hair, deeply set dark eyes, and sad expressions of a distinctly Arabic or Semitic cast. It's likely that some distant Jewish blood flowed through their *campesino* veins. Just the same, close as they may have been, while Oscar, as a patriarch in waiting, looked after the family's livelihood, my father spent his time hanging around the arcades and street corners of town, doffing his hat at female passersby or else consorting with friends, with whom, on the weekends, he frequented the dance halls. Over this his older brother must have frowned. But there was something else as well. Leaving the farmwork to his older brother, my father grew quite attached to his sisters, particularly the eldest, Maya.

. . .

One day, Magdalena brought her new suitor home, to their small flat along la calle Miró, and from the start, Pascual made a good impression on her family. My aunt Cheo, her younger sister, would remember my father from those days as "a quiet fellow" with a certain humble but dignified bearing, that he sometimes came riding down their street on a horse, often with a bouquet of flowers in hand. He seems to have gotten along very well with my religious maternal grandmother, María, as well, though I can't imagine his ever once accompanying her to church, where she, like my mother, took refuge from the sorrows of this world—he just wasn't that way.

While their time in Magdalena's home passed quietly, her visits with Pascual's family would have been far more socially busy, especially on the weekends when they hosted parties, neighbors and relatives coming from all around to their farm on the outskirts of Jiguaní. On such occasions, she got to know his beloved older brother, Oscar, who, she would swear, always liked her, as did their *papi*, Leocadio, an enormously tall, barrel-chested man known for his bodily strength and affectionate nature. (He would be remembered for the ease with which he could hoist up four of his children at a time and for the tenderness of his spirit; but I haven't the faintest idea of what he looked like, as I've never seen a single photograph of him, though he surely must have had something of my father's face in his own.)

The oldest family member, my father's great-grandmother, Concepcíon Dieguez O'Connor, took in those gatherings from a rattan chair set under a banyan tree in the yard. Born in Jiguaní in 1840 of Irish and Cuban parentage, she was just short of her one hundredth year of life; the myth goes that she owed this longevity to her daily cigars and to a regimen of rum and *aguardiente*. She too seemed to have seen something lively and worthwhile in my mother, for Concepcíon often asked her to sit by her side, regaling her with tales of her own youth. Of his seven sisters, however, it was only Maya who gave my mother a hard time. In her mid-thirties by then, and married to Pedro, she often stayed on the farm while he went traveling to the states and on tours to Europe. During his frequent absences, she apparently coveted my father's company at my mother's expense, and so adamantly that in the midst of those fiestas, my mother and aunt often almost came to blows—and if not, they surely had gotten to the point of insults, my mother's favorite retort to Maya, so she would later tell me, being that, instead of Pedro, she should have married her brother. Which is to say that from the beginning, things had never been good between the two women.

Caught in the middle, my father looked the other way, and though his eldest sister no doubt attempted to break them up, the rest of the family liked my mother enough to further encourage her affections toward him. Maya, however, prayed that my mother would go away; and whenever she could, she spread her own vicious rumors about "that Torrens woman," who had the nerve to think she was better than everyone else. Evidently, Maya's dislike of my mother, while not enough to dissuade my father's amorous pursuit of her, still planted enough doubts and misgivings about her character and motives to put off any immediate notions about marriage. Still, at a certain point in the early 1940s, they became engaged: As his *prometida*—fiancée—she doubtlessly enjoyed a boost in his family's standing. How Maya must have suffered.

What my father could have been thinking when he, at Maya's urgings, tore himself away from my mother, and at some point in 1942, having traveled to New York, first walked in through 419's front doors and checked himself out in the large mirrors that, facing one another in the entryway, reflected his curious and perhaps bewildered—or excited—*campesino* face endlessly, is unknowable. He had arrived with money in his pockets, as Leocadio, dying the year before, had left his children an inheritance from the sales of several of their farms to divide among themselves. I like to think that Pascual, leaving my mother behind in Cuba, had made the journey sheepishly, that he missed her. Surely, he had gone to New York first and foremost as a tourist talked into keeping his sister Maya company (and perhaps she had hoped that separating Pascual from my mother would break whatever spell the *Holguínera* had cast over him). Nearly nightly, he and his two sisters made their way to the dance halls and ballrooms where Pedro and the orchestra performed, my father, always a sport and liking to play the big man, spending his money as if there would be no tomorrow. He bought himself some fancy clothes, sparkling cuff links, two-toned cordovans, and, if anything, had no real plans for his future. Still, as good a time as he was having, he would have hardly thought of staying in New York for long, for while he seems to have liked the city enough to prolong his visit, with the months slipping by, he had his own bouts of homesickness and surely missed my mother.

Now, although Pascual had indeed returned to marry her, sometime in 1943, it must have disillusioned her further when, finishing up some business with his brother, he left her alone in Cuba again. (But, before seeing her, he'd gone to a jewelry shop in New York City, where he'd bought her a beautiful diamond ring whose tiny stones were set in an intricately engraved gold band, a ring that she never took off, not even years later on the night when, mugged on a street near where we lived, some hoodlum threatened to cut off her finger.) Finally, after some months had passed, Pascual, having decided to give a life in that city a try, sent her the money to join him; and dutifully, with her heart in her throat—for since her father's death, she had never ventured far from home—Magdalena made her way to Havana with a single valise, the sort of cane suitcase with soft cloth inner pockets that would sit in a closet for sixty years. She took a ferry to Miami, which was only a five- or six-hour trip, before boarding an overnight train bound for New York. Bold in so many other ways, she sat terrified, and demurely so, for most of that journey. When an American fellow, a G.I., tried to pick her up, she didn't have the slightest idea of whatever the heck it was that he said to her; and even if she somehow had, my mother, in her ignorance of English, and as a matter of pride, dared not to speak with anyone. And there was something else: Surely dreading the fact that once she arrived Maya would be in the apartment with her, she made dozens of visits to the toilet, emptying her guts often, so tangled were her nerves. By the time she stepped off that train, her stomach in knots, she was doubtlessly relieved to find my father and Borja, the kindlier sister, waiting for her among the burgeoning Penn Station crowds.

Later, at a certain moment of the day, when, for all I know, it could have been raining, or sunny, or snowing outside, Magdalena too first walked into that building and saw her startled face reflecting back at her infinitely in the hallway mirrors; she probably felt faint as she entered the apartment and looked around. A believer in intuition and prophetic dreams in the first place, thanks to good old Cuban superstition, she needn't have been a sibyl to figure out that her life would never be the same again. No doubt she felt relieved to be with my father, who, for the most part, treated her in a courtly and affectionate manner in those days. Borja, balanced and affable, made her feel at home as well. It's the agitated, scolding Maya who probably gave her one of her dismissive looks the moment their eyes met. With Borja and Eduardo sleeping in the master bedroom, my mother spent her first night in New York in one of the apartment's back rooms—where I would one day stay—beside my father, breathlessly. How strange she must have felt to be there, for to someone from the tropics, New York must have seemed a rather purgatorial and strange place at best, and overwhelming: On some level, she must have despaired—I'd never hear her once say she "loved" the city the moment she arrived—and yet, she was now with her husband. Besides, not knowing more than a handful of words in English, if any, what was she to do?

By then, my father had decided he would stay in New York for the long run. He'd made new friends, for in that epoch, however far away or scattered the Cubans of that city were, they inevitably found one another in the dance halls and on the streets, or just turned up one day, knocking on the door. He'd also started to run out of his inheritance money—some five thousand dollars, I've heard—and, bored with just hanging around the apartment, kept his eyes open for a job. He was a bright man, though a little too trusting of strangers, a country boy with a decent secondary school education from Cuba, which meant that he could read and write and cipher, but what skills he possessed—that of a farmer, work that he had no taste for, and of a horseman who had once spent a year as a mounted postal courier delivering mail in the countryside around Jiguaní—could hardly lead to any job possibilities in the city. (And his English was not so good yet, *sabes?*)

In the end, the only kind of work he, without any particular skills, managed to find, even during those war years, came down to busing tables and washing dishes in one of the restaurants of a famous mid-town hotel, the Biltmore, which took up the entire block at Madison Avenue and Forty-third; it was a job he'd landed through a Cuban fellow named Rubén Díaz, whom he'd met at one of those joints, maybe in the roof gardens of the Hotel Pennsylvania or at the Savoy, where Pedro and the Cugat orchestra sometimes performed. And while he'd eventually work his way up in the kitchens, making breakfasts for on-the-go businessmen in the second-floor dining room and then as a short order cook in the Biltmore Men's Bar—what my brother and I would always more grandly refer to as a "chef" because he wore a white toque—he had started at the bottom, which didn't seem to bother him at all.

He came by that job just in the nick of time, for it wasn't long before my mother had become pregnant with my brother, José. Nevertheless, neither his new position nor my mother's delicate state seemed to slow him down when it came to his passion for New York nightlife, and it seems that while he still had some money, he didn't allow his marital status to get in the way of his primal enjoyments. She found this out when one of his admirers mailed her a barely literate letter. Whoever this lady happened to be, she scribbled down her confessions in pencil and shakily so, her writing and spelling so bad that my mother, waving the letter in my father's face, gloated: "She's not only a whore, but ignorant as well!" Still, her pain at finding out that he had turned into a *parandero*—that is, a roving sort with an eye for the ladies—must have been intense. She'd always say that it wasn't really in his nature, or at least he had never been that way in Cuba (though maybe he was). Left alone in that apartment on those nights, she could have hardly been thrilled when he finally came home at three or four in the morning, reeking of booze, perfume, and who knows what else.

For her part, to add insult to injury, she soon learned, thanks to Maya, about the true nature of her status in that household: as a servant whose job was to cook and clean the apartment and to otherwise tend to everyone's needs. ("I was nothing more than a slave," she'd one day say.) In that inescapable circumstance, my mother became a virtual captive, and whether she liked it or not, each day Maya, home from her job and expecting to be waited on, found new ways to torment her. The insults were one thing, the ordering her about like a Cuban Cinderella another; but the worst of it was that she threatened to put my mother, pregnant or not, out into the street.

Not that my mother lived in complete despair or had no friends whatsoever. My future godfather, Horacio, tended to keep my mother company on those nights when my father and his sisters went out. (Nothing romantic ever took place between them, by the way—for the perennially unmarried Horacio happened to be the kind of man who, if a shapely woman and a handsome fellow passed by at the same time, chose to check out the latter, with a quick turn of the head, a slight redness rising in his face.) It was during those years that another Cuban family, the Garcías, moved onto the block, and here and there, usually at Sunday Mass, which she was allowed to attend with her sisters-in-law, she'd meet some of the other Latinas in the neighborhood—sending out radar, they just found one another. Somehow a few of her English-speaking neighbors took a liking to her as well. Never having any inclination or opportunity to study English, my mother somehow managed to get by with those neighbors with smiles, nods, and a handful of words and phrases. Along the way, she made a few English-speaking friends, who were patient with her syntax or perhaps found her way of talking amusing—among them, and most wildly so, a certain Mrs. Betty Walker, or "*la muda*," from up on the fourth floor, a deaf mute with a brood of kids to look after, whose grunts and wild gesticulations were easier for my mother to follow than any English, the two of them often carrying on in the hall about heaven knows what to any passerby's amusement.

None of her new acquaintances, however, were as gracious or attentive or sophisticated as the forty-year-old Argentine beauty Jacqueline Vidal, who, working as a wartime volunteer in the obstetrics ward of the St. Luke's Woman's Hospital on East 110th Street, had been on hand to assist in the delivery of José, in December 1944. That's how they became friends, not only because Jacqueline, or Chaclita, as she would be nicknamed, spoke a soothing Spanish in a ward where none of the other nurses did, but because she, a musical prodigy on the violin who often performed with her sister María-Luisa on the classical circuit of New York, exuded the kind of cultural refinement that simply reminded my mother of the people she had known during her childhood. Which is to say that, bewildered and stranded as my mother may have felt, it was Jacqueline, whose artistic hands were the first to touch my brother's brow, who became her lifelong friend.

Of course it wouldn't be right to say that my father never took my mother anywhere: She visited Central Park and the Bronx Zoo and saw such landmarks as the Empire State Building, which, however, she never ascended. (In one of the photographs of her from that time, she sits, rather well turned out, on a park bench, looking frostily uncomfortable between her female in-laws, though the one I most like from that period is of my father, dapper in a hat and scarf and topcoat, posed in Central Park, holding with pride a chunk of snow in his begloved hands.) In general, aside from being sequestered in the household like a "slave," my mother, speaking only Spanish, rarely got around on her own. Once my brother was born, however, and she was further housebound save for occasional excursions with a baby carriage out to the park, another complication in her life arose. This had to do with the fact that Maya, having reached her forties, was childless.

As in a fairy tale, Maya simply coveted her nephew with an eye to raising him as her own. But far from adopting a new approach toward my mother—kindness might have gone a long way—she went on disparaging my mother's maternal abilities to my father any time she could, in fact, making my mother out as a reckless soul. This *envidia*—or envy—was so pronounced that my aunt Maya had tried to wrest my older brother away from my mother after an incident over which my mother had had no control. My brother had been crawling along the floor when, by some caprice, he had opened the lower door of a kitchen cabinet just beneath the sink, happening upon a can of rat poison—the rats in that apartment, which came up from the basement below us through a garbage chute and the spaces around loosened steam pipes, were abundant—and this poison José managed somehow to eat, perhaps because of its candied smell. Doubled over, he turned blue and, apparently lifeless, had to be rushed to St. Luke's. (His recovery, after his stomach was pumped, had been, in fact, a close call.) Given her state of mind, Maya, who had come home from her job at Macy's, blamed my mother's carelessness for the calamity. According to Maya, she had proved herself unfit to look after her own son, and, dutifully, my aunt volunteered to take my brother off their hands; and while my father resisted her—though with difficulty, for Maya, as the eldest of the sisters, had practically raised him—he ended up holding my mother at fault. Worst of all, my father, to whom his own blood family remained the most important thing in life, wouldn't tolerate as much as a bad word from my mother about his sister, which is to say that in any such discussions, she never had a chance.

But Maya's efforts did not quite work out for her the way she had hoped. Even her influence could not change my father's mind about my mother, though having an infant in the apartment seemed to make no difference to his nocturnal routines. Now when my father came home, a tie loosened around his neck, at four in the morning, my mother had a crib and a crying infant in the room. Aside from that, it seems that he treated her well enough, even lovingly, but bit by bit, in those years, he slowly began to change. My mother has always blamed it on a combination of that nightlife and his new job at the hotel. He began drinking in the clubs and dance halls, a little at first and then more and more, perhaps to have a good time or to make some liaison easier on his conscience—*But why would he feel guilty? He was a Cuban after all*—or because he sometimes felt homesick for his family back in Cuba, especially for his beloved brother, Oscar. Still, even my mother would admit that his drinking didn't really worsen, nor did his melancholy deepen, until 1945, the year the war ended.

By then, he had started to improve his standing in the kitchens of the hotel; well liked and affable, working around not only other Cubans like himself but immigrants from Italy, Greece, and Poland (whose languages he began to absorb), he found a second home in the Men's Bar kitchen. And though he would have made far more money as a waiter—a job offered to him—he was, as my mother, sighing, put it one day, too proud to earn his livelihood serving others. (And can you imagine what emotions she, raised in a house with servants, felt when treated like one?) So he remained in that kitchen, learning to prepare chicken and lamb and grill seared steaks, got a raise to about a dollar an hour, and, despite some reservations about New York—for there were always people around to stare resentfully if they overheard someone speaking Spanish on the street—felt optimistic about the future.

At some point, he began a campaign to bring his older brother, Oscar, to New York, writing him constantly, and, I suppose, while knowing that his brother would never abandon his life in Jiguaní for good, he did his best to persuade him to visit—much in the same spirit his own life in that city had started. In this, he eventually succeeded, though without any expectations that his brother, a *campesino* to his bones, would ever stay. With four children by two marriages, the eldest aged twelve, and running his own farm, my uncle finally—perhaps reluctantly—consented to make the journey, if only to see his younger brother again.

That autumn, my uncle Oscar rode south to the provincial capital, Santiago de Cuba, to procure a travel visa for the States and, heading homeward at dusk a few days later, was crossing a meadow on his horse when he found himself in the gathering darkness of a storm: At some point, a lightning bolt flashed around him, and, when his horse reared back, he tumbled off his saddle and flew headlong into the trunk of a tree, breaking his neck. I imagine my father and his sisters got the news by telegram, and who of his sisters rushed to Cuba, if any, I can't say. But he lingered, it's been said, in a semiconscious state for twenty-six days—perhaps it was thought he would eventually recover—before he finally succumbed, without so much as ever laying eyes on my father again.

After his brother's death, the sadness of life came to be written all over my father's face, and he must have lamented the fact that instead of showing that other Oscar Hijuelos the excitements and pleasantries of New York, his invitation had, however indirectly, delivered him to the gates of heaven, or hell, or purgatory, or to wherever such kindhearted *campesino* souls go when their eyes close for good: For months after, on his nights home from work, he rarely left the apartment, and assumed the posture and habits by which I would most remember him—by the kitchen table, drinking rye whiskey followed by one glass of beer after the other, a cigarette burning down until it singed the cuffs of his shirt. He slumped in misery, lashed out at my mother, swinging his arms out at her, just because he could not allow anyone else to enter into that cage of his pain. He couldn't hear a thing that anyone said to him, not even his sisters. He'd wince with the realization that certain events cannot be undone, and, blaming himself for that tragedy, embarked upon a sea of regrets.

· · ·

When I was born in 1951, at about five thirty on a summer morning, at the St. Luke's Woman's Hospital, my father named me after his brother, and I suppose for that reason alone, my father always accorded me a special affection. I've been told that as a baby I was good-natured and on the quiet side, that I rarely carried on or cried and had a certain *dulzura*—a sweetness—about me that, I've always believed, must have come from him. By the time I'd entered my infancy, his sisters had finally moved out, relocating to Miami. Borja left when her husband, Eduardo, suffering from a bad heart, became ill, and Maya and her husband soon followed. As for my father? Dividing his days between his job at the Biltmore and home, he still threw the occasional weekend party, as he and his sisters used to, the apartment filling with Cubans and Puerto Rican couples—probably a mix of his friends from the hotel and from the dance halls—as well as a few single strays, male and female alike, from around the neighborhood. On those nights, the drinks and food flowed—my father spending "too much," as my mother would later complain, on sponging *fulanos*, most of whom he'd probably never see again and who, in any case, couldn't give *ni un pío*—a piss—about him; but because he found it almost unbearable to be alone, those parties took place at least once a month, if not more often. His guests came for their doses of Cuban warmth, the congeniality, the music, blaring on those nights from a living room RCA console, and, aside from the fully stocked bar and the ice-packed bathtub filled with bottles of beer, the immense quantities of food, which lay stacked on platters in the kitchen. It wasn't long before the crowd, revved up, would get onto the living room floor, dancing away. And there I would be, the little "*rubio*"—blondie—the cute little *americano*-looking son of that nice guy Pascual, crawling innocently along our living room floor, bounded by a forest of pleated trousers, shapely nylon-covered legs, and kicking two-toned and high-heeled shoes. My brother swears that, innocent though I may have been, I'd roll onto my back and pass the time doing my best to steal a peek at the mysteries residing inside the plump upper reaches of those swirling ladies' dresses.

Sooner or later on those nights, while the music flowed out of the living room record player, which, as with most of our furniture, had been left behind for us by my aunts, with the lights turned low while my mother remained in the kitchen tending to the food or finishing up with the dishes, my father, a sucker for flirtation and a suave *rumbero*, especially after he'd had a few drinks, took to the dance floor, smitten by some woman's engaging glance. By the time my mother finally left the kitchen, she hardly cut an exuberant figure like some of the dolled-up femmes fatales in their tight dresses, whom she thought of as lowlifes. She'd sit back on the couch, her arms folded stiffly across her lap, and, neither drinking nor feeling as jubilantly alive as the other women, take in the proceedings rather somberly.

I suppose that kind of generic Cuban scene of food, drinks, and dancing unfolded in similar apartments across the city circa 1953–54, but in our case, those evenings usually ended on a sour note: For once everybody finally cleared out at some late hour of the morning, leaving behind a disaster of half-finished meals and cigarette-butt-filled glasses everywhere, my mother, unable to forget and forgive my father's treatment of her, would have it out with him. Down the hall in bed, my brother, José, in the room right next to mine or, if we had boarders, in the same room with me, I'd sometimes hear them tormenting each other at night, and loudly so, as if we, their kids, were deaf. And sometimes, I swear, it seemed that we heard things crashing against the walls, plates breaking, hitting noises, and cries—at which point my brother would get out of bed to see what was going on, only to return in tears, having gotten slapped in the face for his trouble. (Here I have to interject that it was from those days onward that my brother formed a poor opinion of my father, a stance that led some years later to out-and-out fights between them on the street, though I never witnessed such and still find that notion hard to believe.)

Not to say, however, that my parents were always at each other's throats; to the contrary, in calmer times, they had their share of laughs and moments of tenderness. He'd sometimes come home with some gift for her, a bottle of perfume or a pair of earrings bought from one of those enterprising vendors who'd go from hotel to hotel, selling goods to the staff at cheap prices. (He must have known every Latino "whole seller" from the Bowery to the Bronx.) Sometimes, I'd see her in the mornings, standing at the end of the hallway by the front door, straightening the knot of his tie and patting down the shoulders of his coat as he'd head out to work. And the fact remains that, however much his attentions may have wandered, they, as a couple, surely fooled around a lot. Once, while crawling across the floor as an infant, I discovered under their bed a white pan of water—a *palangana*—in which floated a wildly distended and somewhat forlorn-looking used condom, which I hadn't the slightest idea about. (At the same time, I can't help thinking of that discovery now without recalling how, on some nights, I'd hear her agitated cries, perhaps of pleasure.) And, as a family, we went places: to Coney Island in the summer, and at Christmas to Macy's for an annual visit to see Santa Claus, or Santa Clows, as my mother pronounced it.

As for the static between them, if it affected me badly, I have no recollection of feeling that way—what was I but a little kid anyway?

●　●　●

Which brings me to that journey I made with my mother and brother to Cuba, in the summer of 1955: It was my father, perhaps in a spirit of largesse or reconciliation, who had paid for our airfares out of his Biltmore wages—$42.50 a week, plus whatever he made in overtime—probably in cash, as he did with all our bills, and since Borja still worked for Pan American airlines, as a bilingual ticket agent in Miami, she had probably gotten him a really good deal for our flight.

I don't recall much, if any, fanfare at our departure, or if my father had even been on hand to send us off—my guess is that he'd gone to his job at the Biltmore—but on a certain morning in late June, someone drove us to Idlewild Airport (now JFK), where we eventually boarded a Pan American airlines clipper for Havana. Since I can't conjure a single moment in later years of my mother ever once relaxing, for even a second, it's hard to imagine that she behaved any differently that day: too fastidious (and vain) to have chewed on her fingernails, when not chatting wildly away with some newfound Cuban acquaintances across the aisle in her one-thousand-words-a-minute Spanish, she, hating to fly, would have been on the edge of her seat and desperate for distractions. I seem to recall that she'd sit very still, back upright, hardly moving at all, as if to do so would have magically jostled that *avion* out of the sky. When the stewardess served us wax-paper-wrapped ham-and-cheese sandwiches, my mother could hardly take more than a few bites. She sighed a lot, looking off into the distance. Later, though she was a first cousin to anxiety, but never imbibed as much as a drink, she must have wanted to during the final leg of our *vuolo.*

The flight took some three hours and had been routine enough until, while crossing over the Florida straits on our approach to Havana, something ignited inside the airplane's left wing fuselage, and just like that, flames started shooting out of its engines. Billows of thread-ridden plumes of smoke, like a rocket's exhaust, spilled into the surrounding clouds, and those silvery gold sheaths of fire seemed to roll back and forth over the wingspan. As the engines sputtered, then fell dead, so exciting to a child but terrifying to adults, the plane breathing ever so heavily, my mother, like so many others around us, made the sign of the cross and began to pray and pray, as if the world were about to end; then she took hold of our hands, squeezing them tightly and only letting go when, after a bumpy descent, we'd miraculously landed safely.

There, in Havana, along the periphery of the airport, royal palms rose in the distance, the sky ever so blue, and as the cabin hatches sprang open and the dense tropic humidity warmed the compartment, we waited while a ground crew wheeled a mobile stairway up to the doors. Shortly, along with a retinue of Cubans and any number of festive, perhaps blasé tourists and commuting businessmen, we disembarked from that clipper and stepped onto the tarmac, where I first breathed the Cuban air.

Later, we caught a bus for Holguín, and during that twelve-to-eighteen-hour journey (I've heard both numbers) as we crossed Cuba, mainly in the dead of night, going from little pueblo to pueblo along the northern coast toward the east, I apparently did not turn out to be a very good traveler. Could have been the intense humidity, or some on-the-run snack we'd picked up from one of the vendors swarming the dusty station stops, but the more deeply we entered Cuba, the more I trembled from chills, squirming about on my mother's lap. Soon enough, whatever I had come down with spread into my guts, so each time we stopped, I'd get off the bus, my mother holding my hand, to vomit into the darkness. (My brother, José, has told me that I did so over and over again.) At some point, my face drained of color, I fell limply asleep on her lap, my mother peering down at me. I have a memory of the bus pulling into another stop, my mother fanning herself with a newspaper, Cuban voices murmuring from the road, where the male passengers, taking a break, stood about outside puffing madly, and inseparably so, on their cigars, columns of bluish smoke curling around them like incense, an almost impossibly loud chorus of cicadas—night bells—sounding from the brush, moths crawling about in agitated circles on the windows, clouds of gnats swirling around the lantern lights. En route again, as I looked out the bus windows, I doubtlessly saw wonderful things: the ocean horizon, like a rising plain reaching up to all the stars, then endless fields of sugar and pineapple, and forests passing, their silhouettes so reminiscent not of vegetation but of contorted shadows standing at attention in row after row, like the dead (my mother along the way touching my sweating brow). Cuba itself seemed enormous to me, and as that night wore on, I probably saw a ghost or two roaming through its darkness—Cuba was full of spirits, I remember my mother telling me—and that sky, I swear, occasionally wept shooting stars.

Then morning came, and a few farmers, black cigarillos in their lips, boarded the bus with caged hens, and as roosters crowed, vendors selling little paper cups of coffee came down the aisle, and the music of a radio—a woman's mellifluous voice, perhaps someone like Celia Cruz or Elena Burke—sounded from the doorways of the houses: I can remember thinking, sick as I felt, that I had been traveling through an immensely interesting tunnel, like that of an arcade attraction in an amusement park, but one that went on and on, seemingly forever.

Once we arrived in Holguín, however, I got better, attended to by my affectionate aunt Cheo and her adolescent daughters, Miriam and Mercita. Our days together went happily enough. Always treating me kindly, they did their best to keep their youngest cousin, a few months short of turning four, well-fed and entertained—oh, but we played in the back, where a mango tree stood, lizards crawling about and a smell of jasmine and wildflowers so strong they left one yawning and sleepy. And while their modest house was just a one-story *solar* and nothing special on a nondescript side street in Holguín, I've always considered it my own little piece of Cuba.

Though I can't describe how the rooms were laid out, in which part of the house I slept, or even where the *baño* with its toilet—what my mother always called the *"inodoro"*—had been situated (think it was in its own shed, just off the back patio, where there was possibly a shower as well), I do know that the mornings smelled wonderfully from the fragrant and dense blessings of a nearby soda cracker factory, and that down the way, along a descending cobblestone street, on a shady corner, stood a bodega where the local *campesinos*, coming into town on donkeys and horses, would stop to have a few drinks, its wooden floor reeking of pungent beer. A mulatto in a straw hat passed his days there, in a narrow space behind a juice-dripping counter, chopping up pineapples, splitting coconuts, and occasionally brandishing on the tip of a machete some chunk of mango or papaya for me to eat. I'd go there with my brother in the afternoons and marvel at the thin and bony hunched-over farmers, whose faces seemed half-hidden under their hats, and at the way sunlight poured in from the back through an open door, casting their shadows into infinity.

For their part, those men, who'd grown up as rustics like my father had on a farm, chewing on their cigars and speaking as if their mouths were stuffed with cotton, must have been amused by the sudden appearance of a small blond boy in their midst. "Cheo's *nieto*," it was explained, the one who came down from New York with his mother, you know, that good-looking brunette who left Cuba with that fellow Pascual and who, however often she smiles, must have regretted it, *por Dios!*—it was written all over her face. They might have rubbed their eyes a few times before getting a second look at me (the story of my life); it took them a while to absorb that such a towheaded boy could have been the offspring of an Hijuelos from Jiguaní. Those *campesinos* would have probably known my father from the old days before he came to the States, when he used to ride the countryside on a horse himself. They would have recalled his languid demeanor and friendly but sad expression, and would have appreciated and respected me and my brother for the very fact that my father's family had been in Oriente for over a hundred years. And in those days when every Cuban from Holguín and Jiguaní knew each other, they would have likely remembered my mother from earlier times, from seeing her at Carnival, or from the local dance halls where she, in her late adolescence and young woman-hood, had so bloomed as a dancer.

And yet, however warmly those *campesinos* might have thought of my mother, they would have still puzzled over the fact that I didn't look Cuban at all.

But, even if they may have been at a loss for what to make of me, they were friendly. The owner always prepared the most delicious Cuban fruit shakes for my brother and me, his machete cleaving into the counter with sharp whacks, the juices dripping down, that taste of what I suppose now had to be *batidas*, which might have been spiked with a little Cuban rum for flavoring, ever so delicious on my tongue. Now and then, one of those fellows would take my brother and me outside and put us on his horse, and back and forth we would go, pulled along the street, jostling by the open-shuttered windows and doorways of the houses and waving at everyone, my head muzzled in its bristly mane, people smiling at us just because we were children.

Later we'd play hide-and-seek behind the trees and go charg-ing like little bulls through the sheets that had been hung up to dry alongside the houses, or we'd sit by my aunt's doorway watching the black laundresses—*negritas buenas*, as my mother called them—go by with their baskets balanced on their heads. About a block or so away, there stood an icehouse—what better thing was there to do than stand by its entrance to cool off or to chew on some of the chips that had dropped from those perspiring blocks of ice into the gutter? I seemed to be always thirsty, so my brother has told me—several times he had to stop me from sipping water from a curbside trough, and it seems that early on, I had already acquired the nervous habit of eating anything offered to me—deep-fried banana fritters, a piece of raw sugarcane, or a strip of *bacalao*, or salted cod (which I had never really liked but ate anyway). One afternoon, while sitting on the curb, I watched my brother, fooling with a hose in front of Cheo's house, turn its gushing spout on a very dapperly dressed man, all in white and wearing a lacquered cane boater, as he rode by on a bicycle. With my brother spraying him with abandon, that scene, at least in memory, played out like something from a 1930s Max Roach comedy: He got off that bicycle fuming and, scolding José, began to chase him around in circles, my brother keeping just ahead of his grasp, until my mother, hearing the commotion, stepped from the doorway and, in her loveliness and charm (or outrage that a grown man would harass a boy, however mischievous, of eleven or so) calmed him down, his anger dissipating in a way that seemed to elude her sometimes when it came to our father, Pascual.

Of course, we'd come to visit my aunts, Cheo, with whom my mother and I stayed, and her oldest sister, María, in whose home my brother usually slept, a few streets away. If there's any one thing I can tell you about Cheo, it would come down to her kindness and demure, self-effacing manner, though it's my guess that there was a lot more to her moods than just that. But as a boy, the only things that registered with me were her kisses, her embraces, her generally sweet and maternal ways. I didn't know that she was a recent widow, nor that she spent her days working in a department store along one of Holguín's shopping streets, and that her life must have been difficult, what with two daughters to look after and support. She never let on about her grief, however, not to my brother and me, and, in any case, seemed to cope with her circumstance by keeping busy—cooking, sewing, cleaning the house, and praying—yes, she was the most religiously devout of my mother's sisters. Mainly she oozed affection, being the sort of woman who spoke only endearments, as with "What do you want, my love?" and "Are you hungry, *mi vida*?" and always with the sweetest smile. I sometimes slept alongside her at night— "*Somos familia*," "We're family," she'd say quietly, and "*Soy tu tía*,"

"I'm your aunt," as she'd hold me close, and I'd half strangle her, returning her affections, so precious and warm she seemed.

Those evenings slipped one into another, without a lot of variation: Once night fell, the unused rooms were kept dark, to save money, I suppose; after dinner, which Cheo improvised over a hot plate or small stove, my cousins serving, we'd listen to the radio. That was a big deal in those days, and very exciting, for most programs, featuring popular music, were beamed in from Havana—acts like El Trio Matamoros (the "moor killers") and singers like Olga Guillot and Beny Moré, among so many others, as well as soap operas and comedies. (And to impose my future knowledge about something I would have hardly been aware of back then, the news bulletins would have occasionally been about the rebel forces of Fidel Castro, then encamped in the Sierra Maestra some fifty miles or so to the south.) Sometimes, we'd join our other cousins, Cuza, Bebo y Macho, y Gladys, María's offspring, and go strolling along those streets, to congregate, as so many other *Holguíneros* did, in the nearest plaza, where a municipal band might be playing and where a stand sold freshly made papaya and coconut-flavored ice cream. ("How you loved your sweets!" my mother would tell me.)

I do recall playing in a small park nearby, El Parque Infantil, where there were swings, and that I'd go there with my cousin Miriam, who, as she has told me a thousand times since, treated me like her little *muñeca*, her blond-haired doll; we also slept side by side sometimes, but the only telling anecdote I know of our time together comes down to something she recently told me: Along that street stood a pepper tree, which I always picked at as if the hanging brilliantly red peppers were lollipops, and that I constantly ate them even when I was told not to, to the point that my lips burned so much that my cousin had to coat them over with honey—I was just that way, and if I take satisfaction in saying so, it's because such a detail reminds me of the fact that, once upon a time, I was a Cuban.

. . .

Altogether, life in Cheo's household unfolded peacefully and without much happening at all, though one evening, I must have been dozing in my aunt's front room, which was her *sala,* whose door opened to the street, and as I happened to look over, I saw my mother and Aunt Cheo holding each other. Perhaps it is a caprice of memory, but one of them was crying on the other's lap—perhaps my mother, lamenting her life in New York, or, remembering his good traits, simply missing my father and wondering what might have gone wrong between them, or if she'd done the right thing marrying him. Or perhaps it was Cheo—with her bottled-up widow's grief and feeling the burdens of her responsibilities and of her own kind of Catholic loneliness, for she would wait her entire life to be reunited in eternity with her husband—who needed her sister's comforting. To be honest, I can't recall just which of those Torrens women felt like falling to pieces that night—or perhaps they both were—but that blurred memory, from so long ago, has stayed with me just the same.

Now, Holguín, unlike the far more raucous city of Havana, shut down completely at about ten at night, with such stillness that a raised voice from some dwelling a block away could be heard, and, after a while, the cicadas took over. In my bed, which I shared with my mother and sometimes my aunt, I waited for the dense midnight humidity and heat to lift—it was a Cuban summer after all—and yet, finally closing my eyes, after tossing in sweat, I'd just as soon awaken to the somewhat cooler morning and rooster calls, and carts and hawkers passing by on the street, cans and bells clanging, ever so happy to do what I, as a young boy, was prone to do, which was to eat and eat things like sugar-covered pieces of bread fried in lard and to sip from my own cup of heavily sweetened *café con leche*. Occasionally, as a special treat, my aunt boiled up a pot of condensed milk, to which she'd add an exotic and deliciously nutty flavoring, so deep and dark that for years, well into my twenties, I wondered just what that magical "Cuban" drink had been. It was one of the tastes I most vividly—and fondly—remembered from my stay in Holguín, and I truly became convinced that its *Cuban* origins were what made that drink so special, as if its uniqueness had been distilled from some obscure roots in the deepest jungle; this was an illusion I held on to until the day came when my mother, breaking that spell of decades-old nostalgia, advised me that my magical Cuban elixir, something I believed had come from heaven and considered better than honey and cinnamon and all the sugars in the world combined, was nothing more than Borden's milk mixed with a few tablespoons of Hershey's syrup.

Along the way, I spent time with my Majorcan-born *abuelita*, who, with sunken but sweet eyes and skin nearly translucent from age, wore her gray hair tied back tautly over her head, in the formal Spanish style. She lived with her oldest daughter, my aunt María, and if there was anyone from whom Cheo derived her gentle and saintly character, it was surely her mother. The sort to sit in a corner and take in things quietly around her, as if contented with a kind of invisibility, she'd suddenly reach her hands out to grab me if I were passing by, just to request a kiss—"*Dame un besito!*"—my *abuela*'s face, so solemn before, softening with happiness. It was in her company that my mother seemed most tranquil; they sometimes shared a bench by the window in the front parlor—I can remember my *abuela*, bathed in sunlight, always sewing some garment—and while they would speak softly about missing each other (perhaps) or of matters concerning my *abuela*'s frailness, for she was not in the best of health (perhaps) or of plans to visit my grandfather's grave together (definitely, for, indeed, they went to the cemetery one day), what I can mainly recall is how my *abuela* treated her second-eldest daughter with utter tenderness, sometimes reaching over to gently touch her face and say, "Oh, but my darling Magdalencita." What my mother felt just then, I can't say, but she always behaved around her with reverence and humility and gratitude, as if to show *Abuela* María that she, indeed, had outgrown the spoiled ways of her youth. She, in fact, never seemed as much at home as she did in those days with her mother in Holguín. (But that's all I can recall about her, my mother's "*santa Buena*" and how they were with one another.)

Now, her namesake, my aunt María, aside from the fact that she bore a strong resemblance to my mother in a way that the gentle Cheo, with her teaspoon-shaped face and sweet smile, did not, I can't remember at all, though her husband, Pepito, remains vividly with me. And not because he was much beloved in the family and known as a good provider and a patriarch, but because he carried me about his country place, a farm, and just about everywhere else we went, on his shoulders. A bookkeeper in Holguín, he had a longish face, intensely intelligent eyes, and a manner that was both serious and warm. He wore wire-rim eyeglasses. (Years later, a balding priest I once saw meditating in a garden in Rome reminded me of him, as if Pepito had returned as a ghost.) One of those Cubans who, never caring for baby talk, always spoke to children as if they were adults, it's to Pepito that I owe one of the few statements that I can actually remember word for word: *"Sabes que eres cubano? No te olvides eso,"* he told me one day when he had taken us up to a beach near Gibara, along the Atlantic coast. "You know that you're Cuban? Don't forget that." That afternoon at the beach, when he had taken off his *guayabera*, the flowing crests of white hair gushing from his chest astonished me. Later, as he carried me into the ocean, I may as well have been riding upon the shoulders of a silver-haired faun, his fur matting in the foam. Laughing and grabbing hold of my arms as I desperately tried to hang on to his neck, Pepito, waist-high in the Cuban sea, began to swing me around in circles, the horizons of both ocean and land spinning around me. I was reeling dizzily when he set me down into the water just in time for a high wave to come crashing over us: another taste, of burning salt water, like brine, in my throat, my thin arms grasping his legs (bony and hairy as well) for dear life, until he hoisted me up once again into the safety of his embrace, Pepito patting my back as I trembled with relief.

Later, I fell asleep under a tree, and I felt drowsy still as my uncle carried me back through the narrow streets of that little sun-parched town, folks standing by the doorways of their palm-thatched houses along the way, calling out and waving at us. At any rate, I guess I can say that on that day, I had been baptized in the Cuban sea.

Now, while staying on Pepito's farm in the countryside outside Holguín, I became deeply fond of nature, or so I've been told. In that *campo* persisted a strong, almost overwhelming scent, not of animal dung or of burning tobacco but of an aroma I still recall from that visit—the air always smelling like the raw inner marrow of a freshly cut or snapped-open sapling branch, redolent of the juices of its white and yellow fringed fibers, of the earth and water, and of *greenness* itself. There were insects everywhere, and blossoms peeking out from the dense bush and forests around us, and at night, when mosquito netting draped the windows, beetles the size and weight of walnuts pelted the walls, with no end to the tarantulas, lizards, and vermin inhabiting the raised-on-pylons under-portion of the house, where the smaller livestock sometimes slept. The crystal night sky over rural Oriente, with a dense sprinkling of stars as seen from Pepito and María's porch, still remains clear to me, but it was the farm's animals that I grew most attached to. I seem to have felt a special fondness for the pigs, into whose pens, to my mother's consternation, I often wandered. Or else I kept chasing after those plump and squealing creatures in the front yard, spending so much time with them that it was easy for me to imitate their guttural swallowing, as if I were a bristly snouted animal myself instead of a spindly boy whom my cousins had already nicknamed "*el alemán*," or "the German," for his looks. Apparently, I pecked at the ground like the hens and caw-cawed like the roosters, doubtlessly running barefoot in their leav-ings. I played with chameleons and bush lizards as if they were my friends.

One morning, when the family had decided to throw a party for their neighbors, Pepito, ordering some hands to dig out a pit in the yard under a tamarind tree, called my brother and me to his side so that, I suppose, we could witness the slaughtering of a pig. The poor thing must have known what was going to happen, for my cousins Bebo and Macho, in their sturdy teens, struggled while dragging it out from its wire pen, and it put up a terrible fight, trying to run away, until with a quick thrust of a blade against its neck, Pepito ended its struggles. (It squealed in terror, snorted, collapsed, and then, trembling slightly, eyes expanded, gave out a final cry before dying.) Soon, they'd dragged it into another shed, where it was cleaved in half, its guts pulled out, and then each side, tied by the hooves, was hung off a hook, buckets left underneath to catch the dripping blood.

The penetrating smell of that pork flesh and its blood made me step away; it was probably a pal of mine, but I remained on hand when those sides were hauled out into the yard to cook over a smoldering pit. It would take hours to roast the *lechón* to "crackling perfection," as the cookbooks might say, but in the meantime, something awry happened—an iguana, crawling over, embedded itself inside one of the flanks. The easiest solution, it seemed, came down to smoking it out, and so they hung that side up under a tamarind tree and built a fire underneath it. However, the wood was too green, or the flame too high, because shortly a column of thick, black smoke went billowing upward into that tree and, at a certain moment, a commotion arose in the branches; soon the tarantulas that had been nesting there panicked, for from its lowest branches, a rainfall of those creatures came dropping down by the dozens, like black flowers, and began scattering wildly in all directions in the yard. There were so many that even the women were recruited to hunt them down, the family rushing after the creatures with brooms and shovels and pans lest they get underneath the floorboards and take over the house for good. Indeed, I remember that.

Somewhere along the line, however, there came the moment when I didn't seem well. My mother's always claimed that I had the worst habit of drinking from puddles in the countryside, especially after a rainfall, and while you'd think that such water—Cuban water—falling from God's skies would be pure as any could be, I came down with something anyway, my face and limbs blowing up, and my manner becoming so listless that I was confined to a bed for days, my uncle and aunts convinced that I had perhaps suffered from an allergic reaction to an insect bite. I don't recall at which point this happened. But those first signs of my illness could have taken place after we'd made a trip to see my father's family in Jiguaní, which was about fifteen miles away, though, if so, I would have been too late to meet my great-grandmother, Concepcíon, who'd died the year before, at one hundred and thirteen, from diabetes. (Her mind was intact and spirits good, even if both her legs had been amputated; among her last words, I've been told, were: "I may have been ugly, but I was lucky in life.") Or perhaps I'd gotten sick, so my mother has also claimed, from something I'd eaten, perhaps a piece of delicious pork, an undercooked morsel, or one I'd picked up off the ground the day when those tarantulas fell from the tree. Or at the beach near Gibara, a prickly mollusk had jammed something vile into my foot, and it had gotten infected without anyone knowing. Or, perhaps, in the midst of some Cuban miasma, for in the woods there were an abundance of stagnant mosquito-ridden ponds, I had sucked into my lungs some germs, or what my mother called "*microbios*." Still, I can't say just when the symptoms of my illness first came over me, and what recollections I have of that little piece of Cuba hardly summon up any moments of particular discomfort. But during that summer when I turned four, from some mysterious source, those *microbios*, which my mother, with an almost medieval panache, would describe as "*animalitos*"—or little animals—slipped inside my body, those parasites (or whatever they were) filling my system with their venom.

Still, whatever ailed me took several months to really manifest itself, and even then, I'm not sure of the day and hour when my mother or any of my other relatives became aware that what I would come to think of as my *Cuban disease* had taken hold, or even if it was noticeable enough to be truly worrisome to them at first. In any event, by the end of that summer of 1955, I just wasn't up to snuff, low of energy, and perhaps even more apprehensive and nervous looking than before.

Maybe I've come to read too much into the slightest of my expressions, but the single thing I have to go by comes down to the only photograph taken of me in Cuba. It was posed in the salon of my aunt Cheo's house in Holguín. Cheo's daughter, the pretty auburn-haired Miriam, with the serious expression of a young girl who had recently lost her father, and my ethereally pretty cousin Cuza were standing beside my mother and brother, his face unfortunately partly obscured. I'm sitting out front on a little chair, dolled up like a little Lord Fauntleroy, my hair blond and wavy, my cheeks covered with freckles, my pudgy knees dimpled, and on my face, if I'm not mistaken, is a look of not just timidity or shyness but of anxiety, as if I knew what was to come.

• • •

By the time we eventually returned to New York, late that summer, I had become bloated and listless, with a constant fever and an overwhelming desire to sleep, a crisis coming about one evening in our apartment when, in whatever manner such discoveries are made, my mother found a shocking amount of blood in my urine. What ran through her mind in such a moment, I can't say, but she must have been frightened to death over what my father might do to her if something bad happened to me. Off in his own universe of pots and pans, steaming soups, hamburger platters, and grilled steaks by day, and coming home to manage as best he could through those evenings, clouds of cigarette smoke wafting through the apartment, it's possible that he hadn't particularly noticed the way I looked, or my lethargy. With his early morning/afternoon schedule at the hotel and his habit of staying up late with his chums, perhaps he just hadn't been paying attention. But whatever his state of awareness, when my mother, in shock or denial, without knowing what else to do, finally let him in on my condition—she must have been shaking and worried out of her mind—Pascual, speaking much better English than she, rose to the occasion. Having a good side—a kind of calmness and a reasoning manner about him when he hadn't been drinking—he quietly tapped on our neighbor's door to use the telephone. But if the elderly Mrs. Blair didn't own one yet (though I remember that, in her hallway not far from her door, a heavy black old-fashioned rotary telephone sat on a table), he probably went down to the corner pharmacy to call our doctor, a Sephardic Jew of advanced years named Altchek, who had an office on 110th and Lenox in East Harlem. In that distant age when New York physicians responded quickly to house calls, he arrived at our apartment within the hour, to find me lying on their bed, barely able to move. Always impeccably dressed, Dr. Altchek, whose dark and liquid eyes, I remember, were filled with both sorrow and compassion, quickly went to work. What examinations he administered I do not recall, though I have the distinct memory of his feeling around my swollen abdomen with his fingers and of his thumb opening my right eyelid, that he shined a light into my pupils. It wasn't long before he, declaring my condition *muy grave* (*grave* is the word my mother always used), told my parents that I had to be rushed to the closest hospital, St. Luke's, fortunately only five blocks away.

It's likely that my father carried me there himself, my mother in a frantic state following by his side, or perhaps they had sprung for the luxury of a taxi ride, with Altchek, no doubt, accompanying us. It's possible that I was so listless as to approach unconsciousness, gone under like my uncle in Cuba after his fall; the truth is I don't remember much about that evening—I probably don't want to, or, as is likely, I had lapsed into a coma. I haven't the slightest idea of the treatments they administered in the emergency room, nor the day of the week, nor at just what hour I had been given a little wristband, admitted officially as a patient, then transferred to an intensive care ward, but that night, as my mother later put it, that *carajo*—the burden—my illness brought my family began.

. . .

No doubt she spent the passing hours nervously, and if my father remained true to form, having already become one of those conscientious fellows—*un trabajador* through and through—who perpetually worries about his image as a worker, he would have stayed in the hospital until it was time for him to begin his daily morning trek to the 116th Street subway on Broadway in silence, likely consumed with anxiety and bewildered. He probably spent that night smoking one cigarette after the other in the waiting room, all the while perhaps thinking about his older brother, the first Oscar Hijuelos, the parallels between us disturbing him. Later at the hotel, on the same morning after I had entered the hospital, while ensconced in the kitchen of the Biltmore Men's Bar with his chums, he probably had his first drink earlier in the day than usual—compliments of the bartender, a *cubano*, who took care of him. At least he must have felt blameless about me, but my mother? Told that I was suffering from a severe infection of the kidneys, she must have despaired at my misfortune and felt mystified by her plain bad luck. Perplexed as she waited in the hospital, her own uncertainties heightened, she must have certainly felt her own twinges of guilt. After all, I had gotten sick in her care and nearly died that very night, and for months afterward, my condition remained, to quote my brother, "touch and go."

Years later, when I'd ask her just what had happened, she'd always look down into her hands, as if just mentioning it left her feeling ashamed. She would always have the expression of a woman who, having tried hard to protect me, believed that she had failed. Sitting with her in the kitchen, I'd get the impression that my mother, unapproachable in so many ways, almost felt that she had no right to me as a son, and that deep down, she wanted to wrap her arms around me but couldn't: It was on such an occasion that she once declared, "But, oh, *hijo*, it wasn't anything we wanted for you."

For the longest time, all I would know was that I had gotten sick in Cuba, from Cuban *microbios*, that the illness had blossomed in the land of my forebears, the country where I had once been loved and whose language fell as music on my ears. Of course, diseases happen anywhere, and children get sick under any circumstances, but what I would hear for years afterward from my mother was that something Cuban had nearly killed me and, in the process of my healing, would turn my own "Cubanness" into air.

The few things I do remember about my initial hospitalization—tubes shoved up me and medicinal smells, and dreary wards, and a terrible loneliness, blood being constantly taken and bitter-tasting pills—seem to have unfolded in the kind of darkness that children experience in bad dreams. Bloated and seeping blood, I must have felt that something had gone wrong, but did I even know? Was I even awake at first? After all, it was common for nephritis to put children under for two and three weeks at a time, sometimes longer, if they awakened at all, and even if I had been aware of it, what on earth could I have been feeling?

They moved me to the St. Luke's Convalescent Hospital in Greenwich after a month or so, and from what I can recall, I was constantly given pills. Nurses pushed along carts on which sat quivering little white paper cups of diuretics and antibiotic tablets, though some of the kids, off in the deeper end, would have been treated for a week or so at a time intravenously; bedpans were the rule, and a mixture of food and children's toilet smells filled the air. Sweets were unknown to us, and what I mainly remember of the food amounted to the blandest of things—like boiled potatoes and carrots, cream of wheat, and possibly skim milk, along with some form of protein, like broiled chicken, but never served with salt, and skinless, a far cry from the euphoria of fat-laced, crispy *lechón*—ah, Cuba, Cuba. What birds we saw went flying through pictures on the walls, and while I have a vague recollection of playing with a set of Tinkertoys and of seeing a few brightly colored toy trucks rolling across a floor, the wonderful nature of daily childhood discovery seems not to have been a part of my stay. I doubt that we did much of anything at all except submit to our treatments and sleep and sleep and sleep. I'd sometimes hear the other children crying, and moaning in pain— from what, I don't know, perhaps from loneliness—but though it's hard to see their faces now, I would pop up in the middle of the night, feeling overwhelmed by the notion that these kids were only fleeting shadows, slipping away and just out of reach from me, on the other side of the room.

Though I spent a year in that place, I haven't a single name of any of the home's doctors or nurses in my head or, for that matter, any sense of what the hospital's staff members looked like, though my guess is that in the Connecticut of 1955–56, they were most likely decent, locally recruited New England folks, and since it seems to have had a somewhat religious atmosphere—here and there crucifixes hung on the walls—I would imagine that a chapel could be found somewhere inside and a chaplain, perhaps an Episcopalian priest, who would officiate over the services, say prayers over the young patients' beds, and console parents when things did not quite work out.

You see, there were others in my ward, some whose renal functions worsened and never quite recovered. It's a fact that not all the

kids who were sent there to convalesce got better, some beds emptying mysteriously overnight. Those who were healthy enough were
allowed into a playroom. That's where I got to know Theresa, a pig-
tailed, sweet-natured girl who, also suffering from nephritis, exhib-
ited the same listlessness and bloated limbs as I: We were cooped
up in the same rooms; our arms ached in the same way from where
blood had been taken; our urine swished, pinkish, in vials; and, in
that isolation, there was always someone around to examine for blood
what we'd left in the bedpan or potty. Breathing haltingly, we shared
the same shocked expression and, like all the kids in that place,
went for months without seeing the light of day, for we were never
allowed outside to romp in the surrounding greens, whose sunny
glare we spied flowing through the windows far above us. If I have
mentioned her, it's because Theresa is the only name I came away
with from that hospital and because, as it would happen, aside from
recalling that we were always playing with alphabet blocks on the
floor and that I'd sometimes see her curled up in a corner, drowsily
trying to stay awake—whatever medicines they gave us knocked us
out—she would be the only fellow patient I'd run into years later,
during my feeble-brained and quite timid adolescence.

Ah, but the anxieties we shared, the treatments I received, and
the isolation I felt during that period would later come back to me in
recurring dreams, the chronic nightmares I'd suffer from well into
my thirties. In one of them I'd feel a rod—possibly a catheter—being
inserted into my urethra, and a flinching over that pain, some nasty
burning in my center; the sensation, as well, of choking on the dry-
ness of pills, of swallowing metallic powders, would come to me,
along with this odd fearful logic that accompanied those rituals: If
I swallowed one of those pills, I'd die, while on the other hand, if I
didn't, I'd still die. Razors with pinheads pricked at my fingertips,
drawing blood, and with so many things entering me, up my rectum
sometimes, injections in the hard tissues of the buttocks, no wonder
so many of my dreams turned into nightmares. In the silence of that
ward at night, with only the humming of machines softly breathing
like the children themselves, down the halls, a haunting darkness

with almost a smothering human nature, like floating shrouds or shadows, which made one cry out, and some other lingering sensations that involved electricity, which would rise as a great shock from inside the body, that plump swollen bag filled with *microbios*, with sludge and Cuban shit, and probably with sins—why else would you be there in the first place? And while all that was going on, I'd begun to forget myself.

I do remember a closet. Since so many infant patients came and went from that place, the children of the ward were dressed in the cast-offs of the children who had preceded them; this apparel was stored in an immense-seeming walk-in wardrobe, smelling of lacquered pine, with shelves that were piled high with trousers and shirts and other items. One day, as a nurse fitted me into a pair of corduroys with a snap-button fly and pull-up straps and a striped shirt, she started barking at me in English to step forward, to lift my arms—commands that I apparently did not respond to quickly enough, for, as I remember, she pushed me inside that closet and slammed the door behind her, leaving me in the dark for what might have been only a few minutes but seemed to me an interminably long time: In the darkness, I worried that those clothes would come to life and, lifting off the shelves like spirits, come tumbling down to smother me. As for being locked inside? It surely reminded me that I was not at home in Manhattan, nor in my auntie Cheo's house in Holguín, nor by the beautiful Cuban sea, nor out in Oriente, dazzled by the evening sky, nor, for that matter, out on our front stoop, sitting beside my father as he smoked cigarettes, watching kids play on the street, or walking somewhere with my mother, whose faces, by then, I could barely recall.

Instead, in its pitch-blackness, it seemed a deep and endless space through which one might fall, or from whose depths might emerge monsters. Shell-shocked, and wishing that someone—my mother, my father, anyone—would come to my rescue, I knocked on the door until that nurse finally opened it, then scolded me about behaving better, to pay attention to her when she was telling me something, and, for crying out loud, to stop being so dense and learn to answer her in English. I don't know how many times this kind of scene played itself out over those long months, but I have a general recollection of feeling a sense of dread (as if the walls would fall on me), harangued (as if I had to watch my every word), and maligned for my ignorance of English.

And my mother? Once I started getting better, it was she, but never my brother, who would be allowed into an inner playroom to spend time with me. While she sat on a bench along a wall, I'd play with some toys by her feet. She always seemed to be talking about something, and frantically—I wish I knew now just what she'd said; occasionally, she'd lean forward to move some blocks around, but I hardly seemed aware of her. She must have at least smiled at me now and then and perhaps affectionately so, but though she may have wanted to hold me, it wasn't allowed—touching was forbidden. Other parents too, I recall, gathered in that room. I've since often wondered what she made of them or might have said to them if she could have managed more than a few phrases in English and shared her worries.

Visiting me and finding that I seemed to have withdrawn into myself, what else could she do but stare at me with dismay, shaking her head at this puzzling sea change, or else sit back in her chair in frustration? What else could she do but sigh, her striking dark eyes widening, as she muttered something under her breath? That same puzzlement would always enter her voice when she'd address me in the future, *"Me entiendes?"*—"Do you understand me?"—becoming one of the stock phrases she'd use to punctuate our every conversation, as if her own son had become a stranger who'd suddenly dropped into her life, an *americano* whose timidity and fears she needlessly (and perhaps selfishly) confused with laziness ("You didn't want to speak Spanish after all!") or with aloofness (*"Por qué me miras así?"*—"Why do you look at me that way?").

I'd often turn away from her, or shrug, or pretend that she wasn't there. It must have killed her.

On one of those afternoons, however, deep into my stay at the hospital, I was allowed to leave the ward and go outside for a while.

I know this because of a photograph, the only one I've ever had to commemorate my stay at that convalescent home. I'm in a heavy coat, bloated and lost and seemingly staggered by the brilliance of spring, my distinctly rounded, very pale face partially washed out by the sun, nothing less than a child's apprehension and bewilderment contorting my mouth. Someone, perhaps a family friend like *mi padrino* Horacio, had snapped it, since my father, in all that time, never once came to see me, and my mother didn't know how to—for I had never seen her take, in all my life, a single photograph (she was not that way). But thank God someone did, for after so many years, even that memory, of me standing in a field, would, like so many other things about that time, have likely been forgotten.

Eventually, there came the day I left Connecticut and found myself in a taxi with my mother crossing 125th Street over to the West Side from Lenox Avenue, where we'd gotten off a New York Central Railroad train. It must have been close to Christmas, for the store windows blinked with colored lights, and pine trees for sale lined the streets. Across the intersections hung banners and enormous glass and wire snowflakes, and here and there along the Harlem sidewalks, vendors were out hawking dolls and toys and all kinds of household goods, crowds of people bumping into each other, enchanting me. I know I wore a heavy wool coat with a hood because my mother kept tightening the cords each time I squirmed about while trying to loosen them from around my jacket collar, and, as would happen a thousand times in the future, she told me, pulling my hands away, "Stop that! Or you'll get sick again!" Then, just like that, we were on our way up that long hill on Amsterdam and making a left onto 118th, our six-story tenement building being the fourth one along that block on the uptown side. As we stopped in front of its gray Doric-columned stoop, screaming kids were inside playing running games like tag and hide in the front hall, among them little Jeanie Walker, the deaf lady's daughter, a little slow in the head but her pretty and expressive face breaking out into a huge grin of happiness at the sight of me: First thing she did was to wrap her arms around me in a hug, but just the same, I had trouble placing her.

Our apartment, number 2, was the first one to the left once you had climbed a few marble steps inside the mirrored hallway. I don't know just what I should have felt when my mother pushed open the front door and I saw a framed picture of Jesus with his burning heart in hand, but it was my brother, José, who led me down that hallway to the kitchen, with its buckling linoleum floors, its pipes covered in rust and mold, and walls streaked with amber trails left by the cockroaches at night. Off my parents' bedroom and directly above our basement boiler, the kitchen's floors were shaking as I walked in. I'm pretty sure it was a weekend day that I arrived, but I can't really say—only that my father, Pascual, or *papi,* was sitting by our Formica-covered table with some of his friends.

"*Recuerdas a tu papá?*" my mother asked me, just as he looked over at me. "Remember your father?" With his heavyset melancholy Gallego face, he seemed friendly enough, and because I did not know what else to do, I ran into his arms, his huge hands gently caressing my back, his eyes, always sad in memory, almost filling with tears over the fact of my miraculous return. My mother then told me, "*Dale un beso*"—"Give him a kiss"—and as I did, my face pressing up against his, a strong scent of tobacco and booze mixed with Old Spice cologne rose into my nostrils. Maybe he had asked me, "*Cómo andas, hijo?*"—"How are you, son?"—or said, "I'm so happy to see you at home," in English. Perhaps he had an early Christmas gift for me, some toy he would have gotten downtown; perhaps he introduced me to his Mexican buddy, Mr. Daniel Martinez, superintendent from up the street, with his languid jowl-laden face and mariner's tattoo on his forearm, or maybe his drinking pal supreme, Frankie the Puerto Rican exterminator, was on hand; perhaps a man I knew only as Díaz, one of my father's fellow cooks from the Biltmore, a dead-on Cuban look-alike for the actor Lon Chaney Jr., also sat by that table—but who knows, it was so long ago. Of one thing I'm fairly certain: My father, in the company of friends and in clouds of cigarette smoke, had exuded, while embracing me, something I hadn't felt in a long time, a simple kindness, which I hungered for; or perhaps, as I sometimes think now, it was pity.

. . .

Then, as I remember, I was taken to my room at the end of the hall, and that too seemed vaguely familiar; one of the few souvenirs I'd brought back with me from my trip to my aunt's—a smallish conga drum with an animal skin head on which was painted the word *Cuba*—had been set in the corner; a bag of toys accumulated during my stay in the hospital, filled mostly with rubber soldiers that some kindly neighbors had bought for me, my mother placed down on the bed. She pulled up on its sheets, the mattress below—"This one is new!" she insisted—fitted with a plastic cover, as she'd been told by the nurses that I'd started to wet myself at the hospital. Though the steam pipes sizzled, as if frying up things in their paint-mottling juices, my mother, despite that terrible heat, went over to the window and gave it an extra push shut. Then, almost cheerfully, she told me: *"Tienes que descansar"*—"You must rest now." And while I didn't feel like napping, and even if it was midafternoon, my mother made me get into bed, explaining that I had been very sick. Naturally, I obeyed. I don't recall that she kissed me, but, in any event, she turned off the lights and closed the door, leaving me, her most frail and delicate child, to stay awake for hours on end, peering out through the window, which only looked onto a desolate back courtyard anyway, wondering what to make of having to lie there in all that darkness.

CHAPTER 2

. . .

A Few Notes on My Past

For the next two years, I rarely went out, except to St. Luke's Hospital for checkups and to a few places in the neighborhood, my mother always by my side. She even felt leery about letting me into the hallway to play with the Walker kids, who daily swarmed up and down the stairs and charged along the marble floors. As for the often rowdy children on the street just outside our front windows, the kind of kids who'd shout, "Hey, Johnny, ya can kiss my ass" and "Fuck yourself, man!" as I watched them playing their running and hitting games and sledding down the hill when it had snowed, I felt nothing less than the purest envy for their freedom. Going out my door, onto the sidewalk, seemed a fantasy.

At some point, probably the summer after I'd finally come home, we went down to Coney Island by subway—a long trip in those hot electric-smelling cane-seated cars into Brooklyn, in case you hadn't the occasion to try that delightful ride out for yourself—on one of the few journeys we made as a family, small as ours happened to be. A photograph: I posed on the boardwalk with my dapper, self-possessed older brother, my father in his looming *campesino* majesty, and my mother, her usual guarded or skeptical expression on her face. I had on a pair of baggy white shorts and a straw hat, and, unless I'm mistaken, I looked plump and soft, perhaps not at all alert, as if I had no idea what I was doing there, not just at Coney—though I recall enjoying the sweetness of its confection-stand air—but with those people, who happened to be my Cuban family.

In those days, with José in school or else working at some part-time job and doing his thing here and there around the neighborhood, and with my pop often at the hotel, getting in as much overtime as he could manage, my mother became the center of my world, often my only companion—and a rather overly vigilant one at that. She constantly washed my hands (and only with Phisohex, the sole anti-bacterial soap that doctors considered safe for the infectiously prone) or else told me not to put things I found on the floor in my mouth and kept after my every move; it seems that I became her full-time job. Sweeping the floors or wiping down the walls, swatting at skittering roaches, she was always *quejando*—mainly about the fact that we were too poor for me to get sick again and about "*los gastos,*" the costs of my medicines and doctors and the hospital visits, some of which my father's union did not cover, my mother reminding me, "In this country, nobody gives nothing away." All the while she'd conjure, again and again, those microbes, which seemed to be everywhere, like the very air we breathed, the dust-mote-ridden light through the window, like God.

She'd go on as well about another realm of which I could have only been vaguely aware: her life in Cuba, and the goodness of the people she had known back in Holguín before coming to America—"*Este purgatorio*"—and about how wonderful a man my father had been to her in the days when they met—"*Cuando él me quería, mucho.*" "If only I'd known what I was getting into," she'd say, without ever missing the chance of attacking Maya. "Borja, yes, she was good to me, she even felt sorry for the way I was treated, but that other one?" She'd shake her head. "That witch . . ." And she'd launch into diatribes against my aunt and into the history of their differences, with stories that inevitably began with "One night that woman" or "That one, the evil sister, *la mala,* thought she could get away with anything, but . . ." Byzantine tales of torment and abuse—my fairy tales—flew from her mouth to my ears, and without her once considering just whom she was talking to, or my age and innocence, as if indeed it didn't matter if I really understood her at all.

Sometimes, she'd take me down the hill along Amsterdam to the ladies' *pelluquería,* or hairdressers, on 122nd Street, which my godmother, Carmen, ran with her younger sister, Olga; in that salon, these Cuban beauties and their female clientele formed the hub of local Latina society, just as Freddie's Bodega and the liquor store next door to it, farther down the block, formed a hub for the Latino men scattered here and there in that ethnically mixed neighborhood. (There was a Japanese restaurant on 119th, a Japanese grocery on 123rd; Irish bars up on Broadway; and, as a matter of course, we'd occasionally see some mysterious-looking Hasidim, with their wild locks of hair, affiliated with the Jewish Theological Seminary, walking on the street. And the center of Harlem itself, on 125th Street, our Times Square, was a tempest of black and Latino and, in those days, Italian folks.) In Carmen's, I just enjoyed hanging around and overhearing the ladies discuss some rather touchy subjects, like male infidelity, crushes, sex, heartthrobs—the sort of things I assume they assumed I couldn't understand, even when Carmen tended to speak to her godson, while smiling and pinching my chin, in both English and Spanish. My mother, in such circumstances, tended to tell Carmen not to bother, with the Spanish at least, but she, my godmother, perhaps flabbergasted at the notion, always went on in that way, saying things like "Magda, you have to give him some encouragements. *No seas tan dura"*—"Don't be so hard on him." She and her sister, Olga, were delicious women, in any case, and quite nice to me. Besides, I just liked the laboratory atmosphere of their salon, with all its space-age-looking hair dryers, ladies in curlers, Spanish in the air, music on the radio, and clients chatting away endlessly in voices that, for the most part, with sunlight pouring down through the window, seemed happy.

And my mother would take me to church occasionally, while my father always stayed home. I enjoyed seeing so many folks dressed up in their Sunday best, the men all wearing hats and ties, and my mother's friends in their veils and florid hats, smelling nice and looking pretty standing on the steps. While the Mass, in solemn Latin, never failed to put me half to sleep, my mother, nodding at the altar and making the sign of the cross, seemed to take it all to heart, even when she couldn't always understand the sermons that the Irish priests—Fathers Ford, Dwyer, and Byrne—delivered weekly to a congregation that, bit by bit, was becoming less Irish and more Spanish. We'd sometimes attend High Mass at eleven, to hear my brother, one of the pipsqueaks in the choir, sing, but even then, if a few people started coughing around us, she get me out of there immediately. (And speaking of religion, at home, my mother often punctuated her observations about life with "*Ay, Ave María*" and "*Por Dios!*" for no particular reason at all; I'd sometimes see her sitting by our kitchen table whispering to herself as she read some letters, presumably from Cuba, and then, having prayed, make the sign of the cross. If it was a letter from her mother, María, in Cuba, she'd kiss the wafer-thin paper it had been written on.)

Now, you'd think that a child in such close proximity to so loquacious and opinionated a woman would have picked up the pieces of that lost "mother" tongue again, just through constant exposure. But, although that's *just what should have happened*, the simple truth is that she never really spoke *to* me but directed her tirades, her aphorisms, her orders, her stories, *at* me. If she'd been a different sort—say, like my loving aunt Cheo—my mother might have gently prodded/eased the Spanish language out of me or, at the very least, gone over the sorts of exercises that most Cuban mothers might with their children, like the rolling of the *rrrr*s through the repetition of tongue twisters like "*Tres tigres tristes,*" or, starting from scratch, taught me just what things were called, or how the Spanish alphabet worked and about *los vocales*, or else, in any case, *gently* cajoling me to speak more Spanish, day by day. Who knows how my feelings about "refusing" to speak it might have changed. But, for whatever reasons, that sort of patience, organization, and attentiveness were just not part of her nature.

Perhaps she thought my Spanish would naturally come back to me or that, quite simply, it seemed too great a bother, given her more immediate concerns. (Years later, she'd say, shrugging, "I don't know why you didn't want to learn," as if that were something that had been offered. And while I now wish she had been more demanding when it came to my speaking Spanish, my guess is that I would have still found ways of pushing that language away.)

Regardless, by then, I remained indifferent, blocked, and somewhat of a spoiled princeling: She may have filled my ears with her thousand-words-a-minute Spanish, but like a good defender, as vigilant about avoiding the absorption of those words as if they were poison, akin to the Cuban microbes my mother always talked about, I hardly ever let those words in through the walls I'd put up. And so, early on, we adopted our own way of communicating with each other: She'd speak to me in Spanish, which I comprehended but resisted speaking, and I'd answer her in English, a language she barely understood and, in any case, never really cared for.

Standing by my window, I loved it when the scissors man, with a grindstone on his cart, came up the hill ringing a bell and, getting a taker, stopped to sharpen those knives and cutlery, the sparks flying off his wheel; or I'd see a ragman going into certain doors where bags of cast-offs awaited him; and, I swear to God, that neighborhood had its share of midgets—maybe they were hooked up with the Ringling Brothers circus and stayed somewhere on 125th Street—but they'd sometimes come waddling by on the street in pairs. Then there were the Italians in their Alpine hats, three men strumming guitars and mandolins, along with a woman, her ears bejangled like a Gypsy's, banging a tambourine, who seemed to appear from out of nowhere—from East Harlem perhaps, or Little Italy—and marched up the hill, serenading the tenements with bel canto and Neapolitan songs. (People would lean out their windows and toss down dimes and quarters wrapped in tissue paper.)

And I'd feel a definite excitement when the coal truck pulled up—yes, that was a different era in New York—and practically backed into our living room, or so it seemed: From its rear dropped a metal chute down into a basement window, where there was a storage bin, and for half an hour or so, the coal, released from the truck, would come rushing below into that darkness, like so much river water (a sound I still find soothing). From the window, I'd watch as well, with some enchantment, what the local Irish cops on the beat called "shenanigans." Our black streetlamps, from the turn of the century, had ornate astragal moldings and roundish ridges that made it easy enough for kids to climb, some three stories high, to their finial tops, usually to place or recover what the local mischief makers had left hanging there—trousers and sneakers, and sometimes even underwear, during that unceremoniously humbling process known as "de-pantsing." They also played three-sewer stickball in the spring and summer, and games like Chinese and American against the walls, and now and then, as I'd wait for my father to come home, fistfights broke out, usually over some girl, someone calling the cops, a squad car or an officer on his beat arriving to break things up—it all seemed so thrilling to me. (Crazily enough, also on that street at night, some fellow, in celebration of his Celtic roots, think his name was Myles, would dress up in a tartan skirt and tam-o'-shanter and, as if part of an invisible procession, move up and down the block, playing wistful airs on the bagpipes.)

Still, if my mother saw me standing by an open window, she'd pull me away and slam it shut. And then, without much of an explanation, she'd threaten me with the notion that I might not ever get the chance to go out; and so I'd sit down, benumbed and cautious, wondering what the hell was going on.

Several times a day, I had to take a regimen of pills, which I got used to, and occasionally some vile-tasting liquids, possibly mild laxatives, but when it came to food, I had to live off my memories of better times. As such, I felt deeply affected whenever an ice cream truck drove up the street with its tingling bells, or when I saw kids coming up the block carrying a white-boxed cheese pizza from the old hole-in-the-wall V&T's on 122nd Street, which they'd eat right there on the sidewalk. (In such a state of vigilance, or food envy, you become aware of every box of Cracker Jacks, every Hershey bar, every thirty-five-cent roast beef sandwich on rye bread with mayonnaise and salt and pepper from Adolf's corner delicatessen that you've seen someone eating.) I could not eat anything with salt, most meats, butter, nor the merest bit of sugar, as my nephritis had apparently left me in a prediabetic state. (By then, my eyes had started failing badly—I had no idea of just why things looked blurry a few yards away and thought that normal; but the deterioration of my eyesight was distinctly related to what had happened to my kidneys, a doctor later told me; neither of my parents, nor my brother, had problems with their vision.) Which is to say they'd put me on a diet that no child of six or seven could ever possibly care for: Whatever foods I did eat—potatoes, carrots, and some meat or chicken—were boiled to death, and never anything as delicious as one of my *papi's* typical weekend breakfasts of fried eggs with steak or chorizos, onions, and potatoes cooked in delicious Hotel Bar butter and smothered in salt, the aromas of which I had to endure while eating bowls of sugarless cream of wheat farina with skim milk. Whatever the doctors at the hospital instructed my mother, invariably through someone translating, she adhered to their dictums religiously, as if she were frightened to death about what my pop would do to her if I had a relapse.

Nevertheless, that regimen was no easy thing for a kid to put up with, especially given that the one luxury we had in our lives involved food. We may have been "poor"—"*Somos pobres*," my mother declared for years afterward—but by the end of each week, our refrigerator practically spilled over with delectable cuts of meat and other victuals that most families in my father's income bracket—"upper-class poor" is how my brother and I came to think of ourselves—would have never been able to afford.

You see, as a short order cook at the Biltmore Men's Bar, my father had worked a special deal with the pantry supervisor at the hotel, an *Italiano* who, for five dollars a week, allowed him to bring home whatever cuts of meat and other delicacies he wanted. He was not alone in this. Earning little despite their membership in the Restaurant and Cabaret Workers Union, local number 6, all the kitchen staff availed themselves of such perks, while management, being vaguely aware of this—and doing the same themselves—looked the other way. (As they did about other things: I grew up eating with monogram-embossed Biltmore utensils and on slightly chipped plates from their different restaurants, and, at one point, an art deco armoire, a cast-off from when the hotel had started refurnishing the rooms, took up a corner of my parents' bedroom.) Daily, those secreted packets of meat came home with my father without fail. Ambling toward Amsterdam, across the Columbia University campus, from the 116th Street subway, with his slightly limping gait—even in those years when he was in his early forties, he'd balloon up and down in weight—he'd walk in through the door at around three thirty or four in the afternoon, a strong scent of meat and blood preceding him, and particularly so if he'd come uptown in an overheated train or in one that had stalled in a tunnel. Tucked inside his shirt and wrapped in muted-orange butcher's paper, those bundles of meat and chicken almost always bled through the fabric.

He'd set them down on the table, light a cigarette, and pop open a bottle of sweating Ballantine beer, while my mother, who did most of the cooking, looked over the contents of those packages: On a normal afternoon, they might contain a few pounds of filet mignon or breaded veal cutlets—what she called "empanadas"—or porterhouse steaks or a big plastic bag of Gulf shrimp too, or several whole chickens, or a slab of Swiss cheese, or a few pounds of finely sliced French ham or turkey breast, not to mention a pound or two of ground sirloin beef or a glowing one-pound brick of creamy Hotel Bar butter— items that, on such afternoons, seemed especially tempting since they were strictly forbidden to me.

Such meats jammed the freezer compartment and the shelves of our buzzing Frigidaire. We had so much of that stuff that I can remember my mother lamenting the waste, often throwing out packages of freezer-burned ground beef after they had lingered too long in the dense frost. In a way, when it came to food, my father was a kind of Cuban Santa Claus or Robin Hood, if you like. For whatever he would bring home, he always shared with our neighbors in the building and with his friends.

My mother did as well. For years, Mrs. Walker, "*la muda*," could hardly pass by our first-floor apartment on her way home without knocking on the door; often enough, my mother found something from the refrigerator for her to take. I can recall watching Mrs. Walker, who, thin and wan, smoked up a storm herself, always letting her facial expressions stretch like rubber in every direction, her hands wildly working the air while attempting to convey to my mother some simple notion, like coming upstairs for a bite—Mrs. Walker spooning her fingers into her mouth and repeating, "Et, et, et," while my mother, savoring a dawning moment of understanding, proclaimed in her heavy accent, "*Jes, jes*—food, food! *Comida*, ha!" and turned to me, saying, "You see, *hijo*, I can speaky the English!"

Sometimes, it would work out that we'd head upstairs into Mrs. Walker's chaotic apartment: Her husband, a bartender working nights, somehow managed to sleep in a room in the back while their kids—Jeannie, Gracie, Carol, Jerry, and Richie—had the run of the house; I mainly remember that piles of clothes were laid out haphazardly all over the place, that she, like my mother, tended to bring in stuff off the street, all kinds of furniture in various states of disrepair lying here and there; and in her kitchen, where we would sit while Mrs. Walker, a nice lady, started to cook some things on the stove—say, some of the steaks my mother had given her—and went on and on about something, which I could barely comprehend, my mother, telling her things in Spanish, with a few words of English thrown in, seemed completely at home with that arrangement. One of those ladies who would smoke while eating, she'd sit down and have a snack, and my mother, sticking to her little finicky rules, refusing anything herself—she'd shake her head, pat her stomach to indicate that she was full—seemed content to bask in their oddly intimate relationship, unrestrained by language. Having a sweet soul, Mrs.

Walker, aware that I had been so sick, would just look over at me and smile, blow me a kiss between puffs of smoke, and then, putting down her fork and cigarette, as she did one afternoon, make a rocking motion back and forth before her stomach, mumbling something in her mangled guttural speech, which my mother, tuned in, seemed to pick up on. In one instance, my mother, translating, told me, "*Ay, pero, hijo, ella dice que fuiste un bebé muy lindo*"—"She says that you were a beautiful baby." And seeing that my mother had gotten that notion across to me, Mrs. Walker would reach over and pinch my cheek.

We wouldn't stay long. I used to think that it would have been nice to play with Mrs. Walker's kids, who had tons of board games on their couch, and the girls skipped rope in the living room, but my mother wouldn't allow me to join them. Maybe one of them might have a cold without knowing it, and, in any case, there was a mustiness about that apartment, perhaps from all the old stuff that constantly accrued in the place, which must have struck my mother as unsanitary. So we'd head back downstairs, *la muda* talking up a garbled storm from her door, a nagging sensation bugging me that I had missed out on some fun once again, and the smell of that nicely cooking steak still in my nostrils.

On some evenings, my father cooked for his pals—steaks with onions and French fries or a simple platter of fried chorizos and eggs—dishes they managed to gobble down even while they continued to smoke (puff of cigarette, bite of food). My father always sent those fellows, wobbly legged and well sated by the time they'd leave, often around midnight—how they managed to get to work the next mornings, I do not know—off with a package or two of chicken or with some cold cuts, his generosity, to his mind, an important part of his very Cuban way of being.

Since we lived near the university, we were sometimes visited by a Cuban professor of the classics, a lonely-seeming baldheaded fellow of middle age, from Cienfuegos, by the name of Alfonso Reina, whom my father had happened to meet one afternoon while walking back from the subway across the campus. The professor always turned up with flowers for my mother and bonbons for her "*preciosos*"

Cuban boys, though I could never have any. His overt gayness, the way his eyes would melt looking at my father and he'd always ask my older brother for a kiss on his mouth, somewhat disturbed my pop, who, in his old Cuban ways, felt somewhat uncomfortable with the fellow's homosexuality but nevertheless welcomed him into our home for a meal and drinks, as long as there was someone else around, like his friend, the sturdily manly (if occasionally falling apart) Frankie the exterminator, as a buffer. He also welcomed into our kitchen one hell of a blessed fellow, from 119th Street, one Teddy Morgenbesser, formerly of Brooklyn, who worked in the accounts office of the *La Prensa* newspaper syndicate and had lucked out by falling in love with a bombshell Dominican babe, a certain Belen Ricart, who had two kids and with whom he lived outside of marriage. Jewish, he'd gotten so Hispanicized by her—and from a pretty active nightlife in the dance halls of the 1950s—that he spoke only Spanish in our home. But from what I could tell, he, with his dark hair parted in the middle, dark eyes, and Xavier Cugat mustache, as well as his way of wearing *guayaberas* whenever possible, seemed quite Cuban, and since I only knew him as Teddy, I assumed that was the case.

My father sometimes took me over to his place. He'd decorated the apartment to resemble, I suppose, an apartment in Havana, with bright fabrics on his art deco furniture, tons of (rubber) palm plants, and hanging beads in the doorways. He had a console on which he played only Latin records, and mostly the big-band mambo music of the 1950s, along with all kinds of folkloric Cuban music, obscure stuff he'd hunted down in Harlem.

On one of those occasions, two things happened that I obviously haven't forgotten. As I was sitting there one afternoon watching the adults drinking away, my father had Teddy pour me a glass of strong red Spanish wine so that I might try it—why he did so, I don't know—but it tasted awful to me; I couldn't imagine why anyone would bother to drink such a bitter thing. ("He's too young for that," my father had ruefully concluded.) Later that same afternoon, Teddy, who owned a reel-to-reel tape recorder, conducted, I guess for posterity's sake, what amounted to an interview entirely in *español* with my father, during which my father, his face aglow, spoke at length about his early days in Cuba, his life on the farms on which he had been raised, and, in effect, a rather straightforward history of his family and of what must have been much happier times, my father attentively noting the death of one of his younger sisters at the age of two from a fever (his eyes welling up), and on along a meandering road of nostalgia and even more tears, to the sad passing of his older brother, Oscar, which, in such moments, he seemed not to have recovered from.

"He was my life, and my blood, who taught me everything I know," he said, patting his chest, which had started to heave, at which point, Teddy, having gotten enough down, concluded the session lest my father get more carried away. Now, if it might seem unlikely for me to recall such exact words from so long ago, I won't dispute that I am perhaps approximating at least the spirit of what he said, but I am now only mentioning this at all to lament the fact that, all these years later, for the life of me, I can't remember the tone and timbre of my father's voice, which remains always soft but indistinct. (As a further aside, about twenty-five years later, long after my father had died, I bumped into Teddy on a bus, and among the things we talked about, I asked him if, by some distant chance, he had any of those old tapes around. The answer, unfortunately, was no, to my deepest disappointment, for I would have given my right arm to have heard my father's voice again.)

Occasionally, if there had been a banquet at the hotel, he'd come home with a box or two of fancy pastries, two dozen chocolate éclairs, and as many creamy napoleons; these too were forbidden to me. It was worse on holidays like Thanksgiving and Christmas, when my father would turn up with a twenty-pound turkey and bags of stuffing, which my mother served with sweet potatoes, garlic-drenched yucca, and fried plantains, people coming over to join us, people eating away, while I'd sit off with some carefully prepared chicken and the usual roundup of boiled vegetables. At least my father was sensitive to my gnawing desires, and the way I'd look at him as he'd sit down before a plate of filet mignon smothered in onions. It bothered him enough that, now and then, he'd ask my mother if she was sure I couldn't at least have a little taste of something different from my usual fare, but she, forced to play the heavy, always reminded him of the fact that, as far as the doctors were concerned, I was still sick, and susceptible to many bad things. He'd nod, smile sadly at me, give a little shrug, and then send me off to bed, where the aroma remained so strong that I could hardly sleep.

So for the longest time, the scent of frying plantains killed me. Not once for several years did I consume anything as lively as a quivery slice of flan, the one dessert my mother cooked, and wonderfully so. And while my parents occasionally sprang for a bar of sugarless chocolate for my delectation, the kind of chalky pasteboard confection intended for old folks and diabetics, every so often a two-pound block of dark German chocolate, over which I would salivate, would turn up in our kitchen. This I'd forlornly watch my brother happily devouring, chunk by chunk. My only consolation came from the fact that my *papi*, feeling for me, often had some ten-cent comic book that he'd bought for me in Grand Central, usually a Superboy or a Flash, which I think he chose because of their torero-red cape and costume. As soon as I'd hear his keys jingling in the door, I'd run down the hall to greet him, his smell of cologne, cigarettes, and meat intact, and find the comic book rolled up in one of his coat pockets; but before he'd hand it over, he'd lean down and say, *"Dame un abrazito"*—"Give me a hug" (or *"Dame un besito, chiquito"*), and once I had, into my room I'd go to follow, as best I could since I could not yet read, the adventures of those heroes by looking carefully at the panels, an act that always remained a high point of my boring days.

In those years, my father seemed not to know what to make of me. I can only recall his kindness, and with the biases I eventually developed toward my mother because of language, I got so attached to him that I came to rewrite my history in the hospital. Little as I remembered about my stay in Connecticut, I just couldn't imagine that he hadn't ever come to visit me during that time. Fabricating his presence in memory, I'd remember my pop in a trench coat and hat, with the smell of rain and cigarettes and cologne about him, standing by the visiting room doorway and smiling gently at me. I'd see him nodding at those other parents, their faces grown taut by worries, and then, inside that room, holding out his arms to me.

What drove that version, which I'd cling to years later after he was gone, came down to the fact that, however flawed the man might have been, he possessed an abundance of down-home Cuban warmth.

Altogether, he was a funny cat, *un tipo bueno*, a tender and affectionate man who had his ways. Once when he had to attend a formal wedding and concluded that his two-tone shoes were too scuffed for the occasion, he covered them over with black enamel paint. And when, in his late forties, he began to get slightly nearsighted and, at first, didn't want to bother with an optometrist, he made do with a pair of glasses that someone had left behind in the bar. (They seem to have worked for a while.) At the hotel, he played the weekly numbers, never winning but kept paying out a dollar a week every Friday for many years, mainly to help out the black man hawking them, a Korean war veteran who had a hook for a right hand. He collected pennies, keeping them in special blue albums, perhaps thinking that they might one day make him rich. He never read books, having neither the time nor patience for them. What he did read: the *Hotel and Club Voice* newspaper, the *Daily News*, and *El Diario*. Also the occasional brochure that someone at the bar had given him, brochures about "Dream Vacation Homes" in New Jersey and on the value of Korean pearls as an investment opportunity being two that I recall. I can remember him far more for his tenderness toward me, at least when I was a kid, than for anything else, but all the while, he had an air of resignation about him and little patience for waiting things out, even gambling. Once, years later, when he took me over to the bazaar at Corpus Christi School and we played a wheel of luck, instead of putting down a few dimes on two different numbers, he put down dimes on all but a few. Of course, the number that he hadn't bet on came out; he shrugged and we moved on. When this Puerto Rican kid, Fernando, got stabbed in the gut in a basement a few buildings away during a hassle with an Irish guy over a girl, and came staggering up the stairway, blood trailing behind him (the sidewalk would bear those stains for weeks), it was my father who went down to the corner to call the police. Afterward, he calmly sat out on the stoop, smoking and telling whoever wanted to listen about what had just happened. In other words, he could be quite laid-back, in a Cuban country boy manner.

And, as I have mentioned, he'd speak to me in English, not always, but when he did, it was with a quiet authority and without my mother's befuddlement and confusion. Whereas my mother remained, for all her life, an ebullient woman, incapable of holding back, her nervous energies flowing all over the place, he comported himself with his younger son with a minimum of words: "Come here," "Go on," "What do you want?" "Ask your mother." And, at least until things got too hard for him, he rarely showed any anger toward me or the world. I just found something comforting about him, even if I would never get to know what he was really about.

Yet, while he offered me affection, that *cubano*, a union man and hotel cook of simple tastes and longings, he never really taught me anything at all, not how to dress (though he could be quite dapper), nor how to dance the mambo or rumba (at which he, like my mother, had excelled), nor, among so many other things, even how to drive a car (he, raised on farms with horses, never would learn). And when it came to something as important as restoring that which had been taken from me, *a sense of just who I was*, I doubt that, as with my mother, it occurred to him that something inside of me was missing, an element of personality in need of repair. Earthly in his needs and desires, he just didn't think that way. Though he never once accompanied me to a doctor and really didn't take much care of himself, he simply must have seen me as the son he had almost lost, and, at first, for the longest time, always deferred to my mother when it came to matters of my health.

After a while, my father began to feel sorry for me. One night, I remember, when my mother was out with some friends, he could not take the wan expression that had come over my face as he stood over the stove, cooking up a steak in butter with onions, along with fried potatoes, in a skillet. Turning to me, he asked in his quiet way, "*Quieres un poquito?*"—"Do you want some?" And though I felt reluctant to answer him, as if to say yes would be wrong, he filled my plate anyway. Unfortunately, my stomach had grown so unaccustomed to such rich foods that not an hour later, I got deathly ill and, coming down with the shivers, had to throw everything up, and took to my bed, worried that my mother would find out; and yet, with my father telling me, "Not a word to your mother, huh?" I passed the night, reeling with the memory, however fleeting, of that delicious meal.

Naturally, I came to prefer his company, which is not to say I didn't care for or love my mother in the same way as my father. If I felt a different kind of affection for her, it had more to do with the way she'd sometimes look at me when I'd speak to her in English, as if I were doing something wrong, or worse, as if I were some stranger's kid trying to give her a hard time. I was too hyper to always notice, too insensitive to become morose, but I can remember occasionally wondering if I were nothing more to her than a burden that she had no choice but to contend with.

Though strict about my diet, she had her inconsistencies. Once she handed me a glass of orange juice in which I saw floating the cellophane body of a dead cockroach, its antennae curling along the surface. When I refused to drink it, she made a face, and, in one motion, picked the insect out with her fingers and threw it in the garbage. "*Está bien, ahora*"—"It's fine now," she told me. And when I still refused to as much as take a sip, she grabbed the glass off the table and emptied it into our sink, all the while muttering, "It's like pouring money down the drain." Turning, she scolded me, "I can't believe how spoiled you are! We're not like *los ricos—la gente rica*, after all!" Then she sat down, oblivious to just how startled and bad I felt.

On another afternoon, when we were in the kitchen, as I sat by the table across from her, eating something, she started looking at me in an odd way. And just like that, she tilted her head back and, gasping, her eyes rolled up in her head; and she cried, "Help me, *hijo*,

I can't breathe!"—"*No puedo respirar!*" Slumping forward, she laid her head in her arms, still as a corpse. What could I do but panic? My stomach went into knots, and I started, without really knowing what was going on, to tug on her dress: I felt so anxious, I thought of running over to Carmen's for help, but, at the same time, I worried about leaving her alone, and pulling at her arm, I kept repeating, "But, Mamá, Mamá, are you okay?" That's when I saw the crest of a smile forming on her lips, and her eyes popped open, and sitting up straight, she triumphantly told me, "Ah, but now I know that you care whether I live or die!" She was laughing while I withdrew deeply into myself, wishing I could slip into the walls: I can remember her telling me, "*Pero qué te pasa?* I was joking. *Fue un chiste!*" When she saw that I hadn't lightened up, she waved me off, saying: "You're too serious for so little a boy." Then I think she pinched my cheek and, shaking her head, left the kitchen, saying, "But now I know you love me. Yes, I do. Now I know."

Okay, so she was a bit unusual and perhaps still as mischievous as she had been as a girl. But the truth is, not having any basis for comparison, nor choice, I got used to her. Still, though she meant well, she obviously (so I now think) couldn't help but let her resentments affect her judgment. Out of curiosity one day, I happened to ask her where I was born. And without hesitating, she said, "But, Son, don't you know, I found you in a garbage can, right out in front." And she took me over to the window, pointing to some cans by the railing. "It was in that one, at the end. I heard you crying and when I saw you, I thought I just had to bring you home." And she, always inventing stories—what she called "*relajos*"—laughed and crossed her heart. "I swear to God that's the truth."

I suppose she wanted me to feel a deep gratitude; I suppose it was her way of telling me how lucky I had been to have been rescued from the hospital, but while I didn't really believe her—for on the other hand, she was always reminding me about how she carried me in her stomach for nine months—a part of me did. Later, looking in the mirror and never really liking what I saw, I truly wondered if the truth had finally come out. Years after, every time I'd hear about that

Sesame Street puppet, Oscar the Grouch, who lived in a garbage can, I'd think of that afternoon.

Not to say that my life in that household with my mother was just a misery—to the contrary, long before I had made any of my own friends, like my pal from across the street, Rich, the ladies who'd come by to see her always treated me nicely. Having a simple liking for my mother's elemental personality, one of them, Chaclita, came by at least a few times a week. Always smelling nice from some mild eau, she wore pearls and, with her dyed blond hair and flapper wardrobe, seemed the most elegant woman to have ever entered our house. She'd bring along bags of fancy hand-me-down clothes for my mother, and, as well, little packages of the European-style marmalades left over from her trips abroad. A sunny spirit who laced her Spanish with French and always spoke of a love affair she once had with a singer named Nelson Eddy, she, in addition to concertizing, taught violin out of a flower-adorned apartment on Morningside Drive. She never had a bad thing to say about anyone, not even my father, whom she must have occasionally encountered in one of his less robust states.

In any event, it was Chaclita who made the effort to show me how to write down my own name. This she did one afternoon as we stood in the hallway, her slender (somewhat bony) hand holding my own and guiding my pencil over each letter across a pad. I did so shakily, and afterward, I couldn't help looking at the name *Oscar Hijuelos* over and over again. Fascinated, and treasuring it as if it had some great value, I took that slip of paper around the apartment with me proudly, until, after I'd left the little exercise out on the kitchen table and gone away for a few moments, I returned to find that my mother had thrown it out.

But to be fair to her, my mother also tried to be my teacher, though she could barely read English. What books we had were the kinds that she either found abandoned under the hallway stairs or in boxes left out by the garbage cans in front of our stoop, tomes, for the most part, discarded by the university folks who, at one time or other, had taken temporary apartments in the building. (I recall a few medical students coming and going quickly, and for a while, there

was a kindly Lebanese professor, prematurely balding, with two little children, living up on the second floor—I think he was a widower because of the way he doted on the little ones—I can remember him winking at me as I'd watch him speaking with my father from our door.) Among the titles my mother collected for our hallway bookcase: a fancy edition of *Oliver Twist* with half of its gold-leafed pages missing, a biology textbook, a volume or two of some outdated encyclopedia, a hardcover copy of *The Adventures of Tom Sawyer*, circa 1930 (which I still have to this day), and other choice sundries like *Agricultural Development in the Middle United States, 1954–1955*, all of which, I think, she brought home mainly because she thought they might be worth something; but she also treated them, at the very least, like decorations, along the lines of the other bric-a-brac that my mother, who could not pass an item left out on the sidewalk, also brought into the apartment.

My lessons, if they can be called that, unfolded with the aid not of children's stories of the Dick and Jane variety, nor any of the classics like *The Little Engine That Could* or of the Golden series, but rather the comics, which my mother called "funny books." My brother, working in a local stationer's, brought some home regularly, as did my father, but we also got some from a teenager named Michael Komisky, later a Catholic missionary priest, who lived in the building next door. A gentle and idealistic soul, his comics were not about crime or adventure but featured animal stars like Bugs Bunny, Donald Duck, and Felix the Cat. These my mother found the easiest to understand. In a tender way, as I think about it now, the afternoons we spent sitting by the kitchen table or lying side by side on her bed, with such comics opened before us, were our most peaceful and unhurried, though I'm still not sure what to make of those lessons in which my mother did her best to improve her quite minimal English alongside me. Just the same, she tried.

"Felis, wh . . . whar . . . whers ar-ray . . . jew . . . jew gaw-gaw-eeng?" And then, she'd stop and say, *"Dejame ver"*—"Let's see now"— and begin the same line again, "Felix, where are you going?" her pronunciation as confounding to me as before. Our movement from caption to balloon, and panel to panel, was always glacially slow, but I didn't mind those lessons at all: I don't know what or how much I learned from hearing the words of Felix ("Yes, I will take this rocket ship to the moon!") as they fell from her lips, but my mother's attempts to meet me midway, as it were, along with her struggles and out-and-out bursts of laughter—from finally understanding what the heck was being said—constituted the only moments that we were together as mother and son when my supposed frailness, my suscep- tibility to infections, my illness, and all the anxieties she attached to me were thankfully absent as a subject of our conversation.

Of course, I had other moments with her, when, forgetting all the crap I'd put her through, she occasionally became almost ten- der toward me. During a time when she worked cleaning up after a kindergarten school on 116th Street in the evenings, I'd accompany her, passing the hours playing with blocks in a corner, while she, not really knowing how to clean at all, went about singing to herself most happily, dusting the furniture and washing the floors and bathrooms until about ten o'clock, when, her work completed, she'd take a few moments and sit down behind the upright piano to pick out, by ear, some tunes she remembered from Cuba. (They always put her in a good mood; walking home, she always seemed a different kind of lady, lighthearted and laughing.) And in the autumns, during a soporific late afternoon rain, falling asleep by her side, I'd feel her pulling me close to her and, sensing her soft breathing, I'd drift off into the most wonderful of dreams. *"Qué tranquilo y sabroso, eh?"* she'd say. "How tranquil and delicious this is!" Later, in unexpectedly good spirits, she'd take me into our narrow bathroom and, singing gaily, wash my hair over the bathtub, the warm spray pouring down on my head, her fingers massaging my scalp, an unexpected maternal sweetness over- whelming me: Everything about that process, from the smell of her perfume and shampoo and the proximity of her body, in its warmth, as she pressed ever so slightly against me, seemed so pleasurable that whenever she washed my hair, I never wanted it to end—and not just for the little niceties of being pampered but because, during such moments, I'd somehow feel a continuity with her past.

"*Te gusta?*" she'd ask me. "Good! At least your *mamá* is doing one thing right!"

And she'd laugh and dream aloud: "I'm doing it for you the same way my *mamá* did it for me, in Cuba." Then: "If it feels so good, it's because your *abuelita* taught me, *hijo*." Afterward, she'd towel my head off, stand me in front of a mirror, and comb my hair. Looking me over, she'd rap my back and say: "*Ya está!*"—"Just fine!"

One afternoon—I was seven—a letter arrived from Cuba, in a nearly weightless envelope. She opened it by the window, at a time of the day when the sun had risen over the tenement buildings across the street, and light came flooding into the living room. Kids were on the street; I could hear them shouting, a ball hit during a stickball game, a car honking, someone calling out, "Run, Tommy, run, ya dumb fuck!" when all at once, as she read down the page, she stopped and looked up, and said, "*Ay pero mi mamá, mi mamá.*" She shrank within herself just then—I'd never seen her looking so petite; she wasn't—and began to softly cry, shaking her head, murmuring to herself. Not knowing what to do, I went over to her, asking, "What is it?" But, as she stood in that shaft of light, she kept on weeping until, just as suddenly, she gathered herself and, touching my face, told me: "*Mi mamá se murió.*" Then, in her English, "Jour *abuelita*, she is now in heaven."

As for my homeschooling, I think that period of studying with my mother lasted for perhaps a year and a half or so, until there came the point when—my father had probably pushed for it—my mother, reluctantly believing that keeping me at home wouldn't do me much good, finally enrolled me in a first-grade class at the local Catholic school, Corpus Christi, run by wimpled Sinsinawa Dominican nuns. The school itself was situated on the Broadway side of 121st Street, just across the way from the Teachers College complex of old turn-of-the-century buildings, its classrooms taking up three floors above the church where I had been baptized, with a rectory where the nuns lived way above.

This happened late into the year so that I had only a few months of schooling at that level. It was just as well—I'd felt terrified and not at all used to being around other children, let alone such an ethnic mix, for the kids in that school, just as in the neighborhood, included blacks and Puerto Ricans and Cubans, as well as Irish and Italians, among others. I felt, from the start, with my mother by my side, tremendously self-conscious and uncomfortable, not just because I'd been apart from normal kids for so long, but because of the way I'd come to believe that there was something wrong with me, for not a day had gone by when my mother hadn't reminded me that my body, like the world, was filled with poisons.

Just being out of the apartment on a regular basis threw me, and in my social awkwardness, I must have struck most of those kids as something of a lost soul. Though I had enjoyed the odd outing with my family into someone's home, going to school scared me, and my face must have shown it. I can recall always feeling out of sorts. In my quietude, I just seemed different from the other kids, down to my unusual last name, Hijuelos, and the face and complexion that didn't seem to go with it. Neither the Irish nor the Spanish-speaking kids knew what to make of me. Given my timidity, as if I'd have preferred to disappear into the walls like a ghost, and, as well, the fact that I didn't have any real inkling how to read, my situation wasn't helped by my mother, who made sure that everyone knew about my condition. While the other kids were dropped off by the entryway doors below, she not only walked me up to my classroom each morning, on those days when the weather permitted me to go to school at all, but, in her broken English, told my first teacher—I believe her name was Sister Mary Pierce—that I was still a very sick child and that I had to be watched over carefully. My fellow students would have probably noticed this without the two cents she'd deliver by the doorway: "My son, he is not so good in the kidneys." And when I had gotten upset one day because the sister asked that we come to class with a ten-cent box of Crayolas, which my mother claimed she could not afford because we were "poor," as I sat forlornly in the classroom, later that morning, my mother, having changed her mind, turned up with a box of those crayons in hand. These she delivered at the door, but not without cheerfully announcing to everyone, "*Mi niño,*

Oscarito, he was crying and crying for them." (I remember feeling stunned with embarrassment and wishing that I could turn into a bird and fly from that room.)

I still missed days, especially if it rained or snowed or if I showed the slightest signs of any fatigue. That my mother refused to let me out of the apartment in the bad weather must have seemed pathetic to some of the kids, but the sisters were more forgiving. (Maybe they thought she was a little troubled and felt sorry for me.) As I got around to becoming, more or less, a full-time student, my mind always wandering, I would feel confused about whatever the nuns were teaching us, as if some part of me deep inside couldn't help but cling to a notion that I was stupid, mainly because I couldn't get my mother's voice out of my head. It took me a while to fall into stride there, having already turned into an overly cautious and suspicious child, somewhat rigid in my ways. For the first few years, I preferred to be quiet during our classes, which began after we'd recited our morning prayers (an "Our Father," a "Hail Mary," and the Credo) and the pledge of allegiance, whose words I could never quite get straight. Having started out later than most kids, I lived in dread of being called on, and lacking self-confidence, I always felt that I had to play catch-up when it came to reading and writing, over which I agonized, all the while thinking that I wasn't very smart. And not just because I was often too distracted by my own anxieties to concentrate well, but out of some sense that my mother and father's limitations, when it came to English, had become my own: Just attempting to read—anything really—I'd feel as if I had to swim a long distance through murky water to fathom the meaning, and, at the same time, though I eventually improved, shell-shocked though I was, I always had the sense that the language was verboten to me, as if I needed special permission from someone to take it seriously. No matter how hard I tried, or how well I did on the tests, I secretly believed that my mind was essentially second-rate—all the other kids just seemed brighter than me.

Told to paint a picture of a house in a field during the sessions that passed as art class, I tended toward using a single color, like green, as if to venture into a variety of colors, like the other kids, remained somehow beyond me. My brushstrokes were clumsy, too wide and sloppy, which was particularly vexing to me, since my brother, José, had not only always possessed an artistic temperament but had already, as a somewhat worldly streetwise teen, begun drawing quite well—for he was already getting locally known as an artist. I also lacked his fine singing voice, having failed to please our well-known choirmaster, a certain Mr. MacDonald, who during an afternoon audition turned me away with disappointment. And as I mentioned in passing before, I couldn't see very well, already squinting and barely making out what the nuns wrote in chalk on the board. It took a while for anyone to notice my nearsightedness, and once my mother began to suspect that something was wrong with my vision, she, holistically minded, or believing in the old wives' tale, resorted to feeding me a bag of carrots a day for months, before finally taking me down to a union optometrist on Twenty-seventh Street, who, for five dollars (upon presentation of a union card), fitted me with my first pair of awfully thick-lensed eyeglasses, my vision so far gone by then that just seeing things as they really were seemed a revelation.

Nevertheless, those eyeglasses, however helpful, added another unwelcome dimension to my self-image: four-eyes. I already had to live with kids calling me an Oscar Mayer Wiener, and though my name would later invite more pleasant permutations among my friends, like Oscar Wilde, Oscar Petersen, and Oscar Robinson, among others, I could never stand it: The name that now seems far more elegant because of my uncle's importance to my family in Cuba, which I wasn't even really aware of back then, became something I never felt proud about as a kid. In fact, I can recall feeling envious over a cowboy's name on *Rawhide,* a show my father liked to watch at night on one of the second- or third-hand television sets he'd buy from a used appliance shop in Harlem. The show's main character was called Sugarfoot, and I suffered greatly that my parents hadn't named me something that wonderful. (Years later, when I first thought I might publish somewhere, I seriously considered adopting the nom du plume Oliver Wells, and to jump even farther ahead, during the kind of journey I could never have imagined making as a child, I signed my name on the guest registry of the archeological museum in Ankara, Turkey, as Alexander Nevsky, the kind of thing I'd do from time to time.)

I never dallied in front of mirrors for long, and when I did, the face staring back at me through the half-moon wells of distorting glass seemed as if it should belong to someone else, not an Hijuelos. (I hated looking at myself: Once, after I'd somehow gotten hold of a water gun, I went around the apartment shooting out any lightbulbs that happened to be near a mirror—oh, but the beating I got for that.) That feeling used to hit me particularly hard when, during the rare outing with both my mother and father into the outside world—a trip by subway to Queens to see my cousin Jimmy and his beautiful wife, María, or up to the Bronx, where my *papi* liked to hang out with his fun-loving friends on evenings so long they drove my mother into fits of despair—I always felt dismayed and vaguely saddened by seeing our reflections in any sun-drenched window: For while I could "read" my parents' faces easily, their dark features so clearly defined, my own, whitewashed by light, seemed barely discernible. Put that idiosyncrasy together with the fact that I was too aware of my body, that cumbersome thing that had gotten all messed up and needed special care and medicines, I sat in the classrooms of Corpus with such self-consciousness that I hardly ever relaxed or felt at ease like the others.

Along the way, however, I experienced my first publication, the moon ditty that appears earlier here in the epigraph. In its simplicity, it says a lot about me back then, and predicts (I think) my later life view. Just something I had scribbled down during class, it ended up in *Maryknoll* magazine—the sisters had sent it to their missions in Africa, South America, Hawaii, the Philippines, Hong Kong, Formosa, and Japan, as an "example of the originality and imagination of a fifth grader." (Mainly, I am amazed that it's one of the few things my mother kept of my doings from those years.)

There's not much more about my childhood schooling to tell, except to say that, in some essential sense, I somehow got through it alone. I read all the books we were supposed to read, though I don't remember any now, and magazines like *Highlife* and *Maryknoll*. On certain afternoons, we had readings from the Bible, which I loved. My favorite story was of Lot's wife turning into a pillar of salt, but Moses's epic tale, from his abandonment as a baby in the reed marshes of Egypt to his last days on a mountain overlooking Jericho, from whose summit he spied the promised land, before dying, broke my heart—and I took that book's stories as pure history, burning bushes, water struck from a stone, descending angels, and all. (Another favorite involved a tale from the book of Daniel, in which the evil Babylonian king witnesses God's own disembodied hand scrawling out words on the wall, the kind of thing I often waited for to happen at night when, unable to sleep, and hearing voices from down the hall, I'd get spooked by the Rorshachian shapes made by the bad plastering in my bedroom.)

Nothing, however, seemed more straightforward than Father O'Reilly's Baltimore Catechism, which, wrapped in blue covers, contained the simple truths that we children were expected to learn and abide by, lest we one day experience the fires of hell. A simple question ("Why do we pray?") was followed by a simple answer ("Because God hears us"). In that manner, as I recall, it offered explanations of sin, salvation, and the immortality of the soul and, as if out of a fairy tale, did not skimp on its depictions of the devil, who came across vividly in wonderfully simple but graphic black-and-white ink renderings as a hoofed, betailed, soot-faced creature with pinched back-pointed ears, crooked bat wings, and long talons for fingers, holding a pitchfork or else cringing in fear and revulsion when confronted with true sanctity. I believed in the devil as well and, somewhat of a blank slate, took to heart all the other dictums we were taught. (By the time I received my First Communion at the age of ten, I truly thought that my state of grace so guaranteed an entry into heaven that, with a child's optimism, I'd think it wouldn't be so bad if I were to be run over by a truck.)

I'd always absorbed religion. For one of the first things I'd ever heard, predating my illness, came down to this: *"Hay un Dios,"*— "There is a God." A God to be respected and feared, a God who ruled the universe through the wisdom of His ways. I don't remember hearing that He, the Father, had ever been a kindly God—that was reserved for His son—but, on the other hand, as my mother used to put it, we owed this world—our very existence—to him, "*el Señor.*" Even if He'd kind of fucked me, at least in terms of what I had once been or was on the cusp of becoming, I truly believed that His presence was as certain as the air I breathed. And why wouldn't I, spending so much time as I did with my mother? In some ways she really went for Catholicism: At the beginning of Lent, a cross made by ashes graced her forehead; on Palm Sunday, strands of dried palm reconfigured as a crucifix were put up on the wall as a reminder of what was to come; Good Friday brought the three o'clock gloom, when, I swear, the world seemed to go dark at that exact moment when Jesus was said to have died.

Easter, however, brought the greatest joy, as holy days went. Even to a little kid, it seemed wonderful that the misery of death was transcended by the flower and sunburst triumphs of the resurrection. And it was fun. I recall that even my father attended the Easter services, my brother singing with the choir for the High Mass, the three of us dressed to the nines, going off together to get lost in that rarified atmosphere of incense and flowers, all the while taking in the mysterious and chilling mystical incantations of the Latin (which my mother always appreciated and possibly understood better than the sermons, which were recited in English). Sweetest of all, for a sick kid like myself, I always felt happy—and curious—to see the other children in their Sunday best, their shoes spanking clean, their hair nicely combed, as they sat up in the balcony, facing the altar, in their own separate section. I enjoyed the sense of being around them, of almost seeming to be a part of a group, even if we sat far away: Quite simply, I often felt alone, though it wasn't as bad in church, where, at the very least, I could count on the company of the angels and saints.

I even had a guardian angel, whom I'd always envisioned as a sword-yielding being of indeterminate sex, with flaxen hair and enormous wings, and Jesus himself, whose picture, which I always admired and felt fascinated by, hung in the hall.

. . .

In fact, I'm pretty sure that, with my protected, coddled, and shell-shocked air, I gave off a somewhat otherworldly and "good" impression, the sort that, later, as I got a little older, provoked certain of the nuns to invite me up to their convent above the school, where I was given simple chores, like sweeping the floors or cleaning their long kitchen's cabinets, in exchange for a handful of candies and fifteen cents or so in pennies. Despite the endless stories I've since heard about cruel nuns, and aside from having the back of my head slapped and my knuckles rapped by a ruler, and yes, my earlobes tugged painfully when, getting older and more pent up, I turned into a classroom wise guy, I have always thought only fondly of those women, who, in their black-and-white wimpled habits and ascetically appointed rooms—narrow, with just a bed, a table, a washbasin on a stand, and a crucifix hanging on the wall—seem now to have been nothing less than sincerely devout throwbacks to some other time.

. . .

Along the way, in the church rectory, the Irish priests must have had some kind of discussion about the changing demographics of the neighborhood, for they began to give Hispanic-flavored sermons. At those nine A.M. Masses when the children filled the galleys, from the pulpit came little parables about a boy and girl, José and María. Typically, these were simple moral tales: María finds a wallet with money in it: Should she return the wallet, even if she has her eye on a dress or her mother could use the money? What should she do? This was the kind of thing she'd ask José. Righteous and good at coming up with answers, he'd advise her to do the right thing. Or they'd feel troubled over some hardship in the family and were thinking resentful thoughts toward others, only to learn that was not the right way to behave. The devil would come to them in disguise and advise them to do whatever they wanted but then they'd meet a gentle and quiet man with the most saintly face, and he would tell José and María to take the high road, never to sin, and in that way they would find their happiness. Sometimes he would tell them his name: Jesus; or it would turn out to be a guardian angel—but in any case, the point of those sermons always came to the triumph of good over evil. And so it went; I would sit listening, surrounded by real-life Josés and Marías in the pews, fascinated and rapt by the telling of such simple tales.

· · ·

Unavoidably, in those years of my childhood, we'd go to the clinic at St. Luke's. I went once a month, sometimes more, for tests mainly. But I hated going. I was already sick of doctors, or at least the anonymity of them, kindly though some may have been. (I didn't like to be touched, palpated, or examined by strangers.) For the longest time, just the prospect of a hospital visit made me gloomy—and I would become so reluctant about those appointments that I could barely raise my head sometimes as I'd amble down the hall, to the point where my mother would call me, as she sometimes did my pop, *"un trastornado"*—or schlemiel loser, to translate it loosely.

Inevitably, I always went, however, my mother tugging at my hands, indignant over what she thought of as my ingratitude. She seemed to believe that I never appreciated the stuff she'd gone through for me—"What do you think I am, a witch?" Now, when I had to abandon my comic books or when she'd disrupted my reveries, which were mainly about becoming like the other kids, and I wasn't in the right mood, I sometimes fled down the hall from her. I'm pretty sure that she first slapped me in the face on one of those days, when, cornering me and fed up with having to chase me around, she really let me have it, the ritual of punishment, or the threat of it, becoming a part of those outings. While heading out for our clinic visits, she didn't help matters by telling me, "Don't forget, *hijo*, that you almost died."

One winter, I was about nine, it was snowing, and just that short trek to the pediatric ward of St. Luke's Hospital on 114th Street required that I get bundled up in a hundred layers as if we were on an outing to the Siberian tundra. I felt manhandled as my mother pulled tight my coat and out we went, down the block, and, as we'd round the corner, heaven forbid I'd stop, enchanted by the soda shop window, where some new cheap toys had been put on display. "We don't have time for that, nor the money," she told me. "One day, when you get better, you can look at whatever you want, but you're still sick and weak—*muy débil y enfermo*—and whether you like it or not, we're going to the hospital."

On any given day, it was jammed full with row after row of mothers and their kids, mostly black and Latino from the projects and Spanish Harlem and even farther uptown, folks who seemed far poorer than ourselves. (My father, after all, had a job.) There just weren't too many white kids around, and, turning heads as we walked in, as if I gave off some bad smell or perhaps because my mother, without realizing it, tended to look upon people of color in a somewhat aloof way, I felt a distinct discomfort every time we had to go there. Aside from that, however, I just never liked having a thermometer stuck up my ass, nor blood taken, nor peeing into a little paper cup behind a curtain while a nurse looked on.

And there were the hours we spent before we'd see any doctors. In those pre-Medicaid days, hospitals like St. Luke's operated on a sliding scale and were in effect, with their steep discounting, much like public health and union-sponsored clinics when it came to treating the more financially disadvantaged folks who had no doctors of their own. The visits cost two dollars, the medicines and tests somewhat more, though not much, but the price for such a good deal—and, believe me, there were mothers in those crowds who couldn't pay even those cheap fees—required that one wait and wait and wait. An eleven o'clock appointment could mean that you might get seen at four, and, as the cutoff seemed to be around five, I can recall more than a few occasions when, after so long a wait, we were told to come back the next day.

C'est la vie, at least with some.

Nevertheless, during those waits, my mother always managed to find some kindred Latina spirit to sit next to, so that they might talk about life and, often enough, the health issues affecting their children. "My son is a diabetic," one might say, or "My daughter has a murmur in her heart," but for whatever reason, my mother, loving any modicum of sympathy, and quite charming when she wanted to be, took a particular pride in trumping the others when it came to me: "*Mi hijo, casi se murío de una infección de los riñones*"—"My son nearly died from an infection of the kidneys," she'd say, a nearly penitent and saintly manner coming over her. *"Fue muy muy grave* [He was very grave]—it's a miracle that he's even alive." And she'd make the sign of the cross, glory be to God in the highest. I tended to feel embarrassed by such remarks, perhaps even more so because they were rendered in Spanish, and that embarrassment deepened when, suddenly, one of these ladies whom my mother inevitably befriended, while noticing how I seemed to have tuned out, leaned close to her, quizzically asking, *"Pero habla español?"*—"He speaks Spanish, doesn't he?" a query to which she usually replied, *"Un poquito,"* her eyes looking afar, her head shaking.

"He spent too much time in a hospital when he was little." And confiding more, she'd add: *"Es más americano."*

For my part, I'd either fidget around, wondering why, if that was so, it seemed something that I should be ashamed about, or, even given that it happened to be true, how I had become so. Though it defined me in those days, that Cuban illness seemed, by my lights, to have always been there, this black hole from which, as if out of a fairy tale, I had crawled into as a little *cubano* and, after a deep sleep, had emerged as something else: a young prince in the making turned into a freak.

When the nurse, usually Irish, finally called us to the front desk for our appointment, we often suffered from the slight indignity of hearing the pronunciation of our last name mangled: Hijuelos, a rare enough Spanish appellation, came out as *Hidgewellos, Hidgejewloos,* and worse. One thing about my mother, having her pride, she took personal offense at the error, often making a point of pronouncing the name properly over and over again for the nurse, so that she might not repeat it the same way ("Okay, okay, lady, what do you want from me?"—as if she, or anyone else, could not care less).

And off we would go, to sit in yet another room, in the pediatric wing up on the next floor. Its waiting room walls, as I recall, were cheerfully decorated with large flowers and suns and bumblebees, and, depending on the time of the year, the nurses would put up cutouts of Halloween pumpkins, of witches on brooms, and pictures of Santa Claus, snowflakes, and holiday trees at Christmas. That room seemed nicer than the one below: At least they had piles of comics and Golden Book fairy tales for me to look at, and I always felt intruded upon when we would be finally called in for my examination.

Our appointments always began with an interview. None of the doctors spoke Spanish, but there always seemed to be a Puerto Rican nurse around to help things along.

"Anything unusual going on with him?" she'd ask my mother in Spanish.

"No," my mother answered, looking down chastely.

"Is he sleeping well?"

"Yes," she would answer, which wasn't quite true, but since I suffered regularly from nightmares, I suppose it wasn't anything my mother cared to share.

"And did you bring along the sample?"

"*Ah, sí*." And my mother would pull out this plastic container from a paper bag, which she, waiting outside the bathroom door, had me fill the morning or evening before. I could never bear to look at it and felt anxious and ashamed as hell when my mother handed it over to the nurse, as, aside from my sense of violated privacy, the sample might contain enough *microbios* to put me back in the hospital.

The doctors were always brisk: They'd examine me all over, and on one of those visits, it was discovered that I suffered from psoriasis, just like my father did. Then I'd get on a scale. I always weighed too much, a mystery since I was supposed to be on a strict diet. The hematology tests were the worst, however—I hated the tube tied around my forearm, the deep pricking that followed, and the sight of my blood filling up the hypodermic, but at least that aversion to needles would one day keep me from becoming a heroin addict like so many of the kids in my neighborhood. Sometimes, a more arcane series of tests, taking up much of the day, required that I go to the nephrology ward. That usually took up another hour or two, and we'd sit around in that room, facing other children, their worried-looking parents beside them, while my mother, hopeful that another Latina might be among them, carefully sized them up. More than once I'd seen her lean forward and, smiling at a "swarthy"-looking Italian or Greek woman, say something to her in Spanish, only to sit back, sucking in air through her lips, in disappointment.

That winter afternoon, my mother had caught wind from a nurse that a nearby room had been occupied by a Latino just recently admitted to the hospital for nephritis, and for some reason, after I had finished with my ordeal and we had gathered our coats, she insisted that we drop in on him to say hello. His wife and two children were in the room beside him. A handsome man with a wonderful smile, he already had an IV line hooked up to his right arm, but, aside from the fact that his face had turned deeply red, as if he had been baking in the sun, he didn't particularly look sick to me. Once my mother introduced herself—"*Soy la* Señora Hijuelos, but you can call me Madgalena"— she began peppering him with questions about what he did and where he had come from (second-generation Dominican, a car salesman in Queens by trade, I seem to recall) and pulled me over to his bed saying, "*Mira*, Ernesto, this is my son. He has *nefreetees* too," she said, as if I still had it, and as if that fact, if still true, would hold a special meaning for him. "But he is already getting much better than he was—as I am sure you will too. *Los médicos son muy sabios.* The doctors are very wise."

"*Gracias, señora*, for saying so," he told her.

A good-natured fellow, with a young and shapely wife, who looked to me both hopeful and on the verge of tears, he wanted to shake my hand, but he did so with difficulty and weakly, for he could barely lift his arm up. Nonetheless, he smiled kindly, and with that, as a nurse appeared by the door, we left the room, but not before my mother told him, "Have faith in God—you will get better!" And to his wife, she said: "They will fix him in no time, I promise you that!" The wife smiled, nodded gratefully, and with that, my mother, feeling as if she had done them some good, took hold of my hand and guided me down the hall. "What a nice man—with such a nice family," she kept repeating ever so cheerfully in earshot of the room, before falling silent. In the elevator, descending to the main floor, however, my mother began shaking her head and repeating, with a little click of her tongue, "*Ay, pero el pobrecito.* Oh, but that poor man. Did you see how scared he looks? And how bad he seems? Oh, but I don't have a good feeling about him at all. Oh, I hope he doesn't die," she said, confiding, "but he probably will."

And that was all. At the doors opening to the main lobby, I almost didn't mind it when my mother went about the ritual of pulling on my galoshes, buttoning my coat, securing my *bufanda* snugly around my neck, and tying, as she always did, the hood ever so tightly, because once we left that sterile place and passed through its revolving doors and out onto the sidewalk, as a snowplow pushed slowly along the avenue, through the carbon blueness of upper Manhattan at five thirty or so, with the buildings across the way resembling misted and barely lit palaces, that most lovely and soul-cleansing of things in this world, snow, was falling everywhere around us.

Behind this recollection is another, of sitting in that same ward one day when I was about twelve and noticing, just across that room, an auburn-haired girl who seemed awfully familiar. She also looked at me in the same searching manner: She wore braces and, in pigtails, with brightened cheeks, had greenish eyes that I seemed to have seen before. My mother noticed her as well and, realizing something, told me: "But don't you recognize that girl? Don't you remember her? It's Theresa from that time when you were in the hospital! You used to play together." She was sitting beside her mother, a somewhat prim and anxious woman, and once my mother had figured things out, she smiled, saying in her best English: "Theresa—this is my son, Oscar, from the hospital," and with that, Theresa smiled and, standing up, startled me—not only because she too, sitting in that ward, had the same lost air about her but because, though she was quite thin from her waist up, I could see that beneath the hem of her violet dress, her ankles were badly swollen. Of course, she was there to receive a dialysis treatment, and, truthfully, she did not seem too happy about that—how could she have been? Still, I did my best to hold a conversation with her: I think it came down to "How have you been doing?" To which she responded with a shrug; and while I sat beside her for a few minutes and I thought we might become friends, I still felt, at the same time, so awkward—and ashamed—of my year in that hospital that I could barely think of anything else to say.

"But you're okay?" I finally asked her.

"I guess so," she answered, shrugging again.

But I knew better, even then: A funny thing, I could almost feel the sickness of her kidneys emanating from her lower back, and from her expression, as if she wanted to cry but couldn't, I saw that she felt trapped by a physical condition that, in her case, had never really improved—and she knew it. At the same time, however, as much as I vaguely recalled playing with her, I really didn't feel a thing for Theresa, my emotions about that hospital stay too raw to revisit, muted. It was probably the same from her end, and so we just sat together for a while, until she was called inside. I never even learned where she lived and have no idea now of what happened to her, for I never saw her again.

That image fades into a conversation between my mother and father one night, a few years after I'd started school. Because I was such a nervous sleeper, they'd sometimes let me fall asleep in their bedroom, just off the kitchen. I'd take that opportunity to listen to the television shows that sounded in the courtyard from the windows of our upstairs neighbors: *The Jack Benny Show* is the one I remember in this instance, a particular episode in which Mr. Benny and his butler, Rochester, discuss what sort of Christmas gifts they should get for Mr. Benny's friends—*"How 'bout a hoss for John Wayne, boss!"* Rochester asks in his cheerfully raspy voice; at the same time, my mother and father had started discussing some insurance policy they'd taken out for me. Assuming that I didn't understand Spanish well enough for them to veil their words, their conversation went as follows:

"Ten dollars a month is a lot of money," my father said. "He seems healthy enough."

"Oh, but, Pascual, what are you thinking? Don't you remember what the doctors told us about his nephritis?" my mother asked. "The kidneys can go anytime again from an infection."

"I know, I know, but he seems so much better," my father said. "And he doesn't look so bloated as before."

"Okay, so what?" my mother told him. "He's only better because I've kept him on that special diet, and the medicines. . . . I'll tell you

I'm sick of being the witch—when I come to him with his pills, he hates me. How do you think that makes me feel?"

"Yes, I know," my father said. "But do you really believe he's going to get sick again? I don't think so, and, *mi vida*, that monthly bill is killing me. So why don't we let it go?"

He lit a cigarette: Someone must have given him a Ronson lighter, or he'd found it left behind at the hotel bar. Its metallic lid clicked shut.

"Why? Why?" she cried out. "Because if he dies and we have no insurance, how will we pay for him?"

"Maybe the union will help," my father said calmly.

"Your union is spit," she told him. "And anyway, what would the insurance company give us back?"

"One hundred and fifty dollars. Maybe a little more."

"On a fifteen-hundred-dollar policy?" she asked. "After all the money we've been paying for him all this time?"

"Yes, that's what the fellow said. I talked to him today."

"But, Pascual, I don't know," she said. "Do we really need it that bad?"

"We always need money," he told her.

"And for what?" She clicked her tongue. "So that you can spend it on your friends?"

"Please, woman, don't start," he told her in the strongest manner he could muster when he hadn't been drinking. "It's just something we could do. That's all I mean. Think about it, huh?"

"Yes, think about it—as if what I think matters to you?" she went on. Then, after deliberating a bit: "Do whatever you want," she finally told him. "But if he dies, you and your drunk pals can get some shovels and bury him in the park. You know?"

"No, no, Magdalencita," my father told her, exasperated. "It's not going to happen that way. Tomorrow, I will call the agent and see what we can do about the policy. And please, don't look at me that way—I just don't think he's going to die, and that money will help us in the end, okay? Maybe I can buy you something nice."

"Yes, something nice," she muttered.

To be honest, once I sort of put what they were saying together, that they were talking about a burial insurance policy, it startled me. I thought about every single picture I'd seen of Jesus being laid in his tomb, and how the priest at church, with his scarlet complexion and rosy cheeks, sermonizing from the pulpit, said things like "Dead, though we may turn to dust, we shall rise again" and all of that, mixed up with Mr. Benny and my parents' voices, somehow left me picturing my interment in Riverside Park (though I would have settled for the woods along one of the terraced walkways of Morningside). And so naturally, I couldn't help but call out, "Good night!" the way I always did whenever I became anxious in the evenings. That night, however, as soon as they heard me, my mother hushed my father—"Pascual, please, lower your voice—and not another word more about the policy," as if she thought there might be some chance in a million that I'd understood what had just been said. I called out again, and with that they called back, "Good night, *hijo!*" which somehow made me feel a little calmer.

Later, after Mr. Benny's show ended, and my parents had managed to make their own peace, it was my father who came to get me; not so long before, he would have carried me down the hall to my room, but I weighed more than one hundred pounds in those days, something I'd just found out while standing on the penny scale at the corner pharmacy. And so he, a cigarette between his lips, walked me down the hallway to my room, and with a little pat on my bottom, sent me off to bed. That same night, I dreamed about a stone rolling away from the tomb of Jesus, and then of myself running across a field, clouds of *microbios,* as frenzied as a plague of flies, chasing after me, and I jumped up, screaming, the sheets beneath me, with their plastic cover coverings below, seemingly catching fire and then becoming, just as quickly, damp with my urine.

. . .

It may be a coincidence, but that same year, we'd come by a 1959 edition of the World Book Encyclopedia. A rather dashing and earnest young Cuban salesman, going from building to building in my neighborhood and concentrating on a Spanish-speaking clientele, had knocked on our door. He must have been persuasive, because, as with all purchases, my mother remained tight about money. I can remember seeing him from the hallway: Drop-dead handsome and somewhat priestly in his demeanor, qualities that left my mother half-breathless, he went into a whole explanation about such a set being indispensible to any child's education and, therefore, to "*el futuro de la familia.*" Later, after she consulted with my father, they signed off on a payment plan and, within a few weeks, that fount of knowledge, shipped in two boxes, arrived. My father called me into the living room and proudly stood over me as I pulled out each cellophane-wrapped volume from its box: After all, these were the only freshly purchased books that would ever come into our house. Looking them over, I was fascinated, thought all of the illustrations, especially the transparencies showing the different systems in over-leaf of the human body, fantastic. My mother stood by the doorway, asking me, "*Y qué?*" And I nodded, thrilled that something so new, even if they were books, smelling so nicely, had arrived.

It's since occurred to me that they may have paid for that encyclopedia with the refund money from my burial policy, but what does it matter? Those volumes would sit in that same living room cabinet for the next forty years, and they did make a difference to me. For I'd consult the volumes for school assignments, as when I'd write little pieces about the War of the Roses or an American state, like Indiana. You know, the kinds of subjects that further enhanced my distance from the hallucination that had been my Cuban past.

· · ·

It was around 1960 when, despite my ongoing "delicate health" and, no doubt, over my mother's objections, my father had decided to send me and my brother down to Miami to spend time with Maya. Though my pop must have suspected that Maya had some ulterior motives—as did my mother, who at that point could not, for the life of her, mention Maya's name without muttering some long simmering aside ("Oh, but that woman hates me; why should we send her our sons?")—he perhaps thought that, deep down, his sister Maya had only good intentions. (I also imagine that, despite the expense of sending us south by railroad, he figured he might save himself some money over the next few months.)

By then Maya and her dapper husband, Pedro, had settled into a new life, and prosperously so. Since moving to Florida back in the late 1940s, he'd left the music business for good, gone to school, and set up a business as a building contractor. I was about to turn nine that summer, in 1960, and my brother, at fifteen, could look forward to earning some extra money working as a hand on one of my uncle Pedro's construction sites. With the city of Miami just coming out of a decades-long state of torpor and decline, my uncle, an employer of more than a few recently arrived Cubans who, at that early stage, had already fled Fidel Castro's revolution, also happened to be the man who, over the next decade, would put up many of the exiled community's new houses.

Whatever my father's reasons, after a thrilling train trip south, my brother and I found ourselves staying in Maya's mightily air-conditioned Spanish-style house in North Miami, whose banyan- and blossom-bush-filled front patio and backyard, jammed with mango and papaya trees, somehow reminded me of Cuba. (I'm pretty sure that the damp earth smell and the florid perfumed air took me back to Holguín, and, at the same time, I felt dropped into the lap of luxury, for they seemed to have it all.) By then, always expecting to be waited upon, I had a softness and naiveté about me that must have left my aunt Maya salivating over my potential for manipulation. I can remember feeling taken aback when seeing Maya (and Borja) for the first time: They shared so many of my father's features—the long-ish, somewhat hooking nose, the sad, vaguely Semitic-looking dark eyes, drooping jowls, and thin-lipped smile—that it was as if I were looking at female versions of him, or to put it differently, at women who were far more handsome than pretty. Since I resembled him in more ways than my brother, my aunt Maya, gasping, then clutching at her breasts, off which hung a gold crucifix, declared, after seeing me for the first time: "My God, but you look just like your father did at this age!" And with that, Maya pulled me close to her and, squeezing me half to death, whispered, as she often would on that visit, "But, child, look at me, can't you feel the love I have for you? And look around you and see what your nice *tía* Maya can provide."

I did, taking in the sturdy glamour of a stereophonic console with a gleaming veneer and rack of recordings from Pedro's days as a musician, walls that were not flecking, ceilings that were not sagging, wall-to-wall carpeting, new furniture and adornments, all nicely clean thanks to a woman who came in weekly. A kind of arboretum took up a room off the *sala*, in which a great twisting tree rose up toward a raised skylight in the ceiling, birdcages surrounding it; there were humming air conditioners, which I considered an unbelievable luxury; modern appliances, including an immense refrigerator that almost took up an entire wall, one side of its interior filled with Pepperidge Farm frozen turnovers, Pedro's favorite, and other treats— all for the asking, she told me. Outside, parked in the driveway, was Pedro's second Cadillac, which also impressed me.

From the start, she kept me by her side; on days when my brother went off with our uncle, Maya would take me over to a shopping center, which was across a highway not far from her home. She'd buy me new clothes, to replace the "rags" that I had come down wearing, and along the way, though I felt vaguely disloyal to my mother, I took in Maya's version of their history, nodding: "Your father made a big mistake going with your mother," she'd tell me. "She tricked him—you know that, and the poor man, with the soul of a saint, fell for it—and what does he have now? But a job that will never get him anywhere in life and a spouse who will drive him into an early grave! Are you listening?"

And while I was too young to really understand the depths of her feelings about my mother's apparent shortcomings, I got the drift: "Without that crazy woman, your *papi* would have been a much happier and successful man. You know, *chiquito*," she said at one point, "without her, he would have certainly turned into something more than a cook, *el pobre*." Then, a little more rancor and vitriol against my mother: "You know that your *tío* Pedro has offered to help your father with work in the construction business if he came here to Miami, but your mother wouldn't hear of it, and that's why he has to work like a slave to make ends meet...."

As she'd go on, I'd drift off naturally: I felt homesick for our apartment, missed my folks, even my mother, and yet, what could I do?

"And your mother," she'd say, shaking her head. "If you nearly died, it was her fault. As I'd always tell your father, 'Be careful with that woman, she'll lead to no good,' and—yes, she's crazy, anyone can see that . . . and careless—if she wasn't, then you would have never gotten sick in Cuba; no, no—that's something that I would never have allowed to happen."

My brother, by the way, took this in from a sly distance and, quite aware as to what my aunt Maya was about, told me, "You know the score; be nice to her and see what you get for it, but don't believe most of the stuff she tells you, hear?"

But she kept trying, day after day; buying me new finery, she'd say: "Now, if you were to live with your dear aunt Maya, anything you'd want would be yours." I didn't know what to make of her campaign, and I can't imagine what she expected me to do, even if she were to persuade me that, in fact, I should leave home to stay with her, as if it were a matter of my choice in the first place.

Along the way, my aunt Maya seemed to have found something quite lacking even in my religious education. She took me to Mass on Sunday in Miami, while her husband and my brother slept in late; I think it was St. Mary's Cathedral, and while, like any young kid, I found those services an agony, so tedious, there came the moment when I, not yet having received my first communion, went up alongside Maya waiting for the Host, though when the priest came to me, and I refused to open my mouth, she shot me a furious look. Later, after I'd lit a few candles for the souls of the dead, and my aunt asked me if I'd put any money in that box, and I hadn't—their glowing aureoles had looked so pretty after all—you might have thought that I'd spit on a grave. After we'd come home, she forced me to empty my pockets, and taking me back to the church, she stood over me as

I put all my coins into the poor box. Then she had me kneel down by the altar to pray. "Oh, what that woman did to you," she repeated over and over again. "And to such an innocent."

On his end, my brother spent most of his days lugging about twenty-five-pound sacks of concrete, which he mixed in a wheelbarrow with water and shoveled into a cable-jointed foundation trench. I know this because I sometimes went out there. Sitting in the shade, in a straw hat, eating an ice cream cone (without anyone objecting) in that infernal heat, I'd watch him working, though from time to time my princely laziness annoyed the hell out of my uncle Pedro, who'd give me an easy job, like washing trowels in a pail, or he'd send me around to collect any loose tools. At lunchtime, Pedro and his workers, speaking in Spanish, would carry on about a wide range of subjects—baseball, boxing, Cuba, that shit Fidel—and about who'd just come over lately, family left back there, and did some of them know the whereabouts of a certain so-and-so from Holguín? At one point, someone recommended a bordello in Hialeah. They never minced words around me: From them I learned about a young beauty, fairly newly arrived from Cuba, who, at eighteen, worked in a house set at the edge of a field and had a *chocha* that apparently tasted clean and sweet as a spring peach. I remember feeling vaguely confounded as to just what they were talking about, but from their cheery smiles, even I knew it was something naughty.

Uncle Pedro, in any case, hired many newly arrived Cubans: One of them, a black fellow, the sort whose sunburnt cheeks looked purple, he referred to as "*mi negrito*," and while my uncle—and the other lighter-skinned Cubans—addressed him with affection, I realize now that, being from the old school and in a city whose water fountains and public restrooms posted WHITES ONLY signs, they might have done so to remind him of his place in the social pecking order. What this *negrito* made of me, so blond and fair, and related to the *jefe*, I don't really know, but when he'd unscrew a thermos and pour the strong coffee he drank at lunch and breaks, he'd always nod my way, winking.

Now, my uncle in his spare time would take me around Miami—

he liked to eat Jewish delicatessen food in one of those art deco diners along the main street of South Beach. Funny to think about him now: this former ballroom dandy who played stand-up double bass with Xavier Cugat, and in his prime dazzlingly handsome, sitting by one of those counters, examining the free multicolored pickles left there for the taking, as if perusing jewelry. If he was religious, he kept it in a drawer. Once at a diner late on a Friday night, at about eleven, on the way back from a Shriners' meeting, where he schmoozed (I suppose) with fellow members to drum up business (he also played canasta with them, while I sat in a room watching TV), he ordered a ham and cheese sandwich on toasted white bread, an act that absolutely shocked me, given Maya's super-religiosity and the fact that, in those days, eating meat on Friday was strictly forbidden to Catholics. When I reminded Pedro, timidly, that he was about to commit a mortal sin, he, obviously a man of the earth and a pragmatic soul, simply shrugged, looked at the clock, and told me, "In Jerusalem, it is already Saturday."

Later, we stopped at a Sunoco gas station, where, within a few minutes, as we sat in his idling Cadillac, a blizzard of green arrowhead-shaped insects, coming seemingly out of nowhere, had overwhelmed the place—teeming like *microbios*. They were so densely packed that one could hardly see anything but the faint glow of some distant highway lamps, and though much of that cloud moved on, enough of those insects remained behind to cover every surface of that place and were so thick in the air that the gas station attendants locked themselves inside: No sooner did my uncle roll up his window than he decided to drive away, and as we did, tearing out of that place, I could not help but wonder if the sudden plague had anything to do with my uncle's attitude about that ham and cheese sandwich. Of course it didn't, but I believed it did.

Generally, Pedro treated me as if it were only a matter of time before I'd grow up and become a more responsible person—for example, he kept showing me tool catalogues from outfits in New York City, where he wanted me to make some purchases on his behalf (why he didn't do so with my brother, I can't say), while Maya, going on nearly daily about all the awful things that my mother had done—"We all prayed for you, nephew, and thanked God Himself when you survived your illness"—continued to treat me as a fairly helpless infant who would be so much better off in her care.

And yet, one day, she, so accusatory toward my mother and her carelessness, fumbled badly. Maya had taken me to the beach, where we walked along the shore; later I romped in the water, shirtless and in a pair of shorts, and though I'd been out in the sun for only a few hours, my fair skin, exposed to that torrid heat without the benefit of any lotion, began to blister. And not in any small way: By the time we'd gotten back home, enormous bubbles plump with oozing liquids—and quite painful—had risen over my shoulders and arms and chest in such an alarming fashion that Maya called in a doctor. (They resembled, I remember thinking, jellyfish.) Soon enough, I was put to bed, shivering, in a back room, its window looking onto an overgrown rear garden with mango trees. A local girl, a some-time babysitter with whom I had seen a matinee of *Psycho* just a few days before, had been paid to watch over me, though she seemed to spend most of her time in the living room with the TV; but now and then, she'd look in to make sure I hadn't tried to pop any of those blisters, which by then were suppurating: I had to take antibiotic medicine, and some kind of cream was placed carefully around the burns' raw edges, or what doctors might call their diameters. But mainly, for a week, until those potentially infectious blisters began to go down, I relived that old hospital isolation again. I can remember falling in and out of some very strange bouts of sleep, thinking, because of all the tropical foliage just outside the window, that I was back in Cuba and getting sick all over again. That isolation so depressed me that I was grateful when anyone ever-so-carefully tiptoed in to see how I was doing, even my brother, who surprised me one afternoon by walking in wearing a Frankenstein mask.

And there was Maya, of course, asking that whatever else I might want to talk about with my mother and father once I got home, not to mention a word about how I had gotten sick under her care; my brother apparently had pledged to do the same.

. . .

As for the revolution in Cuba, which had taken place not so long before, I'll only say that as it had unfolded in the mid to late 1950s, my father fully supported the cause, as so many New York Cubans did. Regularly, he contributed money to a pro-Castro movement based in Miami, and every so often, he went around the neighborhood hawking copies of a magazine, I believe it was called the *Sierra Maestra*, which he sold for a buck on street corners, the proceeds of which he also sent off, however indirectly, to Fidel. My child's take on the revolution came mainly from a Cuban publication, *La Bohemia*, out of Havana, which he'd pick up at a kiosk in Grand Central. I remember it for the heroic portraits of the rebel forces that were featured on its covers. Inside, while I inevitably searched for a wordless single-panel comic strip called *Sin Palabras*—drawn, I think, by one Antonio Prohias, who as an exile later went on to earn an unlikely livelihood through his series for *Mad* magazine—*Spy vs. Spy*—I'd inevitably come across any number of sepia-tone photographs of Cuban patriots who had been jailed, tortured, and shot, their corpses shown lying in the gutters of Havana or on morgue slabs. The same issues also included more than a few hagiographic photographs of Fidel and his commanders.

My father, never a man of too many words, once told me that Fidel Castro was fighting for *"la libertad"*—"freedom." Given that most of his family still lived there, the revolution's outcome meant a lot to him, and on many a night, as his usual cohorts gathered, it became the main topic of their conversations. (That and his job at the hotel, along with work issues and how they all could be doing better wage-wise.) And no more so than on New Year's Day 1959, when word came out that dictator Fulgencio Batista had fled Cuba: A party inevitably ensued, the apartment filled to bursting with friends, and in the smoke-dense kitchen, my father's face aglow from exultation and booze, he could not have been more happy—even my mother seemed unabashedly to share his joy. And while I remember that as a day of a hope fulfilled, I needn't go further now as to the disappointment they, as Cubans, were destined to feel.

Still, while knowing what would happen within a few years to Cuba, it's hard to resist mentioning how my father once had the distinction of shaking Nikita Khrushchev's hand, for in 1958, he and Díaz had moonlighted at a dinner banquet held in honor of the Soviet premiere at the Commodore Hotel during his famous visit to New York. It was attended by some well-known diplomats of the day—Andrei Gromyko, Henry Cabot Lodge, and Cyrus Eaton—and at some point in the evening, after the meal concluded, Khrushchev himself insisted on personally thanking the waiters and cooks, who, as workers, had served him so well. Called out from the kitchen, my father had waited alongside Díaz in his apron and whites as the husky premier made his way down the receiving line, offering his hand to each. Some years later, when the Russians began pouring into Cuba, my father must have considered it a dubious honor, and yet, I think, riding home on the subway that night, after the glamour of such an evening, he, as a former *campesino* from the sticks of Cuba, had probably reeled from the thrill of it all. Such was his life sometimes in that city.

It also happened that my father had been among a group of people gathered around Fidel in 1961 as he, having visited Columbia University fresh from addressing the UN, stood about on its campus, posing for photographs, shaking hands and holding forth with his quite adequate English—back in the early 1950s, he'd lived on West 84th Street or thereabouts for a few months—in one of his last public appearances in New York. What my father must have thought looking Fidel over or if he said something to him, I don't know, but however much he would come to resent the revolution, some part of him must have been impressed by the worldwide attention that Castro, from the countryside of Oriente like himself, had attracted.

CHAPTER 3

. . .

Some Moments of Freedom

Now, if you had met me during my adolescence, when I'd finally started hanging around with the other kids, you probably wouldn't have noticed any anguish in my face, and if anything, you might have judged me a pensive and bespectacled young man, prone to a somewhat nervous joviality. Still, I was an unsettled soul. Scared of heights, I'd go up to our rooftop, some six stories above, and hang over the edge, always clutching my glasses, to get over that fear. (It never took.) And because of the nature of our street, where kids were pissed off at other kids and often fighting, I had no choice but to finally step free from my mother's constraints, for she never wanted me to wander far from the pavement in front of our building, and defend myself. As a kid living down the fact that for years I went out onto the street, it seemed, only with my mother, it was inevitable that certain collisions took place.

I had my first fistfight in those days, or to put it differently, I went crazy lunging after a pair of brothers who for the longest time had been picking on me as I'd sit on my stoop minding my own business. Knowing me as that round face framed in the window, that kid they most often saw with his mother, who seemed so timid and quiet (if not shell-shocked), these two brothers couldn't help but torment me—"faggot" and "pussy" at first, and once I got glasses, a "four-eyed faggot/pussy" among the names they called me. Spitting at me or tossing dried turds (*los microbios!*) my way was the least of it, but what finally tipped the balance was a remark that the meaner of them, Bobby, said to me one afternoon: "Your mother's a cocksucker," a statement I tucked into my pocket without knowing just what that meant.

Later that same evening, while sitting by our kitchen table with my parents and brother, when I happened to repeat it to him, innocently enough, as if I were reporting on the weather—"Did you know that Ma's a cocksucker?"—my brother, without as much as thinking about it, picked up a butter knife and jammed it into my right arm beneath the shoulder (I still have the scar to this day).

"Don't you ever fucking say that again," he told me, his face burning red.

Of course, my mother started screaming at him—slapping him in the face and chasing him down the hall. But once a few days had passed and my gash had started to heal, José had a little talk with me: "Next time one of them as much as looks at you the wrong way, I want you to kick their asses," he bluntly stated.

I suppose he wanted me to do this as a matter of family honor, and because he didn't like the notion of anyone taking me for a chump. By then, he'd already started toughening me up; when my mother happened to be out, we'd go into the living room and take turns punching each other as hard as we could in the arm, until I could barely lift my own, and if he had confidence in me, when it came to going after those guys, it was because I never once cried or gave up—enduring as much as he could give. I never considered that kind of thing as mean-spirited: I supposed it was what older brothers did and never held that against him, though as I think about it now, he probably had reasons to resent me. For while my parents, to some extent, cut me a lot of slack when it came to my avoiding household duties—I had been sick after all, or perhaps I was still sick to them—and my mother, in those days at least, only slapped my face or used a belt on me when absolutely necessary, as when I'd try to venture far from the stoop and refused to answer her summons, my brother had an entirely different relationship with them, particularly with my father.

He hadn't gotten along with him for a long time by then. Too much had gone on between him and my father that went far back to the way he had treated my mother in their early years in New York, and that led to their differences. Or as my mother would put it, my father, so gentle with me, would beat the hell out of him for no good reason.

But sometimes he did get out of line: One night—José must have been about sixteen—when he came home after hanging out with some friends uptown and staggered in, drunk, my mother, seeing his state—and doubtlessly thinking about my father—grabbed him by the hair and pushed him down onto our scruffy living room sofa and started beating him with a broom, and not just whacking him here and there but in his groin, *sus huevos* (she would always tell me that one should go for the balls if assaulted), my brother doubling over, his arms held up over his head, trying to fend her off. She did this while screaming at him at the top of her lungs and promising, as I watched from the living room doorway, that he had yet another punishment to come, for once my father, out somewhere too—and also probably getting a little torn up—walked in, she'd insist, as a kind of emphasis, that my pop also go after him with his own trusty belt.

But he also caught a lot of flak because of me: Years back, fresh out of the hospital, I'd smashed up a set of his prized Lionel trains that he'd paid for himself from his stationery store earnings, just because I could. Instead of punishing me, her poor *pobrecito* son who really didn't know better, my mother took out his justifiable despair on him. (Another beating.) Then too, there had been a night when he limped in badly messed up after a bicycle accident, his leg yellow with a suppurating wound: I can remember standing near him and watching the pus oozing out as he dabbed it with a towel, and the mere fact that he was in such a state, carrying into the apartment the kind of *microbios* that could hurt me, my mother grew hysterical at the danger his injury posed to my health, screaming at him to keep his distance, as if he had done something wrong.

Altogether, he didn't get any breaks at all. One morning after High Mass, when he'd sung a repertoire that consisted of Bach and Michael Praetorius and Monteverdi, thanks to the urbane taste of Mr. Mac-Donald, I'd gone downstairs to the choir room to meet him, so that we could walk home together. We left by a side door along a narrow passageway, where garbage bins were set out; as we were heading toward the stairway, a kitten started mewing from inside one of them, and my brother, rifling through it, pulled out a darling little creature that he fell in love with, happily cradling the gentle thing in his arms. Back in our apartment, he fashioned a cradle for it out of a box, and for a few hours, we had an adorable pet—that is, until my mother walked in from wherever she had been. Without a moment's hestitation she declared it "*sucio*"—"filthy"—with germs and fleas. Complaining that all she needed was one more thing to worry about, she told my brother to return it from whence it had come; I don't know what became of that little kitten, but I've always recalled the way my brother, a tough guy, almost came to tears over that matter.

Still, he had a hard side—how couldn't he? José, or "Joe," depending on whom he was talking to, got around and with whomever he pleased, doing everything that I couldn't: roller-skating, bicycling, staying out till all hours, and, slick in his way, generally navigating away, with a few exceptions, from ethnic hassles. He did, however, come home one night badly beaten up: While riding a train out to the deepest reaches of Brooklyn with some Puerto Rican friends, he was on hand as a gang of white guys, some twenty or so, swarmed into the car, announcing they were going to kick some spic ass. José, off in the rear of the car, had been left alone, his appearance sparing him, but having his pride and a temper and a half, he had stood up and cried out, "I'm a spic too!" Which is to say that those thugs, brandishing baseball bats and chains, turned on him too: It was the kind of story that established his reputation as a noble tough guy in the neighborhood and made him seem heroic to me.

I'd only seen him fight once, rolling around on the sidewalk with a much bigger fellow—I don't recall who won, think some cop broke it up—but in any event, he had a quick temper, and on that street, where just an attitude or a derisive glance—"What the fuck are you looking at?"—could instigate a confrontation, he always held his own and carried himself as someone not to be messed with.

So when it came to those brothers, he would not let me off the hook; not a week after he'd jammed that butter knife into my arm, while we were standing around on the stoop and they came walking up the other side of the block, my brother told me, "Now get over there and show me what you can do!" Then: "*Vete!*" With that came the implication, I knew, that he would take it out on me if I didn't. I don't exactly know what possessed me—adrenaline along with fear perhaps—but I ran charging across the street and in my gleeful madness, caught those brothers completely unaware, flailing at them with wild punches. I think they didn't know what to make of me, and the meaner one, Bobby, whom I'd caught good on his jaw, his head thrown back, ran off crying, the other soon following. What was it but a few minutes of my life? And no big deal—I'm not even sure if I should bother mentioning it now—but the truth is that I kind of enjoyed it, and along the way, on that afternoon, so meaningless to the world, I discovered that I had, without knowing, a lot of pent-up rage inside of me, an anger over a lot of things I could have been aware of, that would continue to simmer under my benign surface, only to suddenly bloom, as it did with my brother, at a moment's provocation.

Afterward, José seemed to feel quite proud of me, and those brothers never bothered me again and, to some cautious extent, eventually became my friends.

            .   .   .

But was I a tough guy myself? That same summer, when I accompanied some kids from my block on an outing to the Steeplechase Amusement Park in the Far Rockaways of Brooklyn, no sooner did we arrive than I, riding some dinky roller coaster, somehow got separated from the group. Once I realized that I couldn't spot anyone I knew, like the nice older girl, Angie Martinez, who had persuaded my mother to let me come along, I began to feel an awful despair, as if roaming through those crowds, something bad would happen to me. The longer I walked up and down that park, teeming with people, the more I felt my guts tightening and a heaviness gathering in my legs, my knees going weak—eleven years old, I felt like crying. I remember thinking that as much as my family seemed overbearing (well, my mother), I might never see them again, and just the notion of not being able to make it back home left me feeling miserable. At the time, I didn't even have a token with me, just one of those circular Steeplechase punch-hole cards good for about ten rides; after about half an hour, I became so desperate that I approached a gang of black kids, all of them towering over me, to whom I offered my card in exchange for my fare home. And while they could have easily taken me off, they flipped me a fifteen cent token anyway, and I soon found myself standing on the platform of the Brighton Beach station, about four blocks away, asking people how to get back into Manhattan; no matter what they told me, I still remained anxious; on the D train for Manhattan, I sat on the edge of my seat, looking at every station sign, until that subway finally rolled into the Columbus Circle stop. Years later, when I'd work in a job involving the MTA, I could never walk through that station without remembering that day. Finally, catching another train, I rode up to 116th Street and Broadway, thrilled to see that its station tiles read COLUMBIA UNIVERSITY.

I can remember feeling, bit by bit, a release of my tensions as I crossed the campus toward Amsterdam, all the while swearing to myself that once I reached my block, I'd kiss the sidewalk.

Of course, when I finally came home to our hot apartment, and my mother asked me what the hell had happened, I just shrugged: I don't recall what she made of the fact that I had come back alone, but by the time I ran into Angie the next day, though I had probably ruined the group outing—"You can't believe how we went crazy looking all over the place for you!"—I had started to feel rather proud of myself, if not so tough or self-assured.

. . .

In those days I remained a reticent soul, especially with Spanish-speaking folks, around whom, fearing the inevitable exchanges, I always piped down. Whenever I went into a bodega other than Freddie's, and my pop and I would head over into Harlem, I had to put up with people—young tough kids mainly—checking me out, and with suspicion (though old ladies were always nice to me). I'd try to shrink into the walls in such places, always felt like I stood out like a leper.

At home, when Cuban and Puerto Rican visitors I'd never seen before came into the apartment, there always seemed to come a moment when one of them would look at my father, his soft voice intoning a slangy, sometimes beer-slurred Spanish, and then at me, whose awkward Spanish was halting, at best, and ask incredulously, "He is really your son?" (*"De verdad, es tu hijo?"* My father, in those instances, always answered: "Of course"—*"Cómo, no?"*—but along the way, his eyes always met with mine, his pupils misting over with a contemplation of genetic mysteries and as well with an awareness of my own history within the family. Though we certainly looked alike, that seemed to make no difference to his friends, for whatever being Cuban was about, I just didn't have it. I got used to that, but I always felt a little ashamed, and generally learned to nod and smile when questions were asked of me, more often than not looking for any excuse to leave the room. (Though some, I might add, became more understanding, especially once my mother said, "My son, *el pobrecito*, was sick.")

I also had some bad luck. At Corpus, during my fifth year there, the school had decided to allow an hour out of the week for Spanish lessons. Our teacher was the school secretary, a certain Mrs. Rodríguez, and while she was a very pleasant lady, her classroom manner seemed hardly soothing, in my case at least. From pupil to pupil she'd go, asking each to repeat certain words and phrases, and while the other Spanish-speaking kids, mostly Puerto Ricans and Cubans, had no trouble at all, when it came to me, I simply froze, my throat tightening along with my gut, and the words I managed to squeeze out, particularly when rolling my *r*s, were so badly pronounced that

Mrs. Rodríguez, out of the kindness of her heart, would go on and on about how I, as the son of Cubans, with a name like Hijuelos, should hang my head low for speaking Spanish so badly.

"Even the Irish kids, *que no saben español*, do better than you!" she'd say. Then: "Don't you even want to try?"

I'd look down, shrug, and she would ignore me for the rest of the lesson, averting her eyes from my glance any time she'd pass along the aisle, each session ending with a coup de grâce, for as she'd leave the classroom, she'd cast a disappointed look my way and, shaking her head, disappear into the hall, mumbling to herself, I was certain, about me. I came to dread those lessons, and after a while, she simply carried on as if I were not there, as if I were somehow beneath her attentions and the worst kind of Latino, who didn't care about his mother tongue, which is to say that at such a delicate time, when a different approach might have made some difference (I really don't know) to my development along those lines, she quite simply made my own wariness about learning it even more intense.

Of course I understood Spanish completely, but for some reason, I felt paralyzed when it came to speaking it—how a bilingual class with a real teacher would have helped me—and with that failing, along with my looks, definitely setting me apart from the other Latino kids (a double whammy, as it were), I remained incapable of finding my way out of the dense wood of my confusions. Naturally, I gravitated to situations—and friends—in which Spanish was not required. By then, in my adolescence, my mother's voice, which had nagged and ordered me around for so long, and my father's, sometimes so calm and measured or else a morass of mumbled, anguished Spanish, had begun to sound to me like voices from a radio, especially when they'd go at each other at night, as if I were asleep again in my aunt's house back in Cuba, eavesdropping on some overwrought and shrill melodrama from another place far away. When my pop's pals came over in the late afternoon, I got pretty good at blocking out some of the dreary things I'd overhear them saying in Spanish—like Frankie the exterminator bawling away because his wife didn't respect him as much as she used to, or about how some new tough boss, an efficiency-expert sort, had shown up suddenly at the Biltmore, making everyone nervous—or my mother's diatribes, once they'd left, about the quality of some of my pop's friends. I'd tune out, however, preferring to listen to anything else, the ambient sound of dinner utensils and plates, the faint hum of television sets, the murmur of more or less calm voices coming into the kitchen from the courtyard—normal life unfolding—which somehow always seemed so comforting to me.

· · ·

Not to say, however, that I didn't appreciate certain things about our family's life, like the food, which I began to eat with abandon once my mother, worn down from her years of vigilance and of taking me to clinics and local doctors like Altchek in Harlem or a certain Dr. Hinkle, a woman, on 119th Street, had given up on my diets. ("If you want to get diabetes, then fine with me," she'd say in Spanish. "And go ahead, become *un gordito:* Get fat!") I think that dam had first burst open down in Miami, during my trip there, when, coddled by my aunt, I could eat anything I wanted. It would have become inevitable anyway, what with my pop and brother always passing me some tender morsels on the sly, fried sweet plantains sending me to heaven. And on the holidays, it became my habit to scoff down pieces of crispy *lechón*, or ham, or roasted turkey and some *boniato*—butter-and-sugar-smothered sweet potatoes, when my mother wasn't looking.

But even before my mother had given up, I already had other respites as well: For some reason, these mostly took place out at my cousin Jimmy Haley's place on Webster Avenue, where his gorgeous wife, María, keeping a tidy apartment with all new furnishings (I remember my mother seeming impressed by that), always cooked up a storm—of strictly Cuban fare. This ravishing lady, buxom and elegant, was always going through the hard labors of stripping the thick skin off green plantains and frying up enough of them to stack high on a platter, more than our little group could possibly ever eat (though I tried). I suppose because it would have been bad form for me not to partake of those meals, my mother looked the other way, though I don't think she could have been too happy about it, since the doctors at the hospital were still scaring her to death about my potential to come down with various maladies. In any event, I liked going there. For one thing, my cousin Jimmy, who spoke perfect English, was someone I deeply admired. If I ever first formed an image of the earnest Cuban male, decent, hardworking, and responsible, it was back then: He had a son a few years younger than I, little Jimmy, and in those years when we would visit, this quiet boy became my friend. Besides, his household seemed always at peace. But if I most enjoyed those visits, it came down to the way my pop never felt the need to load up on booze around them, and my mother, admiring Jimmy and his wife, always seemed subdued and relaxed, commenting always on the appointments of the apartment—the nice linoleum, the newness of their couch—everything neat as a pin. Jimmy himself, handsome, even-tempered, with a laconic tendency toward understatement, seemed as ideal a father as any boy could ever want: He'd talk about his future plans for little Jimmy and seemed keen about sending his son, when of age, to a military school, teaching him how to drive, and perhaps, one day, returning to Cuba as a family, once Fidel left. Altogether, it seemed to me that little Jimmy and his family had it all, but you just never know—for the poor kid's life eventually took a trajectory that almost resembled mine: He got sick in his early teens with leukemia and, instead of recovering, passed on; and his father, so straitlaced and decent, if I am remembering the situation correctly, left his wife for someone else—an outcome that now makes me sad.

The thing is that, after a while, once my mother started looking the other way, I'd devour just about anything I could. I'd join my brother in the consumption of thick ham and turkey sandwiches on rye bread with mayonnaise as a snack, filet mignon and onions or fried veal cutlets on oven-burnt toast for breakfast. On one occasion, we ate our way through what must have been a two-pound chunk of dark German chocolate, from the hotel, which we'd hacked apart bit by bit with a butter knife on the kitchen table. And just as memorably, sometime during a cold November night, when the world seemed endlessly bleak, we somehow managed to devour a box of twenty or so chocolate éclairs that my father had brought home from a wedding banquet, and the two of us later doubled over, guts aching, on a couch.

My brother, always managed to somehow stay slim, while I tended to go up and down in weight, depending on whether, for brief periods, some doctor at the hospital demanded that I resume a strict diet. But whatever diets I went on didn't last long; losing weight over a three-month period, I'd just as quickly put it back on, a cycle I've often since repeated during my life. (Look in my closet now and you'll see three sizes of clothes: in shape, getting out of shape, out of shape.) Actually, getting fat seemed a familial—or Cuban—thing to do. My father, with his devil-be-damned attitudes about food, and God knows how many calories he consumed by drinking beer and whiskey almost nightly, always carried an enormous number of extra pounds, and it didn't bother me to become more like him; I suppose that on some level, it was my way of being more Cuban. (There is a picture taken of us along Broadway, outside Columbia, on the day, I believe, that I had received my First Communion; the suit I wore, incidentally, had been purchased for ten dollars, off a rack in some garment worker's apartment, on 108th, where he sold clothes out of his living room; my father and I sport identical crew cuts, and at ten or so I seem to look very much like his son.)

Besides, I came to think of that bulk, which made the doctors frown, as something that might protect me from *los microbios*, as if taking up more space in the world could make me stronger. (But believe me, even having said this, it had its down side: Now and then, when I'd go with my mother to shop at the cheapest department store in Manhattan, Klein's on 14th Street, or to Annie's on 125th, our inevitable search for trousers in the "husky" bins always left me a little low.)

And no, it's not that I thought about *los microbios* constantly, but it always amazed me to see how other kids seemed so unconcerned about them. On my stoop one day with the deaf mute's son, Jerry, I watched a candy bar drop from his hand to the sidewalk. "No big deal," he said nonchalantly. Picking it up, he made the sign of the cross over it, the way people did walking in front of a church, and said, "Hey, don't you know that's all you have to do to make it clean again?" I can remember being very impressed but couldn't help but wonder how that could possibly be true. (But then, at the same time, I suppose, I believed God could do anything.) Still, it wasn't a practice I'd ever subscribe to: I'd seen enough of the local hounds using that sidewalk to know better, and, in any case, some part of me—the part that looked in a mirror and always felt slightly disappointed—sort of believed that I was still susceptible to all kinds of things that other kids weren't, thanks to those Cuban-born *microbios*, which, despite all my doctors' visits, still seemed a part of me, lurking deep inside the way sins do, inside the soul.

. . .

During those years, the early 1960s—that period of pillbox hats, fifty-cent kids' movie tickets, chewing-gum-wrapper chains, and the Cold War—I was filled with contradictions. Thinking myself a basic nobody, I could behave smugly just the same; I often felt lonely but could be completely gregarious around others, even an occasional jokester, a tendency that would get out of hand sometimes. (Attending the 1964 World's Fair in Flushing, Queens, at thirteen, I brought along a theatrical prop knife that spurted fake blood, and in a souvenir shop outside the India pavilion, where I saw a sitar for the first time in my life, for some reason, I decided to pretend that I was stabbing myself in the heart, announcing to all who could hear, "I can't take it anymore!" An elderly woman, probably a nice tourist from Europe, seeing me slumped against a counter, with that fake blood dripping down my blue wash-and-wear shirt, fainted dead away. I felt a little bad but still ran the hell out of there.) Despite my sensitivity, I was no saint. Devoutly posturing around the nuns at school (as when I'd pray in the kids' balcony at Mass with the fiercest concentration), I'd try to secretly look up their habit skirts, their rosary beads dangling off their cinctures, as they'd climb the stairs. (They wore a kind of baggy black culotte over a large black undergarment; they did not rely upon brassieres but a wrapping of tightly bound white cotton fabric, about a hand's length wide, around their cloth-encumbered chests, the bandage of which I'd sometimes get a glimpse when they'd lift their arms to pray and there would appear a break in the tent of their coverings.) I always became nervous going to my biweekly Wednesday confession, not over what sins I might have committed, but because I felt, as I waited in a line with other kids, that I *had* to confess something: In the darkness of the confessional, the priest behind the grille, I'd make up sins—even claiming that I had "unpure thoughts" when I really hadn't; or I'd say that I had envied another kid for his nice shoes—anything just to hold up my end of the ritual—and having reported my lists, I'd finally confess that I had lied, but only to cover my earlier inventions.

I never consciously dwelled on what had happened to me in the hospital. Yet when I saw a girl at school that I liked, I'd fantasize that I was in a hospital bed, badly banged up and moaning from some crippling malady, while that girl took care of me, tenderly and mercifully, as would a nurse. (Cured and healthy, I'd end up, in my daydreams, marrying her.) But I was always too timid to approach any of them, even after one of the girls at school had given me a Valentine's card that read "*I'm 4 you: I think you're cute!*" That last word, incidentally, confused me so much that I, for some reason, asked my mother what it meant. (Since the word *cute* resembled the Spanish *"cutis,"* my mother, laughing, told me it meant that I had nice skin.) Naïve about many things, I was sneaky. Learning to write, with a loopy script, I took to composing letters—not just to Santa Claus at Christmas (years later, my mother would tell me that she always cherished them, without ever saving a single one), but to comic book companies, claiming I had sent in my subscription money, usually a dollar or so, but hadn't received any yet; most times my little ruse worked, and I used that same imploring tone of voice ("*I am an eleven-year-old boy from a poor family . . .*") to get ahold of the kinds of toys that were advertised in the back of those comics, things like Hypno Discs and magic tricks and, most often, plastic sets of cheaply made (in Japan) and under-cast toy soldiers of the Civil War and D-day. I'd lie in that way because, until I got my own little jobs around the neighborhood, or had begun to scavenge in the basement for two-cent bottle returns, I had no money save the occasional quarter *mi madrina,* Carmen, would give me for simply being nice to her, or the pennies I would scrounge around for in my father's dresser drawer and in the deep silken recesses of my mother's purse when she was out visiting somewhere upstairs.

This led me, along with hearing so often that we were "poor," to a nascent thievish state of mind: I'd often go to the corner pharmacy, where my parents, before we had a phone, used to get their important calls, and, when I thought the counter lady wasn't looking, I'd pocket a candy bar or two as quickly as possible. The afternoon she caught me stealing a Hershey bar, her back was turned, and as I started to make my way out, she grabbed my arm and reached into my pocket for the proof—a lecture, with some threats to call the police, followed, but what has most remained with me was her explanation that she had spotted my theft in an angled ceiling mirror—"Up there, you see it, smarty?" And while I felt much relieved that she, knowing my parents, let me go with only a warning, once I left that pharmacy—it was called Fregents—I took to heart a completely different notion from what she intended: to the contrary, instead of swearing off such things, I resolved to be more careful in the future and not to get caught again.

· · ·

Once I hit the streets with the other kids, I doubt that my mother was happy about that transition. It just happened: My afternoons were soon spent prowling about up and down the block, climbing railings, hiding in basements, and learning how to play basic games like handball against the wall. Eventually, I joined in rougher activities, like a game called Cow in the Meadow, the source of whose pastoral name I haven't the faintest idea of, which involved a simple-enough premise. The "cow" (someone) stood out in the street (the "meadow") and his task involved approaching the sidewalk on either side to pull a kid off the curb, into the meadow, which sounds easy enough except for the fact that once the cow left his meadow and ventured onto the sidewalk, the kids could beat the living hell out of him. What victories, of a Pyrrhic nature, one managed left arms and legs covered with bruises and cuts, and occasionally, as well, someone who didn't like you or thought that you were lame or just had it in for you would go after you for real, and in such instances, the ferocity escalated and what had begun with a good-natured beating intended to strengthen one's character (if there was any motivation at all) turned into an out-and-out fight between the cow and his assailant, though at a certain point, time might be called and the two would be pulled apart until tempers cooled, and the more earnestly intended beatings could begin again.

As distasteful as it might sound, that game, for all its potential for inflicting pain and damage—bruised limbs, cut lips, and boxed ears—always seemed fun: I particularly took to it, what with having so much pent-up *something* inside of me. I'm proud to say that I never went home crying afterward, even felt good that such a formerly sick wimp could hold his own, though I would get beaten with a belt by my mother if I came back with a broken pair of eyeglasses or a torn-up and/or bloodied shirt.

Mainly, I will say this about my block: A lot of tough working-class kids lived on it, and while there were a few serious delinquents among them who spent time away in juvenile facilities for burglary, and in one instance, for dropping a tile off a tenement rooftop on a passerby, blinding him, the majority were merely mischievous, though a few were simply mean. I almost had my eyes put out by this older fellow named Michael Guiling, the kind of teenager capable of fastening what were called cherry bombs, a high explosive, to pigeons. (I know, it's hard to imagine the process, let alone the outcome, but I once saw him tying one of those bombs to a pigeon and lighting the fuse; he let that bird go, and, flying away, it blew up in midair.) He had a thing for fireworks and, for the hell of it, a happy smile on his face, once flung a cherry bomb at my face; if I hadn't stepped aside, who knows what would have happened. (He was just one of those cruel lost souls—years later, sometime in the early 1970s, he'd die of a heroin overdose in the men's room of a bar on 110th Street, most popular with Columbia University students, a dive called the Gold Rail.)

Down the street, toward the drive, lived a giant fellow—six feet five and probably weighing three hundred pounds, his nickname, naturally, was "Tiny"—who had some vague aspirations of becoming a football player. It was he who grabbed me by the back of my neck one lovely spring morning and, holding me there, dropped a dime onto the sidewalk, ordering me to pick it up. When I did, he stomped on my hand, crushing two of my fingers, the nail on one of them to this day oddly distended toward the digit. (Despite hating his guts for that, fifteen or so years later, I would be saddened to hear that Tiny, while having had some success with a second-tier football team in Pennsylvania, died prematurely in his early thirties of cancer.)

The Irish were everywhere in the neighborhood in those days (at least down to 108th Street, below which the streets became more Puerto Rican), but so were Hispanics and what census polls would now call "Other." Unlike some neighborhoods, like around the West Sixties, where different ethnic groups were at one another's throats, waging block-to-block turf wars of the sort commemorated in B movies, the older kids around there seemed to get along. In earlier times, in fact the late 1950s, when I, still camped at home, could have hardly been aware of such things, there had been periods in which gangs like the Sinners and the Assassins occasionally ventured south from their uptown Harlem neighborhoods—north of City College—to stage "rumbles" against the local "whiteys." These were fights born of grudges that began at high school dances with some insult, or a face-off between two tough guys getting out of hand, or because someone was banging someone else's girl, or quite simply out of pure poverty-driven anger and, as well, at a time when the word *spic* was in common usage in New York City, from the deep memory of old, bred-in-the-bone resentments. I'm not quite sure where the Latinos or, for that matter, the other ethnicities in my neighborhood placed their loyalties, but I'm fairly sure that in such instances they joined their white counterparts in these face-offs against that common enemy.

Over those years, blacks had also made incursions onto our block from the east, gangs of them climbing up the terraces of Morningside Park, intending to swarm over the neighborhood, though without much success. Down in the park on 118th, there was a "circle," a kind of stone embattlement that looked out over Harlem, and it is from there, I've been told, that the locals fended off such attacks by raining down bottles, rocks, and garbage cans on whoever tried to race up to the drive by a stone stairway or to climb those walls.

Nevertheless, though those days had passed, but not the prejudices, the possibility of such confrontations still hung in the air, and as a consequence, it was a common thing for the police to patrol Amsterdam Avenue regularly in their green and white squad cars, with an eye to breaking up any large groups gathered on a street corner, no matter what they were up to—usually just smoking cigarettes and bullshitting about girls. Still, the neighborhood definitely identified with that gang-era mythology. When a recording of the musical *West Side Story* first came out, my brother threw a party in our apartment for his friends, with my father, incidentally, stationed in the kitchen, allowing an endless supply of beer and other refreshments into the house, while in the living room, the lights turned low, couples danced to songs like "I Feel Pretty" and "Maria," the record playing over and over again, along with other music—of the Shirelles and the Drifters—but repeating so often that, looking back now, I am sure there was a pride about it, as if, in a neighborhood where mixed couples were already as common as interethnic fights, its songs amounted to a kind of personal anthem for a lot of the older kids. (And to think that the musical itself had been put together by a group of theatrically brilliant middle-class Jewish folks, who, in all likelihood, had viewed such a world from a safe distance!)

. . .

Now, the first party I ever attended, at Halloween, took place in the basement apartment of my father's pal Mr. Martinez, who lived up the street. His son, Danny, later a sergeant in the NYC police department, decorated the place with candlelit jack-o'-lanterns and tried to make their basement digs seem scarily festive, but what I mainly remember is that he provided a plain old American diversion, something I had only seen on TV, a bowl filled with apples for which one would bob, as well as a game of blindfolded pin-the-tail-on-the-donkey, which I had never played before. (Thank you, Danny.) One of their upstairs neighbors was a Mexican woman, Mrs. Flores, who seemed terrified of allowing her little boy, dressed always so nicely and wearing white patent leather shoes, to mix with the other kids. (In his daintiness he seemed another version of my younger self, darker, but just as bewildered as I had once been.) There also happened to be another Latino kid from that block, a diabetic who, sharing my name, was called Little Oscar. Having apparently narrowly escaped diabetes myself, it amazed me to watch him sitting on his stoop as he, with resignation, administered himself a shot of insulin with a syringe. While it fascinated some of the kids, his condition did not bring out pity in them. Unfortunately, so frail and truly weightless, he, just skin and bones, seemed an easy victim to the bullies, and those kids, to my horror, were always picking on him—and cruelly; on at least on one occasion, as he stood with his hand tied behind him to a signpost, they tried to force him to take a bite from a dried piece of dog turd stuck on a twig. "Come on, leave the guy alone," I remember saying, but they didn't relent. (Whatever happened to Little Oscar, for his parents, catching wind of such things, soon got him the hell out of that neighborhood, I hope his future life went well, though I will never know.)

. . .

Slowly, in the years after my illness, I had made my own friends from around, among them Richard, the youngest smoker I would ever know. I can recall seeing him, a few months after I had returned from the hospital, standing outside my front window and showing off the snappy cowboy outfit and medallion-rimmed black hat that his father, often away, had just brought back from his travels. One of the few kids around who'd take the trouble to come visit me in the days when I couldn't really leave the apartment, he'd sometimes climb the rickety back stairway to my window from the courtyard, crawling inside to play and scrambling out when my mother heard us from down the hall. The youngest of a large family, the Muller-Thyms, who occupied two bustling first-floor apartments, one next to the other, across the street, he had four brothers and five sisters (though I knew hardly any of the older ones at all). As families went, they were locally famous for both the brightness of the children and the slight eccentricities of their genius father, Bernard, who had a high sloping forehead and a vaguely Hubert Humphrey pinched-in cast to his face, though with a Dutchman's side whiskers (the only thing missing would have been a meerschaum pipe).

Mr. Muller-Thym had first come to the neighborhood during the Second World War, when he taught swimming to naval recruits at the university. After the war, though armed with a Ph.D. dissertation in the mystical thinking of Meister Eckhart, he had drifted into the business world and, with a brood of growing children, had decided to stay on that block, presumably to save the money he would have spent in a better neighborhood. The aforementioned eccentricities included his tendencies to occasionally parade in front of his windows, which were visible from the street, in nothing but a shirt, sometimes less—and though one would think that his physically candid persona would have scandalized the neighbors, even my mother, crying out *"Ay!"* at the sight of him, at worst found him more amusing than offensive. Publicly, he was civil, always well dressed, and if he stood out in any way from the working-class fathers on that street, it was for both his reclusiveness—I think my father, coming home from work, would say hello to him from time to time, but little more—and the lofty company he kept. (He was actually quite a nice man, always seemed interested in what I had to say, asking about me in a manner that neither of my parents did. "What do you want to do with yourself one day?" "I don't know." "Well, you should start thinking about it soon enough.") A former classmate of his from Saint Louis University, Marshall McLuhan, often frequented that apartment, well into the 1960s before the family moved away; and among the other figures who visited with Mr. Muller-Thym and sat for dinner at his table—doubtlessly on some of those evenings when my pop was sitting around with the likes of Martinez and Frankie the exterminator—happened to be Wernher von Braun, the rocket scientist then with the fledgling organization of NASA, with whom Mr. Muller-Thym had a professional relation as a consultant. (It cracks me up now to imagine this haughty rocket scientist, with his Nazi pedigree and physicist's brilliance, walking up my block to Richard's while screaming kids, cursing their hearts out and jumping onto cars to make a catch, played stickball on the street; why do I see the legendary Von Braun, shaking his head in bemusement over the apparent decline of civilization?)

Once I'd gotten my wings, I'd often go over there, usually in the afternoons, simply because I wanted to get out of my house. They lived humbly enough—there was nothing fancy about the trappings of their apartment—though what first caught my eye, always caught my eye, was the abundance of books in their home. Richard's older brother Tommy, an expansive sort with a bit of Brando about him and much street-inflected bonhomie for his fellow man, to say the least, had his own place with one of his other brothers, Johnny, next door, the floor beside his bed covered with dozens of novels, some of them science fiction but many, I suppose, culled from American classics: Twain, Hemingway, Fitzgerald, and yes, Iceberg Slim are names I recall. Richard himself, the sharpest kid around, had at some ridiculously young age become consumed with history and ancient literature, no doubt because of his father's erudite influence. What can one say about a nicely featured kid, half-Italian and half-Dutch, who reads Gibbons and Thucydides, and the poetry of Catullus and Martial in the Loeb classical editions for his leisure? (At first in translation, and then later, once he had mastered them, in the original Greek and Latin.) His narrow room by the front door was always stacked with piles of such books, which sat atop his bunk bed and on his dresser, the floor, and anywhere else they might fit. He would get a kick out of reciting aloud some particularly grizzly account of a battle or, on the bawdier side, some risqué Roman couplets, a slight and naughty euphoria coming into his expression.

And while it might seem, given the calling I've unpredictably drifted toward, that this exposure to a household where books were so cherished and to a friend with such a voracious mind might have inspired in me some scholarly bent or an early love for reading, to the contrary, I regarded those books in the same manner I would while walking down Broadway with my father when we'd stop to quizzically peer into a bookstore window, never buying any, as if such volumes were intended only for others, like the college students through whose world we simply passed.

On that end, while I tended to dip into my school textbooks and always did well enough to pass from one grade to the next, I continued to read mostly comics, in which I would lose myself, and certainly nothing as complicated as the poems and narratives of the distant past, which, as far as I was concerned, may as well have been written on the planet Mars. In fact, that bookish world always seemed remote to me. During the few trips I'd made (with my mother) over to the 125th Street library, with its musty interior, I always found the sheer multitude of volumes intimidating and chose my books on the basis of whether they had ornate covers. (My mother, by the way, would wait in another aisle, perusing somewhat tentatively a few books that had caught her eye but never taking any out—I don't think she had a card—and if anything, she always left that place annoyed over the way the librarian, a heavyset black woman who, as I recall, always wore a large collared sweater and a string of costume-jewelry pearls around her neck, sometimes watched her, probably, in my mother's view, with suspicion as if she "would take one without her knowing, *que carajo!*") For the record, one of the books I can recall borrowing—well, the only one I recall—happened to be an old edition of *Peter Pan*. I can remember feeling very impressed by the clustered, floridly set words on its opening pages, entangling to me like the vines of a briar patch—a purely visual impression—into which I thought I might delve; but I never made much headway; accustomed to the easy leisure of comics, I found Mr. Barrie's novel, however famous as a children's classic, too strictly word-bound to hold my attention for long. (Or to put it differently, I was either too lazy or too distracted by my emotions to freely enter that world.)

Nevertheless, I liked the fact that my friend had so many books around, including an arcane collection of the writings of Aleister Crowley, in which his father was interested—all so incredibly far removed from my parents' beginnings. On some level, I suppose, I developed a kind of respect and admiration for the intelligence one needed for such things. But if I did so, it was from the distance of someone looking in from the outside, with wonderment, or bemusement, in the same way that my mother, at that hospital in Connecticut, used to regard me.

But we'd also get out, spending quite a number of afternoons roving through the back courtyards behind his building, climbing fences and high walls, to make our way over to 117th Street, which in those days seemed one of the more elegant blocks in the neighborhood. It was a placid elm-tree-lined street whose Georgian edifices, owned by the university, were remarkably ornate, and as much as we felt that we were encroaching on alien territory, as it were, we occasionally managed, just by nicely asking, to play billiards in one of the sunny front brownstone fraternity house rooms (if that's what they were.) And we'd go on the occasional excursion to a nearby park, though Morningside, even then a Harlem mugger's paradise, remained far less inviting than its cousin by the Hudson, where we would go "exploring" through its winding, tree-laden trails as far north as Grant's tomb.

Always fast on his feet, Richard, dark haired and of a slim and compact build, could run around the block, and quickly, without as much as taking a deep breath or working up a sweat, a remarkable thing, mainly given the fact that he smoked a carton of Winstons every week. I don't know how—or why—his habit started; it was always just there. Of his three brothers, the eldest, Bernie, an army officer fresh out of West Point, probably didn't smoke (I would never see him doing so, at any rate), but I think the next oldest, of my brother's age and the most burly of them, Johnny, did, and Tommy certainly (Tareytons, as I recall). It simply wasn't a big thing on my block—if it was illegal for adolescents to smoke, you wouldn't have known that from checking out the street. Kids like Tommy, very much a fellow of this earth, could play three-sewer stickball games and go running the makeshift bases with a fuming butt between his lips, and, as a matter of course, a lot of the kids, having no trouble getting ahold of them, smoked while hanging out on the stoops, singing doo-wop, or in the midst of a poker game, on which they would wager either money or cigarettes. Some guys walked around with a pack stuffed up in the upper reaches of their T-shirt sleeve, by the shoulder, or with a cigarette tucked J.D.-style alongside their ear. Cigarettes were just everywhere, that's all, a normal thing, which, however, I never found particularly inviting except when I'd get the occasional yearning to be like everyone else.

In any event, Richard's household became a refuge to me: It was close by, and the family treated me well. His mother played the piano—I first heard Debussy's "Clair de Lune" over there, and one Friday evening, in the days when Catholics still observed such rules, I consumed my first Italian-style red snapper dinner at their table. But I especially loved going there around Christmas, when they'd put up a crèche and a majestic nine-foot pine tree, their living room table always covered with Italian cold cuts from Manganaro's downtown, and other seasonal niceties, like macaroons and brandy-drenched cherries, the holiday atmosphere so cheerful and strong, what with high piles of presents stacked under the evergreen and wreaths on the walls, that our own strictly budgeted Christmases suffered by comparison. We always had lots of food and booze around, of course, but my father wanted to spend only three dollars on a tree, which we'd get down on Amsterdam; and when it came to our presents, my brother and I received only one gift apiece. I don't recall my mother or father ever having any presents of their own; nor did we celebrate El Día de los Reyes, Three Kings Day, the way other Latino families were said to—in fact, I only heard reference to that holiday many years later; and if anything, after the revolution, when my parents' thoughts turned to their family in Cuba—my mother receiving her sisters' plaintive letters with guilt and sadness—a kind of maudlin spirit became a part of the holiday. Having said this, I can't complain, for even with a humble tree, there was something wonderful about the way the pine smelled in our house, so sweet that not even cigarette smoke overwhelmed it.

At Richard's, the holiday remained the great event of the family calendar—certainly of his own—and while I suppose they were an affluent family relative to our street, they were quite generous and always allowed me to join in their festivities.

I probably envied my friend—he seemed to always receive the best gifts, purchased down at the old FAO Schwarz: hand puppets from Germany and train sets when he was younger, and, during my adolescence, military board games, like Tri-Tactics or Dover Patrol, and Risk, which we'd play on many an afternoon. On those occasions with Richard, whom I admired and respected, smoking away, it became inevitable that I would try one of those cigarettes myself. I was probably twelve at the time, if that, and while I can't remember having any sense of elation at those first inhalations—did I cough or make faces?—smoking at least a few, mainly Richard's, soon enough became part of my days, and the foundation of a habit that would hold on to me, on and off, for many years.

Did I like them? I seem to have gotten used to their bitter taste, and perhaps on some other level I was thinking about my father, of finding one more way of becoming a little more like him. Though I didn't smoke many at first, they kind of grew on me, and a little weary of my lingering self-image as the frail sick son, it wasn't long before, in addition to *comiendo mucho*—lots of food, tons of it—I began sneaking cigarettes out of the half-filled packs that my father would leave in one of his top dresser drawers. I'd sometimes go down into Morningside Park to smoke, where I was fairly certain that my mother wouldn't see me, and while I never lingered long there, it happened that, on a certain afternoon as I stood along one of its glass-strewn passageways, a couple of stringy Latino teenagers, the sort to wear bandannas around their foreheads, coming out of nowhere, held me up at knifepoint. It was one of those occasions when I wished I had the presence of mind to muster up some Spanish, but I'm fairly certain that no matter what I might have said ("*Pero soy latino como tú*"— "I'm Latino like you") it would have made no difference: They didn't like the way I looked, my blond hair and fairness alone justification enough for them to hate me without even knowing just who I was; it would happen to me again and again over the years, if not with Latinos, then with blacks—prejudice, truthfully beginning and ending in those days with the color of your skin. I wasn't stupid, however; I gave them what I had in my pockets—a few bucks from one of my jobs working at a laundry before school down on 121st for this nice man named Mr. Gordon, who'd make his morning deliveries while I watched his shop (and pilfered the loose change on his shelves), and two of my pop's cigarettes, which I had in my shirt pocket.

Eventually, my pop figured me out. Not that he put it together by how many cigarettes were left in his packs—I'd never overdo it—but because I started feeling too slick for my own good. Coming back from some afternoon movie on 96th Street one day, I had lit up one of his Kents only to see my father, peering out a bus window at me as it passed along the avenue. First he whistled at me, a high low whistle that he'd call me by, and gesturing with his hand against his mouth as if her were drawing on a cigarette, he shook his head, mouthing the word *no*. Then he pointed his hand toward me—gesticulating the way Latinos do, his index finger stuck out, and going up and down, meaning I was going to get it. Later, at home, he took out his belt and reluctantly gave me a beating, as always on the legs but painful just the same. Then, hearing about what had happened, my mother got into the act, slapping my face that night and looking strangely at me, as if I were a criminal who had betrayed her, for weeks afterward. Naturally, it made no difference; I adjusted, telling myself that, as with other things, I would have to become far more careful.

·   ·   ·

Around the same time, a picture began to hang over the living room couch. My brother had painted it. Having creative aspirations, at seventeen or so, he had started to make paintings somewhere—not in our apartment, at any rate. Amazingly enough, he had talked his Irish girlfriend from uptown, whose brothers and father happened to be cops, into posing nude for him, that portrait of her, with her burst of dark hair and nice body reclining against a bluish background, going up on the wall. No one objected, and my mother, while probably bemused by his rakish ways, seemed to take a great pride in his talent; in fact, that painting would remain there for the rest of my mother's life—for among other reasons, I think it spoke to her memories of her own cultured father back in Cuba, whose creative blood, she would always say, flowed in my brother's veins.

Of the two of us, José was always the more gifted: Lacking a center, I had a basically infantile mind and no sense of order; I was lackadaisical in my mode of dress, while he, a more sartorial sort, had the kind of instincts that simply amazed me. He knew how to iron a shirt or a pair of trousers to a sharp crispness, and given the challenge of creating a costume for a Halloween party, he once fashioned a gaucho outfit out of some pieces of felt cloth from which he made a vest and, flattening an old hat, came up with a new one with jangles along the brim, the final touch a wrapping in velvet cloth around his waist. (He sort of looked like Zorro and was quite handsome in the mirror before which he posed.) He was sharp in a way I would never be, and effortlessly so, though I doubt that he didn't secretly work hard at it. Above all, I'd always thought, even then, of him as being far more Cuban than I, the Spanish he would speak with some of our neighbors seemingly of a level that I, in those days, could not begin to approach. (*"Tu hermano es mucho más cubano,"* my mother would always say.)

Nevertheless, sharp as he could be, he went through some rough times. Going back a few years, once the Catholic high school he had attended closed down, he ended up at George Washington up on 187th Street, a high school where he always had to watch his back (which is to say, people were always kicking one another's asses) and from which by his senior year he had dropped out. (For the record, my parents were not happy about that.) He worked delivering Sunday newspapers, starting at six in the morning, a job I benefited from, because, working for tips, I'd deliver the missed issues of the *New York Herald*, the *New York Journal American*, and *The New York Times* around the neighborhood once the calls came in at about nine. (There was also the *Daily News*, which most people also ordered, those Sunday editions with their fabulous four-color comic pages weighing three or four pounds apiece. However, I don't recall ever seeing a Spanish-language newspaper like *El Diario* on those racks.) He'd apparently also worked for a gay mortician for a time, around Washington Heights, whose advances in those parlors of cadavers he fended off. Altogether, though he seemed always to have money in his pocket, my brother remained a restless sort, looking for some distant horizon better than what we seemingly had before us. (A pet peeve of his was to the fact that the name *Basulto* still adorned, as it had for decades, the mailbox and bell.)

Generally, he rarely stayed at home, spending more than a few nights away—where, I don't know; wherever he had been hanging out, perhaps at the homes of friends like the Valez family on 122nd or up on a rooftop on a mat. There came a day when his girlfriend's brothers, dressed in their New York City police officers' blue uniforms, began knocking at our door. They knocked because my brother, in the process of painting their sister nude, or at some other point—perhaps during their teenage outings to the piers under Coney Island's boardwalk—had, in the parlance of the day, "gotten her in trouble." She was pregnant, and her family was not pleased.

My father, coming to the door and probably knowing much more than he let on, claimed, as he faced those burly officers, to have no awareness of my brother's whereabouts. (He spoke a low-toned, generally unaccented English, maybe Spanish-inflected in some ways but always calm.) In any case, after several visits with their officers' hats in hand, they stayed away. One of those nights, when my brother had come home with the air of a fugitive on the run, my father, despite their differences, sat him down in the kitchen and counseled him— an unusual thing in our family—as to his choices. Given the situation, I think it came down to the following: Either marry her or get lost. My brother would always say that my father, without a drink in his gut, rose to the occasion and, truly concerned, advised him well. Not so much to take the high road perhaps, but to consider what would be best for his future. For, as it turned out, my brother, eighteen at the time and with a pregnant girlfriend with a cop family to worry about tracking him down, decided to enlist in the air force, and within a few months, he was gone.

CHAPTER 4

. . .

Childhood Ends

The thing about my pop is that he never wanted to hurt anyone. Not consciously at least. He'd always have something of that *güajiro* quietude about him, and while he had his vices, he never sloughed off his responsibilities when it came to work and supporting the household. Much liked at the Biltmore, his nickname was *Caridad,* or Charity, for his giving nature. And while he underwent his occasional metamorphosis from a gentle Jekyll into an oblivion-seeking Hyde, for the most part, people liked him.

I've always remembered him as a man who stoically engaged the mornings. As a kid I always awoke to the sound of his footsteps in the hall, for he'd leave around six for his early shift at the hotel. I'd hear the door opening carefully, the jangle of keys and the turn of the lock, then the door closing shut against the rickety frame; he made more noise than he should have. He'd step out into the absolute stillness of those New York mornings, the city silent and deserted at that hour; only the duration of Sundays, when hardly anything opened in those days, approached them in their quietude. He'd go down the hill of 118th Street to Amsterdam Avenue, a newspaper tucked under his arm, his ambling stride unmistakable, then head up a few blocks south to 116th (the path ascended), where he would cross the Columbia University campus to the subway kiosk on Broadway, seeing few people along the way. Occasionally, he'd meet up with Mr. Hall from upstairs, who worked for the LIRR. They were good friends, though I don't know what they might have talked about. Occasionally, a milk truck or a bus passed by on the street, but generally when he set out to work, he did so by himself.

Into the bowels of the subway he would go, with its dirty platforms and penny Chiclets and five-cent Hershey bar dispensers on the columns, and board his train downtown and eventually over to Grand Central, the seats in those days still often covered in lacquered cane. He'd make that journey, no matter how he might have been feeling, or the weather, even when snow had piled high on the streets and sidewalks. To miss work was unthinkable to him.

Given the way he'd spend many of his evenings, he was probably in a constant state of fatigue—cigarettes, it seemed, helped him keep going. He worked two jobs after 1960, at the Biltmore and at the Campus Faculty Club rooftop restaurant, on top of a high-rise Columbia-owned residential hotel, Butler Hall, a block over on 119th Street. For years he didn't sleep much, and of course, his greatest pleasure remained the company of his friends. His warm manner, publicly, attracted smiles: Sitting out on the stoop, he conversed happily with anyone who happened by. Language was never a barrier. Though I'd grow up with the notion that my father was lucky enough to have mastered English as well as he did, he, in fact, also learned to speak serviceable amounts of German, Russian, Greek, and Italian at the hotel, where the staff consisted mainly of immigrants like himself— which is to say, it seems that he had a facility with language. It amazes me to think that had he been born twenty years sooner, around 1895 or so, he may well have spent his entire life on a farm in Cuba, riding a horse, perhaps alongside his brother, instead of passing his days in the kitchen of a midtown hotel preparing grilled ham and cheese sandwiches and grilled steaks for the usual Men's Bar clientele of boozing business executives, errant college boys, and the occasional famed personality—like Joe DiMaggio and Frank Sinatra and perhaps, in all his years there, Ernest Hemingway. (I will never know.)

A union man, local number 6, he paid his dollar dues weekly and kept a book, somewhat the size of a passport, in which each page, subdivided like a calendar, had a square by the date for each stamped payment. The squares were filled with slogans—*"Buy the Union brand!" "Support your Union brothers!"* He didn't care for Fidel, of course, given what had transpired in Cuba since the revolution, though his sisters, save Borja and Maya, had remained there without complaint, apparently—none of them left or tried to leave, that I know of—and yet when Marcial García would show up, always with a jug of Spanish wine, to speak in defense of the revolution, my father and mother always heard him out without holding that stance against him. My father was a Democrat, always voted so, but he had his prejudices. He never blinked an eye when a Latino, dark as ebony, might come to the apartment, but when it came to American blacks, the sort who lived in the projects above 123rd Street, he would not go anywhere near them. (When I was about sixteen and had made a black friend, a guitar player I'd met from around, and invited him into the house, my father would not allow him inside. "No, you must leave, I'm sorry," he told him bluntly by the door.) Nevertheless, he was quite friendly with our mailman, who was black, bald, and cheery, conversing with him often enough in the hall.

Remember that Cuban boxer Benny "Kid" Paret, who got beaten into a coma at the old Madison Square Garden by the champion, Emile Griffith, because he'd so pissed him off, calling Griffith a *maricón*? His manager, Olga's husband, came by that same night in the aftermath of that brutal pummeling—Benny, after a few weeks, would die—and when Mr. Alfaro walked in, he carried the bucket containing both sponges and the bloody towels left over from that match and set it down by our kitchen table, where he sat for hours drinking with my father, who did his best to console him.

My father had a terribly distended right elbow, from a childhood fall out of a tree in Cuba, his bulbous ulna bone jutting out a few inches beyond the hinge. You couldn't miss it, any more than you could help noticing how his hands were often covered with burns and cuts. As I sat by him one evening, watching him smoke cigarette after cigarette and pour himself another drink of rye whiskey, I found myself staring at his elbow and because I'd always search for something to say, I couldn't help but ask him about why that bone stuck out so far.

"How'd you get that, Pop?" I asked him.

"I got it during the war," he said after a moment, and he tapped at the bone in a way that made the ash of his cigarette drop off. "A German shot me," he said.

"You were in the army?" It was a surprise to me.

"Yes," he said, without equivocating. "I was a sergeant."

"What did you do?"

He shrugged. "*Yo era cocinero.*" He sipped at his drink. "I cooked for all the soldiers and for the generals too."

"Over there?"

"*En Europa durante Segunda Guerra Mundial,*" he added in Spanish for emphasis: "In Europe during the Second World War."

Of course, it was a lie, though I didn't know it at the time. I can only suppose that he made up that fabrication to impress me, his American son. Maybe he did so because war was in the air—Vietnam was just gearing up, and some of the older boys in the neighborhood were going there as soldiers (a few, like Charlie Soto, coming back in a box)—but, even if some moment of patriotic fervor hadn't compelled that story, I don't know if he really believed he had anything glorious to report about his life.

"That's really true—you were a sergeant?"

"*Te juro.*" And he crossed his heart. "I swear it's so."

That excited me, of course, and it left me buoyant. Expecting to go into the army myself one day, I was learning Morse code: I'd sent away for a dime pamphlet about telegraphy and, myopically already half-gone, my lenses as dense and heavy as the bottoms of whiskey glasses, I would sit up late at night, studying those dot dash permutations off a card, without a thought as to how the system had probably become outdated. Nevertheless, that revelation so thrilled me that I actually bragged about my father's service to my friend Richard, from across the way. "You're kidding, right?" he asked me, his mouth pursed skeptically as he took a drag of a cigarette.

Still, for weeks, I walked around convinced that he'd told me the truth, and rather proudly so, though, after a while, I couldn't help but ask my mother about it. The exchange, as I recall, went as follows:

"Hey, Ma, was Pascual in the army during the Second World War?"

"*Qué?*"

"Was Pascual a soldier? You know ..." And I made like I was firing off a rifle.

"*Tu papá? Un soldado? Nunca,*" she said once she grasped what I was getting at. "Never!"

"But why would he tell me that?"

"*Diga?*"

I mustered some Spanish, poor as it was. With her, I always felt like a boat out in some dark bay, sending signals out to a distant lighthouse, always waiting for the light to beam on.

"*Fue mentira?*" I ventured.

"*Sí, hijo,*" she said sadly.

"But why?" I asked.

"*Por qué?*" Her face went somewhere else and then she settled down.

She shrugged and rolled her eyes, and, in the only time I'd ever seen her do so, my mother, smiling, tipped her head back and, with her fist closed and thumb sticking out, as if she might otherwise be hitchhiking, raised and lowered her hand toward her mouth.

"But, *hijo,* don't you know," she said, "that he drinks too much?"—"*Que tu papá bebe desmasiado?*"

Okay: While I knew it, at the same time, a part of me continued to believe him—I couldn't help it.

The hotel allowed him three weeks for vacation, which he always took in the summer, often while still moonlighting at his other job but still having enough of his days free to do what he most liked, which was to go to the beach, usually Brighton, out in Brooklyn. He'd take me along, when I was eleven and twelve, but never my mother, who preferred to stay at home. (Whether she wanted time off from him or not, she had a belief that too much sunshine would be bad for her skin, and in any case, my few memories of her at the beach always find her mainly under an umbrella, her arms and legs and face slathered with lotion.) We'd ride the fan-aired subway down there, always unbelievably hot, of course, and for these outings, I recall, he'd pack a bag of his favorite sandwiches: salami with pickles and mayonnaise on seeded hard rolls, about a half dozen of them (how less Cuban can you get?). He'd put on a pair of trunks (always over-sized) in one of those sandy-floored men's rooms that reeked of salt water, urine, cigar smoke, and compromised stomachs. Then, once I'd changed, we'd find some spot close to the shoreline, where he'd spread out a blanket, wanting to be near the murky water. He drank beers, which he'd bring along in a shopping bag—and in a pinch, there was always some enterprising chap clopping along the sand in a pith helmet and sandals, selling beers out of a Styrofoam cooler. I seem to remember that he also brought along a thermos—probably filled with whiskey, though I can't imagine anyone drinking whiskey in that hot sun—and for my refreshments, a bottle of orange juice. Not one for luxuries of any kind, he'd pull from his bag a little plas-tic, cutting-edge-technology, made-in-Japan transistor radio, hardly much of anything at all, on which he'd tune into a Spanish-language station, a tinny, thin mix of boleros and cha-chas along with an end-less promotional patter punctuating the waterside cacophony, similar radios sounding off from hundreds of blankets around us. He liked women, that's for sure, his eyes never missing a buxom lady's figure, big hipped or big bottomed or not, as she'd pass by or go wading into the water. Occasionally, he'd strike up a conversation with a woman if she were on a blanket nearby, and somehow, despite his girth, he'd cajole all manner of information from her—"Where do you live?" "What do you do?" "Oh, you have kids—I like kids"—the kinds of things I'd overhear him saying in Spanish. Not that he went off with anyone, but looking back now, I'm fairly certain that he enjoyed the pursuit. He did not swim—rather made his way into the water and plopped down into it, falling back on his hands, or else splashed himself with that foamy rush, always keeping an eye on me to make sure that I kept watch over the plump wallet he'd stash inside his shoes, under his shirt and trousers, on the blanket.

The waters off Brighton were not like those blue, crystal clear waters off the coast of Oriente, Cuba, but now and then, I'd catch him as he, sitting up, would look over the horizon with a mostly dreaming expression in his eyes, the way he would sometimes in our kitchen, as if, indeed, Cuba was not far away. He didn't have a whole lot to say to me—we were, on those days, as my mother might remark, just being *"muy, muy tranquilito"*—and after a few hours, maybe four at most, during which I took a few tentative dips in the sea or else examined the half-dead grayish crabs washed up in the auburn sand, it would be time to head back. We'd dress in the same bathrooms and stop for a frankfurter along the boardwalk— and sometimes my father might linger by a railing to have a smoke, the Eiffel Tower–looking parachute drop in Coney in the distance, before setting out for the hour-and-a-half ride home. And while it wasn't much as far as vacation days go—and we'd often repeat the same thing the next day—I enjoyed those outings very much, and think of them nostalgically now.

As I'd get older, we'd go up to the Bronx, a different story entirely, where he'd hang out with his friends at gatherings that began at about three or four on a weekend afternoon. Nothing fancy, they always started out agreeably enough with folks sitting around talking amicably, food, and a lot of it, served on paper plates off a buffet table, and some music blasting out of a record player or radio. Gradually, however, what with the men drinking so much and my father becoming more and more deeply implanted on a plastic-covered couch, I dreaded the moment when we'd leave, usually late at night. The journey home at two in the morning, with nary a taxi or gypsy anywhere in sight along those desolate streets, involved a trek down a long hill, past a row of abandoned buildings, in a fairly crime-ridden neighborhood, maybe number two or three in the city. Uptight and vigilant, I'd hold on to my father's arm, with my pop completely out of it, trusting, even if he'd been mugged a few times before, that we'd manage to slip through to the kiosk stairway of the 169th Street and Third Avenue station without incident (if he thought about it at all). Once on the platform, we sometimes waited half an hour before a number 8 train would finally show up, and even then, that ride back to the West Side, with another wait at 149th and Grand Concourse, could take just as long. Somehow we'd always make it home.

But during those vacations what I enjoyed more at that age were the days when he'd bring me down to the Biltmore, where he'd go to pick up his pay (always in cash and in a letter-size manila envelope, weighted with small change). There was a little office—really a kind of booth—at the far end of a freight dock on the Forty-fourth Street side of the hotel, midway between Vanderbilt Avenue and Madison, that could be entered from the sidewalk. And as my father would speak quietly with the payroll clerk—"This is my son, Oscar," he'd say—I would watch the workers unloading vegetable crates and sides of white fatted beef from the backs of produce and butcher trucks, a process that somehow always enchanted me. Then we'd either go upstairs through a service entrance or make our way back around and walk in through the lobby, a busy place in those days; businessmen came flowing through its brass revolving doors, while bellboys in beige uniforms tended to opening taxi doors and to incoming luggage, groups of tourists and conventioneers milling about. The massive lobby's carpeting was plush, and when you looked above, you saw on the ceiling an ornate Florentine-style fresco of gods flying through the heavens. Just beyond, behind an ornate grille, was a Havana-style palm court, and, of course, as that lobby's centerpiece stood the famed Biltmore clock, with its banquette sitting area, much storied as a congenial spot for young couples to meet up for dates, or where college boys on the prowl might look for girls. (I didn't know anything about the hotel's history at the time—what could my father have told me?—but in conjunction with this writing, I found out that the hotel, some twenty-six stories high and taking up an entire block north of Grand Central, had been built by the Warren and Wetmore architectural firm in 1913, a few years before my father was born. Aside from being the kind of place where the Zionist Conference of 1942 convened and the World Center for Women's Progress held its inaugural meeting, it was at the Biltmore where F. Scott Fitzgerald spent his honeymoon with Zelda.)

Inevitably, we'd end up inside the Men's Bar or the Men's Grill Room, which was entered a few steps down off the lobby through a door by which a sign was posted: NO WOMEN ALLOWED. I recall that it was an old-style oak-paneled room, quite dark and Edwardian in its motifs, its walls decorated with paintings of sporting scenes and nude women, a massive oak bar taking up much of the space, while off to the side were various booths. We'd go into the kitchen, at the back, where my father would say hello to his fellow workers, among them Díaz, the *cubano*. A plate-cluttered and steamy place with glaring overhead neon lights, that kitchen was filled with stainless steel counters, pots and pans hanging off racks, and fans set up here and there to offset the heat of ovens, grills, and deep fryer. A long banister divided the room. Among its appliances, which impressed me greatly, were a battery of six-slice toasters for the preparation of the bar's famous BLT and club sandwiches. I can remember being treated quite well by the staff there—sitting on a stool in the back by a cutting board, watching them cook away, I'd have lunch, anything I wanted, though I distinctly recall always asking for the club sandwich, for we never ate bacon at home, and more than once, my father, a cigarette between his lips, officiated over the making of an ice cream sundae replete with hot fudge topping, whipped cream, and a maraschino cherry, which, placed before me, I devoured. Afterward, once he'd come back from the pantry, we'd head out—down into Grand Central to catch a shuttle to Times Square, and home.

· · ·

He liked to read the *Daily News,* even the funnies, as if studying for a final exam, especially the sports pages, and always took a great interest in the Washington Senators baseball team, mainly because there were some Cubans in the lineup. He took me to see a Mets game once, when they'd just joined the National League and were playing the Senators, someone having given him the tickets at the hotel. (The Mets were horrible in those days and ever since I sat through that lackadaisical game, I've never cared much for the sport, I'm sorry to say.) Having worked a banquet held for a group of Japanese businessmen at the hotel, he came home with a five-thousand-yen note, and, truly believing it amounted to a lot of money, thought he'd have enough to buy a new television set, the sort that didn't conk out suddenly, until he took the note over to an American Savings Bank on 111th Street and Broadway—now El Banco Popular—and found out that it, so valuable seeming, was worth only a few dollars. (I went with him, and embarrassed after speaking to the teller with whom he had tried to cash the note only to learn that cashing it would cost almost as much as it was worth, he shook his head and shrugged. What are you going to do, right?) In his wallet, for some reason, he carried around a bawdy cartoon, always folded up, that obviously gave him a kick. I came across it one day on his dresser. It was of two characters, Harry and Bert Piels, popular advertising mascots for the Piels beer company: They were both bald and somewhat professorial looking—one tall and lanky and the other short and squat. In the cartoon, the short one, with exclamation and question marks shooting out of his head, was locked in an embrace with a nude, buxom, Amazonian woman three times his size, his eyes fixed on her pointy breasts, and a thought balloon with the words *"Oh boy, oh boy, now that's even better than beer!"* rising from his head. (Or something like that: Mainly, I wonder now why he carried it around in his wallet.)

Once, I found a twenty-five-dollar gold piece in the gutter. I have no idea how such a valuable thing happened onto the street, but when I brought it home to show my father, he told me, *"Bien hecho"*— "Well done"—and gave me a dollar for it. (For the record, I also found on the street a two-dollar Confederate bill, which, thinking it worth something, I kept for ages.)

We were always receiving visitors out of the blue—a lot of Cubans who'd recently turned up in the city, just like in the *I Love Lucy* show, which, by the way, my father liked to watch in the reruns. (With *The Honeymooners,* that was the only other show I remember his laughing aloud at.) One afternoon—I was about twelve—he received a few of these new guests: a plump dark-haired couple with an even plumper little girl, in from New Jersey, fresh up from Castro's Cuba, who had heard about a Hijuelos living in New York City. My father was wearing checkered slacks, a short-sleeved shirt, and white tennis sneakers that day—he favored sneakers of any kind on his time off from the hotel, where he would have to stand constantly on his feet—and after bringing them some refreshments in the living room and conversing for a while, he, coming out into the hallway, called me in from my room, where I had been reading comics or doing whatever the hell it was that I would do. He didn't often easily smile at me, but when I— in the midst of my early adolescent can't-be-bothered-by-anything- else stage—lumbered down the hall and the couple stood up as soon as they saw me, my pop, beside himself, bowed as if announcing some sixteenth-century courtier at the court of the Spanish king. In Span- ish, he said, "Oscar Hijuelos, I am pleased to introduce you to Oscar Hijuelos," for that was, indeed, the fellow's name. Blinking affably, the other Oscar Hijuelos, who must have been about thirty at most, smiled and extended his hand to me for a shake. Then his wife by his side said, "*Hola, pariente*"—"Hello, relative"—and I shook her hand as well. We sat down for a while, the other Oscar Hijuelos (to this day I have no idea of the family connection) filling in my father on his doings in this country—I'd heard that kind of thing often, as if it were a drill: no job, no language, some help from Cuban friends, some from the government, the new world so strange, and yet, despite it all, somehow landing on one's feet. That other Oscar Hijuelos, with his wife and daughter, stayed for about an hour. My mother never came home to meet them. And once they left, promis- ing to return, they never did.

· · ·

In the meantime, while all those things were going on, my brother was away in the air force, at first in Biloxi, Mississippi, then in Lack- land, Texas, and eventually in one of the hell zones of the early sixties, London, England, as an air traffic controller. In that time, squeezed between one of those lackluster winter days in our household, when ice formed on the windowpanes, a great snow began to fall. My father, having to go to work, got up that morning with blistering pains shooting across his chest. When he raised his arms, those pains, like rods being jammed into his bones, fluttered down to the tips of his fingers, and even then, when he felt his arms going numb, he, sitting back on the bed, tried to work them out, flicking his wrists wildly, the way people do when their hands fall asleep. But when he tried to stand, it was as if he were carrying a piano on his shoulders. Lulling for a while, he lit a cigarette. And then, taking a deep breath, as my mother dozed beside him, he managed to get to his feet. In the kitchen, searching a cupboard, he found some rum and, swallowing a huge swig, felt his body settling again. At a certain moment, down the hall in our dingy bathroom, the sweat on his face slackening off, he, feeling better and dressing, set off for work. He put on his hat, scarf, and London Fog overcoat, and, despite the snowdrifts, made his way across the Columbia campus to the subway, eventually to the hotel, where he, with those nagging pains in his chest, somehow made it through the day.

I remember nothing of that evening after he'd come home, except that he had gone to bed early. There he had lain all night, tossing and turning and gasping—according to my mother—and while a lovely snow continued to fall, come the next morning, at about five, when my father would usually awaken, he simply could not move. My mother, loving—and hating—him so much, prevailed upon our gentle across-the-hall neighbor, Mrs. Blair, on whose door she banged at that unearthly hour, begging to use her telephone to call Dr. Altchek in Harlem. That great old man, however disturbed from his sleep, turned up by six—I remember that under his topcoat, he wore pajamas—and within a few moments after making some examinations, he, as he had done with me those years before, declared that my father, having suffered a heart attack, should be rushed to the hospital.

That whole interlude of his initial recovery, during which my father spent some three weeks in a fifth-floor room of the Flower Memorial Hospital on Fifth Avenue and 105th Street (thank God for union insurance coverage) with a lovely view north over Central Park, I have to skirt. I will say this: He had his transistor radio to keep him company and, thinned down somewhat with the hospital diet, seemed to be extremely well. I sat by him on numerous afternoons, watching so many of his friends from the hotel and from around come by to greet him. After working more or less steadily at the hotel since 1945 or so, he seemed grateful for the time off, for the outpouring of visitors, and would sit up, smiling in his hospital pajamas, and somewhat optimistically, despite the IV line in his arm. My mother, at least when I was there, never came, not that I remember, though she surely must have. At one point he told me, "Whatever happens to me, take care of your mother."

After he left the hospital, sticking to their diets and giving up smoking, he got even thinner and glowed, somewhat, from renewed health, the bad habits of those years left behind (his body must have been grateful). During that peaceful time, without any shouting in the house, my mother, though still worried about him, seemed far more content, and he, without taking a drink and not yet back working, acquired a more relaxed demeanor. Some things were tough, however—I can recall that we began to run a bigger tab than usual down at the corner grocery store, Whities, where he once used to send me to buy him cigarettes, and at Freddie's Bodega, because he couldn't bring his usual foodstuffs home from the hotel. And perhaps he went through a month or two without full pay (I don't know). But even if we didn't get a tree at Christmas that year, generally, things were good—we finally had a telephone installed, in case another emergency arose, a telephone to whose dial my mother affixed a cylinder lock. And my pop? At forty-seven, he was still young enough to look forward to years and years of life. He felt confident enough to buy the only new piece of furniture that I can recall ever coming into our house, an olive green leather easy chair with one of those extendable footrests, which he got on time payments from Macy's. Nightly, instead of hanging around in the kitchen, he'd stretch out in luxury, watching our always flickering television set.

By spring, when I'd come home from school, we'd pass a few hours taking strolls over to Riverside Park, where he was content to sit on the lawn, watching college girls go by, boats gliding along the water. He didn't need much, though, as I think about it now; he probably had too much time to reflect back on what had happened to him. Sometimes, out of nowhere, while looking around at the loveliness of the day, at the wisps of clouds in the fine blue sky, the sparrows hopping merrily on the grass, or at a lilting butterfly, he'd sigh, and with that, I swear, from him emanated a palpable melancholy—I would just feel it, almost like a shudder, rising from his body. In such moments, I am certain that he, trapped by some dark thoughts or emotions, probably wanted a nice drink. Probably, he felt nostalgic for the good old days when he could just take out a cigarette for a relaxing smoke—he was, after all, a creature of his generation.

* * *

He must have started back up with his bad habits, slowly at first, at the hotel, when, after some three months away, he'd returned to work. Down there, hidden from my mother's eyes, there came the moment, during a midafternoon lull at the Men's Bar, that he'd probably taken his first drink in a long time, and that warming elation, coming over him again, became something he could not continue to resist. And what would go more nicely with a belt of whiskey than a cigarette? After a while, he'd walk into our apartment with his face slightly flushed and think nothing of sitting down and, well, having a smoke. Just as often, coming home, in his trousers pocket, he'd have a pint bottle of whiskey stashed in a paper bag, and soon enough, once his friends started coming over again, the refrigerator began to fill with those sweating quart bottles of beer. My mother, beside herself with worry, became hysterical, and those nights, once his friends had left, of my mother scolding him continually in the kitchen also resumed, but with a difference: Where in times past she had reminded him of his old abuses, my mother now went at his carelessness in the wake of his heart attack—what she called "*un ataque del corazón.*"

"You think you're going to live forever, drinking and smoking? What are you, stupid, Pascual? . . . *Qué carajo,* are you crazy?" She'd go on for hours and in such a manner that, if anything, he took to drinking even more. Worse, he didn't seem able to hold it the same as he used to, for he'd slur his Spanish in ways that I hadn't heard before, and, as well, he'd drink so much that just getting down the hall to the toilet, he sometimes staggered so badly that he would be propelled forward as if someone had picked up the building and tipped it onto its side, or as if he were suddenly shot out of a cannon, or on a listing ship in the stormy sea. He'd sometimes fly headlong so wildly that he'd tumble down and end up slumped over on the floor—I know this because I often tried to help him up, something that got harder as he began to get heavier again, those pounds coming back to him with a vengeance.

The evenings became something of a nightmare to me—to this day I feel a terrific melancholy when it begins to get dark. And not just because of my memories of all the shouting and arguments, but what they led to. No matter how much she tried to reform him, my poor mother, however well-intentioned, only managed in her strident ways to make things worse, while he, falling back on some macho pride, took her pleas (harangues) the only way he could, stubbornly and refusing to change: "*Soy el hombre*"—"I am the man"—was his only answer, "and if you don't like it, divorce me." I heard that word *divorce* night after night, shouted so loudly that everyone in the building did too. I can't blame my mother for seeking her refuge with friends on those evenings, what with my father losing his self-control and falling apart in front of her; at a certain point, once she saw that he was getting a certain way—"*muy borrachón*"—she'd make herself scarce, for if she remained in the apartment, they'd spend half the night circling around the rooms, threatening each other.

But that was not the worst of it for me. Indeed, during those years, on many a night, in the crushingly lonely interludes after his pals, who always visited in the evenings, had left and my mother had gone out, I became his sole companion and, I've since come to think, his babysitter. He would insist that I keep him company (which was fine, even if I would have preferred to just watch our buzzing TV or go over to see my friend Richard) and if I hung in there with him, as an eleven- and twelve- and thirteen-year-old kid, it was because I felt constantly afraid of leaving him alone. So I'd remain by his side night after night in our little cramped kitchen as he'd drink himself into oblivion, until there came a certain point when he'd start staring at me intensely from across the table, his eyes squinting, as if to bring me into focus. A cigarette burning before him, my pop, as if forgetting who I was, would speak only in Spanish to me, and in such a mangled fashion that I wonder now how I understood him. (Years later, while sitting in a bar with a Puerto Rican poet friend, a Ph.D. candidate in Spanish, two incredibly drunk Latino men across from us were holding a conversation about life, but with such slurring that even the well-educated Hispanist beside me could not begin to understand them, though I could.) By then, my father had been dwelling on his mortality for so long that he often cried at the thought of his own passing, and far from concealing that fear—or conviction—he took to repeating a single phrase: "*Voy a morirme*"—"I'm going to die." "*Voy a morirme, hijo,*" he'd tell me. Then: "*Entiendes?*"—"You understand?" his warm liquid eyes glazing over with bewilderment and tears.

I would just shrug or withdraw into myself—what else could I do?

Then he might say, "*Pero sabes que eres mi sangre, y que te quiero*"— "But you know that you are my blood and I love you." And while I realize now just what he must have wanted to hear back—"And I love you too, Pop"—I could never say it, and so those nights went until, at some point, he gave up the good fight and dragged himself off to bed for a few hours of sleep before he'd get up for work for his early morning shift at the Biltmore Hotel, his words of prophesy staying with me long after.

In my way, I suppose, I took out whatever emotions I had from such evenings on other kids, such as the time when I put that cigarette out on my friend Richard's head. (Sorry, man.) I had always gotten along with one of the French Haitian kids from upstairs, this burly, immense, unflappably cheerful boy about my age, Phillipe. It was he and his older brother John-John who once took me into the basement and, setting up a little projector in an abandoned room, showed me the first bawdy film I had ever seen, one of those grainy 16 mm movies you could get in one of the shops along sleazy Times Square, in which the women, by today's standards, were too fat and too ruined looking, but who, with their bushy vaginas spread wide and their doughy flesh, seemed wildly exciting as well as wicked. We also played a lot on the street, and one afternoon, as I stepped out off the stoop, wearing a pair of new Hush Puppies, for some reason, though he didn't have a mean bone in his body, Phillipe shot me a faggy kiss with his lips smacking and chippie-chippie sounds: He was sitting against the stoop's columns and when he did it again as I walked on, I turned and punched him as hard as I could on the side of his face, and his head began bleeding from its impact against the stone. He never did it again.

At the same time, some need made me easily manipulated: I guess I wanted to please others, to have friends. A professor's son, an affable, somewhat handsome fellow who lived around the corner, had brought me along to a party in the apartment of a well-off family whose son attended his prep school. He brought me not out of any intent to broaden my social horizons but because he wanted to beat up some foppish guy for no good reason. In the midst of this friendly occasion, my "friend" urged me, as a favor, to "put this guy straight," and though I had nothing against him and hardly knew the fellow, I called him a faggot, and even when he begged me not to hit him, I did anyway, this professor's son mirthfully looking on.

He also masterminded a confrontation between me and this fellow named Ralph, said to be the toughest guy at the Horace Mann high school. I was out on Broadway and 116th Street when the professor's son persuaded me to fight him, and, man, his reputation had been earned out of real abilities, and what I can mainly remember about that idiotic circumstance is that he turned out to be so tough that I ended up admiring the guy. He had a pretty sister, by the way, who must have been in awe of the fact that I had gone after her tough-guy brother, and from time to time when I'd see her on the street or on the subway, she'd always smile at me, though I was incapable of imagining that she could have any interest in someone from my background. (The irony is that, years later, when I ran into this fellow Ralph, he couldn't have been more friendly, though the professor's son, whom I saw again years later during a period when I was having a lot of success, actually said to me, "Good things happen to bad people.")

For a few years, during that time when my pop got worse, while playing softball in the Harlem league, we'd practice down on the Columbia athletic field near 110th Street and Lenox Avenue, on the very same property that would become a matter of contention during the campus upheavals of 1968. Out of laziness or because I might be late, I'd sometimes take a shortcut through the park, along its deserted paths and, inevitably more often than not, get jumped; I should have known better, but something about the danger thrilled me, or the punishment involved, for even if you'd handed over your change, someone just wanted to have it out with you anyway, and I'd find myself getting into more than a few fights that way. I was lucky not to get stabbed in the gut, like another friend of mine, Pete, did some years later, and I almost had my jaw broken once—or at least it felt like it—but I somehow kept making my way along those same trails, as if, indeed, I was asking for trouble.

But I found other, "safer" means of escape as well. I began to drink, sometimes my pop's stuff, a swig or two out of one of the pint bottles of rum or whiskey he'd keep in a kitchen cabinet—like father, like son, right?—and just enough to lift my spirits slightly, though I never liked the taste. Still, I eventually graduated into absolute intoxication—I think I was twelve—one evening at my pal Richard's across the street. That too was inevitable.

Mr. Muller-Thym, while attending to his paperwork at home, would sit by a table in his living room, sipping champagne, what he called "bubbly." Starting in the mornings, he got through his days in a pleasantly hazy state of mind. Keeping a well-stocked liquor cabinet, he seemed absolutely unperturbed by the notion that his sons occasionally availed themselves of its contents. We'd sit around in Richard's room, listening to jazz on a record player, sometimes to Latin-inflected cu-bop music, which for us, in the early sixties, came down to the vibraphone jazz of Cal Tjader and Mongo Santamaria; again I think his father, an aficionado of Village clubs like the old Half Note on Spring Street, had influenced his son's taste, which veered between the modern and baroque, Bach being another staple.

One night, while listening to jazz in his book-laden room, and smoking cigarettes, we embarked on what had started as a casual experiment involving Coca-Cola, some ice, two glasses, and a bottle of 151-proof Jamaican rum, which Richard had somehow gotten ahold of. I'm not exactly sure just how his mother, Mary, off in the living room watching television, remained oblivious to our doings, but that evening, over the course of several rapturous hours, we drank one potent glass of that sweet cocktail after the other—I found it a revelation that it tasted far better than the wine my father once had me try at Teddy's, or my father's whiskey—and in the madness of that high, we got somewhat carried away.

To confess, the very notion of literally lifting out of my own body as the world went spinning around me seemed a glorious relief. And I never felt so alive! At some hour, I can't say when—I don't remember—I staggered out of there, and getting home so obviously lit up, I received one of the more monumental beatings of my life. I really don't remember a whole lot of what happened—but I do recall my mother dragging me down the hall and putting me in the shower. (*"Cabrón!"* she called me, slapping my face.) And my father? I'm not sure if he had gotten to that point himself—but I think on that night at least he hadn't, because as soon as he saw me that way, he marched right over to the Muller-Thym apartment, where he pushed open their door (never locked), and finding Richard passed out in his room, made his way into the living room, where he had some unkind words with Richard's mother, who for some time afterward did not want me coming to their house.

· · ·

Along the way, something happened on my block: By around 1964, working quietly, the university had purchased every building on 118th Street, and my pop, instead of making his usual rent payments in cash to a management office on 123rd Street, now made them, always in money orders, to Columbia Housing. Unlike everyone else who lived across the street, we were spared eviction, those less fortunate residents, over the course of the year, having been ordered to move out. (And those who didn't want to move, I've heard, were harassed, agents forcing open doors and changing the locks while the tenants were away; the saddest of their victims were old ladies who should have been allowed to stay put. That was the rumor at least.) Most everybody moved—the Martinez family, the Monts, the Cintrons, the Haineses, and the Muller-Thyms among them. (It was heartbreaking to me.)

Nevertheless, just like that, life on my street changed for good. First we lived with the sight of so many of our neighbors packing their things up into trucks, rows of them sometimes lining the block, most leaving by the spring of 1965. Then, for a year we had to put up with the demolition of those buildings, huge cranes and tractors and dump trucks and generators and Quonsets and portable toilets and huge bins piled up with doors, commodes, and bathtubs taking up the sidewalk and street on the other side of the block. Gradually, they brought down those buildings, which had been around since the turn of the century, with demolition cranes. Afterward, they started excavating for what would be the foundation of Columbia's School of International Affairs as well as a high-rise dormitory down the block, dynamite blasts, preceded by a whistle, going off every twenty minutes or so for months. (No wonder I can't stand the clamor of large construction sites.) Nothing good came from it for those who had remained behind: We had to get used to the mess, the noise, and the sudden appearance of guards patrolling the street to keep kids like myself out of those buildings when they were still up—I can remember sneaking into Richard's building not long after it had been abandoned and making my way through that darkness with a flashlight, pushing open his front door (all the locks had been removed) and prowling about the apartment's ghostly empty rooms, where I had spent so much time, all the while feeling that yet another world had been yanked away from under my feet.

But the guards were there, as well, to keep away any junkies from scavenging for whatever they could carry away—copper wiring and light fixtures, for example. Heroin had begun to sweep through Harlem—a lot of drugs were being sold out of the projects along 124th Street and across the way in the projects of 125th Street and along the sidewalks below 110th, those blocks teeming with young addicts. I can recall accompanying one of the local junkies, a really nice guy, to cop his stuff, always a harrowing experience, what with those assignations held in dingy project hallways and with those dealers and their acquaintances, all of them black, frankly not liking whitey (me). On that end, things had been already changing for a few years; I won't entertain any discussion of drugs here, or the ethos of getting high—poor and bored kids, without too many prospects, just liked doing it, and there were enough junkies around that the generally safe feeling one used to have about walking around that neighborhood vanished. (An older kid who lived across the way, addicted but a sharp fellow, used to knock on our door, asking my mother for a glass of water, and at first opportunity would manage to walk through the apartment, with its circular configuration, looking around for anything of value to conceivably take—fortunately, we had little worth taking.) Marijuana, by the way, seemed to have crept in on little cat's feet a few years earlier—kids smoking joints while playing stickball on 120th Street were a common sight. (Most never bothered anyone, just wanting to have their fun, and reefers, at a dollar a stick, were always readily available, just like cigarettes.)

In any event, those demolitions sucked the life out of that street: So many of my neighbors, turned into air. Sure, kids still played out in front, doo-wop singers still managed to get together for their stoop sessions, and I managed to see my friend Richard—who'd moved with his family to a place on West End Avenue in the nineties—but, with so many familiar faces gone, the block often seemed deserted, especially at night, when you'd have to watch your back.

Naturally, during those demolitions, we developed a heightened animosity, as townies, toward the university. I can remember going over to the campus and tossing clumps of dirt and stones in through classroom windows as the students, who had nothing to do with what happened, were sitting for a lecture. (Sorry, my friends.) And sometime later, aside from sneering at any students who crossed our paths, while adopting tough-guy personas, we—I'm talking about myself and a few other local kids—made it a regular practice to head over to the wide street between Broadway and Amsterdam Avenue, by Teachers College, where we'd pass the afternoon prying Volkswagen insignias off the countless Beetles parked in rows out in front: I collected dozens of those things, for no good reason, though sometimes one of us would head down to a pawnshop on 125th Street to sell the medallions for two dollars apiece.

Of course, within a year or so, they had put up the School of International Affairs, right across the street, where Richard's building, 420, had once stood, and, a block south, Columbia's law library, massive structures that to me, knowing nothing about modern architecture, seemed to lack charm. Spared were *la casa italiana*, with the grocers and a soda fountain left intact on that corner, as well as a few remaining buildings on the drive toward 117th Street. Suddenly, students came pouring in through the high glass doors of the new 420 (for that is its current address), and while that was something one came to accept, and even get used to, at night, when the institution closed down, that side of the block became eerily silent and dark. Our apartment, smothered by the shadows of that structure, saw less light during the day. (I've often wondered what my father thought about that building; oh, he still sat out on the stoop, smoking cigarettes in the afternoons, and looked out across the street, as those anonymous students made their way to their classes, and while I'm sure he had nothing against them, he probably missed seeing his friend Mr. Martinez, the superintendent, coming up the block, and the opportunity to invite him in.)

It was pretty lousy from our end, though at least we had a friend in the new housing manager that Columbia had appointed to look after the block. His name was Mr. Foley, a congenial older, white-haired Irish man who always spoke with a thick brogue and who, until then, had worked as a janitor for the Corpus Christi Church; we knew him from there and were always kind to him, and that was a good thing, because in the coming years, he'd look out for us and, most importantly, later on, for my mother.

On the other hand, despite our resentments, when the university held its annual spring fair, with its games of chance and food stands selling stuff like cotton candy, as well as an attraction in which one could pay to take a turn going at some wreck of a car with a sledge-hammer, all of us flocked there, thrilled, as if a carnival had come to town. And some of the older guys did all right with the college girls, in local bars, though the thing that most impressed me about Columbia, as I'd cross the campus, predating the destruction of my street, were the students I'd see from time to time, sitting out on the steps of Butler Library, strumming folk tunes on guitars. I was prob-ably twelve when I first stood enthralled watching a group that did covers of Beatles hits, performing on a makeshift stage in front of one of their student buildings—I think it was Ferris Booth Hall—and somewhere along the line, with all the crap going on at home, I decided that I would try to learn to play the guitar—a pursuit that turned out, in those years, to be one of my salvations.

· · ·

I bought my first guitar, a junky Stella, for five dollars from one of my brother's friends, a dashingly handsome Irish fellow who had sung in the choir with him. On that guitar, warped and never easy to tune, I learned my first chords from a Mel Bay instruction book. On it I played my first Beatles and Bob Dylan tunes. I had my morning job at the laundry, which paid me five dollars a week, and, always working on the side making deliveries for a local printing outfit, I came up with enough bucks to send away for one of those fifteen-dollar elec-tric guitars that were advertised on the back pages of comics. That guitar was also a piece of junk, and I lost heart for a while. (Well, keeping after my father was a part of that loss of heart.)

But then, occasionally, I'd head over to the apartment of one of my school chums, this decent and quiet kid named Bobby Hannon. His mother was Polish, his father an Irish fireman, and they lived down on 122nd Street in one of those cluttered railroad flats that only exist today in the slums. Mr. Hannon, in some ways, with his close-cropped bristled-in-front haircut and etched face, resembled the actor Larry Storch, best known for the TV show *F Troop*. Like my father, he also liked to drink, but with a difference. He fancied himself a musician. On those afternoons when I'd hang around with his son, he'd occasionally take out his guitar, which, as I recall, was a

left-handed F-holed jazz-style Gibson—a beautiful instrument, even
to me. Before becoming a fireman, as a young man, he once had a
radio show in Pennsylvania, in which people would call in and try
to stump him by challenging him to play obscure tunes. So he knew
everything of Gershwin, Porter, Rogers and Hart, etc., as well as any
number of songs by polka musicians, both famous and lesser known.
He had an ear and a half, and once, while reaching over to a table, his
guitar on his lap, to get another glass of beer, told me that there was
nothing he couldn't play. "Try me." Naturally, I was intrigued. But
no matter what I came up with—not Cuban songs, but Top Forty
hits—he'd figure anything out. Just after I'd whistle, say, the melody
of a Beatles tune like "And I Love Her," he'd not only figure out the
chords but pick out the melody (somehow) with one of his fingers
while holding on to his pick at the same time. "Kid's stuff," he called
my choices. He smoked as much as my father, and his face had that
same tendency to rawness at its edges. He was burly, most often liking to wear a T-shirt. With stacks and stacks of Les Paul and Mary
Ford 78s clustered in the shelves above a console, he'd occasionally
put one of them on so that I could hear "real music."

One day I brought my ratty Stella down, and as I played him the
four chords of "Mr. Tambourine Man," he threw a fit, telling me I
didn't know a damned thing about the guitar ("You play like you're
wearing mittens," he said), and commenced, on that afternoon, to
teach me—or at least try to—my first bar chords, and jazzy ones
that made my fingers ache for days. Nevertheless, I'd go back there,
wanting to learn more, and, in time, I could play the square (to me)
turnarounds of pieces like "Someone to Watch Over Me." Afterward,
I'd sit in Bobby's room and feel relieved to hear, off his record player,
the zippier 45s of the day. But I'd pick up stuff all over the place.
Once Marcial García and his family had moved in upstairs and I'd
sometimes end up there with my mother, I learned that he too played
the guitar, but in the classical style, with sheet music for studies by
Tárrega, Fernando Sor, and others lying in stacks on a table by a stand
in his living room. He had a beautiful Spanish guitar from Valencia,
full toned and plump in sound, that, made by an angel, did all the

work for you—that is, if you knew how to play. He taught me some études, which I never quite got right, and because of the craziness in my head and despite all the lessons he gave me about reading music, during which he would fill up blank staffs with the notes written out in pencil, I simply tuned out, in the same way I did when it came to Spanish—some busy emotions in my head preventing, as it were, my momentary concentration.

Still, I loved those lessons, and they brought me comfort, and especially so in that year when the explosions were going off, though I could hardly ever really feel good about what I was doing. If you own a guitar, however, as I learned, no matter how badly you play, you begin to acquire a self-nurturing attachment to it. Often when sitting with my father on those nights when he would go on and on about the perils of his mortality, I'd drift off, thinking about the chords of a song, and in my mind, no matter what the song happened to be, I'd run through its entirety, even some bullshit piece like "Hanky Panky," and coming back, I'd catch him staring at me quizzically, as if I hadn't been listening to him at all.

But I had other teachers as well. Remember Teddy Morganbesser, over on 119th Street, at whose apartment my father had tried to give me my first drink of wine? His squeeze, Belen, had two kids, the first being the fabulously beautiful and *muy sexy* Tanya, who would marry that gallant from my street, Napoleon, and a son, Philip, about one of the sharpest-dressed and most astute, forward-moving Latinos around. (I remember seeing him sitting on the stoop next to mine, studiously reading textbooks from his school.) He was outrageously handsome, with classic heartthrob looks—think of Ricardo Montalbán or, for more current generations, Julio Iglesias Jr., with a beautiful yet manly and effortlessly chiseled face. He was a scholarship student at Fordham and doing well, the kind of slick guy who's conquering the world and I couldn't help but admire. At an early point, he had taken up playing the guitar, and since he, so impeccable in his dress and manner, had set a high bar for his pursuits, his instrument turned out to be one of the most elegant and, I think, pricey guitars around, a curvaceous brass-knobbed Gretsch Anniversary guitar of a shining green luster with a tremolo bar and intricate inlay along the fret board. (Like the perfect woman—in fact, I think, the vast appeal of guitars has much to do with their female shape.)

It was Philip (may God bless his soul, for he, like so many people from my neighborhood, would end in ruin because of drugs) who first taught me how to play that Beatles riff for the song "I Feel Fine." We'd spent a couple of weeks working on it—why he did so, I don't know to this day, except to say he was a generous soul. He had a tender demeanor about him, nodding when you got something right, shaking his head wildly when you didn't. In the half-light of his living room, while he, thin yet muscular, seemed to glow, I tried my best. The rock and roll fingerings were different from the classical, but in the end, I could play that riff, and once I started listening to other Beatles tunes, I figured them out as well, though what would some dumb fuck kid do with useless knowledge like that?

I went to Rolling Stones concerts on Fourteenth Street, at the old Academy of Music, when first-balcony tickets cost two dollars and fifty cents, and, with an empty guitar case in hand, I'd go running from one end of the line of miniskirted ticket holders to the other, hoping to meet some wildly screaming girl. (It sometimes worked, though I was too knuckle-brained to figure out what to do from there.) Over on La Salle Street, some ten blocks away from 118th, I'd hang outside the apartment building where Kenny Burrell, the jazz guitarist, lived, listening to him practicing his scales and tunes. On the same street, in a first-floor apartment, its windows facing the sidewalk, a Puerto Rican *conjunto*, the lead singer in coal-black sunglasses, rehearsed—their repertoire consisted of a few Latin tunes, but mainly they practiced Top Forty songs, a look of resignation and professional "let's get this over with" on the lead's face as he plucked away on his Telecaster. I remember thinking, I'd like to do this. And I'd go down to the Apollo when they had afternoon matinees featuring acts like James Brown and Wilson Pickett and the Cadillacs— and along the way, with my eyes always watching the guitar player in the band, I got some wild idea that I could become a musician.

At sixteen, I'd played guitar behind a neighborhood doo-wop

group that auditioned before a hashish-stoned audience on an open-mike afternoon, singing vamped-up, multi-harmonized versions of popular folk tunes like "When I Die" at the Café Wha? in Greenwich Village. (We cleared out the place.) I'd played in a little band in Brownsville, Brooklyn, with my friend Jerry, who had long since moved away, performing simple rock tunes by groups like the Kinks and Them, as well as some of our own, in more than a few dead-end bars and social clubs in the midafternoon. (I never liked to hang around there at night, for it was a neighborhood where you heard guns popping off in the distance.) And, often enough, while crossing the campus, I'd hear some guy fingerpicking a tune and sit down, just watching his every move. If he sang, that was fine, but mostly I watched the way he played.

Around the same time, a larcenous tendency arose in me. Or to put it differently, it suddenly blossomed. In 1966, a music shop, Levitt & Elrod, had just opened on Ninety-sixth Street, halfway down the block between Broadway and West End. (There's a Salvation Army store there now.) I happened to walk by there one afternoon with a friend just as a delivery of instruments had been made. (My friend's name was Peter, and I suppose we were on our way to Richard's apartment, a few blocks over.) As I looked in, the owners were in the back trying to figure out how to situate things; there were a number of instruments piled inside by the front door, some in packing boxes and some not, among them a stellar four-pickup Kay guitar, which someone had just left leaning up against the front window, and seeing that no one seemed to be watching, I stepped inside and on an impulse grabbed it and began running with that instrument down the street toward West End Avenue. For the record, I was in my first year as a student at Cardinal Hayes High School up in the Bronx, which required that we wear a tie and jacket. Peter, attending a prep school—both his parents worked for Columbia in some blue-collar jobs but put their son in the best school they could afford—was dressed the same; and so, as we bounded down to the avenue, with that guitar bundled in my arms, it might have seemed, in a world of spoiled kids, which is what that neighborhood was to me, that we

were just celebrating a recent purchase, even while the price tag—
$187.50, as I remember—dangled, flapping, off its head. The crazy
thing is that as we went around the corner, a police car was sitting
there, two cops inside having coffee. I told Peter, "Pretend we're rich
kids," and with that, we waved at the cops inside as we passed them
by, and they, not even flinching, hardly paid any notice.

Now, I'm sure if I were a swarthy spic, some dark-skinned Latino,
those cops would have perked up, and, chances are, I would have
ended up at some detention center in the Bronx for the next year. But
it didn't happen that way, and on one of the more delicious afternoons
of my life, I arrived at Richard's new digs, feeling exhilarated.

• • •

I'd also been something of a vagabond performer in Washington
Square on the weekends, going down there to Travis-pick on a guitar with a neighborhood friend who played the harmonica, the two
of us wailing away for befuddled tourists who didn't always quite
know what to make of our "music." Or I'd go to Central Park, where
"be-ins"—impromptu gatherings of music and dance put together by
aspiring hippies—took up the lawn of the Sheep Meadow. I'd bring
my guitar and sit in with anyone, as long as they would let me. A lot
of those kids were middle-class or rich, but playing guitar gave me
an entrée, which I wouldn't have had otherwise, into those circles.
That's how I met that guitar player Nick Katz, and because he had
some good social connections, our little band, whose song lists consisted of covers of famous blues tunes as well as standards by Chuck
Berry and Bo Diddley, got jobs performing at private parties, some
in swanky Park Avenue brownstones—where I got a good notion
of how people with money live—the best, however, in my opinion,
taking place in one of those immense, high-ceilinged apartments in
the Dakota apartment house on Seventy-second Street, in whose
marijuana-sweetened rooms, with all kinds of well-dressed folks in
Nehru jackets and Carnaby Street gear dancing away enthusiasti-
cally, I briefly suffered from the delusion that I was someone cool.

I can recall envying the free spirits I saw around me, particularly on campus, those long-haired kids who seemed at the time to be

about the future. I went through the same thing down in the Village, but however much I wanted to grow my hair long, my first two years at a Christian Brothers high school, with its strict rules about everything, made that impossible (and at any rate, in the summers when I tried to let my hair grow out, my usually taciturn father would take me over to Broadway to get a trim—"You don't want to look like a *marica*, do you?" I recall him saying).

But I still pined away for that freedom. My idols, if I had any aside from the guys who wrote and drew the comic books I still read, were those icons of the British Invasion, from the Beatles to the Rolling Stones, along with some very odd ones thrown in, like the girlish California band the Hullabaloos, whose records I must have listened to a thousand times over, along with those of Manfred Mann, on countless afternoons at Richard's place downtown on West End Avenue, where the experience was heightened by the occasional drink or, if Tommy was around, by the offering of a joint to smoke. (But I had to be very cool whenever I'd come home.) Since I really had so little identity of my own—except as this "son of *cubanos*" who had once been sick and didn't much identify with Latin culture in general, for when I'd hear any Spanish songs, they always sounded passé and locked in some perpetual, unchanging past, and I didn't even consider my Spanish anything I should try to improve upon—I spent those years trying to become anything else but what I should have been, Oscar Hijuelos.

· · ·

While at Hayes, on those mornings when I'd leave my job without a prayer of making all the connections on time to the Bronx, I was often late coming to classes and spent most afternoons in detention. Altogether, it was the kind of school where the teachers, if they thought you were smirking or expressing a less than reverent attitude in class, made you pay for it. Getting slapped, being rapped in the knuckles with a ruler, or having someone squeezing the back of your neck with all his strength until you would finally say, "Yes, sir"—or worse, teachers who were known to take smart-ass kids into the gym and have it out with them in boxing matches—became a part of the daily experience. A good number of those Christian brothers seemed so certifiably gay and effeminate as to become the brunt of jokes, but most were pretty tough Irish guys who, coming up the hard way but taking the righteous path earlier in their lives, would brook no disrespect. If you as much as missed a homework assignment, you were sent into detention for a week and saddled with even more work than you could have dreamed up. I say this fondly because Hayes was good for someone like me, whose attention easily wandered.

Despite my own slothful—or distracted—tendencies, I somehow became a good student, good enough that I seemed to have been viewed by some of the teachers as a special case, someone to be pushed along, no dummy, a kid with problems perhaps but with promise. Half-bludgeoned to do the work, I did pretty well on all the exams and in classes—but in the end, after two years in that school and longing for something different, once their tuition went up to a lordly fifteen dollars a month, I ended up leaving.

That increase in tuition was the excuse I came up with, at any rate. My father, having his pride, insisted on paying for it, but when that new invoice came along, and I saw his face screwing up a bit, I decided that leaving was the most decent thing I could do. Deep down, however, I simply wanted to attend a school without so many strict rules; and for another thing, always feeling lonely, I liked the notion of attending a school with girls. (Hayes had only male students—and the mix, while including blacks, Italians, and Latinos, my neighborhood friends Louie Cintron and Victor Cruz among them, was predominantly Irish.) My parents, by the way, weren't too happy with my choice—my mother seemed puzzled—but I think that while they looked out for me, what with their own problems, they more or less accepted it. Altogether, I don't recall my father having any opinion, one way or the other, about what would turn out to be a stupendous blunder on my part.

To put it succinctly, the educational institution I started attending instead, the Louis D. Brandeis High School, on West Eighty-fourth Street between Amsterdam and Columbus, with its state prison façade, had its problems. Its students were mostly black and Latino and, for the most part, not too inclined to accept the notion of authority.

Transferring from Hayes, where respect toward the teacher was the number one thing, to a school in which students spit at and sometimes assaulted their teachers, in which most classrooms were overcrowded, and where just getting the kids to stop fucking around before every session was a daily challenge to its teachers, threw me for a loop. Some of the teachers were kind to me, as I must have seemed lost half the time, and while I did my best to seem interested in being there, not a day went by when I didn't feel as if I had messed up. Without dwelling too much on how many drug users there were at Brandeis (some 80 percent, I later read) or how many of its students belonged to gangs or had juvenile records, or what it was like in the middle of the day to walk into a bathroom dense with pot and cigarette smoke, with guys shooting up in the stalls, or how one might occasionally encounter a used syringe in a stairwell, or hear about a rape, I will say this: While getting knocked around in those hallways on my way to class—as in some tough pissed-off black dude abruptly slamming his shoulder against mine to start something—I often wondered what I had gotten myself into.

Still, I managed to squeeze by and made my friends, mainly thanks to the hippies there. In that school, those longhairs, mostly white but with some Latinos thrown in, would gather outside after classes and jam. Some sold drugs, a service that was respected (the cops did not seem to notice), but mainly those kids—what were they but sixteen and seventeen years old?—held impromptu music sessions, in the spirit of the day, with flutes, bongos, and guitar. Bringing my guitar, an acoustic, I eventually joined in. For the record, my best friend from Brandeis was a kid of half-Argentine, half-American extraction, who would later play drums in a band with me, and in the aftermath of such sessions, on many of those afternoons, we'd drift off to someone's apartment to play even more music and, often enough, to get high.

I was never good at getting high, by the way. I had such a self-consciousness about my body, and the *microbios* within, that the uplifting removals from one's being that came along with smoking hashish or marijuana eluded me. (I was too uptight and felt more inwardly drawn than I liked; the only thing that worked for me would come with the introduction of a mild beverage like some sweet Gypsy Rose Wine.) In general, however, those were halcyon afternoons: I loved playing the electric guitar, if somebody had one, and while I had to put up with a lot of lead-guitar-playing egomaniacs who weren't too inclined to listen to what other people were putting forth, I slowly began making up my own tunes and, in my way, became something of a songwriter.

Speaking of getting high: My friend Bobby, on 122nd Street, had a down-the-hall neighbor, an Irish kid named Jimmy, a completely slovenly lost soul of a fellow, a mess without a center who, however, taking some LSD in those years, underwent a miraculous transformation of personality. Suddenly suave and self-asserting, he became a drug dealer, of heroin, pot, and LSD. (Among his rumored clients, one of the Rolling Stones when they were in town.) How those business arrangements flourished, I can't say, but despite that change, he continued to live in the same apartment with his mother. In any event, I had been asked by someone in the neighborhood if I knew of anyone who dealt LSD, and thinking about Jimmy, I arranged through my friend Bobby for him to bring me six doses—which cost about twenty dollars, as I recall. What happened amazed me: Bobby met me on a street corner, where we made the exchange, and while I soon passed it on to that someone from my neighborhood and went home afterward, Bobby, heading off on a date on 106th Street with his girlfriend, happened to drop several tabs of that drug and, that night as a good Catholic boy going crazy, swore that he had been possessed by the devil, and, in effect, he, once so docile, tried to take physical advantage of her.

The long and short of it? He ended up in Ward Eight of St. Luke's Hospital, the psychiatric facility there, speaking in tongues.

Unfortunately, his father the fireman, who once taught me guitar, came knocking on our door the next day, frantically demanding of my pop that I confess to having been a part of his son taking that drug. Along the way, he insisted that we see for ourselves what I apparently had done. That same afternoon, as my father and I walked over to the hospital, he finally asked me: "Did you give that drug to that boy?" and because I hadn't—maybe Jimmy had given or sold him those tabs—I told him, quite simply, no, and that was good enough for my pop. But once we got there, I regretted that whole business—never again, I told myself—for that same day, Bobby's father suffered a heart attack, his anguish being so great, and my friend, as we encountered him in the ward, could only repeat a few words—"Nobody loves me," over and over again.

. . .

That same year, 1968, the Columbia riots took place, the buildings down the hill across Amsterdam occupied by the striking students. It struck us as a quite festive affair, what with TV reporters, and spotlights glaring against the walls at night, our block lit like a movie set. All our neighbors made it a habit to gather on the corner and watch the exciting doings, my mother and her friend Olga, as I recall, among them. I went inside the occupied buildings a few times—it was easy if you were a kid. Once I did so with one of the more affable junkies from the neighborhood, and mainly we traipsed about the back stairwells, on the prowl for things of value (I don't recall that we found any), and going into the salons of those buildings where the suffering and gallant students were holed up, it seemed to me, on the face of it, more of a bacchanal than a revolutionary movement. For one thing, they had tons of food, for sympathetic neighbors would fill their baskets, lowered to the sidewalk, with stuff; and they had tons of wine and pot, the rooms filled with smoke; in one place, we saw a rock band performing, and while I had mustered some interest in their movement, I mainly thought it a phony spoiled-kid kind of affair; in other words, like most of the guys from my neighborhood, I wasn't really very impressed, just a little envious of the girls the revolutionaries attracted.

Now, if you're getting the impression that I had drifted into some inner life far removed from my Cuban roots, you've got that right. If I thought in Spanish at all, it was mostly in my sleep, and the gist of my exchanges with my parents usually came down to a laconic few words—"Okay, okay, *te oigo*" or "*Sí mamá, vengo*." And when it came to Cuba, if anything, far from developing a curiosity for its history, for example, beyond what I already knew about Castro, the Bay of Pigs invasion, and the Cuban missile crisis (when we were convinced there would be a nuclear war), and that we had family down there, I couldn't be bothered to learn more. (My mother's own histories were enough, and old to me by then.) I preferred my comics, and sometimes the occasional novel, thanks to Tommy, by someone like Ray Bradbury. (And I liked the randy humor of comedians like Redd Foxx and Lenny Bruce.)

If you'd talked to me in those days, you would have heard a kid who used the terms *chick*, *man*, and *like, you know* almost all the time. I loved *Mad* magazine but also dipped into the kind of arcane publications that one might find only in a neighborhood like my own: I can remember liking Lee Krasner's *Realist*, which basically had an up-yours attitude about the powers that be, and because of the Vietnam War, I could hardly walk across the campus or down Broadway without someone thrusting an antigovernment protest pamphlet into my hands. Because of Marcial García, who was always preaching in our kitchen about the values of the revolution, I had an awareness of both sides of the equation regarding Cuba. (On the other hand, I wasn't the sort of kid to walk around wearing a Che Guevara T-shirt like so many others did.) But even when I had an exile friend like Victor, who'd come to the states in 1962 and knew just how cheated his family had felt leaving Cuba, and their desire to *regresar*—to go back—I remained detached enough to think that such concerns really didn't touch me. I didn't realize that their loss was really my own, a whole other possible life denied to me without my knowing it.

As far as I can tell about myself, back then, I hardly cared about anything except some vague notion of being a creative sort. Lord knows how much my mother had to put up with: When some family from down the street moved out and left an upright piano on the sidewalk, I somehow persuaded the superintendent of that building, Mr. Sullivan, and one of my sturdier friends, a certain Provinzano, to help me bring it up the hill and carry it into the apartment. (I don't know how we managed, but at one point, the piano slipped and, coming down hard, cracked the lip of one of the marble stairs in the entryway—go check, it's still there.) I began to play that piano (badly) and, at one point, putting thumbtacks into its felt hammers, and fooling around while plucking on its strings inside the harp, came up with strange compositions à la John Cage, which I would commemorate for posterity on a cassette recorder.

My pop didn't seem to mind and seemed only vaguely aware of my aesthetic leanings, if they could be called that. On one of those nights when he was hanging around with one of his friends from the hotel, this Haitian fellow, as I recall, he asked me to play something for them (*"algo en español, eh?"*—"something in Spanish, huh?") and when all I could come up with were a few chords along the lines of "La Bamba," he listened for a moment and, with a disappointed expression on his face, poured himself and his friend another drink, shrugging and moving on. I didn't brood about it: If I'd played a Beatles tune for him, it wouldn't have meant a thing; as far as I was concerned, both my parents were really from some other planet. (My brother, on the other hand, who had come home from his air force stint in England and had stayed briefly with us in 1966 while he studied for his GED diploma before he moved out to live in Queens with a young woman, later to become his wife, seemed interested in what I was doing: I think we sometimes talked about my showing him how to play a little guitar, and while, years later, we would often lament the fact that we hadn't tried speaking Spanish with each other back when, it was nothing that ever occurred to us at the time.) No, sir, whatever I was about, a work in progress, as it were, I might have been aspiring to many things but none that had to do with Cuba.

That I was so American, or to put it in the way I prefer, so New Yorkish, didn't bother me much at all, until, as it happened, my wonderful aunt Cheo arrived to live with us from Cuba. She and her daughters and their husbands had come in 1967, thanks to some arrangement that Lyndon Johnson had made with Fidel to allow more Cubans to leave the island legally, of course for money—with which my pop, working his extra job, had helped them out. They were exhausted, of course, after the ordeal, but the reunion between my mother and her sister, whom she had not seen since our visit to Holguín in the 1950s, was joyous. I am not sure what they made of our apartment—I think they were a little disappointed—but whatever might be said about the drabness of our digs, it was surely a big improvement over what they had been reduced to back in Cuba.

"*No había comida,*" I remember my gentle aunt saying, "*y olvídate de trabajo—nos trataron como perritos.*" ("There was no food, and forget about work—we were treated no better than little dogs.")

Theirs was a story that is fairly common to most exiles. Mercita's husband, Angel Tamayo, had run a car repair shop, which had been nationalized some years back during one of Fidel's sweeping reforms, while Eduardo Arocena, married to Miriam, and a most quiet fellow, had been, as far as I know, in the trucking business and harassed by the government for his strong feelings against Fidel. Though it's a cliché by now to mention that they arrived with only the clothes on their back and what they could manage to bring along in a few suitcases, it was, in fact, the truth. I can't imagine how daunting it must have been for them. Still, all of us made do. We had a spare bedroom next to mine—that's where I think Mercita and Angel stayed, while Cheo, Miriam, and Eduardo were settled into the living room, on cots, I believe. (Though now and then, coming into the apartment after school, I'd sometimes hear my mother and her sister whispering to each other as they lay, much as they probably did as children, alongside each other in bed.)

At first, they naturally assumed I could speak Spanish as well as my brother, who came to visit them often, though once it became clear that my repertoire mainly consisted of nods of assent and understanding as to what they were saying—"Remember, my love, when you stayed with us in Holguín?"—our methods of communication, harkening back to my mother and "*la muda,*" often came down to gestures, though Angel, who spoke some English, didn't mind practicing it with me. (One of the first things he said, while noticing my guitar: "You know Elvis? I love Elvis Presley.") Thank goodness, however, that Cheo, despite the displacement she must have been feeling, remained such a tolerant soul: She'd often sit next to me in the kitchen and, taking hold of my hand, recount those delicious days when we were together in Cuba, and in more than a few religious asides, always urged me not to lose my faith in God. ("*Tienes que confiarte en Dios*," she'd say.) I recall my mother apologizing about my Spanish to my cousins—I think she made the effort to remind them about my year in the hospital, though given what they'd gone through, it was hardly a number one concern. What seemed to matter the most, at least to my aunt, was that we were together, and as far as I seemed to be turning out, it made no difference to her, for, as I will always say, she was nothing less than pure affection.

For his part, my father, despite the inconveniences, didn't seem to feel any imposition on his comforts, such as they were. He happily provided them with whatever they needed—walking-around money, advice, got people to drive them to where they had to go, offered to get Angel and Eduardo jobs at the Biltmore, and, of course, fed them to death with that hotel food, and good stuff too. Oddly, he abandoned his bad habits during those three months or so—I don't recall his having much to drink; I think having people around made him happy, and, if anything, when they finally got resettled over in Union City, New Jersey, where there was a big Cuban community, he seemed a little sad to see them go. For once they left, it was back to my mother and father's old patterns; along the way my mother, hearing of how the government and exile agencies had helped them out—Angel, working odd jobs, was soon driving a Chevy, and it wasn't long before they'd made a down payment on a house—couldn't help but feel some jealousy, though I know she truly wished them well.

As for myself? I felt a little relieved to have some relative privacy again, and while I missed them, I welcomed a release from the daily strains—and perhaps shame—I had been feeling about not being Cuban enough to hold a conversation with my own cousins.

. . .

Eventually, at Brandeis, disliking the atmosphere, I became a truant. For every day I attended, I missed another. I always made up excuses about being sick, while in reality, I would be either sitting in some remote spot in Riverside Park, brooding, or in someone's apartment, playing the guitar. The school authorities were perplexed, for when I would come into the principal's office to be counseled, I always seemed like some nice white kid who must have been, in some way, distracted from his higher calling. My grades on tests were always good, but I was always on the verge of flunking out because of my spotty attendance. I had no idea what I was doing there and blamed myself, though I always had an ace in the hole. Somewhere along the line, I had heard that if you passed your Regents Exams, that statewide test of scholastic competence, you could not be failed out of a class. Somehow (thanks, I think, to Hayes) I had gotten 100s in most every Regents exam I took; that is, English, American history, business math (!), and somehow, in lieu of actually sitting through the course, Spanish. Because of those exams, however, I was awarded an academic diploma upon graduation, though my grade-point average remained, based on attendance, abysmal. When Brandeis held the graduation ceremony, my parents did not turn up; nor, for that matter, did I.

. . .

Still, I had enough gumption to demand a graduation present from my hardworking father. For some reason, I had the figure of one hundred dollars in my head, and my pop, wanting to please me, somewhat reluctantly came up with the cash. ("*Eres loco?*" I remember my mother saying. She had good reason—it was well more than a week's pay at the hotel.) I don't know why it mattered so much to me; I always had other ways of making money. I suppose I did so because some of the tonier kids I knew were sent off to Europe or given checks for what to me were unimaginable amounts, thousands of dollars. Or because I wanted some recognition for the fact that I'd dragged myself through school, or simply, perhaps, because I was sick and tired of hearing that we were poor (mainly from my mother). And no doubt something of the spoiled brat in me still lingered. What did I do with it? I pissed it away one night, taking a girl named Diane, whom I knew from Brandeis, to a cool night of jazz, to hear Red Prysock performing at the Half Note, which had by then moved uptown to the fifties. I'd heard it was the kind of club that asked no questions if you had enough money to pay for their five-dollar drinks, and in any case, even as a teenager, I had the kind of serious expression on my face that aged me by a few years. With a bad crush on this tall and pretty girl, I'd hoped that alcohol would make a difference with her. We'd dated a few times, and I even got the chance to meet her mother, in their apartment on Central Park West and 101st Street, and we got along well enough, though I could never get anywhere with her, my biggest secret, which inhibited our conversations, coming down to the fact that I felt too ashamed to tell her much about my family at home; and she was guarded with me as well, though I learned that her father, who was never around, worked as an editor in the film industry. That night I played the big sport, throwing my pop's money away. Red Prysock was good, and we had a table near the stage, but my notion of plying her with rum-loaded tropical drinks came to nothing. She seemed, in fact, annoyed that I was trying to get her drunk, and while she had very little to drink, I, feeling the fool, did my best to get wired myself, which did not go down well with her at all: You see, her own pop, as I would find out one day, had his own problems with alcohol too.

· · ·

In general, however, as much as I might have been a brooding presence, my pop seemed happier than ever in those days. He seemed especially pleased by how my older brother had fared: Since coming back from his stint in the air force, as a Beau Brummel, the sartorial style of Europe having rubbed off on him, he not only made up the credits he needed for his high school diploma but had gotten into Brooklyn College, where he studied art with some fairly well-known painters, who were encouraging of him. Graduating, with that profession in mind, he began teaching art in a Brooklyn high school. Best of all, whatever differences he may have once had with my father seemed to be forgotten.

He'd turn up with the woman he'd married in a quiet civil ceremony, and she, of mixed Italian and Jewish descent, with her raven hair and dark eyes, hit it off famously with both my mother and my father, though from what I could observe, she had taken a particular liking to my father, who, doting on her, kept bringing up, and quite happily so, the notion that he would love to see them bring a *bambino* into the world. I can only recall one moment of awkwardness between them. She had just started working for the city of New York and, over dinner perhaps, the subject of her salary had somehow come up: I don't remember any exact figures—perhaps it was something like seven thousand dollars a year—but that number threw my father for a loop and somewhat saddened him. After twenty-five years at the Biltmore, he had yet to earn as much himself. (His shoulders slumped, he smiled, nodding, but his eyes showed something else.)

That was the summer, of course, of the moon landing. Nightly, when the progress of that mission was broadcast, my mother and father and I would watch it, like most of the country, on television. As Neil Armstrong first alighted on the lunar terrain, uttering his famous speech, my pop, most comfortably situated on his reclining chair, seemed truly enchanted—to think that someone of his generation, who'd been raised on farms in rural Cuba, could live to witness such a monumental act of daring, must have gone through his mind. His lips, I recall, parted slightly at that moment, the way they would when he'd see a baby.

I mention this because it's the only thing I can really remember about the days preceding another journey I'd make. When my aunt Maya in Miami, speaking to my father by telephone, brought up the notion that I go down there for the rest of the summer and work for my uncle Pedro, it seemed a good idea. I would get to spend some time with family and make some money along the way. I certainly didn't object, and while it wasn't the sort of adventure I might have been craving, it was something different for me to look forward to, though I can't imagine that it made my mother happy.

A month or so short of my eighteenth birthday, I was so self-involved that on the day I left for Miami, and my father, sitting on our stoop, wanted to embrace me just before I got a lift down to Penn Station in a neighbor's car, I sort of flinched and waved him off. Maybe I finally begrudgingly allowed him a kiss on my neck, but what I mainly remember is sitting in that car's front seat with my little suitcase and a guitar set in back, and feeling slightly put-upon seeing him smiling—perhaps sadly—at me as he settled on that stoop again and reached for a cigarette. I can recall wondering if I'd been a little cold, but before I could change my mind, the car started up the hill and the last I saw of him was this: my Pop in a light blue short-sleeved shirt, a pair of checkered trousers, and sneakers. He had just gotten his dark wavy hair cut short for the summer, and without a doubt he, always liking to smell nice, had dabbed his face with cologne. Some girl was skipping rope a few steps away and as my mother, Magdalena, watched me leaving from our first-floor window, my father turned to say something to her. Then he stood up to say something to me, and waved again: I think the last words he mouthed to me were, *"Pórtate bien"*—"Behave yourself." Not that I attached much importance to that, and if I said anything back to him, I don't recall.

Of course now I wish I'd been more receptive to him in those moments, but the truth is, I didn't know it would be the last time I'd see him alive.

This is what happened: I'd been down in Miami for a few days and put to work by my uncle on one of his sites, mainly hauling bags of cement around. My uncle, incidentally, as a former musician, took an interest in the fact that I'd brought along a guitar and, on my second or third night there, had me follow him into his garage, where he kept his old double bass, the very one he had played for years with the Cugat orchestra. Bringing it out, he spent a few hours trying to teach me some old Latin standards like "Perfidia" and "El Manicero," my uncle, in Bermuda shorts, attaining such a look of fierce concentration on his face, even if only playing an alternating bass line, while I, trying to fathom the arrangements, did my best to keep up with him. We weren't bad nor good together, but he was not discouraging of me, even if he had better things to do. Along those garage walls were numerous photographs of my uncle Pedro in his glory days, posed on bandstands with his fellow musicians, all in evening coats and tails, an air of glamour about them: Some found him seated in a posh club with celebrities the likes of Errol Flynn, and, as I recall, Desi Arnaz. What he must have made of me, with my longish hair and blue jeans, I can't say, but he, who had once been quite dapper in his time, seemed to have decided that he would have to take me downtown at some point to get me better clothes. As things turned out, there wouldn't be much time for that to happen.

My aunt Maya, by the way, of course, rebooted her efforts to lure me away from home. I won't go into too many details about that— with Cubans, some things never change, and her old animosities and disparagements of my mother picked up where we had left them some ten years before, but mainly she kept to her old mantra that I would be much better off with them and that it was my mother at the heart of my father's problems in life. (I suspect that once we had that telephone installed after my pop's heart attack, she'd had some conversations with him when he could hardly get his words out straight.) But she also had some new tricks up her sleeve: Where before, she'd ply me with ice cream and toys and clothes, Maya, knowing that boys will be boys, did her best to fix me up with a neighborhood girl, a pretty Cuban who, if the truth be told, did not seem particularly thrilled by the notion. Her name I honestly do not recall, though I can tell you that she had longish auburn hair and a figure that in tight jeans was too luscious for me to bear. In any event, come the first Saturday after I'd arrived, we went out to a club near Miami Beach, this loud crazy place jammed to the rafters with young kids, where, at about nine that night as we were dancing—that is to say, while I, considering myself a musician, attempted to dance in that darkened room, its ceiling filled with twirling stars, and the music of Joe Cuba's Latin boogaloo hit "Bang Bang" raging through enormous speakers—I felt this sudden and strange fluttering going up the right side of my body: It was so pronounced that I began shaking my arm wildly, and I must have had a strange expression on my face, for my date, if that's what she was, looked at me oddly. Then, as quickly as it came, it went away.

Sometime later, perhaps an hour had passed, I heard my name announced over the loudspeaker system. It was muffled, the music was so blaring, and at first I ignored it, until, during an interlude between songs, I heard it clearly: It went, at first in English and then in Spanish, "Would Oscar Hijuelos please come to the front office." When I reached that office, my aunt Borja was sitting inside, a look of utter bewilderment and exhaustion on her face. "Come on," she told me. "We have to go home."

Not once did anyone tell me what had happened, but I somehow knew. Back at my aunt Maya's so late at night, I had to pack. My aunt Borja had called the airlines, trying to get us a flight to New York, but the best she could do was to book something quite early in the morning, which is why, I suppose, we spent that night not in Maya's house but in a motel not far from the terminals. I honestly wish I could describe how Maya behaved throughout, except that I couldn't look at her without seeing tears in her eyes, while Pedro, a stoic sort, shaking his head, had hung around by a kitchen table without saying a word—what could anyone say? We left well past midnight. At the motel itself, with my aunt Borja, who could have been my father's female identical twin, in a bed across from me, sighing as she smoked cigarette after cigarette (she lived to be ninety, by the way), I passed the late hours kind of knowing what must have happened but without knowing anything at all—it was as if no one could say more than "Your *papá* has had an accident." I watched TV, an old-time movie: *Enchantment* starring David Niven, one of those classy tearjerkers Hollywood used to make—now and then I'd look over and see Borja wiping a tear from her eyes—and I kept on watching that film until its elegiac conclusion, at which point the station went off the air. Though my journey home early the next morning remains dim, I can remember coming into an apartment crowded with neighbors, and my mother's unbridled, chest-heaving bereavement; Borja's kindness and composure throughout; and meeting up with my brother that next Monday. Sometime in the early afternoon, we went downtown to Bellevue Hospital. There, someone at a desk escorted us to a certain room. It was a simple room with curtains drawn closed. At a certain moment, as we stood there, the curtains opened to a large window, and from some floor below, we could hear a lift operating. A platform came up, and on it rested my father, covered in a dark hooded shroud.

A few days before, he had been working in the kitchen of But- ler Hall's rooftop restaurant as usual, but it seemed to everyone around him that he'd not been feeling well that evening. He had been sweating, his face was flushed, and he had trouble breathing. One of his fellow cooks in that place, a black man who by coincidence was also named Joe—my father sometimes went by that American shorthand—had even urged him to go home, and one of the wait- resses there, a lady named Sally, would remember thinking to herself that my father had seemed rather exhausted and slow-moving, but when she'd asked him if everything was all right, he, in his quiet and self-effacing manner, perhaps worrying about holding on to the few extra dollars he'd make that night, just shrugged good-naturedly and told her that nothing was wrong. Perhaps getting a bit of air might help, he must have thought, and so, stepping out onto the terrace, which had a nice view over Morningside Park eastward to Harlem, he had pulled from his shirt pocket a package of Kent cigarettes in the soft wrapping and, lighting one, had taken a few drags, when, so Sally later reported, he had looked around in confusion, his right arm shaking, and the cigarette dropped from his lips, as he himself, his eyes turned to the sky, collapsed onto the roof tarpaulin.

This happened at nine thirty on July twenty-sixth, about a week after the first moon landing and some twenty-seven years since he'd first arrived in the United States from Cuba. He was fifty-five, and the outpourings of grief at his passing, from his fellow hotel workers and friends from around the city, seemed unending.

. . .

It's hard to explain the supernatural things that happened after he was gone. It was hard to forget him, to put from one's mind that not so long ago, he had, in fact, been sitting by that same table: I couldn't go into the kitchen without thinking about him, and even when I managed to put him from my mind, some remembrance would hit me, just like that. Holed up in my room with the same pack of ciga- rettes he'd been smoking that final evening, for his belongings were delivered in a plastic bag, I'd leave them overnight in a drawer, then find them next morning sitting on the radiator or under my bed. I doubt that I sleepwalked and can't explain how they got there any more than I can find a reason for the way pictures, of my folks in Cuba mainly, fell off the walls at night, or find an explanation for why the front door would abruptly open at around three thirty or four in the afternoon, when he used to come home, even after we'd taken care to shut the lock.

The apartment, in any case, breathed his memories: In the early mornings, at about five thirty, when he used to get up and head to the hotel, I'd awake swearing that I'd heard his quiet shuffle in the hallway, his keys fiddling with the lock. And sometimes, cigarette smoke, though no one smoked inside the apartment—I never did in front of my mother—seemed to linger particularly in the kitchen. (And it wasn't just I who noticed: My godmother, Carmen, coming downstairs to check in on my mother, would sometimes shiver, shaking her head, saying: "He's still here.") It so spooked me that I almost found it impossible to fall asleep without keeping a light on: I'd lose myself in a few comic books or some science fiction novel, or *Mad* magazines, though hardly an hour went by on those fitful nights when I wouldn't think about what had happened. At the same time, if I heard anything, even something as mundane as water humming through the pipes or the rumbling of the boiler beneath, I'd imagine him roaming through the basement, with its twisting passageways, on his way out to visit us. I always expected that, any moment, he'd push open the door to my room, and if I'd happened to finally doze, I would soon enough shoot up in fright. I got to the point that I could not turn off the lamp, nor make my way through the night without listening to a transistor radio: I always dialed past the Latin music stations, preferring the talk shows of Barry Farber, a conservative broadcaster, and Jean Shepherd, whose comical stories, along with Farber's antihippie harangues, simply kept me company.

But the persistence of memory killed me: images of him, drifting in from the permanence of the past, much like the smoke one has blown from a cigarette, going off to the heavens.

The situation wasn't helped by my mother's state of mind. She hadn't been so bad during the weeks that her sister Cheo, coming in from New Jersey, slept by her side, but once my aunt went back home and Borja, another angel, returned to Miami, she really started losing her grip. She went off the deep end—perhaps some old buttons regarding the loss of her father, from a stroke too, when she was a girl, had been pushed—and doubling over with grief, she wandered back and forth in the hallway muttering, despite all the shit they'd put each other through, "*Ay pero, mi Pascual.*" That was one thing, but at night, resting in bed, at first sighing, then tossing and turning, she tended toward talking to herself and, as it were, hosting both sides of a conversation with my father.

"What's wrong with you?"

"Nothing, woman."

"Then why are you looking at me that way?"

"Because you are so pretty."

"Ah, hah, and that's why you abandoned me!"

Then she would call the spirits and witches of her childhood into the apartment, praying to Santa Misericordia and, on her knees in the hallway in a cracking voice, offer her spirit up to God so that she might follow him to wherever he had gone.

I tended to find any excuse to stay out of the apartment, even if I'd just sit out on the stoop at night, where my pop used to, staring out at the lifeless street, where Columbia had put up its new institutional buildings, or I'd go upstairs and knock on Marcial's door—he might show me a few new things on the guitar, and I'd sit watching his fingers work the fret board, all the while sipping a glass or two of dark Spanish wine. In general, folks were really kind to me, even the neighborhood pricks—at least for a while—but I'd have to come home sooner or later and then my mother, seeing my father in me, would start up with all kinds of crazy shit; she couldn't resist letting me know that I was just like him—maybe nice in some ways, but only on the surface, and that deep down she knew I was up to no good and that I was a spoiled prince who'd treated her like a slave going back to the times of my illness, though occasionally she'd mess up and address me as Pascual, and what business did I have thinking that life might be easy, when we all should know that for some folks it will always be a hell. She'd go on as well about how I couldn't have possibly really cared for him and that he knew it—why, I didn't even let him embrace me on that day when I went to Miami and saw him for the last time; she saw that from the window. And for that matter, since when did I care for anybody else, particularly my own mother, who gave her life up for me, I was so obviously wrapped up in myself. Her tone was always indignant, often hysterical, and sometimes she'd yell out Pascual's name in the middle of the night, doubtlessly waking everyone in the building up, but without a single neighbor saying a peep (I'd just hear some windows shutting), and while I couldn't blame her—what a horrid grief she must have experienced—it seemed to me that we had, as a family, so little to hang on to that I resolved to bring us together, as those phone-in radio shows might put it.

But whenever I approached my mother tenderly and did my best to reach out, even speaking my half-assed Spanish and with my heart pricked by thorns; I'd say something sweet: "*Pero, mamá, no sabes que yo te quiero*"—"But, Mamá, don't you know that I love you," or I'd say, as she'd go into a trance, "*Por favor, cálmate!*"—"Please, calm yourself!" She'd not only come back to reality but take the occasion to dismiss my efforts. "What are you saying? Why, you can't even speak Spanish! That's how little you care." And she would start in on me, the way she used to with my father, and that would be enough to drive me back out onto the street, where I'd smoke a few cigarettes, sometimes one of those stale things from the pack left on his dresser, and nursing each one, all the while thinking of him, my little way after all of communing with my pop, who, as it turned out, I would never really get to know.

PART TWO

. . .

What Happened Afterward

CHAPTER 5

. . .

Getting By

My pop's union had contributed a thousand dollars for his funeral expenses, his wake having been held over three long days at the Ecchevaría & Bros. funeral home on West Seventy-second and his farewell service at the church of Corpus Christi. I'll tell you that it was a delight, my brother and myself flanking his open coffin from ten in the morning until eight at night, with the occasional break for lunch, as if anyone could eat, or, as with me, slipping outside to smoke a cigarette. I remember having to buy a new pair of shoes for the occasion, and that my upstairs neighbor Marcial lent me the money for them. I remember that a lot of folks rapped my back in condolence. I shook hands with the mourners as they came by to pay their respects, a few of the fellows pausing to whisper—or sob—a few words into his ear, or someone commenting, "How handsome he looks," or the occasional fellow, drunk out of his brains, with eyes like cracked glass, breaking down like a child—while I hardly showed very much emotion at all.

Afterward, one of his fellow workers from the hotel would occasionally turn up at our door to offer my mother an envelope filled with a few twenty-dollar bills, or in the mail we'd receive contributions from folks who addressed the envelopes to the family of Caridad or Charity. And neighbors, ringing our bell, came by with pots of cooked food or else left them with a note in front of our door. Sometimes an old friend from the hotel, like Díaz, would come by with a package of T-bone steaks. These we, of course, gratefully accepted. Along the way, one of the priests from church sometimes stopped by with an aluminum-wrapped package of something left over from a parish bingo, but no matter what, things were not the same with us as when my pop was alive and brought home that plentiful bounty from the cornucopia that was the Biltmore pantry.

I made a fairly reliable part-time salary (if to work twenty to thirty hours a week is "part-time") in and around the neighborhood. I won't bore you with the details, but on and off for about three years, aside from working as a messenger, I spent my weekdays—and the occasional Saturday—working the afternoon–evening shift at a Columbia University library in Uris Hall, where the business school was located. I mainly tended the front desk or passed my time in the zombie tedium of shelving cartloads of books, all for the regal sum of about $1.35 an hour. We had two bosses, a sanguine and somewhat dissipated boozy gent of late middle age who, white haired, thin but possessing a goose's flaccid neck, liked to hire young boys, and below him, a former undergarment industry manager who, changing professions in midlife, became the subject of an article in *The New York Times,* though I mainly remember him for the fact that his daughter dated—later married—the actor Dustin Hoffman, who, in the wake of becoming known, dropped by the library to say hello to her father from time to time.

In those days, I also had hoped to make a few dollars by putting together a bar band, though my pop's death had turned my hands into lead and my knees so earthbound that it was enough, at least in the beginning, for me to muster the energy to get out of bed.

I'm not quite sure what I did with the money I earned. I suppose I gave some to my mother, though I think that stopped when both our Social Security benefits—which came to about four hundred dollars a month—started arriving, with half of that coming to me, until I'd turn twenty-one, as long as I went to college.

Living at the far end of Flatbush Avenue in Brooklyn, my brother sometimes drove up to check in on us and help keep the peace, but he had, in any case, his own ongoing concerns, while I, as a newly graduated public high school student, had only some minimal ambitions about going to school—mainly to acquire the Social Security money, though I sometimes told myself that I was honoring my father's wish for me. (He seems to have once told me, in one of the few direct pieces of advice he ever gave me, "If you don't want to end up an elevator operator, go to college.") Having barely graduated Brandeis with an academic diploma, I wouldn't have gotten into any college at all if not for the fact that the CUNY system had in those years begun to experiment with an open admissions policy, through which they hoped to draw in and improve the future prospects of even the dregs of the New York City public high school system and, as well, the latest generation of immigrant kids, their grades, at least at that point, not seeming to matter as much as their potential.

Thanks to its often criticized open admissions policy, I was accepted in my senior year at Brandeis into Bronx Community College, on 184th Street and Creston Avenue, near Jerome. That would be the beginning of my sojourns through the city system, for in the next six years, I'd also attend other subway schools: Manhattan Community College, Lehman College in the Bronx at night, and, eventually, the mecca of CUNY, City College, up on 137th Street.

I had, by that point, become quite careless with myself, as if, in some ways, I simply didn't care about anything at all. A story: I sometimes did favors for friends—particularly my friend Richard's older brother, Tommy. I'd cop five-dollar bags of marijuana for him when he happened to be in a pinch. Okay, it was not the smartest or most noble thing to do, but after I'd make my purchase in a hallway at the far end of those stone pathways leading into one or the other of those Grant Houses projects along 123rd Street and Amsterdam, I'd usually head back up the hill, safely enough, and catch a downtown train at 116th Street. One night, however, I'd gotten out late (because my mother, still as a statue, had refused to move from a chair in the kitchen for an hour or so, until I had finally kissed her cheek, at which point she magically awakened) and, copping the stuff, had left the housing projects on Amsterdam, and feeling lazy or out of plain stupidity, I crossed the street and took a shortcut through the housing projects playground on the other side of Amsterdam toward Broadway, where in the darkness, not even midway, a pack of black kids, about twenty or so, as I can remember, came swooping down upon me from behind their hiding places, the bushes ringing the lot, and, surrounding my sorry ass, proceeded to put a beating on me, all the while going through my pockets, tearing off the peace symbol amulet I wore around my neck, and, having taken my nickel bag and a pack of cigarettes, a few did their best to concuss my brain, kicking away at my temples with the full force of their Converse sneakers. It was as if they gleefully wanted to kill me and they might have were it not for one of them—I suppose you might say he was my counterpart in that crowd, the sensitive "nice" one, a somewhat stocky fellow with rolled-up cuffs on his jeans, which were too big for him—who urged his brothers to be cool and leave me alone ("Hey, we got what we need"), and just like that, as quickly as they appeared, they vanished off into what I conceived in my head as some urban Zululand deep within the winding hallways and basements of that maze of project buildings.

Somehow, I dragged myself up from the asphalt and, I think, somewhat in a daze, walked all the way downtown to Richard's place on West End Avenue, where I found Tommy hanging out with some of his pals in a room down the hall from his brother. Rich had by then gone into the army, having been drafted by lottery. (He was probably the most brilliant soldier in Vietnam and probably the least recognized for his abilities—he should have been snapped up for an army intelligence unit but wound up instead tramping about the jungles there, as a foot soldier grunt in the First Cavalry, his memories of those firefights and other inequities to haunt him for the rest of his life.) The kicker: When I walked in, the room was thick with pot fumes, one of his pals having already brought some around. Aside from the fact that I felt as if I had gotten my brains beaten in for nothing, I discovered that I suddenly found the aroma of that burning hemp nauseating—in fact, I wanted to throw up, but as it happened, despite my messed-up state, Tommy and his friends were getting around to their usual nightly business, for after priming themselves on beer and pot, it was not at all unusual for some of the fellows to skin-pop, and later mainline, heroin, an act (finding and hitting the right veins) at which they were quite adept. Though I myself never indulged, I had assisted in the act dozens of times: I'd wrap a piece of black rubber tubing around the user's arm until the vein bulged big, and then, once the eye of blood had seeped into the syringe, unwrap the tightened band. Eyes rolling up in his head, ecstasy following, "What a snap," the user would say, "like coming all over."

It's so tawdry that I would rather not go further into the details except to say that Tommy, a sometime heroin user from about the age of sixteen, would, like many other of the guys in the neighborhood, continue to celebrate its virtues well into his thirties, when all kinds of things would catch up with him.

Though I developed a radar for takeoff artists, there was sometimes little that one could do, as on yet another evening when I got jumped, these three guys materializing behind me right across the street from where I lived, my cheekbone broken and my jaw aching for weeks from getting kicked in the face over and over again. I should have gone to the hospital, but when the cops arrived— someone from across the way had seen them ganging up on me—and asked if I wanted to go to the emergency room, I, detesting hospitals and the very smell of medicine, turned them down; and so they took me up to the precinct house on 126th Street (behind the meatpacking houses that used to be there and a few blocks from the nastiest cop bar in Manhattan, the 7-12), where they had rounded up three suspects— young black men, burly and tough—who sat waiting in a pen. The cops prompted me to identify them and although those young men were smirking and indignant, for the life of me, at that late hour—it was two in the morning—I honestly could not identify them as my attackers with any certainty, or I refused to, even when one of the officers took me aside and urged me to reconsider—"They're *cock-suckahs* after all."

But I didn't give in, even though, having been picked up while running along Morningside Drive, they were probably the guys who'd jumped me, and as they were released, they could not have been more smug—they certainly acted like they deserved to be in jail. The cops themselves were none too happy with me. As I sort of looked more a hippie than a good working-class smart-aleck, they treated me rather disrespectfully, letting me out through a station house side door into the darkness, one of them, however, pissily advising me as follows: "Good luck, Einstein; next time you'll end up in the morgue."

And on one of my more careless nights, when I'd somehow hooked up with a Columbia student who was into some awfully strong psychotropic drugs, I ended up at his place on 116th off Amsterdam, not far from where my mother used to clean the nursery school, stupidly dragging too deeply on a white cheroot that contained pot, tobacco, and a massive dose of angel dust. He was a kind of mad-hatter sort and, as a decent musician, seemed friendly enough, but I soon regretted going there. That angel dust distorts things: turns a twenty-foot hallway into the Khyber Pass, raises the walls into canyons, turns your limbs into rubber, your muscles into liquid, and scrambles the brain in such a way that it is hard to know what is going on. At one point, while I was sitting across from this fellow, whose long red hair spilling from his top hat fell upon his shoulders, he took out a brown paper bag and, asking me, "Guess what's inside?" pulled from it a .38 revolver whose muzzle he put against my head. Then, twirling its cylinders, and with a smile, he cocked its hammer before pressing the trigger. It clicked, no bullet exploded, and he fell back laughing, while I, struggling with that Martian atmosphere, got the hell out of there, leaving the bleakness of the apartment for the even greater bleakness of the street—dark, lifeless, foreboding, autumnal.

Occasionally, my mother and I went downtown to Centre Street to apply for food stamps, for which we, on a limited income, were eligible. I hated going, for we'd have to wait hours the way we used to at public clinics, and for the most part, the clerks handling the cases were late-middle-aged women who'd been forced into taking those positions in lieu of being on welfare. From the start, they gave my mother a hard time, especially when it came to documentation—she had to bring a Social Security card, a birth certificate, a death certificate for Pascual, and, as well, proof that we were "needy," by way of a recent 1040 form (she had none) or a bank book—she had, as I recall, all of two hundred and forty-seven dollars in her "life savings." It would have actually helped if we'd been on welfare, but my mother, despite her grief and shock, remained snooty enough as to swear that, no matter how bad things might turn out, she'd never sink so low as to go on "relief." Those employees who were on welfare, however, sniffing out her haughtiness, gave her a hard time for it: They picked on her Spanish, sent us back to our seats for hours at a time while they looked for some hopelessly "lost" document relating to our case, and only finally came through when my mother or I, eating humble pie, approached them at their desk, politely asking if they might yet approve a new round of thirty forty-dollar-a-month books of food stamps.

Much as I disliked that whole business, I had to go with her as an intermediary—my mother always feeling intimidated by any official documentation in English, as if asking even for food stamps in the wrong manner might get her in trouble. We went, I should add, about once every three months or so, as new rules and glitches were always around the corner, my mother and me riding downtown on the subway together, as she'd go on endlessly about the indignities of having to deal with colored women just to save a few dollars, while I, looking at the subway columns flashing by through the windows, daydreamed, wondering if my father, on his way home from work when he was alive, had done the same.

We also became recipients of government-issue surplus food, like peanut butter, jelly, tuna fish, chipped beef, and condensed milk, which I'd pick up at a distribution center on 125th Street. Packed into large white cans the size of paint gallons, the words NOT FOR

SALE in giant letters written on their labels, and boasting of outlandish expiration dates: GOOD UNTIL APRIL 1992, it seemed the kind of
stuff one imagined would be found in the storage closets of nuclear
bomb shelters. Hardest was finding out just which stores accepted
the food stamps: We had no problems at the local A&P and bodega,
where they knew my mother, but once you walked into a shop in a
different neighborhood, say, some place near Alexander's near 149th
Street and Third Avenue, where there sometimes might be incredible
deals—like "5 lbs. of pig's feet for a dollar!"—she'd have to present
her food stamp user ID, which somehow always offended her, especially if she'd marched up to the counter, having put on one of her
superior airs.

Though she almost became accepting of her terrible loss, my
mother seemed anxious in new ways. Still in her mid-fifties, she
looked at least a decade and a half younger, men eyeing her on the
street—perhaps it was her air of haughtiness or a kind of fleshly
indifference that did them in—but in any case, like her sister Cheo,
she had turned out to be the kind of Catholic to never remarry, preferring to be reunited with her husband in the afterlife. She never got
lonely in that way, though at night, overhearing her speaking aloud
and sighing, I'd wish to God that someone else would come along to
take care of her.

In the meantime, my mother, without any real marketable skills
and still struggling with her English, began to *so* worry about how
we'd manage to survive that she ended up taking classes in typewrit-
ing in some kind of downtown agency. (We had gotten hold of an
ancient Smith Corona that someone had left behind under a stairwell,
and she'd practice on this, for hours at a time, her click-clacking,
tentative and never quickening, sounding through the house: I actually found her attempts at mastering a new skill at her age—she'd
always seemed old to me, more like an *abuela* than a mother—rather
touching, but though she came home with a "typing certificate" from
the agency, her attempts to find a job as a secretary or typist were
doomed, I believe, from the start. She just didn't have it in her, and

after a few months of desperate searching, with a few tryouts in out-lying offices in the Bronx and Queens, she simply gave up.

To save money, she became as frugal as possible. For several years, she hardly ever bought any cuts of meat that were not in fact mostly gristle and bones: frozen turkey legs at a dollar for two, as well as three-pound bags of chicken entrails—livers and gizzards and necks—with which she made her own tamped-down versions of *arroz con pollo,* became our staples.

One of the college students I used to jam with on the steps of Low Library, Steve, a saxophone player who also happened to be a premed student at Columbia, came home with me one evening. After we'd finished playing, driving our patient neighbors crazy, my mother, in a good mood that night, invited him to stay for dinner. However, once he had taken his place at the table, in the seat where my pop had passed evenings (and where, I swear, his ghost still did), and my mother set down before him a plate of yellow rice nicely cooked with tomatoes and peppers, carrots and onions and some garlic, with those chicken necks and gizzards stirred in, he, picking at them as if they were worms, could not bring himself to take a single bite. It was then it first really hit me that, with the absence of my father, no matter what else he might have meant to us, our lives, at least when it came to food, had certainly taken a turn for the worse.

If I'd sometimes felt vaguely curious about the way I'd look in the reflection of a car window or a store mirror—always washed out, nearly unreadable—in the months/years after my pop's death, I couldn't bear to look at myself, even passingly. I remember feeling that the world seemed grotesque to me, and that, as I'd go through my days, my knees were weak and my shoulders tight, as if bearing too great a weight on them. Needless to say, when I actually sat down to study at home, during one of those rare moments when my mother wasn't going on and on about something in another room, I only seemed vaguely aware of what I happened to be reading—I'd stash that information away somewhere—but for the most part I felt like a stupidly wounded animal barely attached to the world and rather benumbed to life. There is something else: I couldn't help myself from looking back over my shoulder, as if I would turn around and see my pop standing on some street corner smoking a cigarette.

The only things that lightened me up were the sight of a pretty female face and music, the latter of which, as you may by now have surmised, happened to be the central passion of my youth. Playing the guitar and writing songs kept me sane and helped me to make friends all over the city. And so I got into the habit of turning up at the school, at least a few times a week, with a beat-up Harmony guitar. There on the steps of Bronx Community, I'd befriended this wiry Italian guy from Co-op City, Nick, who knew his way around a fret board and loved to play bluesy tunes, mainly of his own composition. As the son of an Allerton Avenue barber, he, like me and so many of the others at that school, had been among the first in his family to try out that education thing, and loving music himself, it seemed natural that we put together a band.

This consisted of some kids from my high school, along with a Columbia University football player turned pianist, my old friend Pete on bass, and a hammy, weird-looking tone-deaf singer who could not hold a tune but performed fearlessly, as if lifting outside of himself. Our first gig was at a fashion show for oversize ladies at the Lane Bryant department store, but we mainly performed, if it can be called that, at a locally famous watering hole known simply as the CDR, which occupied the basement floor of a residential building on 119th Street.

I don't recall ever once hearing about or seeing my father drinking there—if he walked into that place at all, it was to cash a check perhaps—and though he had known its affable owner, Larry Mascetti, if only casually, for over twenty years, he wouldn't have had much use for the place otherwise. Aside from rarely spending his money in any bar except to leave a tip for the free drinks he came by at the Biltmore, he would not have felt too comfortable with the clientele, who were mainly Irish alcoholics—in the sense that just about every man above the age of eighteen in that neighborhood seemed to be one. A few black men hung out there, among them a well-known jazz violinist (he later died of cirrhosis of the liver), as well as a spattering of Japanese who'd grown up in the neighborhood, and the handful of Latinos who went into the place to drink would have hardly fit with my pop's idea of what an authentic Cuban or Puerto Rican was about, except as Americanized versions. Most of the people who drank there were decent working-class stiffs, and yet among them were a few bigoted souls who, never taking me to be Latino, had on occasion blurted out within earshot a few references to some "spic" they'd seen around or, more blatantly, about how some "fuckin' spic" had the nerve to give him a sly look—an atmosphere of derisiveness toward Latinos so prevalent that even I, as jaded and pissed off or distanced as I had begun to feel about my roots, took offense.

I felt like a spy moving through both ranks—Latinos I didn't know sometimes gave me the evil eye, while, on the other end, loudmouthed white guys betrayed their own prejudices without as much as giving one damn about my feelings, if they thought of me as Latino at all.

And yet, on a social level, that place appealed to a lot of people: An oasis—literally the only watering hole for blocks and blocks—it was frequented by Columbia University and Teachers College people by day and, at night, by the locals who'd stop there to get tanked up on their way home from work, though there were the occasional drop-ins from the arty, hippie world. One of them lived just across the street, a quite interesting guitar player, Chris Donald, whose girlish dark hair hung down to his willowy waist. He'd always cash the big-time checks he'd receive for playing his white Telecaster guitar in a 1950s cover band quite famous in its time, Sha-Na-Na, that had origi-nated at Columbia. I think the checks were for about fifteen hundred dollars—perhaps his weekly wage, I'm not sure, though I do know that Chris, with whom I had jammed on occasion in his one-room basement apartment, used a good part of that money to buy heroin. For that act, he'd wear period clothes and somehow tame his hair into a passable though wildly oversize Elvis-style pompadour and for at least a few years seemed to be on top of the world, when, of course, in the tradition of the very cool and uncautious, he went overboard one day and overdosed, throwing the universe away on a dime high.

It was a jovially crowded, smoke-filled place that boasted a boom-ing jukebox and had, given all the cops who dropped in, a rather laissez-faire policy about permitting certain things. Some of the regu-lars seemed to always have something shifty going on on the side, but the biggest heavies, it seemed to me, were the cops themselves. They'd sit around in their civilian outfits but always packing revolv-ers, sending out waves of suspicion, world-weariness, and menace. (As in "Do not fuck with me.") They were famously depressed and sarcastic: "How's law enforcement going?" "Fine, how's crime?" With the rare exception, each seemed to me a prince of darkness.

On certain nights, huge amounts of money were openly wagered in the banquettes off to the side, wafts of marijuana and hashish smoke occasionally drifting through the air. For whatever the rea-son, anything seemed to go on those premises. One night while I was in there, the comedian George Carlin, who grew up on 121st Street a few doors up from my grammar school, which he'd also attended and commemorated in an album entitled *Class Clown*, happened to be sitting by such a table, with what must have been an ounce of some white powdery substance splayed across a piece of wax paper before him. Observing this, a ruddy-faced police officer dressed in plain clothes walked over, and while it seemed he had gone over to investigate the situation, it turned out that this cop, whose eyes had the expression of a man looking through a plate-glass store window as if at a curious hat in a corner, had gone over simply to express his admiration that a local boy had made it into the big time, and would he, please, Mr. Carlin, possibly do him the honor of signing an auto-graph. I know this, because I was there just hanging around.

The owner, Mr. Mascetti, by the way, was a burly and cheerful, bald-headed fellow of stout proportions who could have passed as a plump cousin to the musician David Crosby. In the 1950s, before moving on to this establishment, he ran a little bar on 123rd Street on Amsterdam, where, I've heard, the folksinger Burl Ives used to perform. When I first knew him, however, he managed the soda fountain of a pharmacy on 120th Street, where, running errands, I came into one of my first jobs. He had three kids, among them a spoiled son, Butch, who, as it happened, I always had fistfights with, though I owed him or his father my first excursion, at about the age of eleven, to Bear Mountain, something that has stuck in my mind ever since, not only because we had spent a beautiful day tranquilly walking that park's wooded trails, but mainly because he had a car while my own family never made such journeys, not even once.

A good-hearted man rumored to be a member of the genteel petit Mafia—his brother ran some kind of operation in Brooklyn—he might have kept a gun in the back and was probably someone not to be messed with, though he could not have been more kindly toward people—even threw me a couple of twenties when my pop died. Trusting me because of my quiet demeanor, he'd occasionally bring me along with him at night when he'd drive up to another bar uptown in Harlem to take care of some business transaction. In any event, when he heard that I had put together a group, he told me we could perform there any time we wanted to. For a period of a few years, we were to be the occasional "special entertainment" billed as "the 118th Street R&B band." With people having nothing better to do jamming the place, at two dollars a head, on a Saturday night each of us musicians ended up with a nice piece of change.

On some weeks, I took home at least a few hundred dollars, twice as much as I think my father ever earned. But I can't say I did anything meaningful with that money—in fact, I'm not quite sure what I did with it. Being of an age when other kids would go off on three-month summertime excursions to Europe on maybe nothing more than six hundred dollars—a figure I once heard—I never did anything quite so adventuresome, and not because I wouldn't have wanted to, but because, as somewhat of a provincial, it simply didn't enter my mind: At some level, for me, Europe did not quite exist.

We'd play from around nine at night until three in the morning, long gigs that sometimes became wild affairs, what with all the booze and drugs floating around. Among the things I learned on such nights was that you don't have to give a particularly good performance (though we did sometimes) if your audience is stoned. When LSD inevitably entered the picture, and folks began to circle the earth, anything one played seemed to that segment of the audience exalted, serene, and profoundly deep. Most people danced well enough, though some went off into a kind of proto-Aztec hieroglyph frenzy, or else, as in the case of super-medicated Vietnam vets, subdued, very slow, zombie waltzes; and while our repertoire included a few numbers that had something of the Latin rhythm to them—like "Bang Bang" and "Oye Cómo Va"—we were probably the farthest from a Cuban band imaginable, and our audience a far cry from the sorts of dancers my parents once consorted with.

In fact, the closest the bar came to displaying a Latin flavor of a sort came down to the black and Latina hookers from around the Port Authority, whom someone would round up for the occasional bachelor party and bring uptown from Tenth Avenue by the carload. On some nights, these ladies would be out in the back taking care of one man after the other, and occasionally, some of these women blew their patrons in full view of the crowd. I had also seen one of the women splayed across a table and, with whipped cream from an aerosol can covering her privates, submit as one of the fellows, usually quite drunk, went down on her: There were other variations on these oral themes, and a few copulations as well, often enough in the somewhat funky bathroom. Altogether, it was the kind of scene that makes a show like *The Sopranos* seem sexually tame to me now, and it was so absurdly rank—and sleazy—on occasion as to make even the worst of my pop's so-called dance-hall infidelities seem almost innocent by comparison. (And yet, why do I continue to remember that place with fondness?)

· · ·

Tucked back into that period, some months after I had turned eighteen, I had ended up in yet another smoke-filled room, this one situated in the draft board offices downtown on Whitehall Street, where I'd gone to register. Though it's possible that a few in that room were feeling a patriotic fervor about fighting in Vietnam, most of the young men gathered there seemed bent upon getting out on psychological deferments—which meant that one fellow dressed up like Batman, another as a Watusi warrior with bells tied about his ankles, and yet another in a pair of fluffy slippers and diapers; there were some overtly effeminate sorts in there as well, and a gleeful bunch of hippies who were being eyed by the plainclothes cops in the crowd, singing and carrying on, all the while quite apparently high on something powerful, probably LSD. A few others sat, in the manner of soldiers about to go to war, sucking on cigarettes—it was thick as shit in that room—an air of worry tending toward obligation or resignation on their faces. I mention them because, to be honest, when I turned up, I had frankly resigned myself to going to Vietnam, not out of any deep sense of moral obligation or patriotism—as did my friend Richard—but quite simply because I didn't care what they did with me. I filled out forms, answered a few questions in pencil—"How would you feel about confronting an enemy of the United States?" and others that essentially inquired after my interest in self-preservation and soldiering. Strangely enough, my laconic responses to those questions, along with the pertinent bit of information that my father had died the year before, led one interviewing officer to assign me, without as much as blinking an eye, a temporary, six-month deferment—which is what most of the crazies in that room would have been grateful for; and while I had expected to be called back there soon enough, the draft lottery intervened, and in one of those caprices of rare good luck, I ended up with a number so high, in the three hundreds, that I never had to return.

CHAPTER 6

. . .

My Two Selves

In those years, I seemed to have vacillated between two versions of myself: One was musical and hip, somewhat sly, and occasionally wild, the other so completely solemn and conservative of demeanor as to be taken by Greenwich Village hippies as too straitlaced to trust. (When I cut my hair short, I was sometimes looked upon suspiciously by the bohemian sect as if I might be a cop—I suppose that had something to do with my overly preoccupied expression.) The hip Hijuelos smoked cigarettes and liked to get high; like black folks, who I never saw using any other brand, I preferred Kools, maybe a pack or two a night, not giving a damn about health issues. (I was convinced, however stupidly, that by the time I had smoked long enough to come down with cancer, they—the scientific world—would have developed a cure for it.) The other Hijuelos, the pensive shit who looked down on others' self-indulgences and worried about his health, tended toward weight-induced high blood pressure and remained, despite the unpredictability of his mother's moods, complacently disposed toward her. ("*Sí, mamá.*") One did whatever the fuck he felt like doing, lived here and there, made out with the occasional girl, while the other demurely slipped into deep depressions, all the while craving not the escapes of sex or drugs, but *eso de la comida*—Cuban food especially—and the mental comfort foods of comic books and horror movies. That cooler version of myself trudged off one night through Central Park with the guitarist Duane Allman in search of a liquor store and later jammed with him in an uptown pad, while the other, completely insecure but having pretensions of musical grandeur, once boasted to his older brother that he had written the lyrics of a Beatles song called "When I'm Sixty-four." (How on earth I thought I could get away with that is beyond me. I guess I believed they didn't have radios in Brooklyn.)

During that time, the strangeness of my life—of feeling that something had been torn out from inside of me, like a kidney, curiously enough, in my mind shaped like the island of Cuba, that I was as empty as air—gnawed at me every day. The same questions I had about myself kept repeating: Who and what am I? Why is it that I hate seeing what I see when I look in a mirror? Why is it that every now and then I suddenly turn around because of a voice saying, "Cuba, Cuba . . ."? And why is it that I always swear, as I begin to look behind me or turn a corner, that, in a moment, I will come upon all that I do not have—a world, perhaps Cuban, perhaps familial, that for so many reasons seems to have been taken from me?

I tried to be a hippie for a while, but even that did not really afford me a refuge: I'm sorry to say I wasn't very good at it. One summer, I had gone upstate, north of Saratoga Springs, to perform with a pianist friend in a makeshift band at a guitar player's wedding; I knew the bridegroom from jam sessions around Columbia, and, two-timing my own band, for a while I moonlighted with him in a group we put together, the Ravens. He dressed entirely in black, wore dark glasses every hour of the day, had dark hair down to his shoulders, and, altogether, cultivated a look that present-day kids would call Goth. His "old lady," a waitress at the Gold Rail, was all of twenty-two or so at the time and a long-legged auburn-haired fox and a half, as they'd say in my neighborhood. Their marriage, held on the shores of an upstate lake, went off with flower-child aplomb, and the party afterward, with folks coming from nearby communes as well as the city, became one of those all-day affairs, with musicians setting up their amps on a makeshift stage in a field and people lying out on blankets or wading naked in the water, partaking liberally of the booze and marijuana and other relaxants that were in plentiful supply, along with tables of food (of a typical American variety, with some healthfully boring grain and oat dishes).

I'd played guitar with that impromptu troupe of musicians for a few hours, until the mosquitoes and black flies and the heat began to get to me, and, figuring that I'd paid my dues, left to check out the shoreside scene, what with a large number of lovely young women cavorting about in the flesh, along with something else of great interest just then taking place: On a small island some fifty yards into the lake, a couple were going at it with abandon—a woman, her shapely back to us, long hair trailing down her shoulders, straddling some lucky fellow, grinding her hips over him, and most juicily so. A lot of people were watching, among them the bridegroom himself, my friend, whom I sat beside and joined in a smoke (just a cigarette).

Passing some jug wine between us, we took in their lovemaking, watched the woman, her bottom rising and falling, her head turning from side to side, while we said things like "Man, oh man" and "Where'd she come from?" our interest further heightening when, dismounting him, she rolled over and let the fellow go down on her, the two of us shaking our heads in wonderment and blowing out smoke rings, while she not long afterward turned her mouth into a ring and started blowing him, oh, that lucky fellow: It would have remained one of those capricious things that (I supposed) happened at hippie weddings, what with "free love" in the air, an afternoon's drug-induced sexual reverie, if not for the fact, as we soon discovered, that the woman in question, having had her fill of that fellow's masculinity and wading back to shore, wobblingly so, turned out to be my friend's bride.

His response? Shook his head, sucked his cigarette deeply, and, with considerable understatement, told me, "Aw, man, what a drag." Somehow, he had it in him to forgive her—his bride of only a few hours had gotten so drunk that she soon passed out and, in any case, wouldn't remember a thing about what happened, while the lucky fellow, who, I'm happy to report, was a good-looking Latino—and yes, I was a little envious of his swarthy, well-muscled handsomeness—swaggered about with his plump, recently-worked-to-death dick hanging out for all to see, until he learned just who the lady happened to be and, putting on a pair of trousers, duly apologized to the bridegroom. He was so humble as to be likable, and that paid off when later, even more enviously, I watched him going off with another woman. I ended up passing the night, rather uncomfortably, inside a low-hanging tent pitched in a field, swatting away at mosquitoes and unable to sleep, not just because of the heat but because I often had those awful dreams.

That same summer, I was at home one August evening trying to watch television, while my mother, sitting on the couch behind me, went on and on in Spanish about the fact that my life would end up a useless mess. It didn't matter to me. By then I did whatever I pleased in front of her. Smoking openly, I dropped my ashes into the same standing tray that my father used to ("You'll kill yourself with those cigarettes, like your father!" she'd scream), and now and then I'd stretch out in his green recliner, having oddly pleasant memories of him—like when I was little and he'd make a muscle and let me feel it, or my pop, in from the wintry day, setting his snow-dappled black-brimmed hat on the kitchen table and rubbing his hands happily to warm them up and patting me on the head, and how he used to somehow have a calming effect on babies, who always stopped their bawling around him. Such nice memories kept coming to me until, in that reclining position, I'd remember him stretched out in his coffin, and whatever nostalgia I may have been feeling for those earlier times turned into a kind of muted despair, which, of course, I had gotten used to by then.

On that night, I was watching an episode of *Bewitched* or perhaps *I Dream of Jeannie*, a cheery sitcom in any case, when the telephone rang. My mother answered it, called me over: "*Es pa tí*," she said. It was Mr. Mascetti calling from his bar.

"Hey, Oscah," he said. "Can ya do me a favor?"

"What sort of favor?" I asked him.

"Well, it seems that my son Butch has got it into his head that he wants to take a morning flight out of Kennedy to Denver."

"Yeah, so?"

"The thing is that he's—how can I put it to ya—he's been kind of high as a kite lately, if you know what I mean. He's been dropping a lot of something on the strong side—you following me?"

"Uh-huh."

"The thing is, I don't want him going alone with his mind so wacked—*capiche?*—and I was wondering if you could do me the very big favor of looking out for him, for me. There's two bills in it for your trouble."

"You mean you want me to go with him to Colorado?"

"Yessir—I'm only asking because I trust you. Just make sure he doesn't do anything crazy, that's all."

"Okay, I'll do it," I finally told him, not having much else going on.

.   .   .

The next morning, Mr. Mascetti drove us to JFK in his Cadillac, got us there around nine A.M., paid for our tickets at the counter, and then, wishing me well with a slap to my back, took off for Manhattan. We had to wait about an hour before boarding, a very long hour. Having been high all night, on speed and LSD perhaps—who knew—Butch Mascetti had signed on for the duration. Somewhere in outer space, Butch kept pointing his finger at me and laughing wildly, going on about how the interior of the terminal had begun to glow like gold before melting like ice all around him; he'd make whooshing noises with his mouth and scoot around in circles, his hands held out like Superman's, flying, babbling incoherently about the cosmic winds in that place. Not wanting any hassles, I kept bringing him back to his seat; "Be cool," I'd say, only to watch him get up again. The airline staff, mostly young female flight attendants, must have noticed his strange behavior, but I think they were either inured to such doings or simply didn't care enough to boot us off that flight. Finally, we started boarding: I thanked God for that, because he seemed to quiet down.

I took it in stride; when I'd left the house that morning, my mother had been confounded: I had been stupid enough to tell her where and with whom I was going. Her last words to me as I left were "Are you crazy?" for even she knew about Butch's reputation for liking the wild side of things. Well, I was doing it for the two hundred dollars, and because Larry and Butch were my friends, in that order. (Unlike his two lovely sisters, Butch always had a smugness about him, and, as kids, our fights always started out with his making some blunt remark about how I dressed in cheap clothes, or how my "moms" couldn't speak English too well, or how he never liked to go into my apartment because it "smelled funny." The thing is no matter how friendly I tried to be with him, he hadn't changed one bit.) But even if I looked at it as a job, I still couldn't understand how anyone would take a huge dose of LSD and decide to get on a jet plane the next day. (Eventually, of course, I'd find out why. Butch had already dropped the drug at the bar when, out of some idiocy, he decided to call up his on-and-off girlfriend, a girl named Ellie, in Colorado Springs, where he attended college. She had apparently dumped him that very night—hence his sudden decision to fly there, though I couldn't imagine anyone, high or not, going through the trouble just because of a telephone call.)

Once the plane had become airborne, however, Butch seemed to become more contemplative, hardly saying a word, coming down from his high, which was fine with me. To calm my own nerves, I ordered a few glasses of vodka and orange juice from a stewardess, which I sipped slowly, until I began to doze off; then I had a very strange dream. First the wispy threads I always saw inside the rims of my eyes—"floaters"—seemed to become extravagantly beautiful, curling into arabesque flows of script that implied, without using any language, something awfully profound and mystical; and then after feeling completely fascinated by some melodies that I had started to make up in my head, it all hit me: Lurching forward, I opened my eyes to a cabin that had begun bursting with florid colors and seemed padded with an expanding, nearly breathing, foam. Looking my way gleefully and pointing his index finger at me, Butch could not contain himself, laughing, "Got you, sport!"

. . .

A general note: I would not recommend flying anywhere with someone who, out of a controlling motive, would slip into your drink a drug like LSD; I can also assure you that a jet plane—reeking of fuel, carpet-cleaning chemicals, recycled oxygen, bodily gases, perfumes and colognes, airplane food, and, in those days of yore, cigarette smoke, which even for a smoker on that drug smells and tastes exactly like all its ghastly chemical components (from benzene to formaldehyde)—is about the least pleasant place on earth to be. And it hits you that you are locked inside an unimaginably heavy metallic projectile flying through the air, somehow held up in the sky. In that contained, inescapable, and claustrophobic space, I got the jitters so badly that I made it a ritual to go to the toilet about every ten minutes (or however much time) to wash my face and urinate, though at a certain point, with Butch really getting on my nerves, I locked myself inside for so long the flight attendants began knocking on the door to make sure I was all right. (I wasn't and they knew it—from our blabbering and distorted expressions and strange reactions to simple questions, as when a flight attendant would offer a meal, and I'd answer incredulously, "Why?" Later, when we'd finally landed, one of them, a chirpy southern sort, remarked, "It's not every day we get passengers like you."

I suppose this all leads to a certain moment: sitting out in a field in Colorado Springs, perhaps that same evening of the day of our arrival and still feeling the effects of that drug, watching the Pleiades meteor showers with Butch's ex-paramour, Ellie, by my side. I am not sure if that wonderful evening really took place a few days after we arrived, but she, who, as it happens, had also been sick as a child (a very bad heart) warmed to me almost immediately. (I am not sure which Hijuelos showed up, or to which side of me she was attracted, but we spent our nights for the next few weeks together, much to Butch's exasperation—he and I were never the same sort of friends after that again.) What I do remember about her is this: She had long hair; wore wire-rim glasses; had a plain Danish milkmaid's face; had a thin, not full, body; had a father who ran Rocky Mountain Bell; had some poetic aspirations; and had a former boyfriend who had taken his own life after she had rejected him (think she cried in my arms after telling me that tale). Her favorite musical was *Camelot*, her favorite group (unfortunately) the Eagles, and whatever she once had with Butch had lasted only for a few days, if that (and even then I don't know if they ever "made" it—he had the kind of personality that was very hard to get next to). No startling beauty, she had a way of being that really touched me and left me aching over the notion of having to leave her. (I had after all, re-upped for school in the fall: Lehman College at night.)

Parting from each other turned out to be harder than either of us had expected, though Butch, despite having had to put up with the torture of seeing her with someone I think he secretly, or not so secretly, looked down on—*me*—seemed almost mirthful over the thought of her suffering. It really didn't matter: I never saw her again, and if the truth be told, once again I am at a loss for coming up with a happy ending to yet another of my tales.

We wrote each other for a few years, then that stopped, and I really didn't know anything more about her until about a decade later, when Butch told me, as he tended bar in his father's place, that Ellie, for whatever reasons, had committed suicide—and as casually, with a smirk on his face in fact, as if he were reporting a baseball score. Sometime thereafter, Butch himself died in a car wreck, hitting an overpass on the Jersey turnpike while driving his father's Cadillac at over one hundred miles an hour, possibly, as neighborhood gossip speculated, on LSD. That news was broadcast widely, incidentally, on both radio and TV because among his passengers was one of his former classmates at Colorado, Frank Gifford's son, Kyle, who was badly injured.

On the other hand, despite my occasional sorry attempt at fitting in with the hippies, all of twenty-two, I passed a year working in one of the more incredibly sophisticated literature-nurturing jobs of all time: as a salesclerk at Macy's department store. It was actually far better than it sounds, though the pay stank and the store had been going through a decline in those days. I have no idea why I turned up in their second-floor employment office one morning, but I do recall telling the interviewer that I had an aunt, Maya, who had once worked for them in the 1940s, and I suppose that gave me a slight edge. I must have seemed respectable enough, having cut my hair short for my job hunt, and going to college at night also didn't hurt my chances, and so they hired me.

I've since looked back, dreaming about writing the great department store novel, though composing anything else but songs wouldn't have occurred to me back then. My on-the-job training, which came down to learning about "send" and "take" orders and the working of an archaic cash register, lasted for a few weeks, if that, whereupon my floor manager, a certain tall and regal Sicilian, Mr. Trampani, whom I rather liked, put me to work selling curtain rods and window shades, among other household items.

I also had a stint up on the seventh floor selling trendy new items like antigravity pens and neon dial clocks for a department they named Design Seven, where, wearing a blue frock one afternoon, I had the embarrassment of encountering some of my Brandeis hippie schoolmates, who thought finding me in such a straitlaced job the funniest thing in the world. Then, too, I occasionally worked as a flyer, filling in at different departments—shoes, electronics, furniture—a fun rotation since it broke the monotony and repetitious nature of those days, and most spectacularly so during the holiday season, when whatever low morale plagued the employees vanished in the overwhelmingly magical onslaught of Christmas cheer, as the mostly gay display-window staff went crazy decorating the store. That old-time movie *Miracle on Thirty-Fourth Street,* which is set in Macy's, inevitably came into all of our heads—you couldn't avoid it. In the employees' dining room on the ninth floor, stills from it hung on the walls, and a pianist wearing a Santa Claus cap played carols on an upright set off in the corner, next to a little tree: In such an ambience, I couldn't help but daydream about meeting Edmund Gwenn's Kris Kringle in the corridors; also, if you ever wonder where those sidewalk Santas, ringing their bells and going ho-ho-ho for the Salvation Army, come from, in those days at least, you would have only had to look in the Macy's basement employees' locker rooms, where some twenty or so of those volunteers gathered to get into costume in the mornings.

Actually, I never really had much to complain about working there and I did a good enough job, being fluent not in Spanish but in numbers. Mr. Trampani thought enough of my performance to actually tell me one afternoon, "I've had my eye on you for some time, young man," as if delivering a line from a movie, and went on to offer me the opportunity to study, at the company's expense, at their management training school in, of all places, Denver, Colorado. According to him, I would have a wonderful future in retail if I wanted one. But even back then, while I really appreciated the fact that he was looking out for me, I couldn't see myself committing to anything for long.

·   ·   ·

At so young an age, I had, despite my tendency to go off the deep end emotionally, endless reserves of energy. After working all day, about three nights a week, I'd take a series of subway trains and end up at the far northwest Bronx, where I took some fill-in courses at Lehman College. My big goal was to matriculate to City College, where, in the event that I did not make it as a musician, I believed, I'd end up studying to become a schoolteacher of some kind. I became one of those fellows you'd see hunched over a history or math textbook on the number 4 train heading uptown, at around seven at night, later making my way off that El and walking the six or so blocks to the school, as if it were nothing at all. (I couldn't begin to do that now, night after night.) I'm not sure how I managed to stay alert during the unavoidable torpor of those classes—most of the students, many of them older, had full-time jobs and were often low of energy—but we were allowed to drink coffee and to smoke in the classrooms. Some teachers even kept ashtrays handy, but I'd also bring along one of my own (cheap, metallic, the kind sold in a John's Bargain Store for a dime apiece), and if no transit cops were around later, on my way home, I'd have a smoke on the platform, during those endless waits for the train, inevitably thinking, at some point of the night, about my poor father.

. . .

In those years, I had a girlfriend who happened to be into acting, Carol, a lady I met while babysitting my friend Tommy Muller-Thym on one of those nights when he had gotten too high on LSD for his own good. (As when he, a rambunctious soul, would speak of wanting to toss a brick through a police car window.) We were in the Gold Rail bar, where Tommy, in the midst of stunning hallucinations, had attempted to pick up her across-the-hall neighbor, a staunch feminist of a patrician upbringing, as they were sitting by a grubby initial-incised table next to us. According to Tommy, her feminist friend needed a good screwing to get rid of her haughty attitude, and told her so. While that remark did not bode well for his amorous chances, I made Carol's acquaintance, as a sort of equally bemused and neutral party witnessing their verbal parrying.

A brunette, buxom and attractive, she was a very nice woman of some not inconsiderable talents, from a fairly affluent family in Chicago, whose parents, both shrinks, would come to view me, with my street ways of talking and lack of polish (breeding), as something of a Neanderthal whose Cuban roots seemed to surprise them: If I can pick out one incident that would have predicted our eventual demise—and the prevalent attitude toward me on their part—it would be the fact that when I, having hitchhiked to Chicago, first met them, the first thing her father did was to sit me down in their kitchen and administer a Rorschach test, her mother looking attentively on.

(But, hell, what did I know?)

My Macy's job overlapped our meeting, but once I had matriculated to CCNY full-time as a student enrolled in the SEEK program—that anagram for Search for Elevation Education and Knowledge—and I left that store, disappointing Mr. Trampani, a real gent, it was she who hooked me up with one of the strangest jobs I ever had, one of those crazy gigs actors passed around among one another on the grapevine. The job, which paid phenomenally well—some fifteen dollars an hour—involved the kind of placebo versus real-drug testing, a few afternoons a week, for which I happened to be temperamentally suited: pain research. Turning up at the facility, in one of those vast and forebodingly dark buildings that were part of the Bellevue complex on the East Side—I would be given a cup of water and two white pills to swallow, at which point I would wait in an adjoining room for about an hour or so, while they took (or didn't) effect, and pass the time reading. Then into the testing room I would go, led inside by a nurse whose long blond hair reached her waist, and for whom, despite her awful acne-ravaged complexion, I seemed to have developed my usual wounded-animal attraction.

One of the tests required that I keep my fingers steeped in a beaker of ice for as long as ten minutes, no easy thing: Checking out a stopwatch and writing figures down on a chart, which had graphs, the nurse would ask me to rate the degrees of pain I happened to be feeling in thirty-second intervals (I think) on a scale of 1 to 6; to impress her with my macho resolve, I'd usually hold out until my fingers had gone numb (which probably threw the tests out of whack, since, while waiting beforehand, I'd often hear other subjects quickly shrieking their lungs out.) A second test was a variation of the above: My fingers in a beaker, an electric current would be passed through wires into the water, which first registered as a tingle, as if one's hand had slipped into a hornets' hive; then, as she turned a knob, it widened into a more numbing prickly sensation, until that graduated into an out-and-out metallic—and broadening—burning, at which point even I would give up. But along the way, while uttering those numbers, I'd keep looking at the nurse's compassionate face, which seemed to grow prettier and less disfigured each time I turned up as a subject.

The most ghastly—and the only test for which I had zero patience—involved what basically came down to the application of a thumbscrew: Each of my thumbs would be fitted with a clamp through which a blunt screw head could be passed; a kind of elongated paper puncher would be pressed, the pressure raised by increments, the nurse twisting a knob, until gradually the screw nub, progressing more and more deeply into the skin and tissue, began intruding on the bone, at which point it produced a kind of deadening pain that made the right side of my head and the top of my eyeballs ache. Despite my Catholic tolerances and everlasting desire to prove to myself that I was no kidney-diseased wimp, I always called out after no more than a few minutes of that medieval torture—it was creepy, even for a medical group testing aspirins and such, and she knew it, which was why, I suppose, she'd look my way apologetically.

However, the most erotic of the pain research trials involved a heating rod and a tincture of black ink, which the nurse would apply to my bared back, from my shoulders to the small of my back: Wearing a pair of latex gloves, she would spread the ink (or whatever it was) uniformly and gently along every inch of my skin, after which she would further smooth it down with a narrow camel-hair paintbrush, which, truth be told, had the texture of a slightly wet tongue. Taking a long black bulbous-headed device in hand, through whose head she could transmit increasing amounts of heat by turning a dial, the nurse would press it against my skin and slide it about in circles, the remotely pleasant warming sensations, which I hadn't minded at all at first, gradually becoming more intrusive and searing, and this nurse, who must have been Irish, muttering with each increase of temperature, "Are you okay?" Interestingly enough, all that heat sent my blood rushing, and while it hurt an awful lot, it felt great at the same time. That heat, in fact, concentrating in my center, had an incredibly invigorating effect on my friskiness—and she knew that too. Later, while she'd clean off my back with paper towels soaked in rubbing alcohol, I had the impression that it wouldn't have taken much at all to get something going with her, and I might have asked her out, except for the fact that I had stupidly blurted out something about having a girlfriend—but lord, that delicious tension came back any time I got near her.

Along the way, I'd drift back to some of my childhood fantasies of being cured of my illness by some caring nurse, even while the sex/pain thing remained foremost in my mind—what else was there to think about? That strange job lasted only some three months, but it dropped me into a circumstance that, much like love, was both a torture and a pleasure at the same time.

· · ·

Of my teachers in the City system, there were two whom I would credit the most with kindling my first interests in writing. The first happened to teach a basic literature course at Bronx Community, a certain professor Wertheim, who, receiving an essay I had written about one of Bernard Malamud's stories, "The Magic Barrel," whose atmosphere of immigrant melancholy sang to me like a siren perching on a rock, pointed out several instances in which I used easy alliteration in my sentences, crude as they were—*frolicking freely*. In the margin he, a wise guy, wrote something along the lines of *"so here Hijuelos bellows."* When he gave me an A in the course, I felt exhilarated—but aside from doing well, even given my scattered nature, I had really enjoyed the stories, from beginning to end, that were included in the assigned textbook, a Norton anthology of fiction, which I absorbed very much like a sponge, and in that way I first began to fill in the rather huge gaps I had in my knowledge of literature. (Of course, being a sap for emotion, the authors I most cherished, aside from Malamud, included Chekhov and D. H. Lawrence; I still do today.)

Later, at City, a saintly professor, a certain Ernest Boynton, went out of his way to encourage my essay writing—in the afternoons, I'd spend an hour with him in his office as he'd carefully go over my work and explain how I might better develop some of my ideas, a line of other students always waiting outside his door. I grew attached to him; he was young enough, somewhere in his late thirties or early forties, to bridge our age gap. All the students loved him, and he, a nerdish recently married black fellow with thick black-framed eyeglasses and dark rippling hair, a high-domed forehead and pinched-in dimpled chin, had been ever so happy to share with anyone who cared to know news about his wife's expecting a child. It was he who first spoke seriously to me about perhaps becoming an English teacher one day, maybe getting a job in a New York City high school, and he was the first adult who really made me feel that I could do something good—just by putting together a few more or less orderly sentences.

But though I never really took his bookish suggestions to heart, I liked to be around the man just the same, feeling attracted, as I guess

I inevitably would, to fatherly sorts. He was such a nice fellow that God naturally blessed him, of course, striking him down not five years later with a heart attack—the man dying while all the pricks in the world seem to keep on going strong.

· · ·

All the while, I had always been one of those pensive fucks who really enjoyed street jive, the selling of "wolf tickets" by way of outlandish storytelling among BS artists hanging out on the sidewalks. Junkies were the best—really funny in fact, when not falling off the edge of the world, during slow nods that sometimes went badly, as in the case of this good-natured black kid named Alvin, whose sunny disposition did not prevent him from becoming an addict, nor from slipping backward off a rooftop ledge in the midst of a dream. One of my favorite folks, strung out sometimes, sometimes not, was Tommy, whom I would see mainly on the weekends while hanging with his younger brother Richard, finally home from Vietnam and, incidentally, also attending City. Tommy and I would find ourselves just walking around the neighborhood scoping out the action: I don't recall how he made money in those days—he was a college dropout and already a seasoned veteran of the Addicts' Rehabilitation Center on 125th Street, where I had visited him on occasion (they'd give you a little room and several doses of methadone a day, which gave you a kind of high). I think he must have earned some money dealing in soft drugs, though he, when not using the heavy stuff, seemed quite content with just enough to buy a little reefer and the endless quantities of beer, drunk from cans out of paper bags, that he cherished. (Theft has also struck me as a possible source of his income, though I can't imagine that he had that in his nature.) For his own amusement, he liked to concoct the most outlandish tales—of seeing, for example, flying saucers in Central Park, or of going to Harlem and encountering a famous movie star in search of drugs, of having sex with two or three women at a time, stories that were, though hard to buy, easy to enjoy.

I am mentioning this because Tommy, it seemed to me, was destined to parlay his folkloric excesses about city life into an eventual livelihood as a writer. It was the one ambition he had ever professed and spoke about it constantly—I think from the time he was a kid. A short story he had written, in fact, about a young addict recovering in a Harlem rehab much like the ARC (if I am remembering it correctly, he tries to clean up but is drawn back into drugs) made a paperback anthology of young black writers that came out sometime in the early 1970s. It was the only publication Tommy managed, that I know of, and the fact that he had been included in a black anthology didn't bother him one bit. Since he spoke and acted, down to his every *Soul Train* dance move, pretty much like a black man, albeit one without much bitterness about anything, his white skin seemed just a technicality. Just where he had come from, an educated and erudite father and family (and with a brilliant younger brother), didn't occur to him, and though he, with his swifter than swift mind, could have easily, in some other comfortably upper-middle-class setting, aspired to any number of other professions, such as a lawyer or a doctor or a college professor, Tommy just wanted to be himself—this down-home Harlem guy. His love of reading, by the way, never faded as long as I knew him and he is the only person I have ever seen who, losing himself in a narrative while in a state of physical ecstasy, could perk up suddenly to say, "You best believe I can write better shit than this"—about the works of someone like C. S. Lewis or Norman Mailer. "And I will one day, you'll see" was the kind of the thing he'd tell me, his biggest admirer and a true believer in that future.

· · ·

And myself? I liked the florid language of Shakespeare, though watching his plays performed in Central Park often put me half to sleep even when the casts included actors like Kevin Kline and Meryl Streep, among notable others. The blame would go to my short attention span and my own capacity for daydreaming: In the balmy night air, with a few persnickety stars managing to peek down at the world through the harsh New York–down-on-its-luck hazes, I would fantasize not about writing something like Shakespeare but about becoming an actor myself, or at least envying those sorts of folks, in the same way I secretly admired even the most outlandish of rock musicians for having the courage (balls) to get out there in a way that engaged the wider world.

Though there were some prose writers like Hubert Selby Jr. and Pietro di Donato whose work really spoke to me in school—I would see and hear their stories as if I were watching a movie—Tennessee Williams's plays were the first things I'd ever read that made me want to pick up a pen and try writing something myself. (It was that detail of the glowing portrait of the father on the wall in his play *The Glass Menagerie* that absolutely killed me, as if the man were coming back as a spirit from the beyond to revisit—and mutely comment upon—the scenes of a life he had left behind.) But I also loved Mr. Williams's lyric writing style, that tenderness that seemed to permeate all his scenes; and I liked him personally, brief as my meeting him had been. At an antiwar rally held in the Cathedral of St. John the Divine, he had come down from the pulpit after giving a short speech, and as a part of the crowd, I, having cojones and a half, had walked up to Mr. Williams and introduced myself: I'm sure that my being so young helped my cause, but he looked at me and smiled, and we spoke for a few moments. I can remember thinking that there was nothing sleazy about the man, just that his famous eyes, light blue, as I recall, and delicate in their shimmer, seemed lonely as hell.

So, having a few electives to fool around with, and wanting, based on my admiration for *The Glass Menagerie*, to eventually take up playwriting myself—if only as a lark—I ended up enrolling in a drama course. At the time, my teacher, Murray Schisgal, a warm, proletarian sort, was at work on a play, *An American Millionaire*, at the Circle in the Square, and it amazes me now that he was so generous to his students, bringing us down to the rehearsals. There I had the incredible luck of becoming, along with several others, a fly on the wall while the actors—Paul Sorvino, Bob Dishy, and Austin Pendleton—figured out their bits, and Schisgal tried to hammer the play's somewhat amorphous scenes into shape (the show, unfortunately, would end up a flop). He had us write three- and four-page scenes for the acting school students there, which was the first time I ever heard anything I had written read aloud by someone else. (If you are wondering what I wrote about, it was this, as I recall: A man and a woman are in a kitchen. The man is a little drunk, the woman complaining, they have an argument; I can't imagine where that came from.) But, in the end, at least in terms of writing dramatic scenes, I couldn't begin to put down on paper what I had in my head—of course this went back to the way I had grown up. I just circled around the dramatic possibilities, as if I would be disturbing the dead by writing about certain things, and at the same time, it seems that I couldn't quite own up to the fact that I was the son of Cubans, as if it were something I wanted to hide.

"You have some good stuff going on here," Schisgal once told me in his kindly manner as he was reading something I had written. "But how come I'm not hearing any ethnic stuff in this? It's your family you're writing about, aren't you?"

"I guess I am," I'd say.

"Then why don't you run with it?"

"I don't know."

Whatever notions I might have entertained, however, it was Schisgal, puffing away on a cheery wood pipe, who, noticing how I would write inordinately long stage directions but with some panache and verbal intensity, suggested that I might better find my voice by trying another form altogether: "Ever try writing prose, kid?" he asked me that day. "If you haven't, it's something you should consider."

I hadn't, but it was something that was to linger in the back of my head for a long time.

· · ·

I am not quite sure how I made the transition from the kind of super naturalistic (but stiffly guarded) scenes I had put on paper into actually trying to write fiction, but I do recall that it was the writing department's chairman, an affable and dapper fellow by the name of Frederic Tuten (a future teacher and a friend of mine to this day), who suggested that I submit a piece to one of the several fiction writers then teaching under the humble auspices of the City College banner, a list that, in those days, was rather stellar (and serious) in a New York City way. Anxiously enough, and naïve about the difficulties of writing good prose, I spent several nights furiously typing up what I seemed to think might have qualified as a short story, of some twenty-five pages in often misspelled, nongrammatical sentences—a tale about a pretty blind girl, Celeste (a name I took from one of the lovely Parks sisters across the street from where I grew up), trapped in a miserable marriage, who, while having an affair with someone across town, takes the subway and, getting on the wrong train, ends up in a really bad neighborhood where she is jumped and taken sexual advantage of. (Not an iota of my Cuban roots could be found anywhere in it—think I made her cruel husband a Greek or an Italian, and as far as Celeste herself went, I never bothered to identify her origins, though I did have her feeling instinctually frightened by the strangeness of a South Bronx Latino neighborhood, her mugging taking place in an abandoned lot such as those I remembered seeing and playing in during my childhood.)

As for the actual quality of the writing in that piece, it was, I think, rather dense and, in its way, colorful. (I always loved details, though; with the way I thought and still think, order was never one of my fortes.) Joseph Heller, the author of *Catch-22*, taught at City at the time, and I had originally intended to submit my piece for his class—going so far as to scribble in pen *For Professor Heller* across the top of its first page—but it so happened that Donald Barthelme was also teaching there and while I had never read anything by him, my actress girlfriend, Carol, a longtime reader of *The New Yorker*, thought him quite funny and cutting-edge, and planted in my mind the notion I would do quite well with him if I were fortunate enough to be accepted into his class. (Thank you, Carol.)

So one afternoon, I went prowling around the halls of the writing department, which was housed in a long Quonset hut on the south campus, with my short story in hand, in search of Donald Barthelme. Inside the first office, whose doors were not always marked, I saw Joseph Heller, whose face I knew from his book jackets, white haired, regal, quite handsome, in a checkered shirt and blue jeans, sitting by his desk, eating what I think was a pastrami on rye with mustard sandwich (he looked up, asking, "Can I help you?"), and

then moving on, I peered into another office, where sat the ethereally beautiful Francine du Plessix Gray in an elegant French-style
dress, discussing some technicality intensely with some lucky student,
and just beyond, I came to another doorway and saw someone who
might have been Donald Barthelme: Behind a desk and typewriter
sat a gray-haired man of late middle age, in a tie and rumpled jacket,
with remarkably warm blue eyes and an incredibly florid complexion, who smiled at me gently as soon as he saw me.

"Excuse me, but are you Donald Barthelme?" I asked, to which
he replied, "No, my name is William Burroughs."

Of course, I'd heard of him—didn't he write something crazy
about drugs? Oh, yeah, that *Naked Lunch*, which Tommy Muller-
Thym liked? I recall thinking—and though I didn't have any business
to take up with him, he was so friendly that when Mr. Burroughs,
perhaps bored or feeling lonely at that moment, asked me if I wanted
to sit and chat with him for a few minutes, I did. What we talked
about were my doubts and hopes regarding what I had started to
guardedly think of as a potential second vocation behind that of
either becoming a musician (doubtful) or a high school teacher (far
more probable). He was teaching at City as a special visitor, as was
another Bohemian sort, Peter Orlovsky, also somewhere down the
hall; of a congenial bent of mind, he listened to my plaintive musings
patiently, saying things like "Oh, I'm sure you'll succeed at whatever you try, young man." Later, after I'd snooped around about his
past, I was surprised to learn that he had built a youthful reputation
as a drug-crazed sexual deviant who had once shot his wife, a supposed wreck of a human being. But for those ten or so minutes that
I passed with him, he seemed as genteel and kindly as any writer I'd
ever meet, not a single bit of self-centeredness or meanness in his
being—which is to say, he was an anomaly, though I did not know
that at the time. (I didn't even know if he was gay—at least he did
not check me over the way some men downtown in the Village did
during my occasional excursions to see a show or check out music.
Instead he seemed like he would have been perfectly at home in some
midwestern high school counselor's office.)

Looking over the first page of my short story, he nodded with appreciation: "Very nice," he said, rubbing his chin—what else could he say? Whether he meant it or not didn't really matter to me—not then, not now. Above all, his kindness was obviously something I would never forget.

• • •

Barthelme, it turned out, occupied a small and windowless office at the far end of the Quonset hut hall: I found him, with Burroughs pointing from his doorway and saying, "Just follow the smoke," for, indeed, as I got down to that end, a few dense plains of filterless Pall Mall fumes, hanging magically in the air, seemed to lead inside: There I saw Donald Barthelme for the first time. He was wearing a blue denim shirt, sleeves rolled up to his elbows, and reading a *New York Post* with a pencil in hand (was he editing their prose?). He looked, with a longish beard and oval face, like a Dutch sea captain, or a little like a milder, less severe version of Solzhenitsyn. With sandy hair just dropping over his ears and broad shoulders, he seemed a sturdy man in his mid-forties, if that. Surely a writer, if only for his wire-rimmed glasses and nicotine-stained fingers (right hand). He barely looked up when I finally walked in and asked, "Professor Barthelme?" after which, hearing why I was there, he told me to sit down and offered me a smoke. (I happily accepted, puffing away anxiously.) Within a few minutes, however, he had read enough of my piece—which he'd already started marking up with a pencil, mainly correcting punctuation, but laughing a few times, over what I did not know—and without much deliberation gave me permission, by way of a signed note, to enroll in a class he was teaching for beginner's fiction.

I'd take two workshops with him as an undergraduate, and another while (somehow) advancing, on fellowship, into the MFA program at City. All his workshops were wonderfully intimate and easygoing, but, for the sake of brevity, I'll just summarize here my experiences. In my initial class with him, he had us work mainly on notions of form and voice. His first assignment required that we go out and interview someone, and transcribe it in a narrative way. My subject, whom I found along 125th Street, was a young black kid whose life story, already at the age of twelve, would have made many a Fieldston and Horace Mann student faint: addict mother, dead father, brothers in jail. I felt bad afterward—I had asked him too much, in effect hitting the poor kid over the head with the shittiness of his life. Another assignment involved writing a sestina, then a sonnet, after Shakespeare. At the same time, he had us reading crazy books like *Alphabetical Africa* by Walter Abish, *The Blood Oranges* by John Hawkes, and, among others, *The Crying of Lot 49* by Thomas Pynchon, all of which, I have to confess, despite their sophistication, left me, cut from a primitive, emotionally blunt cloth, a little cold.

But I eagerly responded to the written assignments. No amount of work bothered me, as I seemed to have all the time and energy in the world, no matter how cluttered my schedule. For about fifteen hours a week, I helped recently arrived students, mainly from Eastern Europe, with their writing assignments as part of my SEEK work-study program duties—my guess is that my formal English grammar was far better than it is now—and working at that Columbia library, as well as showing up for band rehearsals on the weekends. I still had so much energy left over that at the end of the day, it was nothing for me to spend half the night up by a desk, smoking up a storm while delving into whatever tasks lay before me. (At that age, the early twenties, you can eat, romp with your girlfriend, run around Central Park, romp some more, watch TV for an hour, bullshit on the telephone with whomever for a half an hour, read a chapter out of a textbook, romp yet again, and still have enough juice left over to swim across the East River if you want to.)

Once we finally got around to our first attempts at fiction— though the use of that word *fiction* sounds overly lofty in connection with what I was doing in those days—we settled into a routine fairly common to writing workshops everywhere. Sitting at the head of a conference table (or classroom), Mr. Barthelme listened as his students, having passed out Xeroxed or mimeographed copies of their pieces (both kinds of now-archaic machines were in use in that always budget-challenged school), read from them aloud, while the others prepared themselves to make hopefully constructive comments,

Barthelme presiding as if over a committee. (He must have done the same elsewhere, for he also taught occasionally at the much vaunted Valhalla of writing, Iowa, where the true and glorious future of American letters awaited the world.) I won't go into that process any further, except to say that Barthelme did the brunt of his more insightful work, mainly as an editor, during his office hours—though if a word or phrase caught his ear in class, he might say something complimentary or funny about it. And while he left most of every-thing else to his students, I will say that, as far as I could tell, he seemed to genuinely enjoy his role as a teacher.

My first pieces for him, incidentally, were either earthbound, leaden, and, given the influence of Hemingway, whose work I was then studying in another class, overly formal, or absolutely mad in the spirit of experimentation. Never writing about anything of impor-tance to me, I seemed at my best inventing names—Charlie Lopso was one of them, and Opanio Santinio another, the latter being a stand-in for me. At the same time, I seemed to have somehow become, while reading ancient Egyptian history for yet another class, intent upon writing a humorous narrative about a scribe named Exetus lurking along the fringes of the pharaoh's court during the building of the Great Pyramid—later I became fixated on a bread maker in ancient Rome (which I've always warmed to—the baker reminding me of my father, though I wasn't aware of it at the time—and that setting, in ancient times, wonderful simply because it reminded me of how those New Testament texts always made me feel: hopeful, with-out really knowing just why). In other words, I drifted around like crazy, without much focus or serious intent. Nevertheless, Barthelme seemed most interested in improving whatever fledgling skills I had, which were not many, and though I finished that course feeling I had learned something about writing—perhaps that it really wasn't for me—I had liked the social aspect of it enough (where else did one commune with other students in so direct a fashion?) that I decided to continue on along those creative lines for the hell of it.

I have to say this about City: It was, and still is, about the most ethnically mixed university in the country, a true honeycomb of nationalities and cultural cliques. You couldn't walk down a hallway without hearing three or four languages being spoken—from Russian to Chinese to Urdu. In one of my classes, during the onset of the Yom Kippur War of October 1973, as soon as news of it broke, several of my fellow students, Israelis, got up from their seats and, leaving the classroom immediately, disappeared for the next three weeks. There were Chinese social clubs and gangs around campus, more or less secretive societies whose members seemed to keep themselves out of sight. For the most part unobtrusive, they did have some friction with the black gangs. One afternoon, while walking back from class in one of the main buildings, Shepherd Hall, I came upon a scuffle in which some black guys were doing their best to put a beating on a scrawny Chinese fellow. All I did was to go forward—knowing one of them from a class; he was ex–Special Forces, of recent Vietnam vintage, but a very nice fellow in general, though scary-looking with his Mohawk Afro—asking what was going on, and that was enough, it seemed, to break up the attack, though not without getting my share of dirty looks from my black brethren. In any event, I helped the Chinese guy up, and it turned out that this scrawny fellow, who really wasn't worse for wear, happened to be the head of one of those gangs. Before running off to get his boys, I suppose for retribution, he told me: "Anyone messes with you, let me know."

No one did, though one evening as I went heading down the long hill from City toward the subway on 137th Street, this big black guy came up to me and did this knife-in-a-pocket thing, asking for my money. That's when I explained to him that he was in the wrong place, that the kids who attended City College were generally poor immigrants without much money at all and that if he wanted to go where the students were better off, Columbia University was the place to be. "Oh, yeah?" he asked me. "Where's that?" And I told him—"Just take the train down to 116th Street. Or you can walk." And I even advised him about where he should stand, in front of its entranceway gates along Broadway, and that since money didn't mean much to them, because it came to them so easily, they wouldn't give him any trouble at all. "Thanks, man," he told me, before heading off on his noble mission.

Ironically enough, I had more contact with black folks and Eastern Europeans than I did with the Latinos of City. Yet there was one fellow, a very cool, bone-thin Chilean graduate student with a Fu Manchu mustache and ponytail, whom I'd see from time to time in the English Department. He knew that I was named Hijuelos and seemed quite amused by the fact that I'd turn a deep red when he'd speak to me in Spanish, and answer him with some kind of jive muttering under my breath. After a while, he gave up on that conversational route but noticing that I seemed to have an interest in writing, for I was always turning up with books and clumps of my own work to show around, he began to preach the bible of his own aesthetic preferences—Pablo Neruda, Julio Cortázar, and Jorge Luis Borges. Of the three, I'd only heard of Borges and only because Barthelme, in trying to nudge me away from my purely naturalistic tendencies (and probably lumping all Latino nationalities together), thought he was putting me on to a writer I might consider a kind of kin. But I'd never bothered to check Borges out until the Chilean mentioned him as well: I suppose the fact that he was Latino indeed made a difference to me, as far as taking his advice to heart. Soon enough I got ahold of some of Borges's works (*Labyrinths* and *The Aleph and Other Stories*, I recall) from the Salter's bookstore on Broadway. Sometime later, as well, I purchased a copy of Cortázar's *Hopscotch* and, becoming drunk with those worlds, fell into a swoon that lasted months, as if a ray of light filled with warmth and pride-making energies had struck me from heaven. Soon enough, I went wading into a sea of phenomenal Latin American writers—the most prominent of them García Márquez, whose *One Hundred Years of Solitude* was amazing—but others as well, like Carlos Fuentes, José Donoso, and Mario Vargas Llosa, whose equally wonderful novels were behind the boom in Latin American letters then sweeping the world.

I loved them all, could not get enough of their writings, and the fact those books were written by Latinos stirred up some crazy pride inside of me; and once I got on that trail, I discovered two Cuban writers—José Lezama Lima and Guillermo Cabrera Infante— whose works not only blew me away but left me feeling so good, as if I were back in Cuba or keeping company with Cubans, that I stepped back and, checking out my own work with a recently awakened eye, felt as if, in a way, I had been reborn. For the first time in my life, I didn't feel particularly ashamed of how and what I had come from and, thinking about my father and mother, began to conceive that perhaps, one day, I would be able to write something about them, and without the fears and shame that always entered me.

Of course, that epiphany, and the euphoria that followed it, having its moment, left as quickly as it had come, and the truth remained, that once all that glorious smoke had cleared and I looked over my shoulder and behind me, and felt the indifference of the world—who the fuck would care about anything I would say?—I settled back into the safety of the refuge I had constructed for myself as an *americano* with wavering ambitions.

However, by the time I'd returned to Barthelme's classroom, he'd seemed to notice a marked improvement in my techniques and ear for language. I owed that not only to the wildly brilliant Latin Americans and Cubans I had been reading, but to the bookish influence of the aforementioned Frederic Tuten, who put me on to writers like Ferdinand Céline and Rabaleis and another of his favorites, Malamud, whom I had always liked but had not read extensively. (I even wrote a piece in his class that I still rather like to this day: an account—imaginary—of a boy's outing to Coney Island with his father, which I read aloud, with my voice quavering with emotions I could not yet understand.)

Lest I put you to sleep, I will try to conclude this by mentioning a few other authors whose works I read carefully and whose techniques I tried to understand in those days: Carson McCullers, Saul Bellow, Philip Roth, Peter Handke, Günter Grass, Mark Twain, John Dos Passos, Eudora Welty, James Joyce, Robbe-Grillet, John Berger, and yes, the short stories of Barthelme himself—among others—and if there is no seeming logic to that list, it is because I read everything I could get my hands on, without any overriding design, a kind of madness—or book lust—coming over me. (Speaking of lust, no matter what I happened to be doing in bed, I'd look forward to getting back to whatever I happened to be reading: That's how far gone I had become.)

Along the way, I dove more deeply into the sea of Latin American letters and found those waters increasingly nourishing and warming. Naturally, even among them, there were writers who did not speak to my heart and soul, but they never bothered me to the degree that certain highly regarded mainstream Americans did: Though I admired their technique I never cared for what I will now call the three Johns: Cheever, Barth, and Updike.

. . .

With Barthelme again, I began wanting to write more and more about Cuba. It simply possessed me. Reawakened memories, perhaps inspired by the likes of Lima and Infante (later Arenas and Severo Sarduy), came flowing into me. (And there was something else happening at the time: Hanging around my mother and her friends when they started up with their stories, the details of their lives, and the hardships they'd gone through as newcomers to this country, which had so bored me before, seemed suddenly so interesting. Coming back to my place on Eighty-third Street, I would be sitting by my desk—a fifteen-dollar beauty that I'd hauled up from a junk shop on Amsterdam—smoking cigarette after cigarette and trying to recall, however remotely time had placed it, the little journey I had once made down to Cuba with my mother and brother. There was something life-affirming about that summoning up of images—what was there to see? What did the house look like? What did we do? The smell of things, the taste, the feelings that the night sky seemed to bring out in me. (I'll admit that when it came to Cuba, I had already become a hopeless romantic, an idealizer of that which I would never really know, but which, just the same, seemed a part of me.) And yet, in the midst of such warm feelings, I felt a little queasy at the same time (sucking harder on a cigarette, girlfriend walking in and asking, "Are you still up? And why are you smoking so much?") because the more I wrote about my little corner of Cuba, the more I drifted inexorably into yet another story that was not as comforting: the time I spent in the hospital, that puzzling nightmare that was a part of my life, which I never liked to think about. Once I got to that place, it seemed that I was on the verge of opening yet another door, the stuff of my upbringing that, banging on the walls and screaming, I really didn't have any interest in pursuing because out of a corner of my eye, whenever I looked inside, there were just too many things I didn't particularly want to see again. That sensation shooting up through me had a curious effect on my body—my arms and back would burn up, my skin covering with welts, and a fierce itching such as I had never known before would overwhelm me, and I would swear, no way would I write about that time, which I'd rather forget.

. . .

Still, there seemed something so wonderful about the very notion of writing. I liked it because, quite simply, I could hide behind the pages. No one could see my fair complexion, my non-Cuban countenance. At first I wrote a few strange stories but set them in Cuba—one I called "Invasion of the Star Creatures" or the "Aliens," about this spaceship that lands in Cuba, and whose occupants take on the appearance of Rudolph Valentinos roaming the countryside, finding Cuban women to marry and, eventually, immigrating to the States and becoming "aliens" again. Without realizing it, while scrambling about the CCNY library stacks, as well as those of my local public library, and foraging through the sale racks in Columbia's bookstores, anything even vaguely pertaining to Cuba became a source of inspiration to me, and out of the blue, while writing down every bit of interesting lore and fact and legend I could find about Cuba's history—and feeling nourished by just the fact of coming across the names I'd grown up hearing about, in the elegant and uplifting setting of a book, Jiguaní, Holguín, Girona, and Santiago, among so many others—such discoveries so uplifted my spirits that I couldn't help myself from working into the late hours of the night. Back then, I felt so strongly about entering Cuba, as it were, through the dimension of paper that while slipping inside the very dream I had always carried around with me, I was rarely even aware of the time.

And while I'd hang around on the weekends, playing electric blues and quasi-Latin jazz tunes with my downstairs neighbors, Juan "Ching" Ortíz, an aspiring comic book artist and great musician, and his crazy pissed-off-at-life brother, Eddie, on the bass, and still dreamed a little nostalgically about the fun of performing before crowds of drunk and stoned people with my friends like Nick, who, by then, had decided to focus on his other interest—modernistic painting (shades of Cy Twombly and Ronnie Bladen, to use art-world speak)—another side of me, fighting against my natural impulse to look down on myself, managed to work on. In any event, in the cornucopia of detail that possessed me in those days—because to write about Cuba, no matter how distant the details happened to be removed in time, they somehow brought me closer to an image of my father—I found myself, much to Barthelme's amusement and measured admiration (for I was bringing in twenty pages of not-bad copy a week), writing a takeoff on a Havana guidebook, which, as it turned out, could have existed only in my head, and which, incidentally, made a liberal use of my own brand of "Spanglish," as with my invented term for a Cuban taking a photograph—the verb *snapar.* Shameless, and not having a notion of just how gushing my efforts were—unlike today, when I agonize over a blank page— I quickly accumulated a couple of hundred largely plotless pages, which, however, in describing just about every major monument in Havana and digressively touching upon many another tale—as, say, the story of how the Taino chieftain Hatuey had refused baptism when he was about to be burned at the stake, or imagining Hernán Cortéz walking up a hill in colonial Santíago to his house when he was a governor of the island—I gradually began to sketch in portraits of a largish Cuban family made up of strong-minded women, perhaps like my mother or my aunts, a family who somehow lived in Havana and out on a farm at the same time. Whatever I submitted, Barthelme dutifully penciled in his corrections, and along the way, while reading parts of said work aloud to a class of fairly remarkable students—among them were Ted Mooney and the ever so affable Wesley Brown—I became my own most severe critic.

Still, at least one person thought highly of what I was doing. Among my classmates, there happened to be a young woman who, running a lesbian press out of Brooklyn, approached me after one of those classes: Would I be interested in publishing my "guidebook" with her house? I declined for reasons, I now think, that involved a slight distrust of her sexual orientation—though I also didn't particularly care to make my literary debut with so small a house. Also, I knew that however clever some of what I had been writing may have sounded, it really wasn't very good, or anything that could be called a novel, even if, in those days of the postmodern fragments boom, people were getting away with murder.

A further confession: I wanted to write as cleverly as a Borges or a Barthelme, as magically and lyrically as García Márquez and Juan Rulfo, and, at the same time, as jiveishly as a James M. Cain or an Iceberg Slim, as realistically and tersely as a Hemingway or a Stephen Crane or a Dos Passos, as funnily as a Malamud or a Philip Roth, as ribaldly as a Rabelais and Frank Harris, as soulfully as a Chekhov and Chaim Potok (whose melancholic Jews really spoke to me), as spectacularly verbally as a Joyce or Yeats, and as sweetly as a Neruda—in other words, as Borges himself might have put it, I was everywhere and nowhere at the same time.

Indeed I did read everything I could get my hands on, and since I didn't know a whole lot about literature, and, for what it's worth, given my spotty education, as a tabula rasa, I had no problems finding room within myself to absorb other writers' techniques—in other words, I became a good mimic. If I read Conrad on a Monday, I started to write (somewhat) like him on a Tuesday; if I dipped into one of E. A. Poe's fantasias at bedtime, I dreamed of writing like him in the middle of the night. (My collected prose of E. A. Poe, by the way, which my friend Richard gave me those years ago as a Christmas present, I still have on my shelves today.) Just about everything I read, save for certain aforementioned writers, fired me up, and for at least a few years, while under the spell of Barthelme, I began to reconsider my original notion of becoming a schoolteacher. (Then, thinking about the odds against my ever having a real shot of ever earning a living as a writer, I'd fall back on my old plans.)

I was superstitious as well, always have been. When, for example, I found out that Jorge Borges and I ("*Borges y yo*") shared the same birthday, I went through an afternoon of cigarettes-and-*vino*-fueled elations, swearing that this coincidence was a sign from God that I had been cut from the same cloth as the great Argentine writer. (On the other hand, I also shared that date, August 24, with Lyndon Johnson.) You'd think I would outgrow such a naïve notion, but decades later, while feeling a terrific lack of confidence about writing another book of mine, *A Simple Habana Melody,* which was based on the life of the Cuban Tin Pan Alley composer of "El Manicero," Moisés Simons, who ended up in a concentration camp during World War II—who would believe it, right?—my discovery that he too shared my birthday seemed to me another divine sign, as if the spirit of Simons accompanied me. (And since I'm on that subject, I may as well mention that I also share my birthday with several great Cuban musicians: Benny Moré and Bola de Nieve, who, before I had that knowledge, were already my favorites.)

．．．

As I sat in his office in the Quonset hut one afternoon going over something, Barthelme surprised me by suggesting that I might consider the University of Iowa writing program as a possibility for my future. He apparently had quite a bit of pull there and seemed to imply that if I so wanted to, he could get me in.

"Would that at all interest you?" he asked me that day, almost nonchalantly. "It might help you shape up."

I wasn't quite sure what he meant by the phrase "shape up," but I knew that the idea of going to Iowa seemed revolting—even unthinkable—to me; it just seemed so "white bread." I didn't even consider its reputation as a prestigious first-rate writing school, or that, in fact, Barthelme, a generous but private man, was trying to do me an enormous favor. (I think he must have viewed my work as very raw but promising.) All I could think was No way, answering

Barthelme with a shrug that must have, on some level, pissed him off. Without realizing it, I was turning my back on a golden opportunity: Truth be told, I really didn't feel that I deserved it, nor did I think in terms of a life commitment to a career in writing. In fact, even though I'd later accept a fellowship into the MFA program at City, mainly to defer having to enter the workplace, I never went through a day feeling that such schooling would ever lead to anything. I considered most of my fellow students far more gifted, smart, and ambitious than I; if this sounds like false humility, you have to remember that, while one part of me occasionally believed in myself, the other continued to be plagued by doubts. Despite an occasionally cheerful exterior, I remained privately morose and overly reflective in a way that was the opposite of hip—which, as I will define it here and now, has to do with an effortless and unforced expression of the inner soul. In other words, I continued to be anxious: Sometimes I'd smoke through a pack of cigarettes even if they tasted lousy, left my throat smarting, and gave me the jitters, simply because, having opened that pack, I felt I had a responsibility to finish them. Mainly, I saw that stupidity as a way of passing my time, to forestall the gloom into which I easily sank.

Nevertheless, I seemed to take what I can only think of now as my endless reserves of nervous energy and let it pour into my writing—pages and pages of it, and with a one-foot-in-front-of-another manner, as if, in fact, I were constructing the brick wall of a house. I had a very working-class attitude about writing, as if turning up at a job—I guess that was my pop's lingering influence. As a student, I mainly aimed to please. Though I tended to be guardedly friendly with Mr. Barthelme and remained respectful of his standing (as a critical darling of *The New York Times* and a longtime contributor of fiction to *The New Yorker* magazine, he was at the peak of his reputation), I felt thrilled whenever he liked something I had come up with, even if he, in general, thought I was a little heavy-handed in my treatment of emotions. (Once when I had the hubris to tell him that I felt like I was making clocks when I write my stories, he answered, rather skeptically, "Yes, clocks that go BONG, BONG, BONG!")

Altogether, he didn't seem to mind the notion of hanging around me. One Christmas, he came up to my place on West Eighty-third from the Village with a fifth of Johnnie Walker Red and sat in a chair in the corner while a party of much younger folks raged around him, refusing, incidentally, to touch as much as a morsel of food, his energies dedicated to sipping his Scotch and smoking instead, without much of a word to anyone. And years later, as he did with so many of his former students, he occasionally welcomed me into his apartment for drinks (many of them), but I was most stunned by the fact that when I finally did get married to my girlfriend of some three years, Carol, think it was 1975, and sent him and his wife, Marion, an invitation to what would turn out to be a quite tacky reception, held on the rooftop terrace of a midtown hotel, in a cordoned-off area right next to a busy swimming pool—"You make such a nice couple!"— he honored me by showing up. Throughout this low-budget affair, which my well-off in-laws begrudgingly paid for—only booze and hors d'oeuvres were served—Donald passed his time with his wife and several of my fellow students from CCNY, sitting by a table, nursing his drinks, stroking his beard, and taking in that fiasco with the amused expression of a rather sophisticated man who probably couldn't have imagined himself in such a place in a million years.

. . .

Well, once again, I led a double life. Coming uptown to visit with my mother, I did my best to become a dutiful son, though my mother never had any idea of what I was doing with myself. (When I graduated from City with a B.A., with the distinction of becoming the first SEEK student to have done so, and my mother asked me, "*Qué hay de nuevo?*"—"What's new?" and I answered, "I just graduated from college," she seemed genuinely bemused.) In the meantime, the period of our troubles, which had followed my father's death, when his ghost filled the house, had slipped away. Oddly enough, through death he had become somewhat sanctified in her mind. With his presence lingering in the halls—as if both his struggles and, more pleasantly, his peaceful, stoic quietude in the mornings had left after-traces that one could literally still feel—the reality that he was gone had finally set in. "I now realize how much he loved me, *el pobre*," she would say. For my part, I couldn't disagree: Better to have her speak of my pop kindly than not, though she had, in the meantime, made that apartment a museum to their life together and it would always feel frozen in time.

Now and then I'd turn up with the lady I'd married—they got along well enough despite their long episodes of linguistic confusion—and we'd all take a subway to Brooklyn to spend the afternoon with my brother and his family. Often, when I'd end up with her alone, for my wife was often away on acting tours, my mother could drive me crazy, mainly asking a bit too much about my private life, and why on earth did I settle down with a woman of Jewish ethnicity, instead of a nice "*católica*"? It's the old story, of course, but the truth is I didn't know myself: I was so naïve about Jewish folks, it never occurred to me that she was, nor did I care; her parents, in any case, were not religious, and as far as I was concerned, real Jews were like the Hasidim I'd see frequenting the Guss's Pickles stand down on Essex Street, or those Talmudic scholars in their grave black frocks, from the Jewish Theological Seminary on Broadway. I doubt that my mother had any biases against them, and in fact, when she once heard someone tell her that I looked far more Jewish than Cuban—I'd also heard that I looked more Irish or Polish than Cuban—she happily jumped on the notion, exclaiming, "But, of course, look at his big head—he's got brains!" During those long trips to Brooklyn, when she tended to recount to me the minutiae of her days—from her every meal, conversation, dream, notion, store sale, bargain bought, and numerous "*relajos,*" funny stories from the neighborhood—it seemed that she couldn't bear the idea of silence, as if it would take her to a dark place: I would inevitably think back to my childhood with her, and I'd naturally become a little solemn, even occasionally annoyed. Waiting for a train to come, I'd get up to check out the newsstand or buy some penny gums from the column dispensers, over and over again, just to give myself a breather.

Nevertheless, I came to admire my mother in ways that I couldn't have imagined. In the five or so years since my father had died, she had begun to build a new, fairly independent life for herself. She had her friends, her daily rituals, her doctor's appointments, her continuing education classes in the evenings (English I think, typing, some basic secretarial), her routines at church, at which she became a popular presence (particularly at funerals, where she could manage to either out-mourn the most devastated of mourners, or, if in an entirely different mood, cheerfully sweep into a parlor as if a new and better day had come), her favorite shops to frequent, her little part-time jobs along Broadway, and to my surprise, she began a sincere attempt to read in English, mainly by way of the five- and ten-cent romance novel paperbacks she'd pick up here and there in the neighborhood. But there was something else going on at the same time: Though I had some memories of having seen her, while I sat quietly in a corner as a kid, scribbling something down with a pencil into composition notebooks, I never knew until those years later that she had been in fact resurrecting one of her childhood enrichments: the writing of poetry, at which she had apparently always excelled and which, given the much longer moments of her loneliness, she had taken up with a vengeance.

When I'd come over to the apartment, one of the first things she did was to regale me with some ditties she had just written the afternoon or night before (often involving the departed spirit of my father, and situated in an eternal Cuban garden of her imagination, in which she made her cameos as a bird, a blossom, a winged butterfly, while he entered into those poems as a handsome stranger, a wandering mariner, a confused angel whose heart inevitably held the secret to a lost love), and listening to them, I had to admit that there was something wildly creative, if not out-and-out gifted, about them.

And while she had hardly ever been a reticent soul, with each new outing, her delivery, which she refined after readings for her friends—like Chaclita and Carmen and the women she knew from church—became more brazen, self-confident, and, in her manner, theatrical, as if indeed my mother, who believed in spiritualism, had channeled her father, to the point that she would tremble saying her own words. (Then she'd break out laughing over her own pompousness—"*Soy loca, sí?*" she'd ask.) Those visits were always interesting, if sometimes a little hard to take—even for my older brother, who, speaking Spanish, remained the closer of us to her, because, while José had his painterly aspirations and I had my occasional longings to make something of myself as a writer, it was she—not us—who held court and demanded that we pay her homage as an artist, perhaps the only real one in the family. (After all she had gone through back in the days when she first arrived in America, and for all the *miercoles* she had to endure ever since, I couldn't blame her.)

Here, for the record, is one of her poems:

>Este es mi libro
>
>Este es mi sueño
>
>Esta es la flor
>
>Que perfume mi alrededor
>
>Este es el niño
>
>Que llora porque
>
>Sueña que está perdido
>
>Este es el agua
>
>Que corre sin
>
>Saber que es un río
>
>Este es mi corazón
>
>Que gime y
>
>Ríe a la vez
>
>Porque fue martirizado
>
>Hoy no sufro
>
>No padezco
>
>Sólo confío en Dios

This is my book

This is my dream

This is the flower

that perfumes my room

This is the boy who weeps

because he dreams he is lost

This is the water

that flows without knowing

it is a river

This is my heart that laughs and moans

Because He was martyred

I do not suffer

nor do I want

I trust only in God

Fine as her poetry could be, however, she still sometimes overstepped the limits of our patience. Never a shrinking violet, in her widowhood she had become something else, her personality, always charming and winsome, sometimes bordering on arrogance. *"Son bonitos, no?"*—"They're good, aren't they?" she'd inevitably ask about her poems, all the while expecting only one kind of answer.

But at heart we appreciated her creativity. In fact, in the years that have since passed, my brother, and I have come to agree that, however else our upbringing may have been fucked-up, we at least were given a sense that we came from creative roots—viz., our maternal *abuelo* and our mother. We've even joked about the fact that we are the "skipped" generation. It's the American dream, after all, for the first-generation children of immigrants to exceed their parents and go into certifiably venerated and practical professions like that of medicine or law or engineering, to name a few, with the expectation that their offspring, rebelliously prone, drift off into the impractical field of art. But we had somehow skipped over that, though, I must say, without once taking advantage of the few connections we had to further our progress. To put it differently, if it were not for my brother's practical decision to find a secure job in teaching, or my own eventual luck, we could have easily ended badly, without a pot to piss in or anyone on whose help we could fall back.

By graduate school, I'd actually gotten fairly serious about doing something with the story line that I had been given. Slowly, I began to write about my father—something that never came easily to me—and while on the one hand, I found that process somewhat fulfilling, in that I seemed to be finally writing something "real" for the first time, and felt soothed for a while, I inevitably paid for such indulgences in many ways. Bad nightmares, in which I would see the ghost of my father standing in a shroud in my living room, fire burning through me, and my old choking dreams returned, so that I would shoot up in bed, my heart beating so quickly. And in a new bodily reaction to that stress, horrific rashes, by way of a quickly and magically spreading eczema, would break out all over my chest and back and arms with such vehemence that I wouldn't dare write a word for days. (Ironically, however, having a few smokes and a good slug or two of vodka worked wonders as far as calming me down, or at least in putting me in the frame of mind to forget how my skin would turn into parchment just by contemplating certain things.)

I'd slip, not wanting to write much at all, and then go drifting back to my old pursuits—like hanging around with my musician pals. Or I'd go through periods of getting high again, anything, as an old song might go, to forget that which I was trying my best not to remember. I would also occasionally head down to the bar to see how the old gang happened to be faring, but with the difference that now, since I'd gone to college, some prick would like to ride me about the run of my good luck—"Didn't they figure out that you're a dumb fuck yet?"

At school, my professor Frederic Tuten helped smooth me out. With a Bronx-transplanted European sophistication and bon vivant personality, he made you feel good not only about books and litera- ture but about the calling itself, as if to write was the greatest dream one could ever aspire to. We'd talk about books in a more emotional manner than I ever could with Barthelme, who seemed to be quite methodical in his approach to writing, his passions emanating more from his head, rather than from his heart. Altogether, Frederic, with his union organizer father, German and Sicilian forebears, and working-class upbringing, was far more approachable and easier for someone like me to know. It was he, more so than Barthelme, who encouraged my first efforts at writing a novel—even if I didn't know what the hell I was doing—and, as if to restate the benefit of attending a public college with a quite hip writing department, he put me into a workshop that would turn out to be a once-in-a-lifetime kind of expe- rience: the only class in fiction writing that Susan Sontag ever taught.

We shouldn't have gotten along: Her disposition, taste, haughty manner, and way of being—above the world—couldn't have been more different from my own. And in her utter sophistication and Bohemian snootiness, she was far removed from any woman I'd ever met. Physically, she was imposing; on the tallish side, she had a shock of raven black hair, sans the famous white streak, in those days at least, and an expressive and alluringly intelligent face, her dark eyes intensely powerful: Truth be told, there was something about her that, upon our first meeting, reminded me of some of the more severe nuns from Corpus, as if she too, in some ways, were completely bottled up. She wasn't easy at first. Her once-weekly class met in her penthouse apartment on 106th Street, in a building right across from the Duke Ellington mansion, which overlooked Riverside Park, its entryway and halls, I recall, covered in books. (Another detail of the few I can remember? On a wall overlooking her kitchen counter, she kept a poster taken from a still depicting ancient Babylon from the D. W. Griffith film *Intolerance*. Elsewhere, like half the population of Bohemian New York, she'd put up one of those iconic portraits of Che.) Seated around her living room, we students would listen, riveted, to her every word, as she'd deliberate, often cruelly and bluntly, about a piece at hand: "This is not worth my time," she'd glumly say about someone's fiction. And once, to a young woman who had the strongest aspirations of becoming a writer, Sontag, looking over her words and shaking her head in misery, told her: "If I were you, I'd drop this course right now and forget about ever writing anything again. You just don't have it."

She sent that young woman from her apartment—and that course—crying; afterward, she seemed befuddled, as if she believed she had done the young lady a favor. As a result of that early event, those first classes were nerve-racking for the students, each of us waiting for our own moment of doom to arrive; but, of course, such dressing-down depended on her mood, and, as we eventually learned, her mood depended on the state of her precarious health, for my enrollment in her graduate workshop happened to coincide with the period in her life when she had just been diagnosed with breast cancer. So, faced with the prospect of those treatments—a mastectomy awaiting her—and taking medications, her moods vacillated. Some classes, she skipped going over student pieces, preferring to talk instead about the books she liked—like Juan Rulfo's *Pedro Paramo*, which she considered a masterpiece; and another, "for the voice alone," I recall her saying, Marguerite Yourcenar's *Memoirs of Hadrian*. Once she spoke at length about her own fiction, of which she was quite proud. (Frankly, I didn't get it, having always been somewhat numb-headed to the charms of certain kinds of conceptual, high-toned writing.) She'd talk, as well, about how she went about her own work: "I go through countless drafts, and sometimes spend hours over a single paragraph," she'd say (to my horror!). In her living room, she kept a writing desk on which, just as with Barthelme, she had a typewriter alongside which sat a neatly arranged pile of paper, an austerity about the setup that both of them shared.

Of course, she eventually got around to my class submissions, and because I'd started to write more and more about Cuba, and did so while having many a dream about my father, and therefore wrote of a world that, rightly or wrongly, was rife with ghosts, something about the way I seemed to believe in an afterlife, and my often Catholic imagery, really appealed to her, as did my precocious awareness of mortality. But though she mainly had nice things to say about it—*rich* was the word that both Sontag and Barthelme used to describe my writing (I think it was code for *verbose*)—she could really dislike a passage for a very simple flaw. "This is just no good," she'd say. "This just doesn't work," which would confuse the hell out of me, since, reviewing the same passage in a different context a few weeks before, she had loved it. She'd shake her head distastefully and attempt to rescue it: Often for Sontag, who seemed of the Oscar Wilde "I spent the morning taking out a comma and the afternoon putting it back in" school of writing, the solution, the very change that would restore a passage to its finest state, would, in fact, come down to moving a few words around or changing a period to a semicolon: Then her face would brighten up and all was well with the world again.

And I'd hang around with her after class sometimes. She liked the company. I got to meet her son, David Rieff—he owned a red F-hole hollow-body electric guitar and seemed to enjoy playing country music. (We talked about "jamming, man" once—but it never happened.) On one of those afternoons, she told me that she had always wanted to learn how to play tennis and asked if, when she got better, I would ever be interested in hitting a few balls with her—from her windows, one could see the courts of 122nd Street in the park. She'd also confess that fame was tiring, that the best part of writing came during the actual conception of an idea. She'd talk about going downtown to have dinner sometime—and once when she dropped me off in a taxi on her way to Union Square, she seemed sincere in expressing her disappointment that she couldn't spend more time with me and had to see her publisher at FSG, Roger Straus Jr., instead.

In Sontag's class, as with Barthelme's and every literature course I took as a graduate student, with some real first-rate scholars like Frederick Karl, I received an A—a grade, from one of the leading intellectuals of the day, which, in retrospect, I should have taken as an enormous encouragement about my future prospects as a writer. But you know what? Even when I felt this immediate jolt of elation and truly happy for a few days at such a recognition, once I slipped back into feeling like my real self—not the smart guy who had impressed even such a brilliant writer as Sontag (or Barthelme), but the crude and undereducated snooker artist who still felt like shoplifting every time he walked into a store—all that faded. It would hit me the hardest when I'd go up and visit my mother, bring her some takeout Chinese food, doing my best to hang in there with her, and I'd want to tell her that some big-shot lady, *mi maestra*, really thought I had something going with my work. But it would have meant nothing to her anyway—what would she have known of Sontag or Barthelme—and, you know, once I'd sit down by that kitchen table, where my pop had passed so many nights, I'd remember that I had a certain place in the world, and I'd be stupid to try to exceed it: I'd be better off leaving all that writing business to the real talents in those classes.

CHAPTER 7

. . .

My Life on Madison Avenue

Ey the time I left that program, with the writing of my MFA thesis deferred for the future, I had packed in the notion of becoming a schoolteacher, along with my musical aspirations, leaving them to molder in that realm of passed-over possibilities. At the same time, I did not think of myself as a writer by any stretch of the imagination. Instead I considered myself an appreciator of writing with some hands-on experience of it, some three or so years' worth, though without a thing to show for myself by way of publishing, save a single Barthelme-like short story, which appeared in an issue of a literary magazine called *Persea*. (Perhaps only because it had happened to be edited by one of my fellow students at City, a certain Karen Braziller.)

In any event, I remained far behind the pack: By comparison, one of my fellow students, Ted Mooney, had already published a rather remarkable and much-lauded story, "The Interpretation of Dreams," in the quite prestigious *North American Review*, while another of our first-rate talents, Philip Graham, had come out with a book of his own finely hewn experimental short stories. (Since I'm going there, some of the other students who were writing and publishing wonderful work were Wesley Brown, Linsey Abrams, and Myra Goldberg, among those I remember.) At the same time, I could not pick up a literary journal without seeing something by the Barthelme-esque T. Coraghessan Boyle, or Jayne Anne Phillips, author of the mysterious and fluid *Black Tickets*, or by the most radiantly successful Ann Beattie, another emerging star whose first novel, *Chilly Scenes of Winter*, came out shortly after I had left City, in 1976. That list of emerging talents could go on, but no matter where one looked in those days, I can't keep from adding, it was a very rare thing to see published work by any members of that primitive tribe from our urban jungles known as *los Latinos*.

And while I seemed to have acquired, through my own novice writings, a growing appreciation (or love/hate relationship) for my roots and their Cuban-ness, however skewered by the events that had formed me, I thought it would be years before I could write anything worthwhile. Even then, who out there would publish it? For, in those days at least, it was not as if publishing houses or literary magazines were knocking down doors to find what I would call homegrown Latino/Hispanic writers. As American letters stood, its Mount Rushmore would have been carved with the granite faces of Saul Bellow, John Updike, Philip Roth, and Norman Mailer, with a descending pantheon of names from Barthelme to John Gardner forming the rushing funnel below, while even the greatest of black writers, like Ralph Ellison (whose work I also loved), would have hovered about those bodies like some distantly circling satellite. (Of course, behind earlier successes like James Baldwin and LeRoi Jones—later Amiri Baraka—there were younger black writers coming up, John Edgar Wideman and Toni Morrison being the most prominent. Now try to find a comparable list of Latinos in any discussion of American letters from that period—or earlier—and you won't find a single name to mention.)

Having said all this, I'm turning my own stomach with my self-righteous and somewhat pedantic tone and would prefer to move on to a more exciting subject. And so I will leave it at this: If American readers thought about "Spanish" writing at all, it came down to the highly revered Latin Americans of that day, and even they were being appreciated only by the highbrow liberal intellectuals and some of the better-educated general public. For what it's worth, home-grown Latino writing—Cuban-American or otherwise—if it already existed, wasn't being noticed, nor celebrated to a degree that would have drawn out a somewhat reticent and self-doubting fellow like me: In that way, I was frightened to death of going onstage.

■ ■ ■

Any ambitions that I might have developed weren't helped by my then in-laws who thought me self-deluded for ever having wasted my time in graduate school. Even before I'd married their daughter, they sat me down as someone who wouldn't have much of a future without their assistance and offered to get me, through connections, into the University of Chicago Law School. Of course, once we were to move out there and I started attending classes, we'd need a car and a place to live, which they would most generously provide, as well as their active financial support. But, even without thinking seriously about my future, that whole notion about becoming a respectable lawyer son-in-law, living the middle-class life with all those strings attached, just wasn't for me. (And the mother could be condescending: While discussing seating arrangements for a wedding dinner that never happened, when someone suggested that it might be nice if she sat next to my mother, she quipped, "Then who would I have to talk to?")

Deep down, that marriage wasn't anything I really wanted, which was probably why I got incredibly drunk at my own wedding reception. For the record, that was an easy thing to do: With tons of booze available, but little food, and while the band playing Top Forty stuff kept a lot of the attendees out on the dance floor, several of my friends, and my cousin by marriage Angel Tamayo, drinking on a canapé-filled stomach, got violently ill and, after throwing up all over a table, passed out. I did no better: The only part of the reception I remembered the next day was dancing with my aunt Cheo, to whom, prompted by my mother, I whispered a carefully prepared line: "*Estoy muy contento de que hayas venido a mi boda*"—"I am very happy that you have come to my wedding." She, with her Cuban Edith Bunker sweetness, was delighted and pulled me close, saying: "*Te quiero mucho, nieto*"—"I love you very much, nephew." And I would be able to recall running into some of my school friends and a few of my neighbors from Eighty-third Street, as well as pals from the old neighborhood, and sitting beside Barthelme and smoking a few cigarettes, all the while asking, "So what do you think?" (His answer? "How very interesting.")

But, in general, it seemed that I behaved disastrously: Long after that rooftop terrace had been cleared out, around midnight, as I sat in some diner with my psychologist in-laws, who doubtlessly had many a reason for feeling annoyed with me ("Must you smoke?" the mother asked. "You realize that you drank too much!"), they reiterated the aforementioned plan for me as a demand: "You do realize that we expect our daughter to live in a certain way." Never one to hide my feelings, the fact that my fair-skinned face turned a livid red could not have pleased them much at all. In any event, from that night onward, the days of that ill-advised marriage were already numbered.

For the sake of brevity and to get on with this story, sometime in December of 1976, on a cold and miserable day a few weeks before Christmas, I woke up in our apartment with an awful influenza. I was so sick I could barely get out of bed, but my wife thought I should go to my new job, which I'd held since September at that point, so that "we," as she put it, could use any leftover sick days for a future vacation. Though I had the chills, felt like death, vomited my guts out a few times, and happened to be running a fever, I somehow dragged myself into the rawness of that day and caught a train from West Seventy-ninth Street to work.

On a good day without delays, it took ten minutes to get down to the Times Square station, and riding the front car, I'd get out through the Fashion Avenue exit and walk east along Fortieth toward Madison: There, taking up the southeast corner and right across from the Young & Rubicam agency, stood 275, one of those great old art deco office buildings, with marble pilasters and gilded ceilings in the lobby, that remind one (reminded me, at any rate) of a New York that perhaps only ever really existed in the movies. (Just walking in that neighborhood always brought to mind the films of Fred MacMurray—for I had caught the tail end of a time when a great number of male office workers, the older ones at least, streaming to and fro out of Grand Central Terminal, still wore hats.) Altogether, I just found that ambience—so 1940s–1950s—reassuring, in almost a supernatural, time-dissolving way.

Or at least that's what the daydreamer in me would think, even in the midst of an awful illness. As I'd cut over eastward from the subway, I was always fooling with all kinds of tautologies—feeling, for example, that in the same way I happened to be thinking about what it must have been like back in the 1940s, someone far in the future was also thinking about what it must have been like in the 1970s, a kind of cubist (not Cuban) time thing going on in my head.

Often enough, as I'd zip past Bryant Park, I'd have a book, usually borrowed from the Forty-second Street library, opened in my hands, weather permitting. I'd pass anonymously through that perpetually bustling world in my tie and jacket and overcoat, without taking my eyes off a page except when I came to a light, cars and trucks and buses zooming by ruthlessly, or noticed a pretty girl with a nice figure sauntering along in high heels nearby. Rarely, I should add, did I daydream about writing in those days, at least as a priority, and if you had asked me what I did on the sly, I would have told you that I occasionally messed around with some of the crap I had written for school, in the same way I drew sometimes, or went downstairs to visit and play guitar with my friend Ching, or jammed uptown with my old pals—all my creative outlets being roughly equal in my estimation—just interesting ways of going through my days.

Ah, but my job: Apparently, after finally deciding to get "serious" about my life, I didn't really care what I did with my precious time. I hadn't been looking for work too long and, recession or not, should have been more discerning, but I considered myself lucky to find any job at all. When a certain Mr. Belsky, my interviewer, offered me an entry-level clerk's position with the transit advertising company known as TDI (or Transportation Display Inc.), whose offices occupied the third and fourth floors at the aforementioned address, I, without giving much thought to my future, accepted. Even if it was the kind of work that I couldn't have imagined for myself while a graduate student at City, and there were other things I could have been doing—like taking a gamble and hitting the road as a back-packer to see the world, or, for that matter, following in the paths of so many of my classmates by heading into the relatively serene haven of academia—I simply didn't care how I earned my livelihood as long as I'd somehow remain faithful to "my true self."

Without knowing it, I had become earthbound by certain loyalties—to my old neighborhood, to my friends, to New York, and, yes, even if it seemed contradictory, because she could so easily drive me crazy, to my mother. As a result, a more adventuresome existence just didn't occur to me, as if on some level I believed that doing right by other people was the Cuban thing to do. (One of the few Cuban attributes—family loyalty—I seemed to still strongly identify with.)

At the same time, I can remember that, in those days, I often thought about one of my favorite Tennessee Williams lines, from *The Glass Menagerie,* "People go to the movies, instead of moving," and, while doing so, felt a slight twinge of regret going through me. (Well, a twinge of something, but just a ripple against the much darker feel-ings that often seized me.) Nevertheless, I couldn't have imagined, interviewing for that job, that I'd spend almost nine years there, in various capacities, while doing a pretty good imitation, for all my cool-guy aspirations, of an ambitionless lower-middle-management ad agency schlub, to use that fine New Yorkism. (On the other hand, I'd recall that my father was almost thirty when he came to the States and ended up washing dishes for a time, and I'd console myself with the thought that, comparatively speaking, I was way ahead in the game.)

To give you an idea of the tight job market, I was hired along with a brilliant Yale graduate about my age, David Shinn, later the department head, and eventually, in a new professional incarnation, a lawyer writing judges' opinions for the courts down on Centre Street. We both began work that same afternoon: Our immediate boss was a rough-hewn, bulbous-faced Jimmy Durante look-alike, Richard Bannier, who, as an ex–navy man and World War II veteran, shouted his instructions and stood so close to you that you could read the veins on his nose, the hair in his nostrils, all the while catching his spittle. It was he who first explained to us the rudiments of the outdoor advertising business while taking us around to the various departments in the company, and the folks we'd work with: sales was upstairs, art production in the back, accounting a partitioned-off area just off ours (in which every nervous bookkeeper, some twelve or so and all females, chain-smoked throughout the day, a perpetual fog drifting over them), and after a quick tour through the department that managed the national branches—for TDI had operations in just about every major city and airport in the country—to payroll (which consisted of only one employee, a self-possessed and ever so gentle *cubana*, Delores Perez, after whom, for what it's worth, I would name a major character in one of my books). Lastly, we were introduced to our contracts manager, the man from whom we were to get our daily assignments. He was in his mid-thirties, a little paunchy, with an Elvis thing going on with his always well-lubricated hair, a constant smoker as well (Winstons, "*which taste good like cigarettes should*"), and a rosy bloom to his cheeks. Coming in at seven in the morning, he'd work his brains out until one, then go to a local gin mill and get pickled, afterward holing up in his office for the rest of the day, reading the *Advertising Age* newspaper. Occasionally, I'd catch him blowing his breath into his own palm to make sure he didn't smell of alcohol, and he'd often spritz his mouth with Binaca spray. A jokester, except when higher-ups were around, he, like Bannier, was a very nice man, though somewhat of an acquired taste.

Our department went by the name Central Control. My official title: traffic control assistant. We had six employees in our section, each designated a particular function pertaining to the wonderfully literary pursuit of placing print and illuminated advertising copy into thousands upon thousands of locations nationwide. The media we dealt with included billboards; one-, two-, and three-sheet posters; bus and train car-cards; airport and terminal backlit dioramas (Grand Central station, with its spectacular and numerous dioramic displays and high volume and demographics, being the Taj Mahal of that business); as well as assorted other media, from subway clocks to ads alongside bus shelters, which, in fact, TDI pioneered. (I'm not quite sure what Mr. Belsky actually did, but during my first week there, I spent an afternoon by his side, taking various measurements of a shelter just around the corner from the agency: I think he, a former big shot with the MTA, had a lot of pull, for within a year or so, new bus shelters were being put up around the city, with redesigned structures that allowed for the inclusion of a glass-enclosed frame at the side for the insertion of three-sheet ads, mostly for Broadway shows or cigarettes, the ancient ancestors of those computer-generated ads you see now. But that's the only thing he seemed to have accomplished while I was there, his position, I believe, a payback to the company for some favor in his earlier capacity as an MTA exec.)

Though I had just started out, I soon became responsible for most of the ads that went into the interior of LIRR trains, at the rate of about twenty-five each car, as well as the stand-up ads and dioramas on the station platforms; then most national airports, thousands of spots to be filled, all such work orders done by hand, and our records kept in ledger books, for computers had yet to come into use at the company. (And even then, a few years later when the company finally decided to modernize their inventory system, they were these bulky, time-consuming things that took forever to format and input, while producing reams and reams of hole-punched green and white paper records that were hard on the eyes.) In those days, if you saw a Marlboro Country diorama in Grand Central Terminal or in an overhead display at JFK or La Guardia airports, not to mention any number of other facilities around the country, chances are I had issued the work orders.

Some days, I'd spend the morning making copies of work orders on a Xerox machine, which was always breaking down; afterward, I'd send off a few sets of orders with one of the routers from our warehouse in Long Island City, for use in what we called the "field." Our men, union members all, with ladders, buckets of paste, and brushes in hand, would then spend the next week or so putting those ads up in car after car, and station after station, until they'd have to take any number of them down, the whole cycle beginning again.

It was, I have to say, incredibly tedious and painstaking (to stay awake) work, requiring a good aptitude for numbers (which, being able to cipher in my head, came easily to me), a lot of patience, and an ability to look the other way about some things: The salespeople, having sold X number of spots to an outfit like the Philip Morris corporation, whose Marlboro Country ads were already just about everywhere you looked in the city, always wanted to sweeten the pot with freebie bonuses, which we were continually pressured to fulfill for the big accounts, often at the expense of someone else's space— a fooling with the books process that someone there called "taking from Peter to pay Paul," with a wink.

But the position I would eventually become most identified with at the company involved the very underworld which, on some level, had always made me queasy: the subways. Or to be more specific, the glowing white-dialed clocks, some fifteen hundred and seventy-six of them, with their illuminated ads adorning the platforms. I allocated those spaces but, as well, often went out into the field with my counterpart over there, a roguish Irish fellow named Charlie, who comported himself much like a cop, especially when we'd ride the trains into some pretty rough parts of the city (he'd keep a hand inside his right breast pocket under his coat, as if to imply that he had a gun—I don't know if he did). Sometimes, I'd pass half the day down there, showing executives their ads—how those MTA guys and transit cops do it full-time I can't imagine.

Along the way I learned a few things: Ever stand on a platform and watch a half-full train pass your station for no good reason? It's to keep the train supposedly on schedule. Ever wonder who ran those chewing gum and candy bar dispensers in the old days? The mob. Those machines, never turning much profit, were maintained by guys who were also running numbers. And if you've ever wondered why the system ran so badly for years, it had to do with the resentments the older MTA workers, mostly Irish, felt toward the newer workers, who tended to include Latinos and blacks: Pissed about their incredible entry-level salaries, a lot of those workers, upon retiring, wouldn't bother to divulge the intricacies of switching systems and such. Such were the subjects, among so many others, that came up between me and Charlie while riding around.

Somehow, all of us got through those days, pacing ourselves and finding small routines for breaking the utter monotony of what, in essence, became fairly mindless (and soul-destroying) work. Thankfully, smoking, though never in the mornings, helped me pass the time—all the desks had a heavy hard plastic ashtray stashed in one of the drawers—and, about once an hour, as a matter of habit rather than out of any urgent need, I'd go off to the men's room in the outer hall just to stretch my legs, often (I swear) recognizing Mr. Belsky's brown cordovan shoes just visible along the floor in one of the stalls, where it seemed he'd spend half the day reading *The New York Times* from first page to last; I'd also often bump into one of my favorite people, a quite tall, silver-haired Irishman whose name, by coincidence, happened to be John O'Connor (he'd laugh wildly when I'd tell him that I had Irish forebears and a Cuban great-grandmother named Concepción O'Connor). He had a stately manner about him (paging Buck Mulligan) and, as one of the "go-to" troubleshooters and jack-of-all-advertising-trades, could make his own schedule as he pleased. Like Bannier, another World War II veteran, he had flown nearly a hundred missions as a B17 bomber pilot in the Pacific, and cheerfully aware that he was lucky to have survived at all, never had a bad thing to say about anyone or anybody. (When I once asked him, "How'd you get through the nerves?" he answered: "Booze.") He'd always check himself out in front of those bathroom mirrors before going off to his meetings, or perhaps to see a lady friend, for he was always dapperly dressed. I envied him, I have to say, and the universe in which he seemed to live, for to his generation, the war had been a kind of life-affirming ritual, which my own seemed to have lacked: Hence, a restrained self-confidence emanated from his every pore, while I continued to move through my days without any certainty about myself at all.

My favorite place to hang out, however, while slipping away from my desk, was the art department, where ads would be knocked off for the smaller mom-and-pop businesses in the city, like Zaro's kosher breads up on Lexington, or Gene Barry's Photo Lab on Forty-second, in-house production a part of the deal. The fiftyish art director, who always seemed to be reading the *New York Times* obituaries page, happened to be a nephew of Max Fleischer, pioneering animator of the 1930s and creator of the Popeye cartoons, and aside from sitting me down in an area cluttered with artist materials to show me how he'd prepare typeset copy, with its different fonts, for the printers, or how he'd adjust color proofs—to get just the right tones—trace drawings off a light box, and any number of innumerable techniques that have long since been forgotten, he'd regale me with stories about the New York he had lived in as a kid, in the 1940s. I'd listen to him as he sat over a light box, tracing images onto a piece of translucent paper. He'd freelanced for some of the legendary comic book studios; worked in animation sweatshops, the sort to provide those Harry and Bud Piels ads for television; and, in general, with a nostalgic look in his eyes that my pop would have instantly recognized, championed—just like so many of the guys from my former neighborhood did—the notion that things were simply better in the good old days.

Now, I'm mature enough to know that he was probably confusing the wonderfulness of being young with the mundane realities he had actually experienced, but back then, I thought he might have had a point. After all, I looked into my own past as often as I did the future, and even I had to admit that there was something—perhaps a lot of things—that had been beautiful about my childhood. Still, there was something about life in New York in the 1940s that spoke especially to me—why, I didn't know. As for Mr. Fleischer, there is not much else to say, though I often listened to his stories about growing up in Brooklyn with the kind of interest and respect that made the younger secretaries, among them our scrumptious Puerto Rican receptionist, Myra Lopez, regard me as a bit of a weirdo. Looking back on that period now, I think I used my fascination with other people's stories as a way of keeping my writing, which I hardly touched in those days, alive. Still, at twenty-five, married all of five months or so, I seemed to have, in some ways, a mind-set more appropriate to a man many years older than what I happened to be.

· · ·

Which brings me back around, at the expense of mentioning so many of the other wonderful folks I worked with, to that wintry day when

I turned up at the office despite the fact that I could barely take a breath without having a coughing fit. Bad as I looked, no one said a word to me about going home. It wasn't unusual for the employees at TDI to keep on working through an illness—as some of the higher-ups, pricks at heart, frowned, to use that corporate euphemism, on excessive absences—in fact, I probably caught that flu in the office, where it had been going around. But because of my flu, I was given light duty (mainly answering phones with my rasping voice) and even allowed to take a long nap in the midafternoon, on a couch kept way in the back for the King Perceval production staff, who often worked late hours. Somehow, dosed on cough medicines and blood-pressure-raising syrups from the Duane Reade down the street, I managed to get through the day. (Thank God, it was a Friday.) Finally, heading home, however, I made the error of allowing myself to be swayed from my course by the company photographer Sid, a black dude, who, catching me in the hall and pleading a conflict, begged me to wait out in front with a package that he wanted me to give to a woman. We had no concierge in the lobby—and he hadn't the time to wait for her himself.

"Swear to God, bro," he told me, crossing his heart. "She'll come by no later than quarter after five."

"All right," I told him, even if I felt like death.

So he called her up: "You'll see the dude—a serious-looking white guy—a little mopey maybe, with glasses. He'll have that thing for you, all right, sweetheart?" And he gave her the details of how I was dressed: a dark blue coat with a hood, and a dark red scarf. Then he reached into his coat pocket and handed me a brown paper bag inside of which there was a box about the size of a package of cigarettes, but wrapped tightly in white paper. He took off, rapping my back.

"See you Monday, man; feel better, huh?"

For more than half an hour, I waited in the lobby for her to show up, and then, feeling worse and worse, as I was about to head back upstairs to stash that bag away in a drawer (I never found out just what it might have contained) this fine-looking black woman in a Red Riding Hood outfit came up to me, asking, "Are you Sid's friend?"

"Yeah."

"Well, do you have that thing for me?"

"Sure."

When I handed the bag over, she made happy noises like "Uh, umm" and said, "Yessiree," feeling it through her gloves. Then, as if she hadn't another moment in the world, she took off. "You have a nice Christmas," she called out, turning back to look at me, going to wherever she happened to be going.

The weather had gotten even more bleakly cold in the meantime, a frigid sleet falling, the curbs flowing with sludge, and on such a moonless night the "canyon" of that famous neighborhood—the Empire State Building was just a ten-minute walk away—went floating in an ethereal India-ink black and blue darkness that seemed to both stretch into every direction and at the same time cut right into you to the bones; it was the kind of evening when even the Christmas lights that you saw blinking in store and barroom windows began to bleed tears through the gathering frost on the panes, when not even the sidewalk Santas on the corners of Sixth Avenue, ringing their bells merrily, could work their magic on you.

Somehow, in the same way I had dragged myself to the office that morning, I dragged myself uptown. Climbing out the subway station, at Seventy-ninth, into a Manhattan night when most people resembled shadows, the Edward Hopper yellow-lit windows of the Guys and Dolls Pool Hall seeming to float in midair above Broadway, I couldn't wait to change into warm clothes, eat some hot something, and collapse into bed to watch TV, while my wife, as was her habit, sat on the floor in a negligee, playing solitaire. We lived on the fifth floor (apartment 5I), and as soon as the elevator doors opened, I experienced the strangest intuition that something had changed. Coughing, sweating up a storm, I rang the bell, expecting her to answer—in the old days, she'd quickly welcome me inside—but this time I opened the door to complete darkness. Putting the lights on and taking a quick look around, I could see that just about everything had been cleared out of the apartment, save a futon on the floor, a few blankets and pillows, a small black-and-white TV, and two lamps, as well as some of my things, piled carefully in a corner: typewriter, books, guitar. Shreds of paper and pieces of nylon rope lay scattered here and there on the floors, as well as some old issues of *Backstage* and *Variety* newspapers; plastic garbage bags, filled with her random castaways, lay in the corner; in the kitchen, all the wedding-present cutlery and plates were gone, even a wall clock, but at least some food remained in the refrigerator. A note, addressed to me, apologizing for the way things had played out, had been left on a windowsill.

Oddly enough, suddenly freed up, after an increasingly fallow period of writing, and without much of anything better to do with myself, and after hearing for so long the opinion that the last thing in the world I could ever be was a writer, I started finding my feet in that regard again.

· · ·

It took me a while, though. Getting out from under the ghosts of what my mother referred to as that "*matrimonio loco*," I ended up in a cheap first-floor studio apartment on West Eighty-first Street between Amsterdam and Columbus, a block that, as it happened, had the highest murder rate in Manhattan for a few years running.

I had seen the place, about two doors down from the northeast corner (there is a Korean shop there now), during the day, when I'd slipped off from one of my on-site inspection tours for the company. The block, lined with trees and nearly beatific with sunlight, couldn't have seemed more tranquil—at about one-fifty in rent for about twice as much in square footage, the studio itself seemed perfectly suitable to my modest needs. Only when I actually moved in did I discover that the street's underworld population came out of their hiding places come nightfall. Back from work, I'd have to make my way through a sidewalk jammed with drug dealers and petty thieves, and the entryway, where the mailboxes were kept, was often filled to capacity with some eight or nine enormous black men, not a one, I would guess, much older than twenty. I learned quickly to mind my own business. After a while, those men were actually quite polite to me, stepping aside as I'd come in—"Let the white dude through"—and on one occasion when I politely asked if they wouldn't mind keeping it down at two in the morning, they actually did. Though I got used to them (sort of), they always scared the hell out of anyone who turned up to visit me, except this one fellow I had known from City College, a self-styled poet who, now strung out on heroin, sometimes copped his stuff on that street. By midnight, with my bed just a few feet from the front window, I'd sometimes go crazy as they'd stand out in front talking, talking, talking and whooping it up, a boom box blaring. Only at about five in the morning did things finally quiet down a bit. Still, I rarely got a night's decent sleep, even when I'd resort to earplugs— they were, after all, the looming shadows gathered out in front, just beyond the bars of my window, not six feet away from me.

After I'd moved in with just a bed and a few other items, I got to know one of the prostitutes occupying the apartment across the way, and when I asked her if it was a safe building, she covered her mouth, feeling like she wanted to laugh so hard. "You remember reading last year 'bout that cop, you know the one that got caught by some drug dealers who cut off his head?"

"Yeah."

"And they wrapped it all up in a plastic bag and put it in a garbage can?"

"Uh-huh."

She pointed to one of the garbage cans chained to a railing in front of my window.

"Well, honey, that's the garbage can!"

Despite its criminal element, that street, with some dressing up, was used in several tenement scenes for the Sylvester Stallone movie *Paradise Alley*. That was something else I had to contend with for three nights running—huge generator trucks humming away, banks of lighting glaring away all night, voices squawking through megaphones, and, to top it all, coming home from work, I'd have to show my ID to some security guards just to get to my apartment (as if they, the prick genius moviemakers, owned the city). For all my annoyance, the faux turn-of-the-century streetlamps, much like the ones we had on my block, and other touches, like the old Model T's and carts that suddenly lined the curbs, as well as watching that Marlon Brando of

B actors, Stallone, stomping around, amused me; but then, as quickly as all that had come, much like a dream, it too vanished.

Needless to say, I got zero writing done while I lived there and I was more than a little happy when I finally left after about six months.

. . .

Eventually hooked up with a new girlfriend, I headed back uptown, settling into a fifteenth-floor apartment on West 106th Street. Situated in the back of a 1920s high-rise, its windows looked north over West Harlem and the towers of St. John's Cathedral. (In essence, I had moved back into my old neighborhood.) I most loved the church bells that rang at about eleven every Sunday morning in unison, the clarion of St. John's, the Ascension, Notre Dame, Corpus Christi, and, at the greatest distance, Riverside Church casting an ecclesiastical spell over the world and, in the spring, set every bird for miles around to chirping, their songs inseparable from that chiming. (All right, so I'm going over the top, but New York City was so seedy in the 1970s that one came to appreciate anything that approached gentility.)

I also found myself taking an unexpected comfort in the Latinoness of the neighborhood. (It was a surprise to me.) Not in the sleazy stretches along Columbus Avenue where the proprietary hoods, dominating the corners, bore holes into the back of my head every time I passed, or the sidewalk drug supermarkets of 107th and 108th streets and Amsterdam, which I'd always anxiously slip through to visit my mother, but, in a way I never had before, I became enthralled with the very stuff that hadn't made much of an impression on me while growing up: the mom-and-pop bodegas, the barbershop with its Spanish-speaking clientele, the *botánicas* with their holy statuary and magic candles, the record stores through whose doorways speakers blared (but congenially), the time-freezing music of Tito Puente and Celia Cruz, which hadn't changed in thirty years. Just seeing the *abuelitas* perusing the curbside racks of clothing in front of a store, with their little granddaughters hanging on to their skirts, or some of the paunchy older gents sitting out on milk crates in front of a bodega and playing dominoes and watching life go by, seemed suddenly enchanting to me. I'd find myself standing in front of a shop window taking mental note of every Santa Barbara, Santo Lázaro, and Virgen de la Caridad, and spell-making unguent or curse-breaking candle or love potion in sight. The immense Dominican-owned *almacen* on my corner—a combination butcher shop and supermarket, where you could buy bags of pork chops and chicken legs for under a dollar a pound, and all the Café Pilon and breakaway nougat you could ever want to consume (my mother, knowing of it, used to make special trips there to get a deal)—seemed about as delightful a place to get my groceries as anywhere around. I liked hearing the Spanish spoken there and enjoyed that ambience, with its bins of mysterious Caribbean tubers and gourds, though occasionally, I'd get low whenever the butcher, after speaking a rapid-fire Spanish with all his other customers, finally came to me and said: "Jes, what can I do for you, *sir*." (And just like that, I'd fall into depression, from the disturbing thought that when it came to the culture from which I had come, I would always remain an outsider looking in.)

Well, I guess such anxieties ran in the family. And yet, exasperated as I sometimes felt, a certain kind of creative energy became rekindled inside of me. Something about rediscovering myself and the culture that had formed me needed to be expressed, as did the story I had lingering, like a ghost, inside my head. How to write it, however, eluded me. Save for some enticing fragments, left over from my CUNY years, I really had very little to show for my past efforts. Working full-time and often enough earning a little extra money on the weekends or keeping later hours at the company, whenever I'd finally sit down to write, it was as if I were starting all over again. Sometimes a week or two would have passed before I'd get around again to what I'd come to regard as my "novel." And even then, often under the sway of whatever I happened to be reading at the time—from Borges to Ishmael Reed to Edna O'Brien—the tone and voice changed from week to week. Though I know now (at least in my opinion) that voice comes down to conveying one's personality on paper, back then I didn't have the slightest clue as to what "I"—Oscar Hijuelos, the New Yorkized son of Cubans and former self-doubting acolyte of writers like Barthelme and Sontag—really sounded like. The closest thing I

had, however, to an authentic voice in my head, which I often heard
in Spanish but naturally translated into English, if the truth be told,
came down to something similar to that of my mother.

I did not have a bad life, not at all like that of some of the people
I'd see out in the street begging, or smelling like shit in the park, or
the homeless guy I once saw, while on an inspection, lying on the
subway platform, his head having been split open by an incoming
train. I didn't have much money—think I earned just under eight
thousand dollars annually my first few years at TDI (even then, that
wasn't very much), but I had enough to do what I pleased, which
came down to doing basically nothing. Still enjoying comic books, I'd
make my monthly trips over to an East Side shop, Supersnipe, to look
around—one day I had ventured inside just in time to catch Federico
Fellini buying a stack of back-issue Marvels. (Sorry, folks, I can't help
it.) More or less out of the music scene except for the occasional jam
session with friends, I'd sometimes head downtown to the Lower
East Side and to a venue like the Mercer Arts Center or Max's Kansas
City, at the invitation of my former bass player Pete, then working
as a roadie for the New York Dolls. (Later, he, knowing their songs
inside out, would replace their bassist, who'd left the group.) I'd long
since decided that I found the rock scene a bit repugnant (translation: I didn't have the overtly sexy chops or wild looks to fit into it)
and really couldn't get why people went crazy over certain kinds of
music. (The Dolls, for example, did nothing for me, though I could
see why the ladies liked David Johansen—a hell of a good-looking
guy and a *jamoncito* and a half onstage.) Though I had published
essentially nothing, I can remember feeling superior to just about
anyone I'd meet at such places, simply because I had kept that higher
aspiration in the back of my mind. I even took some pages I had been
fooling around with to Max's one night, and visiting my friend Pete
backstage in the dressing room area—a row of curtained cubicles
that didn't afford much privacy at all—I met the fly Deborah Harry,
lead singer of Blondie (sorry again), also on the bill, and did my best
to win her favor by offering to give her the pages I had written. She
was very polite and kind, surprisingly respectful of me, even though

I was slightly inebriated from having killed time after work in a bar with some of my fellow employees.

Slipping out in the evenings, I liked to listen to jazz at this dive on 106th Street (it's called Smoke now but back then was owned by a shady Colombian who, however, in booking his acts, sometimes displayed a haphazard good taste). I liked sitting by the bar smoking and trying my best to appear as Bohemian as possible, even if by then I had become a hardworking office clone. I'd nod at the most bullshit jazz—what I considered excremental honking, especially on saxophones—even if it drove me crazy. I'd go home late with a headache, usually feeling unimpressed by most of the musicians; but if a guitarist had shown up with some real chops, I'd tiptoe around my living room and pick at some chords on a sweet Brazilian nylon-string guitar I'd bought at an Odd Lot store on Fortieth, trying to figure out what the guy had played. Staying up until some ridiculous hour, I'd manage, as my pop used to, on just a few hours of sleep; then my workdays in the office would begin all over again.

· · ·

In that time, I really didn't have much contact with writers—just on a very occasional basis, as when a friend would call me up and say that so-and-so had a reading somewhere. Otherwise, it was a rare thing for me to spend time with anyone talking shop. At work, the only well-read person there was my counterpart, David. As I recall, he had some literary aspirations of his own: A Faulkner and Thomas Wolfe aficionado, he also wanted to write a novel, perhaps about his upbringing in western Pennsylvania, though, working hard in the office and putting in a lot of overtime, as the sort of conscientious sort whom bosses loved, he never got around to the point of having anything to show me. I did spend the occasional evening hanging out with my friend Wesley Brown, who was then writing a great novel called *Tragic Magic*, and I'd bump into former colleagues on the street—all of them seemed to be getting wherever they were going much more quickly than I. While walking down Fifth Avenue one sunny autumn afternoon, I ran into Philip Graham. On his way to the offices of *The New Yorker*, where he was about to publish a story, he could not have been in a more ecstatic state, while all I could think about was what I would hopefully eat for dinner.

I had so few friends in my life who seriously read books, let alone writers, that I felt myself very much a loner. (The women in my office read on the subways and during lunch, but mainly Jackie Collins novels, though I noticed the occasional Robin Cook book in the mix, while the men read hardly anything but magazines and newspapers.) Still, I managed to find consolation in the libraries nearby on Fifth Avenue—I spent a lot of my lunchtimes haunting the stacks of the Forty-second Street and the Mid-Manhattan branches, rarely coming back to the office without some interesting tidbit by an author I'd never heard of, to help keep my head together and my hand upon the pulse of literature. (Yes, if you were about twenty or thirty years behind.)

In the nice weather, I'd sit out on the steps (daydreaming, looking off) while the most beautiful and shapely secretaries sunned themselves around me, or came sashaying along in their tight skirts and high heels—of course I noticed them, but I doubt if they noticed me. And what would they have seen anyway but a youngish bookworm wasting his youthful energies and time on something as ephemeral as reading? Occasionally, I'd head out with the office gang on a Friday after work to make the Upper East Side disco scene, partiers jamming the sidewalks at nine in the evening as densely as commuters did Grand Central Station at rush hour. On those nights, hundreds of folks swarmed into those clubs to do the "hustle" and show off their latest moves, while I, dragged along and never going anywhere without at least a paperback stashed in my pocket, stood off to the side, or huddled by one of our tables, sipping a four-dollar watered-down gin and tonic out of a plastic cup, taking everything in, and occasionally, to some of my more lively coworkers' dismay, actually flipping through some pages of a book. I did so even when it was nearly impossible to read anything but a girl's fly figure in a room whose main sources of light came from dim candles, cigarette tips, and a galaxy of disco stars, elongating like peacock eyes as they swirled across the walls.

Inevitably, there was always someone around to pull me out onto the dance floor and I'd sort of go along with the fun good-naturedly— in the same way I once did when it came to Latin dance parties— without much expertise or self-confidence. Though I'd occasionally remember some fancy flourishes that I'd picked up from watching my father and guys like Tommy, with his Motown dance steps, I never felt at ease. Still, I took solace in the fact that I knew of very few writers or, for that matter, musicians who danced much at all. Thinking that my guarded ways and introspective manner were understated and cool, I doubt if any of my office friends shared that opinion: No doubt about it, I probably came off to them as a bookish wallflower.

I'd also hang out at the Pierpont Morgan Library on Thirty-sixth Street, which, in those days, despite its fifty cents admission price, was hardly ever crowded. I liked the way that books, encased behind beehive glass, rose in great cabinets from the floor to the ceiling, and the old manuscript pages from the illuminated Bible they'd put on display. My favorite objet d'art in the joint, however, happened to be a reliquary, said to have been the property of Constantine's mother, Helena. It contained a piece of wood, a splinter really, that was said to have come from the "true cross," and a fragmented nail said to have been used during the crucifixion of Jesus. I'd just stare at that for the longest time, feel that I was somehow communing with the past, like a Borges character, and then, I'd leave that ambience of the early twentieth century and reenter the madness that was midtown Manhattan at one thirty or two in the afternoon.

.   .   .

Altogether, in terms of keeping any sense of myself as a writer alive, books made a big difference, as did my occasional trips down to West Eleventh Street, where I would spend a few hours talking with Donald Barthelme, who, for whatever reasons and despite the fact that I was a nobody, always made time to see me. These visits entailed, from the very start, oddly familiar evenings that began no later nor sooner than five thirty. Donald, sitting across from me, an ashtray and a bottle of Scotch set out on a coffee table, chain-smoked and drank as quickly and as much as my pop used to, but with the difference that he did not speak a mangled Spanish nor go into sad meditations

upon his mortality. (Thank you, Donald.) I wish I'd been more attentive to recording our conversations like so many literary sorts do—if
I had felt that I were literary, I might have. What I do recall of those
evenings came down to the manner in which he'd extract information
from me about his other former students ("And Wesley, how is he?")
and make inquiries about my former wife ("Oh, I'm sorry to hear that
it didn't work out") and my current job ("You do what!" and "Are
you sure you don't want me to put in a call to *The New Yorker* to see
if they'd have something for you?"). In turn, I'd ask him about his
stories, or mention something I'd noticed in one of his longer works,
like *The Dead Father*, or, intending to butter him up, make him aware
that I had noticed some new translation of one his works on the wall
shelves behind us. On at least a few occasions, I offered to set up a
jam session with some of my jazzier friends for him—though I had
never seen the kit, he apparently played a high hat and snare drum
(he always refused). Making him laugh, I'd come out of nowhere with
an offer to provide him with the kinds of tickets that were readily
available as freebies to the employees of TDI—for the Ringling Brothers circus and Friday-night boxing matches at the Felt Forum. ("No,
thank you," he'd say, stroking upon his beard.) Along the way (I'm
compressing here), we'd speak about any number of things—injustice,
as when an actor friend of his had been stabbed to death on the street
for no good reason, and how lousy it was that his friend's widow, a
Swede, as a consequence, had been deported; or the capricious habits
of certain writers—he always talked about Thomas Pynchon (whose
writing I found opaque) as having a penchant for hiding out in closets
when he'd visit someone; or we'd slip into a civil discourse: The government, of course, charged too much in taxes, and as far as salaries
were concerned, at least for writers trying to live honestly and without
ostentation, we once arrived at the figure of one hundred thousand
dollars a year as a reasonable wage. He'd ask me about Cuba—was I
planning to go?—a question that always made me feel a little guilty,
as if I should, though as soon as I'd leave his apartment, it would seem,
as always, unthinkable. Much as I loved the guy and felt thrilled to

be with him, I'd wonder how he would feel if he had to contend with censorship, or if he came home one day and found someone else living in his flat, or woke up to find that his bread and butter, *The New Yorker*, had been nationalized, his salary cut to a tenth of what it had been before. I do not recall, however, voicing these questions to him, though I wouldn't have put it past me.

Of course, we'd talk about books. Deeply opinionated, Donald, in essence, had little patience with forced sentimentalism and false profundity (paging John Irving), and always tried to steer me in a certain direction. And while I don't care to further elaborate on his tastes, those evenings, fueled by goblets of Scotch on the rocks, always arrived at a certain moment when he, growing impatient with making small talk, would cut to the chase: "And are you writing anything these days?" he'd ask me. And when I'd tell him, "Sure," he'd simply say, "Okay, send it over and let me see what you're doing."

It's quite incredible to me now that he would make such an offer (though I also think it was his way of winding up the night) and that I didn't take him seriously enough to follow through. I was too uncertain about my work to risk embarrassing myself—and I didn't want to waste his time. Nor did I want him to think I had regressed in terms of technique and progress. (I fantasized that my former classmates were advancing way beyond me at a dizzying rate.) Above all, though I didn't realize it, I obviously had a lot of my father, Pascual, in me: a fatalistic, nearly passive attitude about life that didn't allow me to take advantage of real opportunities. Even then, I believed that just hanging around someone like Barthelme was a kind of credential unto itself.

Inevitably, for the longest time, no matter how often Barthelme brought up the subject of my work—teaching part of the year in a new position at the University of Houston, he even telephoned me now and then over the years to see how I was progressing—I managed to put him off. And when he'd revisit the notion of my attending the University of Iowa—some three or four times over a six-year or so period—I never took that, or his other efforts to help me, seriously.

. . .

Still, I kept fooling around on a typewriter at night and on the weekends, while accumulating stacks of unfinished scenes, vignettes, and, I suppose, what might pass as chapters of something about the way I had come up in life, too raw in both content and style, I thought deep down, for anyone in the publishing world to really care about.

Besides, I had developed a new interest. Born of a flair that I had for gesture drawing and the fact that I had been a junkie for comic books, the children's literature of my urban youth, for a time I wanted to become a cartoonist like Charles Schultz or Mort Walker. To that point, however, my pursuit of that vocation, which I occasionally spiced up with nighttime life drawing sessions at the Art Students League and National Academy of Design, with the random gorgeous (or homely) model as my subject, had only yielded a few strange children's stories, an endless procession of birthday and Christmas cards that I made for friends and family (how I loved Christmas), and, given the recession-bound world of those years, some ridiculously obtuse ideas for syndicated strips.

The closest I came to breaking into the biz I owed to my guitar-playing buddy Ching, a zippy draftsman who would later gain momentary fame as the artist of *Krypto the Superdog* for DC Comics. During one of those weeks when the repetitious nature of my office job had been getting to me, it was Ching, then an inker for DC, who suggested that I go over to their offices during lunch one day and chat with an editor over there, a fellow named Paul Levitz, who might be able to help me with some work. Not as an artist, however—I just didn't have those chops—but as a scriptwriter. Though it wasn't anything I'd particularly wanted to do, I gave it a shot, coming up with a story some eight pages long, about two brothers, the first a vampire, á la Dracula, and the second a vampire hunter, á la Van Helsing; I thought it was pretty good, sensitively written, etc., but he called it, to my surprise, "too literary" and highbrow for the average DC reader.

. . .

Along the way, I came up with some writing that didn't make me completely ill: in one instance, a narrative of some length that I'd written in a month or so of such sessions, involving a Cuban woman of an indeterminate age, remembering her childhood in Holguín, and a later romance with a fellow from the countryside. I have it somewhere, haven't read it over since, and what I mainly recall is that it had a rather lyrical and nostalgic tone. Tightly written, during one of my anal phases in which I tried to be as "literary" as possible, I lavished upon it nearly every exotic word I could find in a dictionary and thesaurus. (There was no such thing as blue, rather it was cerulean, and pink became roseate and so on.) Xeroxing a few copies of it in the office, I sent one off as part of an application for some grant, and the other became the writing sample I attached to my application toward a "working fellowship" at a well-known writer's conference in Middlebury, Vermont. Later, it thrilled me to learn that I had been accepted: I mean, what else would a young man working a nine-to-five full-time job want to do with his precious days off in the summer than wait tables?

· · ·

This took place during the last weeks of August 1979, just as I was about to turn twenty-eight: the conference, involving rustic housing, antique barns, and an ambience somewhere between that of a college campus and a wooded Zen retreat, had a pecking order that began with the paying writer aspirants, then the working fellows (like myself, usually folks who hadn't published much), then regular, better-published fellows—minor stars as it were, whose only duty was to show up and read the auditor's work (only if they wanted to)—and upward to the staggering Olympian heights where the great literary geniuses of our time apparently resided. Among those staggeringly great literary geniuses: John Irving, Tim O'Brien, Howard Nemerov, and the pharaoh himself, John Gardner, with his head of flaxen Prince Valiant hair. I, for one, had not read his famous and brilliantly titled *Sunlight Dialogues*—I'd peeked at it and found it, well, a bit on the plodding side, but what the hell did I know? I did read his *On Moral Fiction*, which, in its general attacks on many a postmodernist author, seemed to single out the work of Donald Barthelme as a model of the very worst kind of writing. However, it was one thing to read of such an opinion, quite another to breathe it in the air.

Upon disembarking a bus to join my fellow "waitroids," as we came to call ourselves, and settling in a cabin with several new friends, I had no idea that, for the two-week duration of the conference, Gardner's ideas about nearly everything would be taken as God's word spoken on earth, among them his disparagements of Barthelme. In such a world, Barthelme was a Satan—he would have laughed at the notion—but what surprised me the most was how often I overheard attendees, coming fresh from a lecture, parroting Gardner's sentiments: One man literally spat on the ground, telling me, "Barthelme is full of shit!"—and there was worse. That hit me as a shock to my system, for aside from witnessing a little sniping and some hurt feelings in workshops, while at school, I had hardly experienced such viciousness from anyone and had simple-mindedly formed the notion that most writers respected and cared for each other. As much as I stood outside of it, I saw the literary life as a kind of brotherhood, a noble pursuit in which literature seemed an answer to the tawdrier aspects of existence. In other words, I was naïve, stupid, uninformed, green, and hopelessly idealistic despite the fact that, given the way I had come up, I should have known better.

Of course, I had my job: With about twelve or so other fledgling writers, I spent those weeks getting up quite early in the morning to serve and bus the first of the day's three meals, in a converted barn turned into a massive dining hall, where some two or three hundred people, eating in shifts, sat down at a time.

The biggest rising star and resident sex symbol? John Irving, dressed in leather and riding around on his Harley-Davidson motorcycle. At a reading he, handsome and Byronesque, held forth with the seriousness of a lama about to raise the dead: His prose electrified the audience; women sighed at the sight of him, as if he were a Sir Galahad in the flesh. (I don't remember what he read—think it was a chapter in progress from a new novel—but, in its verbosity, one could sense the careful brick-by-brick masonry of his breathless prose.) As someone to wait upon in the mornings, however, he was not particularly pleasant—he'd flash you a dirty look if you picked up or served a dish while he was in the midst of saying something—though he was not nearly so bad as a quite famous children's author, of distinctly European origin, who at a certain point told me, as I served a glass of wine from the wrong side—only because someone was standing in the way—"Don't you know anything about etiquette and proper dining? You should serve beverages from the right." And John Gardner? He seemed affable enough but always gravely disposed, perhaps because of a hangover, which everyone seemed to have. He too held forth often about some high-toned *miércoles* or the other, his brightest and most adoring devotees always vying for his attention. Where Irving seemed to be the resident sex symbol, Mr. Gardner was more a papal figure or a shaman. He could not go anywhere without someone trying to slip some story or fragment from a novel into his hand. (He'd look it over, quickly, make his appraisal, and recommend another writer to help with that work.)

One evening, he held the audience spellbound with a reading from his latest, the gothic, very interestingly written *Grendel*. Privately, however, his modus operandi was to comment on the weaknesses of someone else's work—in one instance, after a reading by Tim O'Brien, he "confided" in me, as he must have with everyone else he spoke to, that the story, while interesting, didn't really work in terms of its prose. (Sorry, Mr. O'Brien.) He was a trickster as well: Before a large gathering, he had a page of prose, the opening to a book by an anonymous author, projected onto a screen and asked his audience if it seemed an amateurish work, and, if so, how it could be improved upon. People wrote frantically in their notebooks for some twenty minutes, after which the suggestions were read aloud. It was something about an apple and a tree—and after dissecting the responses, which he mostly disapproved of, he revealed the identity of its author: Norman Mailer. The piece he had planted turned out to be the first page of the forthcoming *Executioner's Song*. As the audience members murmured among themselves, Mr. Gardner beamed over his own saturnine cleverness. Still, at the breakfast or dinner table, Mr. Gardner could not have been more polite, and though there was something Napoleonic about him (he was quite a short man, though with a Viking visage, like a Thor), he seemed to go out of his way to be kind to the waiters, which kept him in good stead with us.

* * *

As waiters, we actually had an advantage over everyone else in that we had a built-in community, whereas many of the attendees, arriving as strangers, had to endure a great deal of loneliness and, as a member of a large anonymous crowd, a low standing in the strict pecking order of things—until, inevitably, at one of the post-reading nightly barn dances, where the booze flowed and love flourished, they'd find a companion. (Also, I'm sure, as they'd gather with small groups of writers in workshops or in a meeting room and share, often enough, quite intimate information with one another through their prose, that too became a way of finding a kindred spirit.) More exclusive were the senior faculty cocktail parties that were held in a house called Tremont, which we, delivering liquor cases there, nicknamed Delirium Tremens. Since one could attend only by invitation, few of the waiters ever saw its interior: I only went once, and caused a row, as I had snuck inside through the back. The cocktails mainly took place (as I recall) in a cozy parlor with a fireplace, the mightiest writers on the planet talking literature with their favorites, who, I happened to notice, were, with perhaps one or two exceptions, the best-looking women at the conference. It was so blatantly sexist and hypocritical, given the air of sanctity hanging over people like Mr. Gardner, that even the more misogynist pricks I knew from the advertising world (and believe me, I met one every day) seemed, by contrast, far more earnest. What took place there was so blatant—one of our crew of waiters, a quite beautiful southern girl, had fallen under their spell and tended to come back to her quarters dead drunk and disoriented at three in the morning—that I couldn't understand how those same folks could look at themselves in a mirror without sensing their own darkened souls, let alone participate in discussions about morality in fiction. (No wonder they were so awful in the mornings.) I recall having a brief and somewhat pleasant conversation with Gardner about Tolstoy before getting kicked out by an assistant to the gods.

("Are you aware that you've broken the protocol here?") Mainly, I remember leaving Delirium Tremens with the impression that, for some of those writers—not all—the conference was mainly a way of what my friend Tommy would call "pulling some beaucoup pussy."

• • •

After about a week, there were afternoon sessions devoted to student works. One delicate-seeming young man, his voice trembling, read a too lyrical and tender narrative about a son following a broken-down drunk through a small midwestern town at night and its resolution and climax, at story's end, is the narrator's discovery that said broken-down drunk is his father; the audience, so seriously disposed, dissected its various elements quite thoroughly, though never too bluntly nor cruelly, and generally seemed to like it, while I, having lived with such a father (except my Midwest town happened to be situated in West Harlem), felt almost contemptuous of the way it ended, as if the guy didn't really know what he was talking about— *A pop like that is just there from the time you are old enough to become aware*. In those moments, for whatever my reasons, I formed a notion that I have since, rightly or wrongly, usually clung to. This I shared with just about anyone I could that day: *Stories often end just where they should begin*. It wasn't a particularly brilliant insight—a lot of writing is thinking aloud on paper, and necessary if only to discover the real heart of a story—but I can remember realizing it was the first opinion about craft or an approach to narrative I'd ever voiced aloud.

Though I found an infinite number of things that put me off about such a place, something about that kind of environment— which is also true with art colonies—in its wall-to-wall nature, as it were, tends to push you into the center of whatever creative dream you are pursuing (or avoiding), whether you want it to or not. Quite simply, there were enough people around who sincerely loved the notion of literature as to embolden someone like me to give a reading one evening from that longish narrative about Cuba.

I had to fortify myself with red wine, and, as I recall, I often paused to light a cigarette, which helped dampen my nerves. Still, I had a hard time of it: Even at City College, I had never read anything

so directly hooked up (at least in my mind) with an abstracted, somewhat more vocabulary-wizened version of my mother's voice, that is
to say, her more charming Cuban, non-nagging side—a voice that I
had cloaked in dazzling language. (The kind of language to impress
novices, and to win literary prizes, if you have the right grad school
provenance.) It tore my guts up just to read it aloud—at certain
points, when I came to parts about the *campesino* who enters her life,
I had to stop because my breathing became so halting. Later, a friend
told me that I had turned a livid red, and then, alternately, as white
as parchment. It was such an emotional experience that, finishing
up, I had to take off alone. Wandering through a meadow, not far
from where Robert Frost kept a cabin, I looked up at a brilliantly
clear night sky, the Milky Way hanging low, and, strangely enough,
felt my father's presence all around me—or to put it differently, perhaps I felt his absence—but, in any event, I stayed out there for more
than an hour, confounded by the whirl of emotions that was sum-
moned up by what I had written; as it's been said that all roads lead to
Rome, anything I wrote eventually, however veiled, in some mystical
way, led back to my pop.

I continued to think about him, at some point, every day, long
after I returned from that conference. Hanging on to his coattails,
everything else about my life, from my childhood illness and the sadness I felt growing up, followed behind the images I had of him. In
fact, though I was haunted by his memory, it remained something I
hadn't been particularly aware of, until, like a thief, at some moment,
it would come up behind me. Once while attending the play *Da*,
about an Irish man's tribulations with his father's (often humorous)
ghost, there came a scene in which the father stands atop the roof of
a house, and because it brought back to me that image of my father
standing on the rooftop of Butler Hall the night he died, I lost it
completely, and would have broken down crying if it were not for
the public nature of that place. (My girlfriend, by the way, without
knowing it, once took me for a surprise birthday dinner at that restaurant. There I had tried to eat, without letting on that my father
had died not ten yards from where we were sitting.) Oddly, for all

the times I passed by the Biltmore Hotel, on Forty-third and Park, I never felt tempted to look inside its front lobby, which, I've been told, had remained largely unchanged from earlier years. (I don't know if I was afraid to walk in there or if, in my mind, the old Biltmore of my childhood is the only one I wanted to see.) And at Christmas, despite all the frivolity and parties and drinking and screwing around that came with that season (oh, the things I would see in the office when people were really letting loose), I'd feel a special melancholy. Something about working downtown in what the kids in my neighborhood called the canyon, with the hawk—the wind—at my back, always seemed gratifying to me in a strangely ghostly way, as if, walking in a crowd along the avenue, I could picture my pop, back when he was alive, among them.

I knew he was dead, but memory is a bitch and, with a daydreamer like myself, could make the past seem imminent. And though his presence has faded in its power from my mind by now, back then, I had such a strong recollection of him physically, and of his manner, it wasn't much of a stretch for me to wishfully impose him upon the anonymity of a crowd.

At night, I'd worry about falling asleep and seeing his ghost. Whereas I used to wake up with a jolt, inspired perhaps by the agitated emotions and repressed memories of my childhood, I'd now awaken, my heart beating wildly, from the impression that my pop was just outside in the hall waiting for me, as if he wanted to take me with him. One night I walked into the darkness of the living room, where I saw my father, or the shadow of him: He spoke to me, in Spanish of course, saying: "*Soy ciego*"—"I'm blind." And then he said: "*Por favor, abra la luz*"—"Please, turn on the light." When I did, he told me, "Thank you," and simultaneously vanished. I swear this happened—dream or not, that's what I saw and heard. After a while, it occurred to me that I had some demons to exorcize, but each time I sat down and tried to conjure the world I'd come from, and wrote about my father—honestly—the sensation that I was tampering with the dead left me feeling so anxious that by the time I'd get up from my desk, after scratching at my forearms and wrists while smoking cigarette after cigarette for hours, my skin was a bloody mess. This went on for a long time, each little fragment that I came up with (and threw into a box) bringing with it a price, by way of rashes and sores.

In my self-mortifying Catholicism, I eventually came down with the worst case of eczema, so bad that even folks in my office noticed. My arms, chest, back, and neck were raw and dry; high-strung and feeling guilty, I lived with a *picazón*—an itching—that drove me crazy and intensified every time I'd sit down to write. It got to the point of being so painful that I felt myself on the brink of giving up on that novel, if not on writing entirely. It just wasn't worth it. I was in such a bad way that no hydrocortisone cream made a difference, and I had to sleep with my arms held out over the sheets, anything to keep the fabric from touching me. (I even went to a dermatologist—and that wasn't easy. She told me that she hadn't seen such a bad case before and seemed puzzled that nothing she prescribed seemed to work.)

I was at the height of that discomfort when I had a lovely dream: Walking in a meadow, maybe in a place like Cuba, in the distance I beheld a river, and in the water, there stood a man. As I approached, I could see that it was my pop, Pascual, awaiting me. There, he told me, shaking his head: "*Porque te mortefiques?*"—"Why are you tormenting yourself so?" And with the kindest of expressions on his face, he, reaching into that water, brought up cups of it in the bowl of his hands, which he washed over my arms, my face, my back. I don't recall exactly how it resolved, but I do remember feeling a sense of relief, and, though a dream it may have been, in the morning when I awakened, my skin had cleared of it soreness.

CHAPTER 8

. . .

Our House in the Last World

My work on that book, on the weekends and on most nights after work, became a passion which my mother, amused when I'd ask her questions about Cuba or about what she recalled of my childhood, thought of as my nice new hobby, which she went along with. At the office, where I was rarely seen without a library book in hand, I always got through my duties as quickly and efficiently as I could manage, so as to allow myself more time to write, while some of my coworkers, needing the overtime pay, were far less hurried. I didn't like working past five, if it could be helped, and some days I worked so frantically that I sometimes missed lunch, my midday meals coming down to a candy bar eaten out in front of the building, followed by a few cigarettes afterward. (I always waited until past noon to have a smoke: I had watched too many people climbing the subway stairs on Fortieth Street wheezing and often stopping before reaching the top just to catch their breath, only to pause on street level to light up a cigarette.) I had long since begun to dress more casually, abandoning my ties and jackets for blue jeans and a shirt, as if I were the office Bohemian. Still, now and then, I'd get offered a better job with more duties—on one occasion, I was asked to run their office in Seattle, a position that would have paid me more money (though not enough) and came with an impressive-sounding title: VP of operations. (I turned it down.) Other opportunities arose along the way (I will not bore you), which I also turned my back on. After a while, management left me alone.

And although I am perhaps sounding rather blasé about my situation there, the fact remained that for every good day when I felt that I was doing the right thing by remaining a willing more or less middle-rung lackey, as long as I could pursue my "art"—the way I'd think about it during my more pretentious moments—there followed two or three days, sometimes a week, when I would take a good look in the mirror and realize that, approaching thirty, for all the wonderful gifts I supposedly possessed (music, drawing, writing), I was, in fact, a hack, a poseur, and, worst of all, a classic underachiever. Like my friend Tommy, I talked a good line, with the difference, however, that I believed it was he who had the real talent. (Another truth is that I considered my older brother, José, more deserving of achieving, so to speak, our family's first artistic success. Having said this, I am not even sure now if, on some unconscious level, I held myself back as some kind of crazy nod to Cuban familial order.)

. . .

Despite the tedium of my daily routines—or perhaps because of them—I began to slowly accumulate a lot of pages, of scenes and dialogue, all the while searching for a voice that somehow sounded like "me"—this fellow, a New Yoikah, with Spanish words, drawn from memory, zipping through his mind like so many *pajaritos volando*, as my mother might have put it. At a certain point, when I'd decided that I needed a formal opening, my superstitious side got the best of me. Taking a pad along, I left my apartment one Saturday morning and headed over to St. John the Divine cathedral, where I spent some five hours sitting in the knave pews, taking in the organ practice, the piped-in choral music, the ambience of that Episcopalian altar (almost as soul-reaching as a good Catholic altar) while scribbling out, in a most elemental manner, what would become the first chapter of my novel. I went back there on occasion, or, if the weather was fine, I'd sit in the cathedral's herb garden, fooling with scenes, all the while trying to fight off the nagging depression that would suddenly come over me in waves, shooting up from my knees. (The thing about being inside a church: I just didn't feel alone—even if I didn't see a single soul; just the notion that someone *might* be there peering at me from some timeless, perhaps beautiful place, bolstered my spirits enough to make it all just a bit easier.)

Of course, it was all autobiographical—the first chapters (getting a lot of it wrong) trying to reimagine my father's courtship and marriage to my mother: To help me along, I'd pore over any maps of Cuba I could find, usually in an antiquated atlas, the sort I'd come across down in Fourth Avenue's Biblo and Tannen bookstore; just perusing the cartography of Cuba, with its profusion of mysterious names, like the parts of a body, and those etched and writhing lines, sinewy as vinery, that constituted its rivers and roads and borders—all of that fed my imagination. Even if it had been years since I last stepped on that soil as a child, I'd find my pop's hometown of Jiguaní and trace its route to Holguín, and though I would just be looking over a piece of wafer-thin paper, it was as if I could go back there again. I'd remember that he had once worked as a mail carrier and imagine him riding over the countryside on a horse from farm to farm, cocoa and coffee plantations and dairy centrals abounding, a satchel of letters in his charge. I'd hear the birdsong ringing out from the forests, blue sky and verdant hills surrounding him, and the rain coming down like a waterfall at four in the afternoon, and smell the clay earth giving off a cooling perfumed exhalation, then the heat and humidity rising from the ground. Best of all, I would imagine him as a young man, tall and thin in his saddle, and astride his chestnut mare, as he'd make his leisurely way down toward the Sierra foothills: Simply put, in those bits of research, he'd come back to life!

They, of course, journeyed to America and had two sons, the older named Horacio (after my godfather) and the younger—my stand-in, or doppelganger, as the educated folks say—Hector, I took from a Puerto Rican guy about my age, who worked behind the counter of a liquor store on 105th Street. While I'm at it, I called my pop Alejo—liking its similarity to the Spanish word *lejano*, "faraway" (but also in homage to Alejo Carpentier, the Cuban writer)—and my mother, or someone much like her at any rate, Mercedes, which was my aunt Cheo's name. As for *mi tía* Maya, whom I could only see at that point through my mother's eyes, I made up the name Buita—which, I suppose, had something to do with *buitre*, "vulture."

Gradually, I began to fill those pages with the spine of what I perceived as my life, up until the time of my father's death. Yet, while I felt that I was probably making some progress toward becoming a writer, *if that's what I really wanted to do*, in that process of digging up the dead (and resurrecting them, as it were), I began to experience some very bad nights of restless sleep and disorienting dreams again. (As it would turn out, I'd go through that same upheaval with later books, but this was the worst.) My nightmares got so bad that my girlfriend at the time, a sharp lady on her way to a Ph.D. in statistical analysis at Teachers College, often thought aloud that a little psychological counseling might help me achieve a creative breakthrough and recommended that I see a therapist. But coming from a culture (*cubano*) and neighborhood (mainly working-class) where, quite frankly, something as bourgeois as therapy was not only unheard of but spurned as a rich man's indulgence, I couldn't even begin to take such a suggestion seriously. "Oh, really?" I'd say, feeling somewhat offended. And yet, often hitting a wall (sometimes literally), I eventually did.

The fellow I hooked up with happened to be a *cubano* who, as he would tell me, had left the island disguised as a priest and, coming to the States from Spain, to which he had escaped with a Vatican delegation, worked for IBM for a decade before commencing his studies for a Ph.D. in psychology, his specialty dream analysis. (He was also something of a humanist, having been mentored by Rollo May.) When I met him for the first time, probably around 1980 (I do not exactly recall), he seemed everything that I was not: tall, dark featured, somewhat macho, soulful, pensive, with a strong but charmingly Cuban accent, and he had the handsome if slightly serious face of a *Asturiano* matador. Above all, he was a Cuban from Havana, which, it surprised me to learn, actually meant a great deal to me. (Even so, I had my doubts at first, enough that once when I visited Donald Barthelme, I couldn't help but ask him if he had ever seen a shrink. His answer: "I have found them, upon occasion, useful." Drag of cigarette, gulp of drink.)

Still, it took me a long time to trust his judgment enough to allow him inside, as it were. But eventually, he became of use to me, at least in the way a priest can be when you go to confession. During those sessions, I learned a few things. It was the first time anyone had ever told me that the kind of year I spent away from my family as a four- and five-year-old would have produced an acute sense of anxiety and depression, insecurity, nightmares, mood swings, and melancholy in anyone (oh, thank you!). But it was all the more traumatic in my case, he reasoned, not only because of the nature of my illness but because of the way my circumstances had, in effect, severed me from my roots (no big news). My darkness had been further aggravated by my sense of guilt related to watching my father, or "*tu papá*," descending into a purgatory of self-injury and, the big payoff, his death—something that I, experiencing a survivor's sense of helplessness, had obviously not yet come to accept. (The flip side came when this psychoanalyst, being a *cubano* and naturally superstitious, and as someone who had, in reality, almost become a priest, cast doubts on whether anyone could be *truly dead*. He—the antiscientist and a hater of *ese comermierda* Fidel, who had outlawed the open practice of Christianity on the island—simply believed in God, and in ghosts, and in spirit transmissions. In other words, bless his soul, he was not your typical psychoanalyst.)

Though I left many of those sessions feeling better, I also wondered if I had turned into some kind of faggot. (Go to my old neighborhood bar and tell one of those wasted guys that you felt depressed and he'd look you over and say: "What you need is a drink and a fine piece of ass.") Sometimes, I felt so stupid about that therapy that I'd stop for months at a time, only to go back. Most sessions I treaded water, though; once, in what must have been a case of transference (or time travel), the interior of his office somehow became that of a rustic house in Cuba, down to its deeply green smell of palm leaves and dampened earth (swear to God). Somehow, he came to represent for me some paternal Cuban archetype, as if my father and the *abuelos* I had never known had been magically combined in him. For a few minutes, I had a sense of belonging. On the heels of that experience, which was like a waking dream, he told me, in a voice that sounded just then so much like my father's, "But don't you know, *eres cubano*. You are Cuban, after all."

While I am a little embarrassed to have disclosed such a thing, those sessions, despite the formality of the circumstance, offered me the kind of internal encouragement that I could never get anywhere else, not from my family nor any of my friends. And the process of talking about my dreams, which, in any case, always had either a terrifying or mystical aspect to them, really got the gears in my subconscious working, and even helped me come by the title of my novel one night. It was on the spine of a book, along one of the shelves, the *H*'s, in the used bookstore around the corner from my mother's apartment, where I had gone walking in a dream. Noticing my name on the spine of a book, I pulled it out and saw my novel's title for the first time: *Our House in the Last World.*

For what it's worth, I simply don't know where else that title could have come from, except my subconscious. It was just there. Having said that, I can't help but point out that were it not for two missing letters—*c* and *j*—one could spell my name, Oscar Hijuelos, from it. I know it's not much, but at the time that little coincidence, even if it is a bit forced, imbued the book with a magical glow.

Good things happened: Sending off the first chapter to a foundation, I received a grant. It paid three thousand dollars, before taxes, a fortune to me at the time, not enough to live on but an encouragement. (I do not remember what I did with that money.) The best part of receiving such a grant, the CAPS, came down to some of the folks I met through it. One of the judges, a Puerto Rican living on 115th Street in East Harlem, Edwin Vega Yunque, or Ed Vega, called me up. He was a novelist, and a fine one at that, who, however, in that climate when no major New York houses published Latinos, had gone critically unnoticed in his own city. (Or to put it differently, completely ignored by the major newspapers.) He treated me well, however, invited me over to his apartment, where, as it happened, I got to know his daughter, Suzanne, an aspiring guitar-strumming singer back then, who, I recall, often performed downtown at a place called Folk City. Ed was a Buddhist, married to an American wife, and as a writer knew just about every Latino author in the city, among them a Puerto Rican poet, Julio Marzan, and the Guatemalan David Unger, both of whom became my friends.

It was just a happy time: Through Vega, I made my debut as a writer, reading from my own work before a Latino audience at a poet's hutch up in the South Bronx—just a storefront with some folding chairs and a podium on Jerome Avenue. That initiation took place before the kind of down-home crowd you only find in the ghetto, with kids, mothers, pregnant women, old *abuelitas*, teenagers, and your rank-and-file local poets and teachers responding to your work with both seriousness and enthusiasm. (Afterward, tons of food was served from tinfoil-covered plates, along with beer.)

I also did a reading back then in an East Harlem apartment— think it was at Quincy Troupe's home: I don't recall just how long I read from my work—mostly black folks were in attendance, and while I stuck out (as always) and met one hell of a grouchy poet in Amiri Baraka, I felt really good to be hanging out with that crowd. (In a way, outside the office, I had started to lead a secret life.) And yet the reading that made the most difference, with Wesley Brown, took place up at City, where I filled in as a last-second replacement.

It turned out that the audience included one of my former class-mates at City, Karen Braziller, who had published my short story in her review, and her husband: They ran a small downtown press— Persea Books, whose offices were on Delancey Street in the same building that once housed *Mad* magazine (I remember those kinds of things). Having read from a portion of my manuscript, I think it was the husband who inquired whether I had anything else along those lines. Not long afterward, I turned up at their door in their building off Gramercy Park East with a couple of shopping bags filled with the fragments and longer narratives I'd been fooling around with over the past few years: These represented what would become, after intense amounts of work on both our parts, my first novel.

Taking a few years, the actual process went more or less smoothly, and at a far less hectic pace than what publishers would demand today. About the writing itself: typewriters, ribbons, pen and pencil, notepads, white-out, scissors, erasers, Scotch tape, and rubber cement were the tools I used to produce the final manuscript.

As for the editing, I benefited from the expertise acquired by my former colleague at CCNY, Karen Braziller, then a senior editor at E. P. Dutton but assuming those same duties for their press. Spanish proofreading was done by my friend Ed Vega, with whose corrections the novel passed muster. Finally, when it came to a cover, we settled on a painting, found in a book in the New York public library (I think), an early work, circa 1945, by Philip Guston entitled *If this be not I?* It included so many elements that figured in my novel—columns, a stoop, a figure in what looked like a chef's toque, and distant tenements—that it seemed the only choice. Over the title, a generous quote from Barthelme, while on the back one found a fairly stern picture of me, going through what I guess was a "Russian author" phase, in a beard.

But until it was actually published, even as I continued my weekly routine at TDI, that book seemed an abstraction, whose eventual quite public nature I hardly even thought about at the time. I doubt, in fact, if I could have written that book were it not for the feeling that it would somehow remain an intimate and private affair: How else could one go ahead and dive into certain personal ordeals and write about them unself-consciously? Somehow, it hadn't occurred to me that the novel would be read by some of the people it was actually about.

But it wasn't just that: I agonized over parts of *Our House* in a way that few people could ever imagine. And while I've since learned that it's not really worth draining yourself emotionally (like I am doing now in this memoir) for what some cooler-hearted folks might categorize as quaintly visceral, as a younger person, I couldn't help myself from striving to establish, through a book, some sense of just what I had experienced. Even when the catharsis you go through can leave you feeling euphoric or incredibly sad, the fact that you've allowed some fairly deep and personal secrets to escape into the world doesn't hit you until it actually gets out there, *coño!*

As the date of release approached, I had been told that one can never know about reviews, but bit by bit, over a period of a few months both before and after publication, a number of newspaper reviews, around fifteen in all (which seemed a colossal validation of my work), came out, and all favorably, about the novel. This crop included the *New York Times* Sunday book section: A certain Edith Milton reviewed *Our House* along with a novel by a Korean writer, Wendy Law-Yone, *The Coffin Tree*. And though I didn't realize it at the time, as kindly as she spoke of my writing, she was the first to pigeonhole me as an "immigrant" writer (translation: "ethnic" spokesman for the primitive people known as Hispanics in those days).

Strangely enough, when Ed Vega reviewed the novel in a literary magazine, Vega, though he really liked it, he pointed out that while it had been quite professionally produced, it was badly lacking in Spanish copyediting. ("Hey, man, uh, you remember that you proofed it?") Nevertheless, I felt so buoyed by these attentions and rich—I'd made four thousand dollars for my five years of work!—that for the first time in my life, I actually believed I had a writing future.

As it happened, so did the kindly people I worked alongside at TDI, who offered me a fairly large amount of car-card advertising space on the New York city buses at a rate that even I could afford. What's more, my art director and our production department came up with the artwork for me, while I provided the written copy, which, for the record, went: "*A family's journey through three worlds: Cuba . . . America . . . and the Unknown!*" Afterward, a friend of mine, Eddie Egan, head of Bristol-Myers's production, prevailed upon some of his Chambers Street acquaintances, who operated some of the bigger presses in the city, to do him a favor by printing those ads up for free.

In short order, not a month after the book had come out (on little cat's feet), some several thousand car-card ads for *Our House* were

276 · *Thoughts Without Cigarettes*

gracing some of the more primo bus lines in New York City, among them the much-coveted Fifth Avenue route. And so it wasn't long before a shopper heading down to Saks or Lord & Taylor on the number 5 line could look up and notice a deeply processed advertisement for *Our House* right next to one for Marlboro cigarettes. In fact, each bus would have had four or five of them. Other lines, covering Manhattan from east to west, with some extending into the Bronx and Brooklyn, on buses otherwise advertising the likes of *The Mists of Avalon*, also conveyed the not too spectacular news that a writer named Hijuelos had apparently arrived. Entertaining visions of popular success, I soon learned, however, that no matter how many buses ran ads about a novel, the books had to be in the stores. Only a few that I checked—think Scribner's and some others downtown, as well Salters on 113th and the Book Forum in my neighborhood—had copies. Now and then, someone from the office would come over to my desk with a copy of *Our House* for me to sign. And what I usually heard was this: "Oh, but I had to look all ovah the place, just to find it." (This, before the days of Amazon and ebooks and iPads.)

But people couldn't have been nicer. I got bottles of booze in the interoffice mail, with notes of congratulations, and one of my partners, Charlie, in subway clocks even took me out to lunch: "So you really fuckin' did it, didn't you, kid?" Folks from my neighborhood also appreciated the effort, given that I had captured something of the way they came up. And while very few of them bought my book—I can count those who did on one hand—my pal Richard purchased two, for himself and his brother Tommy, who, as I soon learned, had formed his own opinion about it.

I bumped into Tommy in the park one afternoon, and the first thing he did was to slap me five.

"Good for you, my man," he told me. "I read your book, and I liked it, though I would have done a lot of things differently." Tommy took a drag of a cigarette. "And better, you hear?"

"If you say so." I looked off, leaves whisked up by the wind in pinwheels along the cracked park pavement.

"But the thing is, that novel doesn't really count 'cause, like, it's your story, and real books are about other shit, you know?"

"Yeah, maybe," I said.

That day, I made sure not to seem at all above him in any way: In fact, I told him that I couldn't wait to see what he was writing himself—even offered to help him in whatever fashion I could. But it was as if it didn't matter. Lighting one of his Tareytons with the butt of another, and offering me a sip from his can of beer, he said, "Nah, I'm all right—don't even think about it, man." Then we talked about hanging out again, and, parting, we kind of embraced. Leaving him, I hadn't the slightest notion that I'd never see that beautiful and rambunctious dude again.

. . .

My older brother, for what it's worth, made no bones about telling me that my mother had been upset by the book (as if she could read it?), that she could not bear any of the passages about Pop's drinking, and that, on top of it all, I had gotten a lot of stuff wrong. And he thought that my portrayals of family friends like Olga were offensive—that I had no business describing her (or someone like her) as the kind of vainglorious *cubana* who would parade around in negligees and brassieres, and undress, to reveal her fabulous figure, in our living room.

"You know that she's going to feel offended by that, don't you?" he told me.

In the end, I believed him, and took to skulking up my block whenever I'd visit my mother. Worried about running into any of the folks I had portrayed, I had almost gone ducking behind a car at the sight of Olga coming out of my mother's building one day. But she saw me: "Oscarito, come over here!" she ordered. I did.

"Why are you avoiding me? I'm not going to bite you."

"I know."

"Well, there's something you should hear," she said, with the severity of the Old World Spaniard she, with her curled Coco Chanel hairdo and intensely dark features, resembled. "I read your book, and I will tell you, *mi vida*, that I loved it!" And she flashed me a sweet, toothy smile. "And thank you for putting me in it—you got me right."

Indeed, Olga, in her sixties, well past her prime by then, seemed to have enjoyed the fact that I had more or less described the way she had once been as a shapely Cuban bombshell, whose mere glance left men breathless. But she did chastise me about other things. "You were too hard on your mother. I don't blame you," she said. "She could be difficult, but you were still too hard on her." She did not mention my pop, though she must have been thinking about him as well. Happily though, as I went by her on the stoop, on my way to see my mother, whose face peered out at me from behind the venetian blinds, Olga gave me a kiss on the cheek and a slap to my bottom. Her final appraisal, as I blushed: "We're proud of you. *Fue un libro, muy muy lindo!*"

And my mother? As my brother had surmised, she wasn't too pleased by whatever she had managed to read of that novel. Having come a long way since my childhood, in terms of her ability to understand written English, she had made it a monthly ritual to visit the corner bookstore and return with a bag full of romance novels, which she'd go through methodically, with, I believe, the help of a Spanish-English dictionary. Otherwise she passed her days working in some Harlem-based version of a temp agency like Manpower, or else she, knowing every Latina in the neighborhood, made some extra money watching the comings and goings of customers in a friend's clothing shop along Broadway. However she spent her days, she seemed to have enormous amounts of time to read, though I think it took her weeks after I had given her an inscribed copy of *Our House* to get around to deciphering the text. Once she began to, however, she became quite circumspect about it. The only things she ever had to say about that novel? "Why did you have to write me in that way? *Yo no fui tan mala!* I wasn't that bad!" And, as I recall: "Yes, your father was a good man who could be angry with me sometimes. *Pero me quería mucho.* But he loved me very much."

(Of course there was more to her reactions than those few words: Sometimes when I'd come over to see her with some Chinese food from Broadway, while sitting across the kitchen table from her, I'd catch her looking at me wistfully, as she used to when I was a child, as if I were a stranger who had somehow learned all about her. At least once, she told me, in such a moment: "But I never wanted to hurt Pascual in any way.")

She once mentioned that she could never get past a certain point (I never knew if the text became too difficult for her, or whether she could take only so much of her own life, however roughly, thrust back in her face), but whatever she may have felt about that book, my mother took the trouble to carefully wrap her copy in plastic so that it would not become worn-out on the shelf. Learning how impressed her *New York Times*–reading friends, like the Zabalas sisters and classy Chaclita, were by the fact that I had been reviewed there, she took to keeping a copy of that notice in her purse, ever willing to show it off to anyone she bumped into. Obviously her pride over the fact that she had a published author as a son overrode any reservations or hurt that my mother had surely felt over what she perceived to be its content.

． ． ．

For my part, I can recall riding the subways uptown from work and thinking that even if that book couldn't ever sell very much—I think maybe only fifteen hundred copies had been printed—I had begun, in some small way, to make something of myself. But aside from that feeling—ever so fleeting at three o'clock on a dreary afternoon— virtually nothing else had changed in my life. Though I had avoided the fate of so many would-be writers, I kept at my full-time job.

Still, I had my occasional moment of glory. Not long after *Our House* came out, I got a call from the Endicott bookstore on Columbus Avenue and Eighty-first, then one of the great independents in Manhattan. Their manager, a lady named Susan Berkholtz, asked me if I wouldn't mind coming by one morning to sign some books, and since I hadn't ever done anything of that nature before, and because it felt like such a professional thing to do, I eagerly accepted. Leaving my office at about eleven, I made my way uptown. When I came in sight of that store's two massive front windows, I almost fell over: One of the windows had been filled with pyramids of *Our House in the Last World*, copies adorning the wall in a row, and nothing else. It seemed the fulfillment of a dream, and, once inside, I passed the next hour or so by the front counter euphorically signing my book for the occasional customer—perhaps twenty in all, not a bad turnout. Afterward, Ms. Berkholtz, later an agent best known for representing Latino authors, had me sign some stock copies, and that also left me floating on air. Beaming with accomplishment, I sipped a cup of coffee, and thanking all her employees, I walked out of the store sometime after one, intending to go back to work.

But once I got outside again, I couldn't help feeling overwhelmed by the moment. I was filled with such pride that instead of heading downtown, I thought, "To hell with it," and hailed a taxi instead, giving the driver my mother's 118th Street address.

I found her in the kitchen preparing a big pot of lentil soup, one of her favorite meals, as she had become quite a health food nut by then, and one bent on preserving herself into eternity—she was just a few years short of seventy. (Her dresser drawers, aside from containing a number of artifacts from her life with my pop, and religious pamphlets and rosaries, also brimmed over with Spanish-language magazines about health and diets.) When I walked in, after giving three quick trills of the *timbre*, she was surprised—and vaguely delighted—to see me in the middle of the day. She felt put out, however: My mother hadn't gotten around to making herself up or bothered to get dressed. She wore only a robe and seemed as if she had not awakened too long before, and though she told me to sit down, and started to putter about the stove, I just said: "Mamá, get dressed, I want to show you something."

"*Sí?*" she asked.

"*Sí, mamá*, a surprise."

"Ah, *una sorpresa*," she replied, rather happily.

It took her a while: Years later, I'd learn the hard way that her side of the family had arthritic maladies in their blood, and as she moved deliberately but slowly about her bedroom, getting dressed, I could hear her giving little cries of "*ay, ay, ay!*" Finally, she had gotten herself together, and, escorting her down the street, rather impatiently, as I couldn't wait for her to see that window, we finally reached the corner, where I hailed another taxi. By then, because of my mother's rheumatic condition, it was always an operation getting her in and out of any vehicle, but did I care? My moment had arrived! No matter how often my mother asked me where we were going, and why, the only thing I could say to her, and gleefully so (you know, like a good son), was that she would soon enough see something to make her happy and proud of me.

So we hurried downtown, and even though only an hour at most had passed since I'd left that store, by the time we pulled up to the curb, the window had already been changed, Umberto Eco's *The Name of the Rose* now in the place of honor so briefly given to me.

Having no choice but to take her inside, the only thing I could show her were a few of my books on a shelf. The staff seemed embarrassed, as did I, but afterward I took my mother to a pastry shop nearby and bought her some napoleons, the sort my pop occasionally brought home. I don't think she ever had a clue as to how crestfallen I felt: At least I got some insight, right there and then, into the nature of that business.

As for those bus ads? They ran for about three months, and though my novel did not fly off the shelves, the enticement that I would produce a similar advertisement and space for a paperback induced a fellow named Pat O'Connor, at Washington Square Press, to spring for the paperback rights, a big twenty-five hundred dollars (half of which I split with the publisher). In exchange, they'd benefit from another ad campaign. I recall riding buses and seeing people looking up and checking out that advertisement, and occasionally I'd run into a friend who'd noticed it, but if it made my name and book known to the public in any way, I wasn't particularly aware of it.

Only once did it make a real difference. I think the paperback ads had started to run in the autumn of 1984, and that same October, I came down with another one of my horrific flus. Having become the sort of person who would do everything in his power to avoid seeing a doctor, I reluctantly decided to drag my sorry ass over to St. Luke's emergency room one night, but only after I had started coughing up blood. (That scared me: Despite my plaguelike symptoms—bad stomach, aching bones, diarrhea, scorched throat, and burning nose—I had managed to continue smoking my Kool cigarettes until I could barely swallow.) Once I got to that waiting room, filled with every variety of junkie, alcoholic, stab victim, abused wife, and sick child, as well as a contingent of bloodied and bruised homeless people, I fell into an immediate gloom. Not only did going there again remind me of my childhood visits to that place, but I knew that however bad I felt, I'd have to spend half the night waiting.

Up by the desk, manned by a Puerto Rican nurse who had the hardened demeanor of someone who had seen every possible permutation of human suffering, her porcelain face a mask of cinnamon indifference, I filled out a medical questionnaire and handed it to her. As she looked it over, her brows rose with interest: "Hijuelos? Where would I have seen this name before?" I didn't connect anything with it and shrugged. But then something hit her: "Oh, yeah, I know, I seen it on a bus—the numbah eleven Amsterdam line— could that be?"

"Uh-huh."

"You wrote a book, is that right?"

"That's me."

"Well, for God's sake—good for you." And she smiled. "Lord, I wish I could do that—oh, the things I've seen! You wouldn't believe it." Then she took a good long look at me—at my deathly sweaty pallor, my bloodshot eyes, my drooping body—and, leaning forward, confided: "Tell you what, to save you time, I'm gonna admit you right away, okay, honey?"

"You kidding?"

"Why would I kid an author"—she pronounced it Arthur—"like you?"

I ended up getting out of there about an hour later, and it took me almost a week to get better; and when I did, I dropped a copy of the paperback of *Our House* off at that ward, inscribing it to that admitting nurse, whose name, it turned out, for all her toughness, was Daisy.

And that, ladies and gentlemen, was about the extent to which those bus ads helped me.

. . .

In the interim, a few interesting things happened: At one point, enriched by my final advance of some eight hundred dollars or so, I flew out to Southern California to visit my former down-the-hall neighbors from Eighty-third and, while staying in their complex in San Diego, began a poolside romance with a twentyish divorcée in progress who happened to be a former Miss Los Angeles. I won't dwell on the tawdrier details, though I will say that after I had come back to New York, we often spoke by telephone in the evenings. As it happened, these took place during a period when, for reasons involving one of my cousin's husbands, my line was tapped.

You see, back in 1983, the FBI had listed my cousin Miriam's husband, Eduardo Arocena, who had stayed in our apartment back when, as their number one most wanted fugitive. He was suspected of having been the head (and founder) of an anti-Castro organization, Omega Seven, and of ordering or carrying out the assassination of a Cuban diplomat. Personally, I found it hard to believe that Eddie, *un hombre muy callado*, a quiet and gentle man, could be behind such a thing, but the truth was that he had been on the lam, as they'd say in gangster movies, for some time (though it had not stopped him from calling me up the previous Christmas to wish me well, while also proclaiming, "*Viva Cuba libre!*")

Eventually, the search became so intense that the FBI sent two officers over to 118th Street to interview my mother, and though she had fallen back on the claim that she spoke "too leetle Engeleesh," one of the officers, a very well dressed American "Negrito," as she described him, naturally hit the clutch and slipped into a ridiculously fluent Castellano—Castilian Spanish—that dazzled my mother. (That's what she mainly talked about for weeks—about how that

American black man had spoken such a refined Spanish.) In the end, she had nothing to tell them; she certainly did not know of his whereabouts—why would she?

Nor did I, but that did not stop the FBI from messing with my phone. Suddenly, I'd pick it up and hear all these clicks and sonic hums, and switches—even voices in the incredible distance, ever so faint but audible, saying things like "Roger that" and "Roger out"—whistles too, sometimes so loudly that I'd have to pull my head away. (My brother and mother experienced the same disturbances.) This bugging happened to coincide with my Southern California romance. Calling me nightly, she loved to go recount the details of what we had once done, what she would do the next time she saw me, the places where she ached inside, how she was touching herself just thinking about me, and, along the way, moaning as she'd breathlessly bring herself around—in short, a bit of phone sex. What those agents made of it, I can't say, but on a few occasions, I'd hear a click, and static and screeches, as someone (I think) listened, until the poor guy on the other end couldn't take it anymore.

As for Eduardo, the poor soul, eventually apprehended and tried, was sent to jail, where he continues, I think unjustifiably, to linger to this day.

. . .

All in all, I really didn't have much to complain about. As a Latino writer—no matter how I looked upon myself, that's what I happened to be—I had already done quite well. My book had come out with a New York house, a very rare thing; I had been reviewed in the *Times*, an even *rarer* occurrence for a Latino writer; and, best of all, along the way, I found a place, however peripherally, with my own special community of writers. Not just the inner-city thing with friends like Julio Marzan and Ed Vega, but in a scene so erudite, yet social, that it was to become known as a hub of Latin American literature in New York City.

Situated in a McKim, Mead & White Georgian brownstone on Sixty-eighth Street and Park Avenue were the offices of the Americas Society, an organization dedicated to the promotion of cultural ties between the United States and our hemispheric partners: Canada, the Caribbean Islands, and Central and South America. Also known as the Center for Inter-American Relations, its ground floor boasted an art gallery, whose shows were mainly dedicated to exhibitions culled from the Latino diaspora to our south. On an upper floor, reached by a winding robber-baron staircase, were several ornately appointed salons in which all manner of programs, from music recitals to business lectures, along with a profusion of poetry and prose readings, literary panels, and such took place nearly every night of the week, each event followed by cocktails.

I'd first caught wind of that place while lugging my corrected manuscript of *Our House* around a book fair on the East Side. A friend had suggested that I introduce myself to a woman at one of the booths, a director of programs at the Americas Society, Rosario Santos, a transplanted Bolivian who couldn't have been kinder when I shyly (terrified of the notion of having to speak Spanish with her) introduced myself and, eventually, left her that copy. In turn, she had passed it on to her deputy there, a vivacious, wildly attractive young Hispanist, a certain Lori Carlson. One of those rare creatures unable to resist helping others, she, upon reading *Our House*, later hosted me as the special guest speaker at a program of her design called Books and Breakfast. On that occasion, just after the novel had been published, I gave a reading from it and answered questions for a small gathering of mainly Latin American businessmen, all before the hour of nine in the morning, after which I went off to work, attending to my subway clocks. She also assigned a *cubano*, Enrique Fernandez, to write a critical—and as it would turn out, quite positive—piece on *Our House* for the literary journal she edited, *Review*, an honor, as far as I was concerned, given the incredible caliber of the authors whose work she championed in its pages.

Ms. Carlson, whose Grace Kelly looks and sweet temperament turned more than a few heads, also officiated over a number of literary evenings in which a nobody like me could not only attend *charlas*—lectures—by some of the most prominent writers of the Latin-American boom, but afterward find himself rubbing shoulders (bumping into literally, the rooms were so crowded) with the likes of Mario Vargas Llosa, José Donoso, Luisa Valenzuela, Carlos Fuentes, Elena Poniatowska, Octavio Paz, Ernesto Cardenal, and, among so many others, the towering, Lincolnesque Julio Cortázar. (Which is not to say that there weren't any non-Latinos around. Two I can recall were the poet/memorist William Jay Smith and the novelist William Kennedy, fresh from winning a Pulitzer for *Ironweed*. He couldn't have been more cordial and respectful of me, and took pains to pronounce my last name as accurately as he, married to a Puerto Rican, could. Both he and Smith were real gents.)

I also made the acquaintance of some Cubans there, among them Héberto Padilla the poet, as well as the greatest of Cuban novelists, Guillermo Cabrera Infante (a wonderful man), whom the center had first introduced to an American audience. Other Cubans turned up, sometimes from the island, like Pablo Armando Fernandez, but since one side always boycotted the other, you never saw the pro- and anti-Castro writers in the same room at any given time. (Somehow, after attending a reading by Fernandez, I met his father, who, at hearing my story of my Cuban/American conflicts—which is what I tended to talk about with some folks—he told me, "Well, being half-Cuban is better than not being Cuban at all.") Another Cuban writer, who would become most famous posthumously in a film, *Before Night Falls*, Reinaldo Arenas, thin and wan, and wretchedly broke, also frequented the center and had gotten his first job in New York, teaching writing, through its office. I happened to have met Renaldo, whose short and slight body was topped by an implausibly large head, his skin quite pocked, his handsome features ever so tender, in Books & Co. on the East Side one evening. We spoke (in Spanish—how I did it, I do not know) about the fact that he had grown up in Holguín, where my mother came from; I told him I had just published a novel, and he seemed quite touched to meet a kindred soul. (I gave him a copy of *Our House*, which I got off the shelf and paid for. He accepted it, while confessing he couldn't read English. "*Pero gracias, hombre,*" he told me, handing me his card in exchange.)

Most impressively, the center also hosted one of my idols, Jorge

Luis Borges, whom I met briefly, and whose hangdog but beatific otherworldly face I have obviously not forgotten. Altogether, those fetes, which welcomed everyone, were of a moment that would never be seen again, a moment when such a place, like the Americas Society, afforded two worlds, that of Latino and non-Latino, the opportunity to come together and celebrate the grandeur of a shared culture. (I am not certain of too many things, but I will venture to say that I doubt the word *spic* had ever been uttered, or even thought of, in that building.) Compared to any American literary cocktail party I'd ever attend, those evenings seem now like some distant dream.

I may have had an ordinary job, and I may have had a hundred doubts about myself as a Latino, and all kinds of gripes about a million things, but, lordy, when I'd leave that center, I'd feel really good about my Latin roots, and in a way I never had before, even if, by the next afternoon, after trudging through one subway station after the other and catching a few stiletto glances stabbing into the back of my head, from Latinos who didn't like whitey, that glow of belonging— and relating to that literature—might ebb and eventually fade. All I know is this: Since those days, I've never again experienced a literary scene so inclusive, nor so nurturing through the sheer heft of intellectual sharing, nor one in which being a Latino writer really counted for something.

CHAPTER 9

. . .

Roma

In the autumn of 1984, when I had become a member of PEN—a big deal to me—I was recruited to partake in a gala reading with some two dozen other authors, commemorating their first International Writers for Peace day, held downtown in that organization's West Broadway headquarters. For the program itself, each writer read some statement or poem or bit of prose relating to the notion of peace; and while I had huddled with my friend Richard, from my neighborhood, coming up with a selection of quotes from the ancient world, of the "Thou shall beat thy sword into a ploughshare" variety, and had worked hard to put together what I had hoped would be an interesting presentation, I soon decided that I had perhaps put in too much effort, when walking into that jammed room, I overheard the poet Jane Cooper, gravely intoning, and with a quivering voice, the lyrics to "Blowin' in the Wind."

I turned heads there, mainly because, of all the writers on hand that day, I had been the only one to show up wearing a suit and tie. (Norman Mailer, for example, appeared at the podium looking quite hungover and wearing what seemed to be a wine-stained turtleneck sweater.) Sitting down next to Allen Ginsberg, he had nodded, smiling, at me. When his turn came, he got up and read some crazy-sounding poem of easy beatnik rhyme—something that had phrasing along the *Nagasaki, Kill the Nazi, Kamikazi* line which the audience of die-hard lefty aesthetes deeply appreciated, but which I, as usual, didn't get. (No offense to Allen Ginsberg fans, but I essentially thought the guy had a racket, though I will admit I was about as uptight as any young author could be.) I remember, however, feeling that I had made a connection with Ginsberg, and in what I considered a friendly Cuban manner, I patted him on the shoulder when he came down from the stage and took a seat beside me again.

When my turn came, I threw everyone in that room by reading from my selection of quotes about war and peace from antiquity. And while it was probably not the most exciting thing I could have done, at least it was brief, which, I've since learned, crowds really like; Ginsberg himself seemed to appreciate the effort. In fact, if anyone had seemed to have watched me carefully, it was he, with whom I made bespec-tacled eye contact quite often from the podium, Ginsberg nodding repeatedly at my words. Later, when I returned to my seat, he even tapped me on the knee. Afterward, however, when I got a chance to speak directly to Mr. Ginsberg at the cocktail party, he seemed puzzled that I had even approached him. He asked me two questions: "Which magazine are you with?" To which I answered, "None." And then, more surprisingly, he asked, "What are you doing here?" which really threw me, since I had been sitting next to him, had been introduced as the Cuban-American author of *Our House*, and had thought him rather attentive during my little discourse. It was in that moment that I first learned that a lot of pretending went on at such events, and that even writers, not to be confused with anyone else, were required to first and foremost wear the appropriate Bohemian apparel.

· · ·

And another moment I still cherish today? Through my publisher, I believe, I had been paired to give a reading with Bernard Malamud at a Presbyterian church fund-raiser on the West Side; I am not even sure of the exact occasion, think it might have been for the Columbia Literary Review, but I felt so honored to be sharing the podium with Malamud that it has remained one of my favorite readings to this day. The poor man, I should mention, was then dying from cancer, and so far gone as to be nearly unable to communicate, so deep was his depression. But he was thoroughly professional and, with some difficulty, read from a new work in progress, his age-mottled hands trembling and his voice wavering and low. Somehow he soldiered through. Afterward, when I had the chance to speak with him, he seemed half-dead to the world, until, taken by the devastating smile of a female friend who had come along with me, he found a momentary resurrection. Looking into her eyes, Malamud, buoyed by her presence, seemed to have slipped out from his suffering frame of mind, his posture straightening, his voice, though still delicate, more lively, his eyes for the first time that evening losing their melancholy. I have no idea of what they spoke about, something about old movies perhaps, but once she left him, he underwent a transformation back to the Malamud beside me, the writer who, like his characters, lived in a universe that always spoke to me, of pain and longings and grief. It was probably his last public reading.

And perhaps you're wondering whether any Cubans ever showed up to my readings. They sometimes did. Even back then, I had a little Cuban fan base, word getting around, mainly among the females, longtime New Yorkers mostly, who, like my parents and aunts, had come here long before the revolution (they were the Cubans I mainly knew). But every so often, as I'd give a reading, I'd look out and spot someone, arms folded severely across his chest and with a no-nonsense seriousness upon his face, a man affiliated with some anti-Castro organization, on hand to check me out: I could always tell—and for years afterward I'd know them from their severe disappointment that my writing rarely commented on or openly attacked Fidel Castro or his regime; my work just wasn't that way, and as a consequence, I have sometimes seen these kinds of *cubanos* get up, disgusted, and leave the room while I happened to be in midsentence.

. . .

For all of that, however, once the luster of my debut faded, I fell back into the routine of my days at the agency—living for the weekends, occasionally plodding off to the library at lunchtime (I will forever feel grateful to the nice Puerto Rican librarian who had ordered seven copies of *Our House* for the Mid-Manhattan branch.) Only occasionally did I feel as if my life had changed, as when some creative chief from another agency, knowing me from around and remembering that *Times* review, would call me up to offer me a job as a copywriter. In fact, for a brief time, I was tempted to move over to Y&R—which was just across the street—but somehow couldn't bring myself to do it. By then, I had slipped into what I suppose might be called a postpartum depression, and while I had started to fool around with a new novel, something about a Cuban building superintendent named Cesar Castillo, lingering in the perpetual underworld of a basement (*la ánima del Pascual?*), I began to feel that my book's publication had been a fluke, viz., thinking that had I not known the editor from CCNY, nothing would have happened in the first place. And, without realizing it, I still strongly identified with my pop.

Mainly, I'd become melancholic like him, out of the blue. I have the distinct memory of riding the subway home and thinking, as I held on to one of those poles in the center of the car, that I was probably hanging on to the same one that my pop did as he'd ride back, in a forlorn state of his own, with his scent of meat, cigarettes, and booze, from work. (Same line, same cars, the same passing rush of tunnel girders in the darkness; why not?) And it would hit me that perhaps my life would never really be different from his, and all at once, I'd wish to God that I could become someone else.

I had been feeling especially awful one October night in 1984, another of those cold miserable New York evenings, when the black slickened streets, runny with distending lights and misery (now I'm thinking like Ginsberg, *carajo!*) seemed to define the world. I'd always found blue Mondays hard to take—like just about everyone else who worked downtown—but after I'd turned thirty-three, an age that held a lot of symbolic weight for me as a Catholic, and my life, after the publication of that book, had seemed to flatten out again, I didn't really know what the hell to do with myself, except to continue on in a job from which I would never be fired—for they knew they had someone smart on the cheap. With that realization, the prospect of trudging through yet another workweek on automatic pilot, as it were, became more and more of a burden. At thirty-three, I was old enough to feel that I hadn't a whole lot of time to piss away, and though I thought about quitting nearly every week, the company's generosity with those transit ads (and well-wishes for my career, such as it was), and the fact that I really didn't have anything to fall back on, nor the nerve to just say "fuck it," kept me there, though on some days I'd feel like I was going out of my mind with boredom.

It was one of those evenings when just about everything seemed off, faces elongating in crazy animal ways; the pizzeria guy, stout and sturdy, looking to me like a bull through the glare of his window; the panhandlers coming off like jackals and seeming more devious than usual as I'd just walk on ("Hey, baldy, I'm talking to you!"); the subway stairwells, gutters, and sidewalks smelling pissier (and shittier) than before, and when not even the notion of buying myself a few dollar bottles of wine and smoking half a pack of cigarettes, while watching some bad horror flick on TV, cheered me up. One of those what-on-earth-are-you-doing-with-your-life evenings. I was in the kind of mood where just to hear *español* spoken on the street irritated me—as in *"What the fuck did you all ever do for me?"* When I walked into the dollar shop to buy some toilet paper, even the gossiping sweet-natured old Latina ladies by the counter, whom I generally felt charmed by, got on my nerves. (So maybe I was a white motherfucker after all.) Just a lousy night altogether, and on top of it all, I couldn't believe that I'd have to get up and start all over again the next morning. (I'd leave at eight thirty-five; somehow I'd always get to the office, hustling, by nine.)

In this lousy frame of mind, I walked into my building entranceway and got my mail. Occasionally I'd receive a "fan" letter—in the same way I kept every review for that book, so I did the letters, maybe ten in all, which I'd answer with as much grace and gratitude as

I could muster. Mainly I'd contend with the same roster of bills—"*Bullshit, bullshit, bullshit,*" I would say to myself while flipping through them.

That evening the mail included a creamy envelope of some thickness, whose return addressee was an organization I had only just recently heard about, the American Academy and Institute of Arts and Letters. I couldn't begin to imagine what it might say. I was sitting in my living room, smoking a cigarette, when I tore it open, and even as I reread the thing, I could hardly believe its contents. I must have read it a half dozen times when I finally realized its significance. That letter, quite simply, offered me an extraordinary opportunity: Would I, the recipient, be willing and available to accept, if so offered to him, a paid year's residence as a writing fellow at the American Academy in Rome? The fellowship would come with a monthly stipend, a travel allowance, living quarters in a villa, all my meals, and a studio. It was to begin in the autumn of 1985. Among the things that hit me in those moments was my recollection of a photograph I had once seen of Ralph Ellison, taken in the sunny courtyard—or *cortile*—of the academy's villa. I had always thought that going to a place like that would be a dream, and you know what? I didn't even have to think twice about it. Would I be available? Who were they kidding?

At the awards ceremony itself, in May, which was held in the institute's amphitheater, after a rather tony luncheon with various other artists and award recipients on the institute's stately grounds on 155th Street and Audubon Terrace, I received my Rome Prize. The presenter was a rather plastered, towering, and hunched-over John Galbraith. Beforehand, I'd been told that he would first read a citation about my work and then shake my hand, but either he forgot about it or they had changed their minds. "Oh, to be a young man again, going to Rome," he told me, with a handshake. "How enviable." And that was it.

Still I waited for him to say something else, and when he gestured for me to leave the stage, with a shoving motion of his upraised palms, I looked out at the audience and shrugged, cocking my head about, as if he were some kind of nut, and brought down the house.

I also remember Jerome Robbins smiling warmly and winking at me as I proceeded offstage, and hearing my mother occasionally, sitting out somewhere in the audience with her friend Chaclita, emoting— "*Ay! Ay!*"—during the ceremonies. I recall urinating in the turn-of-the-twentieth-century Mark Twain–era urinals downstairs between Harold Bloom and Robert Penn Warren and feeling as if I had finally arrived!

It was quite a pleasant affair, really the high point of my life to that point, and the first "graduation" ceremony in which I was involved that my mother ever attended. (They even had a photograph of me, along with some samples of my manuscript in a display case, which impressed her very much.) I am not quite sure what my mother made of that rather haughty crowd, but she enjoyed the hors d'oeuvres and wine (unusual for her to drink at all) and nearly fainted at the sight of Jacqueline Onassis, whom, at one point during the reception afterward, she discovered standing just next to her.

"*Ay, pero por Dios,*" she exclaimed, patting her chest while holding her gold neck chain crucifix in hand. "If only your *papá* was alive to see this!" Ms. Onassis, for her part, was gracious enough to notice my mother's genuine excitement and smiled at her. For months, all my mother talked about "*Jackie y yo*" with whomever she bumped into, and years later, having decided to try her hand at writing a novel, she came up with a wild scenario about time travel, in which Onassis figured as the reincarnation of Marie Antoinette, or something crazy like that.

. . .

That next summer before my thirty-fourth birthday, after a heartbreaking farewell to my friends at TDI—after nearly nine years with that company, I was too sentimental for my own good and may have broken down at the party they had thrown for me—I went off to Europe for the first time in my life.

Flying to Madrid and lugging a valise that I'd stupidly filled with books, few clothes, and, among other things, a passport holder stuck under my shirt, I didn't have the vaguest idea of what I was doing. But arriving in the land of my forebears, I felt surprised by just how much my Spanish blood meant to me. It just hadn't occurred to me before. (These were sentiments that the Spaniards, in their atheism, their newly digested post-Franco freedom, and their hard-nosed somberness probably found quaintly bemusing.) I was stunned to see so many fair-skinned and blond Spaniards, especially in the north (*"They look like us,"* I wrote my brother.) I lived happily, ineptly on occasion. It thrilled me to hear *castellano* as only the Spaniards could speak it, with all their Arabic flourishes, the *theta* and *rrrrrr*s rolling like a waterfall (yes, I know I'm pushing things.) While thinking that I couldn't really speak much Spanish, I found myself forced to use what I knew, and after about two weeks there, while staying in pensions and having to navigate the markets and shops and museums of that city, I started speaking and writing it—even sent my mother a postcard entirely composed in Spanish, detailing my "adventures," such as they were. The younger women in Spain, it seemed to me, were either femmes fatales, like some of the shapely Guardia Civil ladies I saw standing on the corners in their tight khaki uniforms, holding machine guns, or intellectual, schoolteacherly sorts—at least the ones who spoke to me. It took me a while to let go of certain images in my head—like the electric dusted air of the subways, sleazy Times Square, the projects, the shit of certain neighborhoods, and, of course, that other something that I'd always carried around with me, the baggage I had from my upbringing. I liked it that life in Spain went a certain way, that I didn't ever have to worry about getting jumped and that I didn't have to keep my radar turned on or go through all the endless nonsense of seeming perfectly calm when finding myself in a lousy neighborhood, as often happened to me in New York, though once I went south, I couldn't help but feel a distrust for the inordinately friendly and aggressive Moroccans, who always seemed to be on the make. (I was right, at least about the younger ones, whom I'd encounter hanging around the bus stations or following me down a street, calling out, "You speak English? . . . *Etes-vous Français? Esperate, Aleman!*") After years of adhering to an early schedule, I didn't have to worry about getting up at any particular hour, and when I finally got around to breakfast, I'd usually end up in a bar, where I'd smoke a few cigarettes, eat a buttered roll, and drink brandy with my coffee. (God bless any nation where the workers begin their day in that manner.) For lunch, living off tourist-menu specials, I ate more rosemary grilled *merluza* and olive-oil-drenched potatoes and drank more cheap red Spanish wine than I ever would again in my life. Along the way, I became grateful for any opportunity to engage with the Spaniards. Once when two young (and very fine) girls came up to me in their school uniforms on the street selling lottery tickets to raise money for some orphanage, I didn't even hesitate to buy them, so thrilled did I feel that they looked me in the eyes and presumed that I was a Spaniard. In the Prado, where Picasso's *Guernica* hung behind a massive plate of glass, protected by two machine gun–bearing soldiers (I'd never seen so many weapons being held out in plain sight before), and where, in the pretentious manner of the daydreaming young, I decided that Velazquez's *Las Meninas* had to be my favorite painting of all time, I'd sit around for hours in the overheated rooms, feeling as if I'd won a million dollars in some contest.

At the Escorial, that storied royal residence north of Madrid, I felt the heaviness of Spanish history everywhere around me, and it made me sad. I already tended to think about all the people who had died in this world, and in Spain, perhaps because of the aged cripples and maimed survivors of the civil war who were still to be seen begging on the streets everywhere, the fleeting nature of existence followed me about like a ghost. In Seville, I wandered about the Gypsy neighborhoods, on the outskirts of the city, whose passageways and streets were too narrow for police cars to go through, seeking out bars where I might hear authentic flamenco music. (It was a miracle that someone didn't rob me.) In Guernica, my heart stopped: I had gone into a slot machine parlor one evening, feeling smugly self-assured that even if I had been rarely accepted as a Cuban Latino in the states, I could at least pass as a Spaniard, *más o menos*, in Spain when an old man cast a dirty look my way, and then, further shattering my delusions, raised his right arm, his palm held straight up, and saluted me, saying: "*Sig Heil!*" Then he spat on the floor.

On a long train ride in an acrid car reeking of tobacco, animals, and soot across Gallicia, I ached with an inexplicable feeling of belonging (my pop's side of the family were Gallegos after all) and yet, at the same time, I could not produce a single name of a relative or a town to visit there. (That ached as well.) On such a train, one couldn't help but fall into conversation with the farmers who traveled on them: One such farmer, feeling deeply touched (the more educated the Spaniard, the less touched he or she felt by my nostalgia for those roots) by the fact that I was by ancestry a *paisano*, and thinking me a rich American, offered to sell me a farm of some twenty hectares for (converting from pesetas) roughly fourteen thousand dollars. (How interesting that would have been, had I had that kind of money.) Later, I made like a pilgrim, visiting the sacred cathedral in Santíago, but oddly, though I'd been told that it was a very special place—even some of the guidebooks said that it had a mystical air—I, who considered myself cut very much from my mother's cloth, and therefore superstitious, felt nothing at all in that place. Among my other excursions in Gallicia, I took a ferry out to *la isla de* Cies, an island off the Atlantic coast of Spain that had been reconfigured with dunes and trees and white sands and driftwood in the manner of California beaches after Franco, smitten by a visit there and, as a dictator, able to move mountains if he so liked, had ordered it done. I saw my first nude beaches there and narrowly escaped getting beat up by a gaggle of older Spanish women who had happened along the same spot overlooking a cliff where I, *el stupido,* had stood posing before a camera on which I had set off a timer; as those women approached, and I ducked into the bushes, the camera, set on top of a rock, clicked as if I had been waiting, in fact, to get shots of their tanned, spectacularly drooping bodies. (During the two-hour journey back, I had to contend with their accusations, their scornful expressions, and the fact that they told anyone they could that I was "the one with the filthy mind." Did I care? All I knew was that I wasn't standing on a subway platform somewhere deep in Brooklyn on a hot summer afternoon.)

Traveling all around the Iberian Peninsula, I ended my Spanish journey in Barcelona, where, indeed, many of those Catalans were as fair (and sometimes balding) as I. Roaming its streets, I couldn't help but wonder where my maternal grandfather's family had once lived, or whether my mother and her sisters had been aware of such landmarks as the Parque Guell or the other insanely ornate buildings Gaudí had designed, during their visits there as children. I wandered the old quarters of the city endlessly, bought countless novels from the kiosks off the Ramblas, editions of works by García Marquez, Borges, Italo Calvino, Vargas Llosa, and Neruda, to name a few, for my planned Spanish library in Rome. (I swore that I would get through every single one of them.) I haunted the guitar shops of Barcelona, trying out one instrument after another, no matter how much it cost, despite a budget of about one hundred dollars. Eventually, I bought a real beauty, manufactured by the House of Struch in 1985, an orange wood, mellow-toned guitar, which sits in this very room behind me as I write.

On the very day I was to leave for Rome with my new guitar in hand, my valise weighing even more from newly purchased books, and my head dense with recent memories, I got a little careless and allowed my radar to turn off. Overdoing the *vino* (and cigarettes) at lunch, as I made my way to the central station in Barcelona, all the while feeling as if I were Mr. Slick New Yorker, my wallet with all my cash vanished, some fellow having picked my pocket in the crowded square.

Fortunately, though I had nothing more than a few pesetas in change left, I had kept my ticket and passport stashed inside my shirt; brooding, I settled into my second-class compartment and was wondering what I would do over the two-day journey to Rome for food when into that car came four cheerful, not-bad-looking Spanish nurses in their late twenties, from Merida. They were toting picnic baskets filled with food and wine and chocolates, and hearing the story of how I had been pickpocketed, took pity, and tenderly so, on this *americano*. Europe? God, I loved it!

· · ·

Though my nearly two-year stay in Italy probably deserves far more space than anyone's patience should allow, I will frame this little part of the book as a love story of a sort, for no sooner had I arrived in that city than did I become intoxicated with the Latino-ness of Rome and a lifestyle that, every day I lived there, somehow conformed with my memories (perhaps) and fantasies (definitely) of what life must have been like in Cuba before the fall, or, in the machinations of that long-ish narrative I had been fooling around with, Havana itself.

Rife with birdsong, blossoming gardens, high arching palm trees, and tropical vegetation everywhere, as well as a populace of outspoken, charismatic, friendly, occasionally curmudgeonly, styl-ish, and earthy people—with no end to the dazzling women, of all ages, there—Rome, that "great outdoor museum," as Malraux once put it, pressed so many wonderful buttons inside me that for much of my time there, I became a new and improved version of myself, still tightly wound but, for the most part, really enjoying my life for a change.

Just walking those streets, especially in neighborhoods like Trastevere or by the Aventine, I'd stroll through the markets, absorb-ing, with almost a hunger, not just the scents of the marvelous breads and herbs and flowers that were everywhere, but the bel canto of the Italian language itself, which, for some reason, I felt far more at ease navigating than even my ancestral *español*. In fact, I used the Span-ish I'd more or less improved upon during my recent travels to help me get along with the Italians. (Down in Naples, the Italian almost sounds like Castilian sometimes.) They understood me completely, and, because it was not my emotional turf to defend, I eventually flourished, or at least more easily in a street-friendly getting-around fashion. Though I attempted to decipher the daily newspapers, which were always remarkably slangy, and the writings of Borges, Cortázar, and Calvino in their Mondadori translations—incredibly, as in Spain, "literature" could be found in the racks of the sidewalk kiosks along-side Donald Duck or *Paparone* comics, religious tomes on Padre Pio, and some of the raunchiest porno I'd ever seen—it wasn't anything I came close to mastering, at least not in the way that a few good solid years of study would have afforded me.

Nevertheless, I loved visiting the used book shops of Rome, where

I indulged my interest in graphics and printing, often coming away, for only a few dollars in lire, with some fantastically illustrated volume, its production values incredible, with colors as deeply realized as those one remembers from childhood. My purchases included an antique edition of *Le Avventure di Pinnochio* by Carlo Collodi and a version of Dante's *Divine Comedy* as told by Topolino (Mickey Mouse), as well as a turn-of-the-century star book, among other items, which I have continued to treasure to this day.

It wasn't long before my second-floor room at the academy filled with such books, as well as the occasional knickknack from the market. Humble by any standards, it looked out onto a courtyard with a fountain and two high pine trees, its gravel paths often sounding with the footfall of visiting scholars and fellows, Italian voices murmuring upward along with birdsong—it was Borges who said his favorite word in English was *nightingale*, while I would think that *uccello* would qualify as mine in Italian. My furnishings included a bed, a desk, a few lamps, two chairs, and dresser. The room had a sink but no toilet, and I depended upon a communal bathroom for showers, etc. On a stand sat a heavy black telephone with a rotary dial, which I used mainly for calling the *portieres*, most of whom spoke quite good English, though one of them, the night man, appropriately named Orfeo, used only a Roman dialect that for some (like myself) was nearly impossible to understand. International calls always had to go through a special operator, and one would have to sometimes wait and wait, before finally giving up. (Though I had no one to call.)

• • •

Arriving at the villa, in addition to my room, I had been given my own little studio off the edge of a Tuscan-style garden—a run-down tile-covered shed with cracked windows, endless drafts, spiders, and salamanders, that was wedged up against the ancient Aurelian wall, which the Romans, back when, had built as a defense (it's been supposed) against the barbarians. (In the spring, it would overflow with wisteria.) My windows had a view of an unbelievably serene and beautiful landscape, of orange-blue Roman skies and umbrella pines, and among the buildings in view, sharply defined like mannerist

silhouettes in the twilight, a sixteenth-century domicile that Garibaldi had once used as a headquarters during his defense against the
French, and where Galileo, at a time when a country road passed
through those grounds, had once stayed. (The walls of such buildings
and of those surrounding the garden were riddled with bullet holes.)
I'd climb a series of cracked disintegrating steps, the path overgrown,
to get to my studio, and there, when I was not wandering the city, I
sat by an enormous desk before a little Olivetti. With pads of paper
and a pile of manuscript that I'd dragged around Spain in my suitcase
(as if they were songs), I'd set out daily, more often than not, to fool
around with my second novel, which had already started to take on
a new direction.

If you will recall my uncle Pedro, of the Cugat orchestra, then you
can perhaps imagine how, in a moment of insight, I transformed my
superintendent character, one Cesar Castillo, into a musician whose
band, the Mambo Kings, had once performed here and there in New
York City in the 1950s.

Back on 106th Street, long before I'd left for the academy, I'd had
this notion for my book—of a superintendent who had once had a
glorious past, though just what that past was about, I really could not
say. But gradually I got some clues. As I'd ride the elevator, its operator, a soulful and quite melancholic fellow of middle age, from the
Dominican Republic, named Rafael Guillon, would begin singing
to himself, as if withdrawing into an inward dream. His voice was
so moving, so resonant and rich, that I'd sometimes invite him into
my apartment during his breaks. Taking hold of one of my guitars,
he'd commence upon a bolero—classics like "Solamente Una Vez"
or "Historia de un Amor"—and with such a professionalism that I
just had to ask if he'd ever performed publicly. To that he answered:
"Yes, back in my country, I made a number of records, and I was
somewhat well-known."

I'd wanted to ask him how on earth he had ended up spending
his days in an elevator—the very life my Pop had once cautioned me
to avoid—but he preempted me, simply shaking his head and looking forlornly out the window as if at his own past, the way my father

used to: "*Pero no sé lo que me pasó,*" he told me. "But I don't know what happened to me."

Of course his broken heart moved me greatly, and, as a small homage to the man, when I'd later get around to creating an orchestra called the Mambo Kings for that novel, I'd name one of the musicians after him. (The good news about Rafael, by the way, is that he later retired and moved back to the DR, which he had always missed so much.) Then too, my memories of every wonderful Latin band I'd ever heard performing on the nearby streets below—at block parties on 108th and 107th—or rehearsing out of their apartments in the Bronx and Brooklyn and over on Tieman Place came back to me as well. Another inspiration? One of my downstairs neighbors, a first-rate bass player, Raul, with whom I would occasionally jam, worked full-time as a bus driver for the MTA. He too once played in different Latin bands that never quite made it. In his company, I'd think about how unfair it was that so many fine musicians, with chops up their asses, could end up having to scrape by with daytime jobs while they played music to feed their souls. (At the same time, I could not help thinking about the first-rate mambo band that once performed at a Corpus dance, real pros, stoically playing rock tunes like "Tequila" and "Do You Love Me?" for the kiddies, their lead singer shaking his maracas with the most disconsolate expression on his face.)

Of course, I had my own limited but accurate memories of what it felt like to be playing at two in the morning in a smoky and crowded bar, on some nights when you felt like it and on some when you didn't. I also knew something of how much young musicians really have dreams of making it, and how easily those dreams can be crushed, the world being, I think, somewhat cruel, and how (so easily) one's moment could so quickly pass.

However, without a doubt, the biggest influence on my creation of Cesar Castillo had to be the glamorous career my uncle Pedro once had as a performer with the Cugat orchestra back in the mambo epoch, a life played out in elegant louche café-society venues that, as a source of inspiration, I wore like an inherited glove. (But even Pedro's story had its own sad ending: In the early 1980s, he had gone into a

Miami hospital for the removal of a mole from beneath the lobe of his right ear and the surgeons, messing up, had somehow cut into a major artery, whose bleeding could not be stopped; hence, my image of Pedro, in a white tux and tails, seated by a table in some club with my aunt Maya—in Havana and New York—overflows now with crimson.)

Along the way, I had attended a Santeria ceremony over on Columbus Avenue with a Cuban playwright friend—I loved those sweet old black ladies, the *santeras* who, gentle as sparrows, not only exorcized demons but cooked up a storm in the kitchen. It was through that playwright friend that I met Chico O'Farrill, a bandleader, arranger, and composer whose Afro-Cuban jazz pedigree involved working with the likes of Charlie Parker, Dizzie Gillespie, Machito, and Chano Pozo at their peak, and harkened back to the glory times of Havana nightlife in the 1940s. Though one of the Latin greats, he had been reduced to mainly writing jingles and background music for television and radio advertisements, and while he still participated in recording sessions with some quite famous musicians, Celia Cruz among them, the moment of his greatest glory had also passed. Physically slight, with a face that seemed reminiscent of both Salvador Dalí and Xavier Cugat, he was rather curmudgeonly, at least when I first met him, for he valued his privacy and only spoke to me as a favor to his friend. Still, over drinks, he provided me with a sense of Havana's nightlife circa the Batista era—none of it being anything I hadn't already suspected, viz., the sleaziness of the mob's influence in Havana, the bawdiness of certain of its clubs and bordellos, and the hardships of coming up as a musician in a city in which even the finest talents were but a dime a dozen. Then, once he'd decided that enough was enough and politely booted me out, I left his apartment, feeling somewhat grateful for the information, and without the slightest suspicion that years later we would become rather close friends.

Ultimately, however, it was Cesar Castillo himself who worked his own magic. I conceived him as a cross between my pop (in the sense of his fleshliness and drinking) and a heartthrob (now dated) like Victor Mature, with touches of both Frankie the exterminator and Mr. Martinez the superintendent. He wore the gray utility uniform of my uptown super, Luis (who, a cocaine addict, would do any job for the money, and, constantly wired, died at about age forty from a heart attack), with his smells of plumber's gum and incinerator ash (as well as tobacco). With so much information floating in my head, I still hadn't figured out just who Cesar Castillo happened to really be, when, as I sat before my desk one day, I envisioned him coming out of a basement into a courtyard, singing in a wonderful baritone, but, at the same time, carrying in his arms an old record jacket on whose cover I first "saw"—cross my heart—the rubric *The Mambo Kings Play Songs of Love.*

Still, I already had a tentative title for that manuscript—*The Secrets of a Poor Man's Life*—while the name Mambo Kings, for Cesar's orchestra, simply occurred to me while noticing how on old mambo recordings, which I'd come by in secondhand shops and places like the Salvation Army, musicians such as Perez Prado would be referred to as the King of Cuban Swing, or the King of the Mambo, and perhaps I had seen in Spanish the phrase *"El Rey del Mambo,"* but never once "Mambo King," which I came up with by simply inverting the old terminology from the 1950s.

Once I'd figured out that my humble super had been a mambo king, or *the* Mambo King, as he would become known in the novel, I still saw him in terms of a contradictory personality: On the one hand he was rambunctious, wild, life loving, woman chasing, devil-may-care, blatantly sexist, big dicked, and altogether, even when long past his prime, herculean in every way possible (or to put it differently, a man of the earth and of a triumphant body, until his vices got the better of him). At the same time, because I'd always identified that feeling with being Cuban, he had a tendency toward melancholy and so many soulful memories that he seemed to be two "selves," as it were. That dichotomy puzzled me, until one day I realized that Cesar Castillo was, in fact, two persons: Hence his younger brother, Nestor, came into the world, or, as I thought of him, he had always been there, lingering inside Cesar Castillo's head.

A far more measured and poetic soul, but devastatingly sad, Nestor Castillo was an infinitely talented musician, and the sort to sit inside a tenement window strumming a guitar while writing a heartfelt bolero about, at least in the beginning, the Cuba he, as an immigrant living in New York, had left behind. Once I had figured that out, it became a matter of placing the stories of these two Cuban brothers in the context of Cesar's memories of the past.

And so, as they say, that novel began.

■ ■ ■

Without detailing the further processes of that book, at this moment at least, I will say that its writing, which I had pursued so tentatively back in New York, now took on a bloom as radiant and all-consuming as the city of Rome itself. In other words, those wonderful Italo-Latino energies that were flowing into me, so alive, so varied, so intensely felt, began to find their way onto the page. It was as if Rome had become my Havana—and held out such strong resonances for me that I, sitting in my study, a cigarette burning in a tray (MS, an Italian brand, which English speakers had nicknamed for their pungency Massive Stroke), along with the occasional glass of marketplace jug wine (so young that within a few weeks, it would be good only as paint remover), found the words gushing out from me, like so much water from the Acqua Paola down the hill. Though the heating in that shed was faulty and halting at best, and the coolest air seeped in through the cracked windowpanes, I loved every moment of it. Stricken by some romantic notion of being a writer, and thinking of the composer Chopin, I'd even gotten hold of some mittens and cut off the tips so that I could keep my hands warm while typing. On occasion, when it became too damply cold, I'd put a lit candle on my desk and warm my fingers from the flame—so very nineteenth-century that it delighted me. As a wintry twilight fell, and Venus started her ascent over the Aurelian wall, winking at me, I'd sit back and remember that not a year before, at that same hour, I would have been sitting by my desk at TDI, waiting for the clock to count down to five.

Though the villa and grounds had once seen better times, I

learned quickly that coming to the academy was an honor, and for most of the fellows there, a competitively driven one. Among them were pre- and postdoctoral classicists and art historians, architects and architectural scholars, conservationists, city planners, experts in Italian Renaissance literature as well as aspirants in the field of Italian studies, who had been culled from the finest universities in the United States and, in some cases, Europe: Harvard, Princeton, and Yale graduates were well represented at the academy, but even when they came from other universities, there could be no doubt as to their drive and brilliance, for they were the crème de la crème of young scholarship. Added to this mix were returning former fellows, now tenured professors on sabbatical from some of the most prestigious universities in the country, to take up half- and full-year residencies devoted to studies and writing, and, as well, the occasional invited honored guest.

During my year at the academy, of this group, the two most notable were Dorothea Rockburne, the artist, and one Leon Krier, architect, town planning theorist, and Prince Charles's right-hand man when it came to London architectural conservation, with whom I became rather friendly—mainly because the two of us had a shared interest in *fumetti,* comics, which took us all over Rome to visit shops.

On the other side, among the nonacademics, in a separate class unto themselves, were the fellows in the arts—painting, photography, sculpture, and music. In my year, they were a rather talented but temperamentally uneven group that included one burly older painter, who, having applied to the academy some fifteen times over the years, arrived with a smoldering contempt for the spoiled brat "careerists" surrounding him. He resembled, incidentally, a Thomas Nast rendering of Saint Nicholas, down to his bulbous nose and gray scraggly beard, though he, dressed usually in a lumberjack's shirt and coveralls, hardly ever behaved in a jolly manner with anyone—and remained particularly belligerent toward me.

When I'd first turned up at the academy, I'd made the mistake of mentioning to him that my Rome Prize had come out of the blue, awarded to me from afar, from within the mysterious star chambers of the American Academy and Institute of Arts and Letters, as I'd never applied for it; and though I'd said this so as to separate myself from the ultracompetitive folks there, for I'd never hustled anyone (or ever would) in my life, nor had I ever been one to "look around a room" to make possible connections, it did not go well with this man, who, until we became friends, made my life and that of the other fellows generally miserable. A perpetual presence at the downstairs bar just off the main *salone*, he tended to linger there without company, as most people, once seeing him, changed their plans. It seems that he was mainly a confrontation junkie, insults ("I've got more talent in my pinkie than everyone else here put together") his general means of communication. But he must have also been crazy—his paintings, mainly portraiture and Roman cityscapes that were constructed by mounting blotchy dashes of paint one upon the other, seemed the work of a madman (at least to me). One day, when I'd shown up at the bar with a nice-looking woman I'd met in Rome, he nearly proved it, almost pushing me over an edge; ogling her body lasciviously, he leaned close to me, asking if I could do him a favor.

"Like what?" I asked.

"Like letting me fuck her," he said, pointing her way.

I was holding a beer mug at the moment, and if not for the fact that I would have been kicked out of the academy for good, I would have punched him in the face with it.

・　・　・

But my dealings with him were the worst of that stay, aside from certain moments of the ghastly, unbridled snobbery I occasionally encountered. After my years at TDI, never a hotbed of intellectual activity, and with my plebeian education ("City College? How quaint"), I was unaccustomed to academic speak and the incredibly long-winded conversations I'd overhear at the dining room tables. Though I enjoyed attending the academy lectures, in which one could get up and leave, I found that certain people were best avoided, and, along the way, I may have offended, without intending to, more than a few of them.

Still, in those days I made the acquaintance of a photographer in her mid-thirties named Barbara Beany, an expat who had married an Italian, whose roundish and expressive face always seemed swollen, her cheeks of a deep rouge coloration: Working for the academy, she had sought me out, and while I hadn't been aware of just why, I always felt an inexplicable kinship with her, as if I knew much more about her than was possible. But I could never put my finger on it, until I learned that she suffered from bad kidneys. A sunny personality, despite her difficulties, we'd often stroll the academy's back gardens, talking about her life in Italy and my book, which seemed to have touched her. Ever so quiet and gentle in her manner, I realize now that she, indeed, knew that her days were numbered.

Leon Krier and I were friendly enough that he invited me to London for New Year's. My first autumn in Italy, we'd palled around quite a bit in Rome. On the evening of one of that city's greatest (and rare) snowstorms, we had driven down to the Vatican, its piazza abandoned, and gone hiking in a state of elation through its three-foot-high drifts, talking about the monumentality of its architecture (in fact, we'd drive around Rome to obscure hill towns discussing nothing else). We'd make countryside excursions, his wife, Rita Wolfe, a painter, often joining us. But as I said before, we mainly caroused about for books. He'd invited me to London out of pure kindness, and though I had come down with an awful flu (my annual friend), I kept my assignation, having booked tickets on Ethiopian Airlines, the cheapest fare I could find. The day I left for London, I was on my way out to Fiumicino on a bus when traffic completely stopped on the highway. Suddenly, dozens of police cars, sirens blaring, went whizzing by, followed by ambulances, then military vehicles. As we waited, someone listening to a portable radio mentioned that some kind of attack had taken place in the airport. A few hours later when we were allowed to proceed, I arrived at a chaotic scene— hundreds of people and airline employees wandering about in a daze (so it seemed to me). At one side of the terminal, near the El Al and TWA counters, large paneled screens were being wheeled into place, while airport workers in janitorial coveralls stood on ladders, steam-blasting blood and other matter off the bullet-pocked walls. Even then I had no clear idea of what had happened, nor would I until, after an endless wait, my late-morning flight made it into London's Heathrow, sometime after ten that night, when, as I recall, tanks were lining the airport route. Only when I made it over to Leon's place at Belsize Park and turned on the "telly" did I learn that I'd witnessed the aftermath of the terrorist attack known as the Rome Massacre.

■ ■ ■

Mainly I enjoyed myself: I learned to play something that vaguely resembled tennis on a court outside the academy library. I'd whack at balls with an ebullient kitchen helper named Rocco, later the operator of an ice cream truck in Rome—"*Ciao*, Oscareeno," he'd call out to me, ringing its bells. Every morning, despite my afternoon habit of smoking, I'd go jogging around the scenic grounds of the Villa Doria Pamphili Park, some five miles or so—and effortlessly so; a former aristocrat's estate, resplendent with a birthday cake mansion, it was one of the more elegant retreats in Rome. I'd run through there daydreaming about the kind of life I'd have if I were to stay there for good, or what a pity it was that my father had never experienced such a day. I enjoyed watching the priests in their meditations and the kind of misted and cool mornings when the park was practically deserted, when you got a sense of how things once used to be.

One morning while "footing," as the Italians called it, I thought I was experiencing a hallucination: Rounding an upgrade and coming down upon a stretch that opened to a vast field bordered by a corridor of umbrella pines, before me lay encamped Garibaldi's army, that is, about two hundred movie extras dressed in period costume and shakos, lolling about the misty greens, with muskets in hand, for a Franco Nero production! On yet another morning, on my way back to the academy from an all-night party, I saw Aguirre himself— Klaus Kinski, standing in front of the Pantheon in an open raincoat whose fabric he began flapping like a bird's wings, as he turned in circles, obviously stoned out of his mind, in a glory over the gilded sunlight passing like honey over the square.

. . .

Though I liked to keep to myself, I loved going on what amounted to the guided tours—or "walks"—that the resident classicist in charge, Russell Scott, who somehow always reminded me of Stan Laurel, conducted to key spots in Rome; and when the academy made an autumn field trip to archeological sites along the Amalfi coast and below—from the baths of Baie to Paestum—I loved every moment of it and found Italy never less than breathtaking, even on the bleakest days.

During that trip, I became quite friendly with our bus driver, and in the evenings, while most of the fellows stayed at the hotel, he, an older man, and I would find the local social club (usually in a tavern) and play the Italian card game of *scopas*—I forget how it worked now, but playing it well depended on keeping track of numbers, particularly combinations involving the number seven, and since I was good at basic math, I tended to win every time, confounding him. He was another one of those salt-of-the-earth Italians with whom I felt perfectly at ease, and in the small towns we visited, I found myself, without quite knowing why, drawn to the *paesani* and their way of life—of course, now I realize that in them I saw something of my *campesino* father.

On that occasion, I roomed with Professor Scott, who told me that I had a propensity for talking in my sleep on those nights, in a jumble of Italian, Spanish, English, and (apparently) some Portuguese (so he said), some other side of me, expressing an almost confident feel for languages, coming out. (On those same evenings, I also got into the habit of composing little quasi-poetic bits, mostly easy rhymes about my day's observations: One that I remember, about a mythological painting in the Naples museum, went: "Aphrodite in her nightie feeding Aries tasty berries.")

. . .

And breathing all that fresh myth-ridden air scrambled my brains as well. In one of those towns by the southern coast, I had another of my ecstatic moments, for going out to look at the stars one evening, I got caught up by the moonlight's play upon the horizon and imagined (or saw how people could imagine) the likes of a towering Neptune rising out from under the shadows that went mysteriously swirling under the surface of the restlessly churning "wine-dark" sea. At an academy dig in Tuscany, an Etruscan-Roman-Lombard site known as Cosa, I watched a white mare and a stallion frolicking in a meadow, the late morning light doing strange things to their forms, and saw how easily some imaginative ancient could have taken them from a distance to be centaurs. At the edge of a Bronze Age Garden of Eden called Filotosa, in Sardinia, I saw a field of olive trees and under each a netting of white upon the ground, on which, among the olives that dropped, the peasants, their caps pulled down over their brows, slept as peacefully as if they had always been part of a timeless dream, that spell following me everywhere.

Back in Rome, I spent many a morning in the forum, hanging around classicists and developing an interest in archeology, so much so that in the coming years, for some six seasons, I'd devote my summers to digging out trenches and hauling wheelbarrows of *fangi e sassi* by the Temple of the Vestal Virgins, in the *area sacra*, an ongoing excavation supervised by the aforementioned Russell Scott. (If you don't think a place can be haunted, then I suggest you go prowling through the Roman forum at six thirty in the morning, when the very upturned stone and marble columns seem to ooze spirits—mists literally rising from the corners of long-abandoned villas (at least they would for me). In fact, once the word got out that this Hijuelos was a soft touch when it came to digs, I moonlighted on several others, up in Cosa and in Campania to the south. I was so smitten by the notion of seeing the ancient world that I decided to visit Egypt in the winter. I was in Cairo when the army went into revolt and burned down several Giza hotels, among them one not far from where I had stayed. Later, I made it up the Nile to the island temple of Philae where Antinous, Hadrian's lover, was said to have drowned himself; and although I fell deathly sick from a stomach malady along the way, by my journey's end, with Karnak and Abu Simbel and other such marvels behind me, I felt, archeologically speaking, gloriously fulfilled.

And yet, at the same time, throughout those touristic travels, as

I went jogging along the dusty palm-lined roads by the Nile in the early mornings, or crawled up a narrow shaft into the antechamber of the Great Pyramid, I had a nagging premonition that something sad had taken place back home, a strange and inexplicable feeling that accompanied me back to Rome. And this, unfortunately, came true. On the evening of my return, I walked up a hill toward the Academy's back gate, where I bumped into one of my favorite fellows, Josefina, a Sardinian princess, who happened to be a classicist. After we had chatted a bit I made my way through the gardens and the villa complex itself. In my room, I sat down on my bed, when, wouldn't you know it, the telephone rang. It was about ten thirty on a Sunday night, the world so still. One of my old neighborhood friends was calling me from New York.

"I got something bad to tell you," he said. "Tommy Muller-Thym's dead."

"Oh, man—what happened?"

"Well, you know he had some bad stuff going on with his liver, that's all," he told me. "Went out alone and blind in a house upstate."

The details of our reminiscences about him—as a gifted, funny, and super-bright dude who should have had a good life—aside, the loss of him killed both of us, but what could one conclude except that some things "just *bees* that way," as my friend put it.

It took me a long time to get over that; and, though I knew he was gone, I brought Tommy's jive spirit with me, wherever I went. That next summer, when I traveled all across Turkey visiting archeological sites, the most splendid of which, if one should care to know, were that of mystical Efes, where Saint Paul preached in the amphitheater; Sardis, with its collapsed temple to Saturn; the ruins of Pergamum; and, to the east, Nemrut Dag, the fantastically strange mountain tomb of one of Alexander the Great's descendants, Antiochus I, whose summit—forgive the tourist-guide speak—afforded one an incomparable view of the rolling steppes of Asia, Tommy came along with me. Then, of course, with time, his presence, as with so many memories, faded—though I am glad that he is with me again, as I write these lines down now.

. . .

Okay, so you must be wondering what all of the above has to do with the fact that, at the same time, squeezed out here and there, I had been working on my novel about Cesar Castillo, who, as it turned out, had a brother named Nestor; well, the answer is this: absolutely nothing, except in the sense that such travels and interests set free another part of my heart and soul, which, until then, had been almost entirely bottled up. And that, in a phrase, helped me with the writing of it.

Making the Castillo brothers musicians, like my uncle Pedro, I knew they had left Havana in the late 1940s, to pursue the mambo scene in New York City, and that, as with most immigrants, their first years, while coping with a new language, a strange new environment, prejudice, and an inevitable sense of displacement (as well as elation)—the latter of which I often felt myself in Rome—were difficult. They'd have a moment of triumph, which I could never quite figure out—that is, until one afternoon, on a lusciously fecund spring day, when I was sitting in my studio and trying to decide whether to take a walk down to Trastevere or to remain by my desk searching for a solution. For some reason, just as I was about to leave, I began to recall how as a kid watching television with my pop, we delighted in the *I Love Lucy* show, and not only because of the comedy and give-and-take between Desi Arnaz's character of Ricky Ricardo, a Cuban nightclub performer in New York, and his endlessly charming but zany American wife, Lucy (a match-up, incidentally, that I have in the decades since seen duplicated countless times), but because of how familiar it seemed to us whenever Ricky's relatives turned up at his door from Cuba: I'd always wondered about those folks and the lives they had lived. And while I often entertained the notion of writing something about those walk-on characters, it hadn't yet dawned on me that such an idea could be of use to me in my novel about a former Mambo King looking back on his life. And yet, right then and there, in my studio in Rome, it occurred to me that the brothers, fresh from Havana, had once appeared at Ricky's door and, as musicians and singers, would perform on the stage of the Tropicana nightclub, as did so many of Ricky's Cuban friends. Of course, as part of their backstory, set in the real world of the novel, he'd have to discover them somehow, and so, at a moment when I still felt greatly tempted to lose myself in the perfumed warmth of a Roman afternoon, I forced myself to type out the following lines:

> One Tuesday night in 1955 the Cuban bandleader and television personality Desi Arnaz walked into the Mambo Nine Club on 58th Street and Eighth Avenue to check out the talent. Someone had told him about two Cuban brothers, Cesar and Nestor Castillo, that they were good singers and songwriters who might have some material for Arnaz to use on his show. . . .

The song they perform that night is one that Nestor Castillo had written for a love he'd left behind in Cuba, "Beautiful María of My Soul"; in some ways it was strictly a product of my life in Rome, and of my closet religiosity, for the name María first came to mind, in terms of that novel, on the Good Friday evening before Easter of 1986, when I had gone to the Colosseum to watch, among crowds of Romans, Pope John Paul II preside over the procession and ritual known as "La Via Crucis," or the stations of the cross. Through a sound system that thundered, echoing through the farthest recesses of the ancient center, an Italian cardinal with one of the most resonant and deeply rich voices I'd ever heard, began to recite the story of Jesus's passion and death. Now and then, the name Maria would burst through the narrative—

> *Allora, Maria, la donna di Gerusalemme. . . .*
> *Gesu, il Figlio di Maria. . . .*
> *Cristo Gesu, nato dall Vergine Maria . . .*
> *Santa Maria, Vergine del silenzio e di misteriosa pace. . . .*
> *Il cuore in piena per l'empatía con la tua morte e il tacito*
>   *dolore di Maria. . . .*

—all the while enchanting me in such a manner that I allowed that name to roll over and over again in my mind, until at a certain moment, long after I'd left that wonderful processional, in the middle of the night, I shot up in bed, not from any bad dreams but from something that came to me as if out of the Roman/Havana air, a simple line, "La Bella María de mi Alma," which I just had to scribble down lest I forget that subconscious rumination.

But aside from that divine inspiration, it also helped to have a beautiful woman in my life, about whom I will now briefly speak.

. . .

One October evening, about a month after I'd arrived at the academy, I'd descended a steep stairway into Trastevere, and there, just before the final steps leading from the Via Scala and the maze of cobblestone streets beyond, I came upon the apparition of a stately Asian princess, perhaps from the court of Kublai Khan, performing the mundane task of walking her little fox terrier. She was rather mysteriously dressed in a cape with cowl and high leather boots, and while I could not quite make out her face, half-hidden under the silken scarf she had wrapped around her mouth against the misty rain, she cut such a spectacular figure that I, deeply under the influence of a Dante lecture at the moment, couldn't help but ask, "*Sei* Beatrice?"—"Are you Beatrice?"

But that just made her laugh, and noting my accent, she told me, in quite perfect English, "So you are an American?"

By some miracle (thank you, Lord), I found myself following her into Trastevere, where, among other things, I learned her name— Sojin, or "pearl"—and discovered that my status as a fellow at the American Academy in Rome quite impressed her, as, in fact, it did so many Romans. Later, sitting in a café where the waiters knew and doted on her, I first saw her face and could see just why they—and, as I'd learn, just about every vendor and storekeeper in Rome—did so. Without dwelling excessively on the virtues of her appearance, I will only say that, as I later got to know her and we started going out to places together, it was nearly impossible to walk even a block— in any quarter of the city—without some Italian fellow (and God, half of them were always on the make) coming up alongside us on, foot or on a *motorino* and sometimes in a car, to make some jovial rascal's remark to her in Italian along the lines of "Why don't you lose the four-eyes"—or "the bald guy"—and come and have some fun with me!"

For some reason, though I don't think it thrilled her, she forgave my flaws ("You are a refreshing change from the usual handsome and superficial Italian men," she'd told me) and, stranded more or less in a foreign land, far from her home in Seoul, Korea, and perhaps craving the opportunity to end up one day in America, seemed to think me far more intelligent and sophisticated than I happened to be. She loved that I hailed from New York, and the fact that I was a member of the *cubani* people pleased her as well. While I didn't conform, in any way, to her notion of what Cubans were supposed to look like, she, having taken the care and effort to read my first novel, out of some mixture of pity and real affection came to idealize me, even if I happened to be going bald and dressed too much, in her opinion, like a beatnik. (To hide my receded hairline, I rarely went anywhere in Rome without wearing a red or black beret, or a baseball cap.) She also liked the fact that I didn't mind spending money on her— whatever she wanted or needed, it never bothered me to throw her some bucks, especially since I'd have to practically force her to accept the money, as she found it embarrassing, but never so much for her to refuse in the end. Still, I am not so sure what she saw in me, though, in fact, I really did go out of my way to be good to her.

In my eyes, she was something of a James Bond girl, if I may: incredibly sexy—she had posed in various states of undress for a number of Italian magazines, among them *Playboy* (for the very reason that she never showed me any of them, I'd search for pictures of her in the used magazine shops that were virtually everywhere, in Rome; I never found any). From a well-educated background, she had also an adventurous past. Having run away from a strict boarding school in Korea, she had traveled throughout Asia and, with a German boyfriend, spent a year trying to get rich through the sleight-of-hand export of electronic goods from Hong Kong into India. Somehow, she had ended up in Italy. When we met, she had been keeping company with an older Italian man who wasn't treating her too well, though she had her own little place, in a sixteenth-century building, off the Via dei Panieri (street of the bakers) in Trastevere. Her downstairs neighbors were three young gay men, two of whom, donning wigs, dressed up as women and worked a trade as oral hookers at the Stazione Termini. They were so convincing as women that I hadn't the slightest notion that they were men, until one evening when we were visiting, to demonstrate to Sojin some subtlety about the art of love, the prettier girl pulled off the stockings of the other and went down on her who turned out to be a him, even as we were sitting there sipping wine. ("Madonna," I remember hearing her mutter, under her breath, in embarrassment.)

The Romans were sex crazed in some ways. Up from the academy was a place called the Bar Gianicolo and on Saturday nights, it became a rendezvous point for stylish Roman couples to meet before adjourning to sex parties—orgies, if you like—or so my lady friend told me. I believed her. The few times we went in there together on a Saturday night for a coffee, men always approached her. One evening a couple came by to drop a card on our little bistro table: I don't think I was part of the deal, but in any case, she, thinking that they, despite their elegant finery, were what the Italians called *schifozi*—what my mother called *gente baja*—was not the sort to have ever taken them up on that kind of thing.

. . .

She wasn't very good with money, spending most of it on clothes. At one point, to pay for her tuition in a fashion design school located just off the Piazza Farnese, she worked as a showroom model for designers in the city; another job that kept her in the fashion loop took her down to the Piazza di Spagna, where in a leather goods shop whose name escapes me now, she waited on the wealthiest of tourists, among them, she'd casually mention every so often, the occasional movie star. She drove a Fiat 500, a piggy bank on wheels but commodious enough for us to make a few trips south to Naples, where we scoured the rebranding fashion salons for bargains. Out at Capri, she almost got me drowned by accepting a boat ride into the bay with a couple of Mafiosi, who kept urging me to try water-skiing—one of those fellows, who could not get his eyes off her, had a perpetual erection inside his gold spandex and kept whispering to his chum what seemed to me some rather sinister notions. But if they were devious hoods, they obviously decided that murdering me wasn't worth the trouble. (For the record, once we made landfall again, I would not talk to her, beauty that she was, for a day or so. On the other hand, looking back on it now, I find it incredibly funny.)

She was really a cheerful and good-natured woman, bright and outgoing: The gardeners and crew at the academy and all the gate-keepers liked her—every week, someone or other would ask me if we were going to get married. (A funny thing: Even Francine du Plessix Gray, a beautiful woman herself, visiting the academy with her husband, the artist Clive Gray, always seemed unable to take her eyes off of Sojin when she happened to be around.) The only people there, in fact, who seemed to resent her were certain of the female academicians. Though Sojin spoke Japanese, Chinese, Russian, German, Italian, French, and English, one such academician always referred to her as the "bimbo." I'd look the other way—what did I care? We were having a nice time together, no matter what we happened to be doing. After all, it was all part of the dream I seemed to be living in Italy, whose lovely and quite passionate energies slipped bit by bit into my writing, while my own affections for that woman, later to be displaced and abused, seemed so real and something that I then believed would never be forgotten.

I stayed on in Rome for almost another year after my fellowship ran out, and because I had some money saved and no particular place to go, I rented a largish apartment some ten blocks from the academy, by a marketplace, its back windows looking out over a series of descending terraces and gardens. There we lived as tranquilly and, I think, as happily as possible, though I did have an upstairs neighbor, a red-haired Sicilian actress, who might have wanted to have something with me (or perhaps with Sojin). In another flat in the same building, a kept woman, also of dazzling good looks, who, bored to death with her arrangement with a rather solemn fellow from Milano, would sometimes take me with her to see the opera. (Sojin,

I am certain, thought we might have had something between us but didn't seem to care.)

In that residence, while left alone, I worked on my novel, but it was something that slipped in and out of my life; weeks would go by when I wouldn't write a word—namely because, quite frankly, I didn't think anyone would care about such a book—and thusly bored, I'd look around for something to do with myself. That came down to music. Walking along the street, if I heard someone with any kind of chops playing an electric instrument, I somehow mustered the nerve to ring the bell. Eventually, I had my first real success with a bass player, Stefano, who not only invited me up to jam but produced a huge chunk of hashish—or *cioccolato* (which the Spaniards were also crazy about)—to enhance our performing pleasure. In turn, he knew of a few other musicians, among them a guitarist (with a ton of equipment), a keyboard player, and a drummer, and getting together every weekend in the basement room of a warehouse-sized bakery out by the Via Appia, we started to put together a repertoire of mainly reggae and Eric Clapton covers, which these Italians, hash- and potheads to the core, particularly cherished. But once again, I had a capricious musical career: We played a few gigs in the homes of friends, a blues bar in Trastevere (to a house that would have been empty were it not for our friends), and, that next Christmas, a dance party at the academy, for which we received permission to rehearse on the academy grounds (unheard of, I believe) and whose high point, at least from my group's perspective, came when they were all invited into the academy dining hall for dinner, a great honor, no matter how spotty the food was in those days. (And our performance? Not too bad, as I recall, and quite nicely dressed up by Sojin swaying to the music.)

I really enjoyed their friendship—but once they found out that I had my own place, with two bedrooms, my apartment became their lovers' retreat; these Romans, cool as they could be, lived at home with their families, which would pretty much be their story until they'd get married, and even then, having one's own domicile wasn't a certainty; housing was so tight in that city, unless you were a foreigner renting, that young couples would go anywhere they could to make it: At night the road behind the academy, a street on which stood religious institutes and priestly housing, was often lined with rocking, bobbing automobiles whose windows always seemed to be steamed up in the winter, and in Trastevere, there was a Thai bar and restaurant right off the Via dei Panieri, a massive joint with bamboo décor, that rented curtained booths to young couples for the evening so that they would have some privacy in which to pass their amorous time—a venue, by the way, that most academy folk did not have a clue about.

My musician pals were no different, and after holding a party in my place, where we just hung out smoking this and that, with lots of wine flowing, most took turns with their girlfriends in the spare bedroom. Having a soft heart, I'd lent my favorite in the band, a great guitar player named Sandro, an extra key, but once that got out—and it did, as he couldn't help bragging about his special in with me—I'd find myself in the situation of having to use a coded door ring when I'd come home, for copies of the key had been made. But, even then, that didn't always work: Poor Sojin once came in to find my bassist friend in bed with his girlfriend. After a while, with someone wanting to come over nearly every day, it became an impossible situation, especially in terms of my writing, and I found myself in the unfortunate position of having to dislodge my Italian friends from that apartment—at first they cooperated, though rather sullenly, a moratorium finally agreed upon—then that would fall apart, someone ringing my bell, which could be heard all through the building, at two in the morning. What else could I do but let him and his girlfriend in?

Oh, they were grateful all right, but between that and my discovery that after almost two years in Rome, I had run out of money, a check cashed at a local Banco Nazionale having bounced, it started occurring to me that sometime soon, I would have to leave that city and the wonderful, occasionally cantankerous people who inhabited it.

CHAPTER 10

. . .

Another Book

Not that I wanted to leave, however. That notion not only left me despairing, but my girlfriend, taking my sudden decision the wrong way, thought that I had made up my poor financial situation. After treating her so well, and playing the sport with just about everybody I had met in Rome, I'd gone through a good amount of money, and far more quickly than I ever thought possible. (Every so often I'd take the Sicilian and the beauty from upstairs in my apartment house to the toniest restaurant in the neighborhood for lunch, a joint called Il Cortile, where I once spied Marcello Mastroianni holding forth at a table.) Not that I even began wanting to abandon her—far from it—but the scene that took place when I told her about leaving ended rather badly. With tears in her eyes she claimed that if I really wanted to stay, *we* could find a way to scrape a living together, or, if I cared for her, I would bring her back to the States, a notion that scared me. Really, there wasn't anything to be done. Stupidly, I had put a wall between myself and our future, shutting her out and never really giving any other possibilities much thought at all.

But as indifferently as I behaved (I had to be out of my mind), I also didn't have a dime to my name, and I learned quickly enough that I didn't have anyone in my life in the States (New York, at any rate) with the means or disposition to send me as much as the cost of my airfare back: In fact, I only managed to get home because of a deal I quickly made with a Hispanist professor at Swarthmore, who had written me in Rome earlier that spring requesting that I give a lecture to his students there—about what, I didn't know—in exchange for my airline ticket and three hundred dollars, just enough to get me back on my feet when I'd arrive.

Still, aside from tearing myself away from Roma and the easy lifestyle there (except for rush hour, when every Italian raced home at two hundred miles an hour just so they could do nothing), I had hardly thought about New York or the people I'd left behind, and when I did, opening the door to my own memories, I'd sink into a profound *You came from shit and to shit thou shalt return* depression. Bingeing to get over it, I'd smoke and drink cheap, not bad, wine to the point that, yes, my kidneys would ache so deeply that I'd feel *almost* tempted to see a doctor; and then, feeling better, after a day of misery, the thought that I really had nothing to return to, after all, would lay me low again.

Sojin, at least, remained gracious to the end. The day I left, in early May, she drove me to the airport and we said our good-byes, promising, of course, to see each other again as soon as possible. As I crossed over into the passengers-only lounge, I could see her mascara running down her lovely face as if she already knew that getting back together, given my departure and mercurial temperament, was unlikely, if not impossible.

After I landed midafternoon in JFK and worked through the traveler's usual rigmarole, I took a bus back into the city and nearly passed out from how gray and run-down Harlem looked: The same avenue that had so thrilled me as a child upon my release from the hospital, and where I had spent countless afternoons as a teenager shopping or hanging out here or there with my friends, seemed so hopelessly ugly that I quickly started to sink; I'd gotten so used to

Roman aesthetics and the tropical colors of that city, the sun-baked crumbling walls and balcony gardens, as well as the Californian/Mediterranean blueness of its sky, that for the first time in my life, I had some insight into the visual despair that Cubans of my parents' generation—and for that matter, my exiled cousins—must have experienced as newcomers here. Whatever charms the city had always held for me—and however much I may have fed off the energies and variety of our citizens—would take me months to appreciate again. In the meantime, I felt so glumly disposed that I could hardly believe that not twenty-four hours before, I had been in bed with a remarkably beautiful woman whose spectacular looks, I quickly decided, not a single woman in New York could begin to touch.

It wasn't just a matter of physicality but of spirit: So many of the faces I glimpsed that day seemed hardened and angry and so generally pissed off at life as to distort even the finest of their features grotesquely. Of course, I was under a spell, unexpectedly missing not just the woman I'd left behind but Italy itself: New York women seemed plain and mean in a way that I had never realized before, an impression that lasted for months, until, of course, I got used to the city again and, making my own inner adjustments, became more and more the dumb shit I had always been. I'd also arrived looking sharper and better-dressed than ever before—a fashion designer, Sojin had done everything in her power to break me of my badly wanting sartorial tastes (okay, if I told you how many people have since looked at me and declared: "But I thought Cubans were supposed to be sharp dressers," you wouldn't believe it), though the air of upgrade and refinement I now exuded—and my sudden discomfort over my old surroundings—left me, always the loner, feeling even more estranged, and probably too delicate for that world, as if, in a carryover from my childhood, I had reentered into my Lord Fauntleroy mode, albeit as an adult version.

. . .

In my absence, I had rented my apartment to a friend of mine from CCNY. I'd already hooked up with some yuppie willing to fork over almost twice my monthly payments to live there, but when my friend called me up, newly moved out from another place that he shared with a woman and his adopted son, with my own good fortune, I felt so bad for him that I bagged my agreement with the first fellow, throwing some ten or so thousand dollars away in the process. The problem, however, was this: Though I'd written him from Rome that I would be needing my place come the end of April, a date I had arbitrarily chosen and kept pushing forward, and he'd had plenty of notice to leave, when I finally got home, expecting to find my place vacated, I discovered that my friend had hardly packed a toothbrush. In fact, the apartment seemed in a state of chaos, with clothing, boxes, and books and magazines and newspapers strewn about everywhere, but among the things I hadn't expected to come across were the Black Power and Elijah Muhammad posters he'd plastered on the walls. Additionally, his adopted son, then about six years old and a rather troubled kid, had done a fair job of increasing the local cockroach population by stuffing cookies and other foodstuffs he presumably had never wanted to eat inside my couch, which is to say that my apartment had become infested with them.

But somehow I wasn't angry or particularly disturbed: My friend, a quite laid-back fellow, seemed hardly bothered by those conditions, and while I felt less than happy to be back in New York, just stepping into my apartment, with its sweeping views of Harlem, seemed to make it easier. Besides, I'd almost learned to relax in Rome—why become an uptight, anxiety- and complaint-ridden New Yorker again, when I had a newly found sense of gusto and (so I thought) savoir faire? Once he'd explained that he had made plans to get everything out that next weekend, I somewhat settled down. He'd already found another place in the neighborhood and just hadn't gotten his act together: So, everything was cool, right?

Not really. We were on our way out when I asked him if there'd been any mail beyond the occasional batch he'd sent to me in Rome. That's when he hauled out a box filled with a number of thick TOP PRIORITY envelopes from the IRS and Department of New York State Taxation, some of which were well over a year old; I got a sick feeling seeing them, and maybe it was jet lag, but my stomach went into knots, as it always used to: "How come you didn't send me these?" I asked him.

"Well," he said. "I didn't want you to feel hassled—I mean you were having a good time, right?"

Then I opened one of them: Apparently, I owed quite a lot of money in back taxes. How that happened, I can't say, but I'd neglected reporting the few grants I'd received in the past, and, it seemed, they'd caught on to me. With penalties, the amount I hadn't paid them, long since officially delinquent, came out to about eight thousand dollars, as of a month or two before. Having almost nothing to my name, and always stupid about money anyway, I suddenly saw the good deed I'd performed on behalf of my friend in a new light. As I put it to him, incredulously, "Man, I'm fucked," to which he, no doubt placing my misfortune in the context of the fabulous time I'd probably had, just looked at me and shrugged: "Uh-huh."

. . .

There was something about the threatening tone of those IRS notices that did a number on whatever residual well-being I'd returned with from Italy. Within a week, once I'd gone through what amounted to a hero's welcome among my old neighborhood friends—as if I'd come back from some distant war—and had on my third day, as if risen from the dead, gone to visit my mother, whom I hadn't seen in nearly two years, the first thing I thought of as I walked back into that haunted apartment and looked around was, I can't believe I grew up here—while the first thing she said to me, in apparent delight, was "*Hijo!* Oh, but what did you bring me?" I decided I had no choice but to try to work something out with the IRS.

. . .

I think the office was situated somewhere on Suffolk Street downtown, in a massive but cluttered room filled with some one hundred or so cubicles, each with its own fluorescent lamp overhead, an auditor, and some poor unfortunate turning purple, shaking, voice rising, his life ending, pleading his case. In one of those cubicles, I faced a black woman in a polka-dotted dress and white-frame glasses, somewhere in her mid-fifties, whose eyelids continued to blink unexpectedly, as if the yellowish light in that windowless room hurt her. I had walked in wearing an Italian scarf wrapped about my neck, a fine silk shirt, pleated trousers, and soft leather shoes; sitting down and presenting both my paperwork and my side of the story, all the while trying to impress her with the notion that I was above doing something as tawdry as evading taxes, I must have come off like the biggest fop in the world.

"I really hadn't anything to do with what happened with those taxes—you see, I was living in Europe for the past year or so, in Rome, in a villa for a good part of that time—studying and writing, in a community of brilliant scholars and artists—and while I was away, I prevailed upon a friend of mine"—her blinking eye did a double take on my use of the word *prevail*—"to look after my affairs. But you see, my friend seemed to have not thought the papers you sent me too important, and because I had been working on a novel and of course traveling throughout Europe for much of that time, I hardly ever had the opportunity to inquire after such things and . . ."

As I went on, she wrote things down in pencil on a pad, occasionally looking up at me and uttering, "Uh-huh," just as my friend had, her face betraying an opinion, so recently formed, that I was some kind of idiot trying to plead hardship to someone who had to spend her days in such a lifeless soul-destroying environment: I really didn't have any excuse except that I had a friend who probably had his own problems or, without realizing it, had indeed fucked me—but I could have been kidnapped by aliens as far as that office's directive about obtaining monies owed was concerned: It just didn't matter. After listening to my excruciatingly banal excuse—in essence, that my life had been going too well for me to be bothered with such things—she put down her pencil and smiled, though not widely.

"Mr. Hidjewlos," she told me, "I am very sympathetic to your circumstances, but if I were you, I'd go out as soon as possible and find a good accountant. We've got some restitution coming to us."

It would take me over a year and a half to pay the IRS and New York State their back taxes, but while I'd remain mystified by how my good deed had backfired on me, at least one nice thing came of it:

My downstairs neighbor, directly below my apartment, was a black psychiatrist who used to hate my guts and accuse me of being a racist because, having to turn up at TDI most days, I'd be forced to bang on the floor at three in the morning to get him to quiet down. A cool night owl with some kind of state-of-the-art stereo system, he loved to crank up his speakers when the whole rest of the world tried to sleep, while he listened to the cool jazz of WGBO, whose programming came through my floor so clearly I could make out the DJ's words, and every riff, every drumbeat, every agitating sax regurgitation of forms and musical motifs I'd heard a million times before—to the point it would drive me crazy. I'd tap the floor with my knuckles, then pound at it with my fist, and he'd turn it down a little, but then, just as I'd be slipping back to sleep, it would get louder again, until finally I'd have to go downstairs and knock on his door.

Barely even looking at me, he'd say, "All right, all right." But I'd have to do so every night. After a while, I'd get so agitated, I'd take my electric guitar and, turning my amp down against the floor, crank out the craziest and most irritating blues riffs you'll ever hear: More than once, we'd have more than a few unkind words, his opinion coming down to this: "You are only complaining because you hate Negroes and are a racist."

I'd pretty much forgotten about that, when, having returned from Italy, I heard the heavy bass of some moody Miles Davis tune coming through: This time, though, when I tapped (not banged) on the floor, he turned the volume down really low; guess he must have thought I was my friend. Eventually, he caught wind that my friend had moved out and when I ran into him a few days later, he told me: "At first, I couldn't believe it was you who rented out the apartment to a black man."

And with that he offered me his hand: That was the one good thing that happened.

• • •

That next year, regressing into an anxious state of mind, and forced to hustle around for money, I became a voracious smoker again. Because I didn't want to start up with another full-time job downtown, which I could have wrangled through connections—how could I become a copywriter after I'd won a Rome Prize?—I found myself taking on any kind of teaching job, though not at any university: I just never considered myself accomplished enough to teach writing on a college level. (There was more to this: I wasn't in any loop—while most of my former classmates had, at that point, been teaching in different colleges for the past ten years or so, I, a latecomer, would have been lucky to land a few courses as an adjunct, but even then, as I always had, I felt as if I needed more experience as a writer before presuming to teach others—something that apparently hasn't bothered entire generations of creative writing teachers.)

I ended up working at three venues, as it were: One was a suicide ward at the Gracie Square Hospital, the other a terminal cancer ward at Payne Whitney. And I taught at the Amsterdam House, an old-age home up on 112th in my old neighborhood. For suicidal, seriously depressed, and troubled folks, I learned that you had to establish some very specific writing rules: "Please, no blood from orifices or from any acts of violence. No mention of the devil or the use of the color black." That kind of thing. Among my students was an Ursuline nun, somewhere in her late fifties, who, descended from Italian nobility, had slashed her wrists simply because she woke up one day and realized that she did not believe in God and had therefore wasted her life. She wrote, however, remarkably spiritual poetry. The terminal cancer ward was more problematic. Whereas most crazy people, in my experience, enjoy being told that they are, indeed, crazy, there is nothing one can say to someone dying of cancer to relieve him of that ultimate disappointment and agony.

Falling back not on what I had learned from Sontag or Barthelme but from my own mother, whose poetic strivings over the decade or so since my pop's death had grown more sophisticated, I had them write about the most important or happiest days of their lives—in prose or poetry—and for a short while, at least, I seemed to have lifted some of them out of their own bodies and miserable fates. And I found that it helped to adopt a tender, almost priestly manner with them: It helped that I do believe there is something (unimaginable) awaiting all of us (owed to my Catholic barbarity or, as some prick psychiatrist once said to me, to my lingering childhood fantasies of finding "Daddy" and therefore salvation). Mainly, I just tried to emulate the kindly people I knew, and that seemed to make a difference to them, though there is no amount of preaching or kindness that can take the place of morphine. The old-age home was the happier experience: Among my students was a 107-year-old woman, a former doctor from Missouri, who had maintained a lucid mind while her body had shriveled up to the size of a small, gnarl-limbed child's. (Hers was the story of how she became the first female doctor in her state.) Though I never cared for the smell of musty death in such a place, nor the natural melancholy of the aged, I felt at least that I was easing their exits from this life in some little way. Heading home with a few dollars in my pocket and happily lighting up a smoke, I'd feel some sense of accomplishment until, at some later hour, I'd take stock of myself and realize that at my age, thirty-six, I really wasn't anywhere at all.

．　．　．

Yet, having to make quarterly payments to the IRS, I was hardly making ends meet—thank God one could pay such cheap rents back then. Once my grant-funded jobs ran out, however, I went back to working for Manpower as a file clerk—but it left me so depressed that I quickly gave up on it. One day, out of the blue, I received a letter from an upstate arts group located in the town of Lake George, offering me a teaching job for some six months, for which I would be paid the regal sum of five thousand dollars: It wouldn't solve most of my problems, but it wouldn't hurt.

Eventually, as well, it hit me that the only way I would ever be able to pay off my debts was to sell a book. That's when my agent, Harriet Wasserman, came in: I'd known her since 1984, and though I'd never earned her a dime in commission, nor given her anything to shop around, she provided me, as had Barthelme, the kind of encouragement that folks starting out in the business need. From time to time, I'd have lunch with her or she'd send me off to meet an editor to whom she had talked up my talent. The two I recall meeting, before I went off to Italy, were much admired old-school publishing men, the likes of which no longer exist: Harvey Ginzburg and Corliss "Cork" Smith, classy fellows either of whom I would have, in fact, been happy to work with. Though I had first been referred to Ms. Wasserman by my editor at Persea, she had no interest in my staying there. (Nor did I: One of their mantras, though most often true, but which a person from my background just didn't want to believe, had it that I should never expect to make any money as a writer.) Unfortunately, I didn't have much of anything going on in those days. As far as I was concerned, that novel about those two Cuban musicians, which I had been writing on and off for the past three years or so, and which I hadn't bothered to show anyone, didn't even begin to strike me as the kind of book that mainstream publishers would be interested in, mainly, I think, simply because its subject matter was Latino.

The newspaper of record certainly reflected that: As someone who can remember coming to *The New York Times*, which I used to deliver as a kid, only later while in college (when it seemed a distinctive step up in terms of syntax and vocabulary from the papers I had been raised with), the fact that I never saw any reviews of Latino-authored books in its pages seemed to be a sad comment on how little publishing had changed since my first novel had come out. What Hispanic- or Latino-surnamed authors they did review, or that bookstores and publishing houses cared about, came out of the "Boom"— García Marquez on the top of a heap that, however wonderful, left little room in the public imagination for those writers, like an Edwin Vega, who, coming up the hard way, with nary a connection in the outer world, remained unknown to New York publishing and therefore to a mainstream audience in America.

My agent must have seen in me the potential for bridging that gap. I think a lot of it had to do with the way I looked: She was Jewish, and because I had been sometimes taken as so, I am sure she considered me more "sellable." In such circumstances, my non-darkish/non-ethnic looks probably struck her as an asset, and the truth is that, whenever I met up with such editors, like a Harvey Ginzburg or a Cork Smith, the barely visible hesitation on the part of someone trying to reconcile my face with my name ultimately became an expression of relief. And that alone must have put them at ease. (Well, perhaps that all just happened in my head. At least on one occasion, I learned that the fact that I *was* Latino could be off-putting. When my first novel came out, I gave a copy to my next-door neighbors, some five elderly Jewish sisters, who had, at first, been delighted, only to later knock on my door and return it, one of them saying, "Oh, but we thought you were Jewish. I'm sorry, but this is not for us.") Nevertheless, even after the minor success of my first "immigrant" novel, a genre which, as I would learn, seemed to have very little to do with "real" literature, I still couldn't muster much faith in myself as a writer nor, for that matter, in my novel about those *cubano* brothers who go on the *Lucy* show. Instead, I found myself longing to write something truly "literary." (Translation: having nothing to do with my Cuban roots.) At a certain point, I decided that it was time for me to "shit or get off the pot," as my older brother, with his fondness for blunt sayings, would put it. Either I would write a book or forget about the whole thing—maybe go back into advertising or follow that other nascent dream, of becoming a high school English teacher.

In any event, having put in a successful application for a residency at the MacDowell Colony some months before, I spent six weeks or so that autumn, in 1987, holed up in a cabin in the New Hampshire woods, working with all the sincerity I could muster on a "literary" novel. Under the influence of just about any writer I read or heard—poets swarming through that place and giving nearly nightly readings of some kind—my prose took on a delicacy and fineness of language that I had never thought possible. The story, some two hundred pages' worth of it, tapped into some of the longings I must have felt as a kid in the hospital. In that novella, a group of terminally ill children (somehow) realize their situation and, though dying from unspecified causes, (somehow) manage to organize an escape from their home and into the woods, where they (somehow), as I recall, hook up with a magical entity, a witch who lives in a cottage, who restores them to health, but only briefly. (I remember hitting a wall and wondering how to get the hell around it.) I must have been thinking about Ken Kesey's *One Flew over the Cuckoo's Nest* and the story "Hansel and Gretel" at the same time, but however I had constructed that story, I deliberately went out of my way to avoid mentioning my Cuban-ness, while aspiring to a style that was lyrical, erudite, and, so I thought, beautiful.

. . .

Coming back with what I considered a masterpiece, the kind that would establish me as more than a promising "immigrant" voice, I finally decided to show it to Ms. Wasserman. She read the manuscript quickly, over a weekend, and called me up so that we might have a lunch to discuss it.

"That novella," she later told me in some Lexington Avenue restaurant, "is about the worst and most pretentious thing I have ever read in my life." Then, shaking her head, she said, "Look, just put it aside. Take my word for it."

This may sound strange, given the previous buildup, but, though I had written the thing, it had not come from my heart (though I carried an eternal image of terminally ill children inside me) and the whole process had been torturous. While one part of my psyche, benumbed from an overexposure to too much lyrical poetry, had been persuaded that it was good, no matter what anybody might say, another side of me, the one whose skin had started to break out again into dry raw patches, suspected that it was a piece of treacle. Come what may, I felt a tremendous sense of relief at her appraisal. There was something else: I liked the fact that she could be so bluntly honest with me, which is to say that in those moments, I felt as if I could trust her, at least when it came my writing.

"So what else have you been working on?" she asked me.

A curious-looking woman, very plump and short, her visage a cross between that of Gertrude Stein and Queen Victoria in her later years, and with a florid style of dressing that, depending upon flowing scarves and ankle-hem dresses, harkened back to the fashions of the 1920s, she, in fact, conformed to what one might have fantasized a slightly eccentric agent to look like. Indeed, in the coming years (over almost two decades), I'd learn just how eccentric an agent like her could be, but at the time, I felt nothing but pure gratitude that someone who represented the likes of Saul Bellow could have taken so much interest in someone hardly known to anyone except back in my old neighborhood, and then only as the "guy who wrote that fuckin' book." Above all, however, it was her expertise that I needed.

"Didn't you once tell me you had something else in the works?"

"Well, that other thing?" I said. "It's about these musicians from Havana." And I went on to fill her in on some aspects of my story, such as they were. She couldn't have been happier to hear about it: Two Cuban brothers who end up as walk-on characters on the *Lucy* show? She loved the notion.

"But get me some of those pages as soon as possible," she insisted. "And I'll read them over and see what I can do." Then, as I looked off, as I sometimes did in moments of discomfort, she tugged at my sleeve. "I mean it," she told me. "Don't forget."

Living alone in those days, I could do whatever I pleased in my apartment: smoke, drink, and eat at any hour, get up at three in the morning if an idea hit me, go out when I felt like it, watch Bozo the clown on TV if I wanted to, jam with musician friends, put out cigarettes in the wall, turn on a bed light in the middle of the night to read, and, among so many other things, I could work at my own pace and never worry about having to clean up what someone else might call a mess. Not having outgrown the shopping-bag method of writing left over from *Our House*, once I had to actually come up with some pages from my book, which was then still entitled *The Secrets of a Poor Man's Life*, I emptied several boxes of that manuscript out onto my living room floor, and, in the only aesthetic clue (aside from paying close attention to false sentiment and good language) I'd taken from Barthelme, a collagist at heart, I proceeded to arrange and rearrange them into various piles, aiming to achieve, as Cortázar had done in *Hopscotch*, a novel whose chapters and narratives, such as they were, flowed into one another as atmospheres, not so much in any order but through the associative power of what the characters' emotions conveyed; or, if you like, almost musically, which was exactly the effect I'd wanted, though I'd never really thought of it as so until I actually laid it out. Without realizing it, I already had much of the novel's supporting structure—its framework—including a number of short experimental sections that were written in the voice of a young boy, my stand-in, as it were, and who, for the sake of a potential narrator with an inside, highly subjective view of the story, happened to be Nestor Castillo's son, Eugenio: I liked one particular bit in which he describes watching the *I Love Lucy* show with his uncle Cesar, a superintendent and former Mambo King, and that made for the opening. I followed that up with what I believed to be a pretty sound portraiture of Cubans in New York in the 1950s, the ins and outs, literally, of Cesar Castillo's sex life, as well as the inner torments of his brother—perpetually pining away for a woman he'd left behind in Cuba, María. Somehow, so many little bits I'd written, with so casual a freedom—and therefore happily brimming with tons of life—fit together so perfectly that, at a certain moment, I suddenly understood how jazz musicians feel when, thanks to some clever arranging, all their crazy-shit riffing falls into place, to make something that you've never heard before.

Once I had put a couple hundred pages together, a lot of them with cigarette ash burns, wine and juice and who knows what else stains, I was almost tempted, because of my usual self-doubts, to rearrange everything again, but in some moment of practicality, I decided to say to hell with it and, catching a subway downtown, dropped the manuscript off at my agent's office.

· · ·

Then I tried to forget about the whole thing: It was not as if, after all, I lived in a writers' world or had a lot of colleagues to mull things over with. In fact, I'd be fabricating a lie to say that I expected anything to come about from that vocation, and if I had any hope for that manuscript, it came down to a simple desire to pay off my bills. Approaching my late thirties, and having turned my back on an advertising career—to think I could have run a Seattle office or worked at Y&R writing copy like *"You can taste it with your eyes!"*—I really didn't have any other prospects in my life, except for that book. What else could I do but hope that someone would be interested enough in it to offer me an advance?

However, it wasn't only about that: I seem to recall having a sense that writing books was a noble pursuit, akin to bringing some light into the world, and while I can't begin to put myself in that idealistic place again, I'll only say that, back then, it was my naïve faith in the value of literature that also kept me going. At the same time, I couldn't begin to imagine an interest in my work. Who, after all, published Latinos? And what were they going to do with a name like Hijuelos, and who the fuck could care one bit about a lowly spic superintendent's life and a bicultural world that, with links to the one I had been raised in, no one had ever written about, except me in that first book, *Our House*, which, to this day, has mainly remained forgotten? Of course, I wondered what sophisticated readers would make of the fact that my main character, Cesar Castillo, father of that universe, drank too much because of the woes of his life (Yes, of course, a cliché, I could imagine people thinking), or of the fragile Nestor Castillo, whose obsessions with a woman (and country) left behind, as well as his memories of nearly dying as a child, closely paralleled my own. Would those two seem pathetic? Or too emotionally blunt for any readers?

. . .

Thankfully, I could depend on my family—or my mother specifically—to help me forget about that little corner in my life. In fact, when I'd head over to 118th Street to visit her, she, having her list of required gifts—some food, a dessert of some kind (chocolate ice cream), and a bottle of wine (for she had developed a taste for it in later years)—would speak with admiration about how my older brother had everything together—kid, wife, house, reliable union job—while, at the same time, she'd imply without exactly saying it that I'd turned out to be a *trastornado,* or screwed-up loser. Indeed, I really had nothing going for me except some vague creative aspirations, which in that neighborhood, where most of the kids grew up to become cops and firemen and union workers (or else junkies, con men, and criminals), meant becoming a bum, or as I'd often hear, a "hangout artist." On some level, she must have felt sorry to see her son floundering, and though I think it finally hit her that I might have been bright, I'm sure she didn't think I had much to show for my efforts, except some fleeting worldly experiences. And I think she secretly suspected that I was broke, for a few times when I brought over Chinese food, my mother offered to pay for it—something which, for a woman who watched her every penny, was a remarkable gesture of generosity (or pity).

On the other hand, she could really rub the vanity of my situation in my face. Oh, she'd tell me about every son and daughter of a friend to have landed a good job, how many kids they had, where they lived, or conversely, perhaps in an attempt to make me feel better, go into some of the local tragedies—that my old friend Bobby Hannon went crazy; or that Philip Ricart, Belen's son, who, once dapper and supremely well composed, took too much LSD and became a street person; and so on with one sorry story after the other, like the fire that had, the past winter, swept through a hotel in Quebec, in which one of the beautiful Haitian sisters from upstairs and her daughter, vacationing there, had perished, or that she'd just run into Mr. MacElvoy, whose sixteen-year-old son, on the brink of becoming a seminarian, had been murdered one Christmas some years back—and how shattered he remained over that—or that one of the priests at Corpus was a repressed homosexual, and that Frankie, from the pharmacy on 120th Street, still lived with his mother and drank too much . . . in her way, rightly reminding me that much worse could happen to a person than being out of work.

Sometimes, too, she'd spook me, staring at me strangely—especially if I'd made the mistake of lighting a cigarette: "So you've forgotten how you almost died, huh?" she'd say. "Go ahead, kill yourself." Then she might lecture me about health food and vitamins—"When was the last time you went to a doctor?"—before going off into a momentary spell, fixated on my eyes, and coming out of it, she would say: "*Sabes cuánto te pareces a tu papá?*"—"Don't you know how much you look like your father?" The kicker is that while growing up, I'd always wondered why, if I looked so much like my father, who in my eyes was *muy muy cubano,* no one ever took me as a Cuban.

One day, while pondering that long-standing mystery, I asked her, "If Pop was so Cuban and I look just like him, how come nobody ever takes me as so?" Laughing, she answered: "*Tu papá?* Why, he never looked Cuban at all!"

Seeing her was always wonderful and awful at the same time. Feeling both inspired and drained by my mother, once I'd finally get home to my apartment, the first thing I'd do was pour myself a hearty drink (usually wine, my other favorite, vodka, being a luxury) and light a cigarette—and if the right frame of mind hit me, I'd feel a momentary bliss and almost an optimism about my future as a writer. But just as often, depleted and my spirits low, I couldn't even begin to muster the strength and will to imagine the things that would, shockingly, happen with that novel.

By the time my agent started sending the novel around, we'd decided, during the course of a telephone conversation, to change its title to the far more swinging and cheery *The Mambo Kings Play Songs of Love,* which, if you know that book at all, was the name of a 33 LP album Cesar Castillo and his brother, Nestor, had recorded back in 1955 or so. There were several literary houses that my agent had considered sending it to, among them Farrar, Straus & Giroux, but she'd already been trying to interest one of their more upcoming young editors in my work, an Exeter/Ivy League sort with poetic credentials, Jonathan Galassi, who I had met briefly in her office, years before while working at TDI. Thin, intensely bookish in his looks, he dressed in the manner that one supposed certain editors did: button-down shirt, jacket and bow tie, loafers, and, I recall, wire-rim glasses. His handshake was neither here nor there, though his manner was never less than affable, if, however, a little too patrician for my taste—but then, in those days, most editors were. At the time, I hadn't realized how lucky I was to be introduced to such an important fellow, that as a Latino, I was being afforded the unique opportunity to break through such a long-standing literary barrier into a world that, worshipping the likes of F. Scott Fitzgerald and John Cheever, had yet to give Latino writers a chance at all.

In fact, I was hardly able to remember his name when, one evening a few weeks after she'd started sending the book around, my agent called me with the rather startling news that this same Mr. Galassi had been ecstatic about the manuscript and wanted to make an offer. My reaction? You're kidding me, right? By that same Friday, he did—for an amount that I initially turned down; I simply needed more money to finally settle up with the IRS, as well as to cover my expenses, agent, and further taxes. I didn't expect them to come back so quickly, but that following Monday, they did. Within a few months, I received a check for half the advance, enough to settle my tax situation and to pay my expenses during that year when I'd actually get down to finishing the book.

. . .

I worked on most of that manuscript on 106th Street. It was a rhapsodic time. Relieved of my financial burdens and having nothing to lose, I "filled in" the life and histories of the Castillo brothers, whose musicality I wore like an inherited glove. Along the way, I drowned in mambo music, my KLH record player running from the earliest part of the day, when I'd come back from jogging around Central Park (nothing like a smoke afterward, by the way, when you're feeling all oxygenated), until the evenings, sometimes even past midnight. But did I care? I was still young enough to possess an endless-seeming energy, and though I had never thought in a thousand years that I could end up at a publisher like Farrar, Straus & Giroux, the very notion that I was possibly on my way inspired me further. I worked tirelessly, chain-smoking like a motherfucker and only rarely taking time off to hang around with some of my musician friends. After a while, the ordinary business of going out on errands, to shop for groceries or to buy cigarettes, became an imposition. I don't recall just when I handed in a "completed" manuscript or how long afterward it was returned to me with suggestions, but the process went smoothly, nearly effortlessly, as everyone over at Farrar, Straus & Giroux had seemed to have fallen in love with that book, even if they were uncertain as to how it might go over with the critics and public. (It had tremendous amounts of sex in it—why wouldn't it? I had enough naughty schoolboy Catholicism left in me to fill a cathedral, and my hyperawareness of bodily functions and of the body itself spilled over into the book in ways that left me, once so frail and sick, cracking up over its sexual possibilities.)

And the editing? Despite his upper-class airs, Galassi, as it turned out, proved to be a superb editor for that book, allowing it to breathe in every way and urging only truly prudent changes. With a musical thing going on in my head, I treated word repetitions like beats—and sometimes it worked and sometimes it didn't. Fortunately, as the author of a fine book of poetry, *Morning Run*, he was linguistically savvy enough to stanch my gushing use of certain words, like *lumbering* in reference to Cesar Castillo's sexual attributes, which, early on, had occurred some fifty or so times. He was also splendidly judicious in other ways—I don't think we had a single argument over anything at all. (It was just a different time altogether: Now everything is done over the Internet, manuscripts like this one electronically transmitted and much of the work done without actually speaking or spending much time with anyone—the impersonality of it all is staggering to old-school writers like me.) By contrast, meeting with Galassi, with my unruly, marked-up, held-together-by-chewing-gum rewrites in hand, was a joy. We'd work for a few hours in the morning, then head out for lunch somewhere near their offices by Union Square, to just relax and have a few drinks—at least I did—and later I'd take the subway back uptown feeling as good as anyone could over a professional relationship.

I also had a pleasant experience with the in-house copy editors, the sort of ladies who walked around with pencils tucked behind their ears and seemed to swarm, paper in hand, along the hall of that publishing house, whose walls were lined with books and shelving like library stacks, to check out their facts. I got along particularly well with a longtime employee, a Puerto Rican woman, Carmen, whose tender loving care in regards to that manuscript—and the capricious Spanish I employed—made a wonderful difference not just to my novel but to me. The fact that she so liked it made me feel good, as it represented its first success with a Latino reader. (And that left me happier than anything else: For once, with my writing as my own front man, as it were, I was being accepted.)

The final touches, at least at that stage, had to do with conceiving of a book jacket. A well-known cover designer, Fred Marcellino, had asked me, through Jonathan Galassi, if I had any ideas that might be of use to him. Since the novel's title followed the style of a 1950s mambo record, I sent him about four record jackets from that time: He especially liked one of them, which featured a sultry-looking blond babe of the 1950s, whose image he lifted and put on the cover of my book. (The cover, incidentally, turned out great, though a few years later, the designer's use of an actual image of a woman from one of those jackets, the model still being alive, would involve me in a lawsuit, in which I was held at fault.)

Along the way, other things seemed to be cooking. A friend from my Brooklyn days, an art scholar and entrepreneur, Jeffrey Hoffeld, had told me that the founder of a gallery in which he had once been a partner, Arne Glimcher, might be interested, as an aspiring movie producer, in taking a peek at *The Mambo Kings Play Songs of Love*—even in its early uncorrected form. Since I had nothing to lose, I went along with the notion. A few months later, I met with Ms. Wasserman and we went over to Glimcher's place on East Fifty-second, an opulently maintained art deco high-rise apartment building of 1930s vintage (so I would guess), across the street from where Greta Garbo supposedly lived. He occupied a duplex penthouse overlooking the East River, and the first thing that impressed the hell out of me as I walked in was the fact that his entryway floor was inlaid with an antique second-century Roman mosaic of a maritime theme; his walls were covered with paintings from his gallery, the Pace on West Fifty-seventh, all by famous artists—Robert Rauschenberg, Jim Dine, Chuck Close, and a portrait of him in broken pottery by one Julian Schnabel, among others; talk about money. I can remember trying to behave as if I were not already in over my head, though

Glimcher, younger then by a decade than I am now, could not have been nicer, nor more accommodating, and seemingly humble.

I would imagine he, as a professional gallery owner, took an enormous pride in discovering new talent, and I suppose that same tendency had followed him into the movie business. I was apparently that new talent, and he did everything to charm and impress me. He spoke of spending a lot of time with "Sigourney" on the shoot for *Gorillas in the Mist*, of his many industry connections and his absolute determination to make my novel into a film—though it had yet to receive even a single review. With passion, he spoke about many of the novel's themes—the close yet troubled relationship between the brothers really hitting him in a personal way—and of course, of how he, of a certain generation, had been raised on the mambo and the cha-cha-cha. And that song I had created on Nestor's behalf, "Beautiful María of My Soul"—"Oh, you'll see what I'll end up doing with that. We'll get a first-rate composer in, I promise you."

He spoke of making my novel into a film with such confidence that, after a while, it started to feel like a foregone conclusion—such matters as an agreement for a movie option as a precursor to a contract, a necessary formality, would be forthcoming to my agent in no time at all.

That day, I got my first sense of why the man, as I'd learn, happened to be one of the most successful art dealers in the world: He was good at making you feel that his intentions were really your own. And he knew just which buttons to push. On our way out, while leaving it that I would meet him at some future point in his favorite restaurant, the Four Seasons, to talk over things further, he telephoned his chauffeur, a former cop named Bob, and gave him instructions to take us wherever we wanted to go in his limousine. I was startled. The only time I had ridden in a limousine before was for my pop's burial out in Long Island. After dropping Ms. Wasserman off at her place on East Eighty-sixth, I found myself being shuttled uptown toward my old neighborhood like a pasha. I liked his driver—a real working-class man, of Sicilian roots, the sort with whom I always got along, a real salt-of-the-earth fellow. We talked, mainly about the

Howard Beach area of Queens—my brother's second wife had a lot of family out there, and that Italian connection opened Bob up as if he were an old-time chum and confidant. Eventually, he told me how much he thought Mr. Glimcher was worth—a stupendous amount. "And that's not includin' the value of his artwork, *capiche*?" I used to think that he was just confiding in me as one working-class guy to the other, but I can't help wondering now if I was set up, those incredible numbers meant to further impress me.

I do know that riding in a limousine made me feel both well-off for the first time in my life and also somewhat embarrassed. Asked "Where to?" I had him stop at a picture frame shop on West Eighty-sixth, and then I went right next door into a comic shop to look around. My next destination in that fabulous limousine? Some exotic bar on the East Side or downtown in Soho? No: the Food Town supermarket on One hundredth Street and Broadway, where I bought some groceries. Afterward, when I came out with my bags (chicken, potatoes, carrots, tomatoes), I thanked Bob for his help and told him I didn't mind walking for a bit. (It didn't seem a healthy thing for me to be seen pulling up to my building on 106th Street in such a rich-looking vehicle.) He just nodded, tipped his cap, and drove off, while I made my way those six or so blocks, my head spinning with a deepening wariness about the possible direction in which my life might be headed.

. . .

You see, I was no budding Jay McInerney, a novelist famed for zestfully embracing the bounties of his success. I simply didn't trust that world. And while I appreciated the attention I seemed to be getting from the likes of someone like Mr. Glimcher (who at a different point took me into the inner sanctum of his gallery and had his assistant bring in one Picasso oil after the other for me to view and even touch if I wanted to—Unbelievable, if only my pop could see me, is what I actually thought), I felt tremendously grateful for the opportunity to get out of New York when the occasion arrived.

My teaching stint in Lake George came along at just the right time, during that nerve-racking prepublication stage when my manuscript was being turned into page proofs for a bound galley. My appointment as a resident writer, which was to last some six months, began in the autumn of 1988—think it was late October when I first arrived. There, in a meeting room in a former courthouse just off the lake, along Canada Street, I taught a weekly workshop in creative writing, free to the public. My students were a wonderful group of locals, consisting of both the well-heeled and well-educated country club folk—doctors, lawyers, and dentists among them—and struggling working-class mothers, along with a handful of normal middle-class people, with some quite interesting backwoods folks and retirees thrown in.

I lived in a mountainside house overlooking the Hudson River, about twenty miles north of town, with a couple who had kindly offered to put me up for practically nothing. The husband, an ex–Benedictine monk, taught art at a local college and made totemic sculptures that he sold throughout the Adirondack region, while his wife, who had tracked me down on behalf of the arts center in the first place, ran most of its public outreach programs. I won't go much into my life there except to say that, as sojourns go, it was about as far removed from New York, or for that matter, Italy, as any place could be. I learned to drive a stick shift there, however, good for maneuvering a car over the mountains, and I made a lot of friends as well. It turned out that the art center's director happened to be a singer with one of the best-known country rock groups in the region, the Stony Creek Band, with whom, in that latest incarnation, I began to perform as a sit-in guitar player, at local country clubs, barn-style dances, and in the kinds of Adirondack joints that would have found their New York City equivalents in the leave-your-guns-by-the-door discos in the South Bronx of 1982. That was yet another life, and brief as it had been, I loved being away from the buildup for the book, and that distance made dealing with such chores as correcting the manuscript a bit easier.

I also signed that option with Glimcher's Pace Productions, having entrusted all the contractual business to my agent, who, as I would eventually learn, was also in over her head, having little practical knowledge of the movie business. But I much enjoyed the Lake George area while my stay lasted, and then, of course, as I'd received news that a bound galley of my book had been finally produced, and that there were things I'd have to do, I returned to New York.

Once home, I did my best to maintain a kind of cool among my old friends from the neighborhood. They tended to have a blasé attitude about my profession, as if anyone could do it, and when it came to the folks I'd meet while visiting my brother's in-laws out in Howard Beach, where they'd hold backyard barbecues a few blocks from where John Gotti lived, I'd feel so out of touch with the writing world that, whenever someone asked me what I did, I hardly thought it worth mentioning, though I inevitably would. ("Oh, yeah, your brother told me you write stuff—like what, spy novels?") Most people were nice, but among some of the strangers I'd meet, the writing profession seemed a bit on the scammy side, and more than once I'd hear something like, "So, okay—what do you do for real work?"

During that time, it seemed that I always had some duty to attend to in regards to the prepub biz of the book. Learning that *Publishers Weekly* felt strongly enough to request an interview with me, I found myself putting on another hat—as a self-believing writer who'd always had a vision for that novel, while, in reality, I'd hardly even figured out any way to talk about it. For that matter, as a publishing world "guinea pig" from the Latino community, I'd have to brace myself for any number of questions about the ethnicity of my writing and about the status of Latino writing in this country—but, so warned my agent and anyone else at the house I happened to talk to, I would have to be careful not to offend anyone by stating the obvious fact that, on the surface of things, no one, to that point, had seemed to give a shit for the intellectual and creative life of my/that community. Never claiming to be a spokesperson for anyone except myself and, so I thought, believing that my first novel *Our House in the Last World* had already presented my take on the issues pertaining to my Latino identity, I learned soon enough that, on just about every occasion, I had to explain myself all over again, even if jokingly so—"I know I don't look or act particularly Cuban, but it's just a disguise to find out what folks really think." That alone was enough to make me dread the very notion of speaking to any journalists at all.

Still, I tried to look upon it as part of my job, though I couldn't have begun to predict how much the baring of my soul (as in this book) over the years would become a part of my life.

That's probably why I welcomed any opportunities to slip uptown, though returning to my neighborhood and spending time in the old apartment always provoked a melancholic detour into Memoryville— which, like religion, was good for creativity but bad for living. Or to put it differently, the same melancholy that bled through the Mambo Kings continued to pour through my veins. Though my agent told me that all kinds of good things were about to happen—"Just watch how your life will change!"—I'm not sure that it was anything I wanted to hear. Perhaps that's why I went out of my way to keep my feet on the ground. Not once forgetting where I had come from, I allowed myself to become more deeply entangled with my family duties, and these mainly came down to looking after my mother ("As I once took care of you, now it's your turn to take care of me," she'd say). Every so often I'd take her to the hospital for her checkups (with which she had become obsessed) or to such and such an office for some document, or, as often was the case, out to visit with my brother in Staten Island (or the "Latin from Staten Island" as went the name of an old rumba of the 1930s).

As with earlier times, such trips required of me great patience, not only because my mother, as if trapped in a certain groove on a 78 RPM record that skipped, could not restrain herself from going over her life with my father, but because, in her mid-seventies and slowing up from the more typical maladies of advancing years (though her mind remained as sharp as ever), just getting her around—on foot to the subway, and then to the ferry boat—seemed interminable, a two-or-so-hour trek that *felt* like a day. Oddly, even back then, as I'd walk slowly across the flagstone promenade of Columbia, my mother holding on to me so tightly, the same feelings that dogged me as a sickly child—of wanting to break away and run off to some far-away place—came back to me, and I'd wish to God that I could have somehow managed to have stayed in Italy, or, at any rate, somewhere else. At the same time, I came up with the notion that my Cuban identity, however New Yorkized, required that I do the right thing and never, never turn my back on my family, no matter what other desires drove me. And why?

Even I didn't have a clue, *coño*.

Frankly, I wasn't sure if I was cut out for the literary life, whatever that may have been, in the first place. From what I had observed of it, from my safe distance, it didn't always treat people kindly. Over the past decade, Donald Barthelme's reputation, for example, had seemed to sink and sink into a kind of near-oblivion. Where once his books were reviewed on the front page of the almighty *New York Times* Sunday Book Review and greeted as masterpieces, by 1989, his works had been relegated to a quarter page in the back of that publication. Where his experimental fictions had once been considered timely, relevant, brilliant, and cutting-edge, he had been most recently eclipsed by Raymond Carver, whose surgically precise but often maudlin prose had become the new standard of excellence. (And all the more so after the poor man, a reformed alcoholic who often wrote of those trials so transcendently, died of cancer in 1988.)

Surely this sea change affected Barthelme's spirits. During my visits with him on Eleventh Street, just as I had returned from Rome and about a year and a half later, he had seemed, in terms of his own creativity, somewhat of a lost soul, a writer trapped by his self-imposed restrictions and obviously perplexed by his own disenchantment. Confessing to a writer's block, he once told me that he would love to write an autobiographical novel but thought that he couldn't, as it would be a betrayal of his aesthetic and of what people expected of him. (The closest he came to doing so was a lovely story called "Bishop.") I didn't quite understand his resistance to a bit of change, but what concerned me more was the horrific doubling-over cough he had developed by then. On those evenings, keeping up with him as a smoker seemed a stupidity—he had gotten to a point when his episodes became violent, his face turning such a deep red that the only way he could soothe his burning, nearly rupturing throat was to down, in one quick and continuous gulp, a full goblet of Scotch, and only then would that retching abate. Though he didn't seem to flinch at my suggestion that he should write whatever the fuck he felt like writing, he blew up at me when I suggested that he see a doctor: "Mind your own business," he snapped, lighting up another cigarette. "I know what I'm doing," he told me. "Trust me."

Then, feeling better, he poured me another Scotch and said: "Okay, one more, then you have to go."

We did speak a few more times and remained on a friendly basis, and when I finally received a galley of the *Mambo Kings* I *almost* sent it to him. Despite all the work I'd already put into it, there were a few paragraphs in the novel, as well as some passages, that I just had to rewrite, and because I wanted to impress him, I decided to wait until I'd had a chance to put in my changes and planned to give him the finished version instead. In the meantime, Donald, through his friend and colleague at the University of Houston Ed Hirsch, a poet who had won the Rome Prize in Literature that year, 1989, traveled to Italy and took up a three-month residency at the American Academy, among the happiest and most carefree of Signor Barthelme's professional life, he and the Eternal City having gotten quite well along. The only caveat is that when Donald finally returned to Houston, with worsening symptoms, he was found to be suffering from throat cancer, by then at an advanced stage. Shortly, the following happened: On a midsummer day in July, while in the hospital, with his wife Marion by his side, and, as I've been told, somewhat sedated on morphine, he was sitting up in his bed when, at a certain moment, he slipped into a coma from which he, lingering for two weeks, never awakened.

The craziest thing? When I first heard about it, I kicked myself for having held my novel back from him (as if my changes would have made much difference in his opinion), but beyond that, I kept thinking that he had been one the few people who had ever looked out for me, and that he was about my pop's age at his passing.

(In fact, Donald passed away on July 23, my father July 26, twenty years before.)

. . .

By the time *The Mambo Kings Play Songs of Love* came out that August of 1989, it was already a fairly well-known entity within the industry: FSG, a house so brilliant at creating a buzz about a book— and in a way I have never since encountered—had practically started a riot at the American Booksellers Association meeting that spring by giving out their advance reading copies along with a canvas bag bearing an image of that book's cover. I'm told that people had swamped the FSG tables and that within a few hours, every last one had been scooped up. Prepub reviews were as good as could be hoped for, and several foreign publishers bought the rights early on. It also seemed that some important newspaper reviews, among them one in *The New York Times*, were imminent, though the official word within the house was not to expect too much, a notion that they held on to until at a certain point, the *Times* requested that I meet with one of their staff writers for the Sunday Book Review—I did so in a bar around the corner from where I lived. (Mainly we discussed how I had come up with certain notions behind the book, the *I Love Lucy* angle, a bridge between American and Cuban cultures, most intriguing him.) Once FSG learned that a little interview would be included with the review, they began to think *The Mambo Kings* would be given a fair amount of space, though to what extent, they could not predict. (They were already on a roll; two of their books, one by Carlos Fuentes and the other by Mario Vargas Llosa, had landed spectacular front-page reviews, but they did not expect anything like that for me: They were Latin American Boom writers after all, while I, as a homegrown Latino—and therefore of far less interest to the general American public—could hardly expect the same stellar respect.)

And yet, come one Sunday—I do not recall the date; I think it was midmonth—my novel made it to the cover of the book review (the literary equivalent, in those days at least, of a musician getting on the cover of *Rolling Stone*). The female critic could not have been kinder, despite the book's high content of macho shenanigans, lauding the work as a great literary *immigrant* novel, the review accompanied by a dandy pen-and-ink illustration depicting a swirl of Cuban musicians shaking maracas and playing drums in a lively jam. I could not have missed it. For even if I wanted to avoid the subject—and a part of me wanted to—I would have heard about it anyway, for my agent, publicist, and editor, among others, called me as soon as they received the news. That was quickly followed (or preceded, as the *Times* book review could be had a week in advance) by a Friday review in the daily *Times* by the star-making/career-withering Michiko Kakutani, who gave me a high-toned rave, though, once again, for my wonderful *immigrant* novel. I was so naïve as to write both reviewers thank-you notes—as I would have done at the ad agency, where if someone looked out for you, some gesture of appreciation followed. I never heard back from either one of them.

Wonderful reviews in just about every newspaper in the country soon followed—literally over a hundred of them (for it was before the Internet killed the newspapers) within a two-week span. (The fifteen or so reviews I received for *Our House*, by comparison, were a drop in the bucket, and that book remained so little known that for years after, people assumed that *The Mambo Kings* was my first novel.) As much as I'd swear those reviews made no difference to me, I still put each carefully away in a box and occasionally took one or the other out to read over again, especially if it had spoken of my book in outsize terms. (Some implied that it was a modern American classic, certainly a breakthrough in terms of Latino literature in this country, and sometimes they actually admired the writing!) To further stroke my ego, *Vanity Fair* did a piece about me (and a review), accompanied by a photograph in which I happened to look somewhat smug and dapper, a cigarette burning in my hand. (The shoot, complete with a willowy and beautiful photographer, took place on the green behind the article writer's brownstone on Sullivan Street: half-Cuban, Wendy Gimbel was one of the great early supporters of that book and of my later work.) And since a British edition would be coming out that following spring, I interviewed with a number of their magazines, even posed for a photographer from British *Vogue*. That same week I went down to a Soho studio and did an international radio broadcast alongside the Panamanian singer Ruben Blades, who, of

Dutch ancestry, had a Cuban mother. That, along with the Beatles—the group that had inspired him to first become a musician—was our point of connection, though he had done a double take when my mind went blank after he'd told me that *su mamá* had come from La Regla, across the bay from Havana, even if I'd mentioned it in *The Mambo Kings*.

Then a *New York Times* article on me came out in the daily arts section. A certain Peter Watrous had come by to talk with me about the musical elements in the book, but what I had been mainly interested in was the fact that he played some guitar. Though it was not mentioned in the piece that resulted, he ended up staying in my apartment until a late hour, and we jammed.

As I had been booked on several big-time television programs, the *Today* show and *Good Morning America* among them, I had been urged to get contact lenses, but I simply couldn't. I was so used to seeing myself in a certain way that the thick drowning-in-water lenses I'd always lived with had become, in effect, my eyes. (Or as I have often since thought, a buffer between myself and the world.) Instead I compromised and spent a small fortune on a pair of thin, specially treated antireflection lenses, cased inside a fancy French frame. (They cost about two and a half weeks of my pop's old salary—that's how far gone I had become.) Nevertheless, as one who had ducked out of any speech class, appalled at the notion of seeing myself captured on a video camera at Brandeis High School, the prospect of going on live national television somewhat terrified me.

Once I got down to the NBC studios at Rockefeller Center, however, a kind of nostalgia for homey old-time TV hit me, and, thinking of Ralph Kramden and Desi Arnaz (and how my pop had liked them), I almost calmed down, though never completely. I'd never worn so much makeup in my life, and it surprised me to see how my black interviewer, Bryant Gumbel, a true gent, appeared absolutely gray under the normal light. (Seeing him in that makeup, I could only think of funeral parlor cadavers.)

In any event, though I would not say that my first appearance was a disaster, I did distinguish myself by rolling my eyes around like BBs whenever Mr. Gumble asked a question that either discomfited me or seemed stupid. ("Why Cubans?" . . . "Why Desi Arnaz?") I also went through that broadcast with the feeling that my head was too big ("*mi cabezon,*" my mother sometimes called me) and, as I always have, felt a little jarred by the way some of the staff regarded me as I walked in, with an interior double take upon finding out that the balding, fair-skinned blond guy was the "Cuban-American" writer scheduled for the show. Sitting under the tremendously bright arc lamps, I couldn't help but check myself out in a monitor to my side. Accustomed to never really seeing my own eyes, I had no notion of just how well they would read through my new lenses—or how much I seemed a nervous beady-eyed jerk—but at least I could console myself with the fact that I had pupils that came across quite intensely on camera.

I went on a fifteen-or-so-city tour after that, reading at bookstores overflowing with people. The best of it was that I met some really nice Latinos and, among them (us) in every city, some Cubans, a long long way from home, Americanized exiles, professionals mainly, who, despite whatever bones they may have had to pick with that book—too much sex, or not anti-Castro enough, or too obsessed with the character's *pingas*—appreciated my absolute love for Cuba. Though I met my share of dainty older Cuban women who thought parts of the book a little saucier than their conservative Catholic dispositions allowed them to enjoy, they too flooded me with something that I could never get enough of: affection—nothing too gushing but just enough to leave me with a tender feeling. And my American readers, if I may use the term? They were kind to me as well, no matter where I went traveling in the country. I found myself visiting many a fancy household, usually gatherings scheduled around my time off, in fairly opulent settings, local high society taking pride in hosting me as their guest. Occasionally, a musician, relating to my book for its insights about the profession, would turn up to make a gift of one of their recordings to me, or a beginner, wanting to break into the music scene, would ask my advice.

But I'd also encounter the sort of person who seemed disappointed when they met me. "I thought you would be swarthier, and more . . . Ricky Ricardo," someone actually told me. Or else they wanted to hear something different from a New York accent, or to see something in my body language and manner that was more distinctly Cuban. (Perhaps they wanted me to come out dancing the mambo or smoking a cigar in a white panama hat.) Sometimes I'd get hit up by a Latin American scholar, who, addressing me in ethnographic terms from the audience, wanted to turn my reading into a symposium about *his* knowledge of Cuba. Sometimes, a lefty, usually a super-liberal who had traveled to Cuba as a political tourist, or had gone there as a college student to chop sugarcane, would denounce my novel for failing to sing the revolution's praises. I did my best to be polite, but it often pissed me off: I'd thank God that I could slip out the back and have a smoke. All along, of course, what else could I be but myself?

And yet that was not enough for some folks who almost seemed angry that the face and personality behind the conception wasn't what they wanted it to be. I knew them by the way they'd stare at me during my readings, or when they didn't laugh at my jokes, and ultimately, more often than not, I could tell just which ones were bound to get up and leave in the middle of my reading.

Sometimes, at midnight, in a hotel room in Portland or Minneapolis or St. Louis—could be anywhere—I'd lie down on the bed, feeling fairly exhausted, and man, the first thing I'd wish I could be doing (besides smoking a cigarette) didn't necessarily have anything to do with women (even though at every venue, there seemed to be someone interested in getting to know me) nor with the prospect of making some money (which was what my agent always talked about) but with the small ways I had of making myself happy—as when I'd sit down with a really good guitarist, like my old pal Nick or the best jazz player I knew, a fellow named John Tucker, whom I met years before on the steps of Columbia University's Low Library, to jam for a few hours, leisurely and without a worry in the world, a glass of wine or two by our side, a cigarette burning in an ashtray—just like it happened sometimes in my novel, to my characters Cesar and Nestor Castillo.

That same autumn, once I'd come back from the tour, I started teaching creative writing at Hofstra University in Long Island at night, a job I had gotten through a writer friend, Julia Marcus, before the book came out, as a hedge against going broke. It required an hour-and-a-half commute each way (subway, train, bus), a real pain, but at least it got my mind off the hoopla and that constant feeling that something both wonderful and awful was happening to me. Though I had enjoyed meeting the majority of my readers, it didn't take much of a curious expression, on the part of both Latinos and non-Latinos, to make me feel that, once again, I had become the receptacle into which people's prejudices poured: Altogether it made me feel like some kind of lab specimen. Aside from escaping that scrutiny, however, I discovered that I simply enjoyed being around those Hofstra kids, most coming from what I would call a nouveau middle-class background—and, who, in most cases, seemed to be the first in their second- or third-generation post-immigrant families to make it to college. One of my classes started at eight, the other let out around six, as I recall. Coming home one evening, I found the very patient and affable writer Richard Price waiting outside my apartment on a stairwell. He had called me up out of the blue, having found my number in the telephone book, but I was so distracted in those days that the time of our meeting had completely slipped my mind. No matter—we ended up having a bite to eat, whereupon he asked me if I would ever be interested in writing scripts for Paramount, with whom he had some kind of arrangement as a scout: I was dense and provincial-minded enough to politely decline, though we remained friends thereafter.

In general, that whole period threw me. I met all kinds of people. George Plimpton invited me over to one of his famous *Paris Review* parties, where I found myself rubbing shoulders with Norman Mailer, Kurt Vonnegut, and Gay Talese, among other authors of note. That same night, I had dinner with the writer Peter Maas and Mr. Plimpton—George, as he asked me to call him, offering to conduct an interview with me for his literary journal. Though I told him I would have to think it over, I had already made up my mind to avoid it, my own stupid modesty (infernal *can't really succeed too much* reticence) getting in the way. But I also believed that it was something that should come later in one's career: After all, what had I written at that point but only two books? (Later, he would publish an interview with me in *Newsweek* magazine entitled "The Reluctant Mambo King.")

Around that time a well-known Latin musician, of the old New York school, invited me over to his place on the West Side, where he did his best to get me high on coke—think he saw it as a perverse test of character. I declined that as well. Later, though I had long before interviewed the great Afro-Cuban composer Chico O'Farrill for my novel, I became a regular at his parties, where my local success was greeted warmly by some, skeptically by others. (I met musicians like Johnny Pacheco, Paquito D'Rivera, Mario Bauzá, Graciela, and of all people, Desi Arnaz's pianist and arranger, Marco Rizo, a truly sweet man.) Of those, Mario was my closest neighbor, literally living around the corner from me on 105th and Amsterdam: I'd go jogging in the mornings and find him sitting around on some milk crates with friends in front of a corner bodega Havana-style—he'd laugh at the sight of me, Mr. Slightly Chubby Four-Eyes, jogging by, his head shaking like Ray Charles's, the man rapping his knees. Inviting me up to his apartment a few times, he wanted me to write a book about his life story—I proposed that we do it with a tape recorder, and it made him really happy, but it became one of those things that I kept putting off and off, as my career got busier, until Mario, coming down with a cancer that racked his entire body, died a few years later.

While teaching my classes at Hofstra, I attended numerous literary fetes where I first befriended Paul Auster and Francine Prose, and many other writers as well—I won't bore you with such a list— but, after a while, as much as I enjoyed such an opportunity, I became somewhat befuddled by the fact that for as many events and literary gatherings as I attended, I rarely encountered another homegrown Latino author. A strange tale, however, about another "me." I had gone to a party and, introducing myself to several people, received a frosty reception. A slightly tipsy young woman told me, "You can't be him. I met him last night. He is dark haired and swarthy and noth-ing like you." Apparently, I soon learned, there was someone going around town impersonating me: Later, when someone from FSG turned up and explained that I was indeed Oscar Hijuelos, several of those folks came up to me to apologize; a few days later, I even received a note from the same woman, profusely begging my pardon. I wrote her back a one-word reply: "Uh-huh." And while I much appreciated my access to that world, and being that rare creature, a Latino writer suddenly in the spotlight, I felt put off by the fact that I seemed, for the most part, to be "it," as if I had become a temporary member of an exclusive club that, unless you had connections, was nearly impossible to get into.

. . .

Part of me wanted to step away; the other, my public persona, had no choice about the matter, especially after my novel had been nomi-nated for both the National Book Critics Circle and National Book awards. Part of the process, involving the latter, entailed a public reading at the National Arts Club. My fellow nominees included Amy Tan (*The Joy Luck Club*), Katherine Dunn (*Geek Love*), and John Casey (*Spartina*). Introductions made, each of the authors read from their books, though as I listened I felt somewhat annoyed by the general propriety of the selections, and while I had originally selected a section in which the Castillo brothers meet Desi Arnaz and his wife at the club Tropicana, in the spirit of livening things up, I made a last-moment change, choosing instead to quote from a monologue in Cesar's voice about all the women he'd deflowered in Cuba back in the 1940s, and—who knows what I was thinking— while Mr. Casey, I recall, read a description of a man whitewashing the hull of his boat in his backyard, I lingered on a passage wherein Cesar Castillo, in quite wonderful language, I thought, describes his methods for preserving a woman's virginity while entering another of her, uh, most intimate places (which, by the way, I first conceived in Italy, where they are obsessed with anal sex). I should have known better, but then I am fairly certain that winning the award was one of the last things on my mind. Needless to say, I think I shocked most of that rather conservative audience, which seemed to consist to a large extent of genteel white-haired New York society ladies, and in the end, my book did not receive the award—the genteel John Casey with his whitewashed hull and prose did.

On another evening, a few weeks later, after the winner had been announced at an elaborate banquet we all headed uptown to the famous Knopf publisher Sonny Mehta's apartment on Park Avenue, for a late-night party, and the main thing I can remember about that evening was my sense of relief at being away from all the photographers and reporters; at last it all seemed to be at an end. As a side note, however, I have to mention my mother's reaction. News of my nomination naturally made it into the Spanish-language newspapers like *El Nuevo Herald* in Miami and, of course, *El Diario* here in New York, a Latino writer, the son of immigrants, rising to such heights, a first. She'd call me now and then to ask whether I'd heard any news about winning it. Explaining that it didn't work that way, I'd hear a sigh on the other end. Nevertheless, it gave her bragging rights with her friends up and down Broadway and Amsterdam for the month or so while the selection process lasted, until all the excitement seemed to have ended as quickly as it had come. I took her out to dinner one evening with my brother, not long after the winner had been announced, and she was especially solemn, even moody.

Finally, I asked, "*Pero, qué te pasa, mamá?* What's going on?"

"*Ese premio,* what happened with it?"

"What, the National Book Award?" I shrugged. "Let me tell you, with all the odds against me, it was a miracle that I was even one of the nominees. But it was still an honor."

"*Ah, sí, un honor,*" she conceded. And then, thinking about something intensely, she turned to me, her expression one of severity and disappointment, and for a moment I could see balled up in her eyes everything that my pop had to contend with sometimes. Looking away, through the restaurant window, she said: "Yes, you were one of them," and she shook her head, adding, "*Pero no ganaste.* But you didn't win," a failing on my part that I believe she took as a personal slight.

. . .

Oh, but it wasn't all so contrary an experience: I spent an evening with William Gaddis and his lady companion, Muriel, eating Chinese takeout food and talking about literature in his East Side apartment. And once Mr. Glimcher's good taste in books had been verified by all my good press, he brought me more closely into his circle. Invited to dinner, I was to meet him on a certain corner on the East Side—and there, as I stood waiting one autumnal night, I saw the apparition of Pablo Picasso from his Braque period, with his thick dark hair combed in a half-moon crest over his brow, his eyes intense, demeanor solemn, standing alongside a column. He turned out to be Claude Picasso, the great painter's son, somewhere in his early forties, one of my dinner companions. Also to join us, another of Mr. Glimcher's friends, Sigourney Weaver. Of course, I enjoyed meeting them, but at no moment did I feel relaxed or that I fit in with such people, though they were perfectly open and friendly— Claude, a photographer, even offered to translate my work into French. Besides, with certain kinds of people, I would become more the listener—I've always hated small talk—and though I'd walk away from such an occasion feeling as if I had acquitted myself—for, as I recall, Ms. Weaver offered to fix me up with one of her actress friends—Mr. Glimcher, a keen observer of humanity, as an aside told me, "You really don't get just who you are, do you?" (That was his version of something my mother would cryptically tell me one day: "Your problem, *hijo*, is that you are *too much* like your father.") Whatever the reason, after such heady occasions, the sort that any number of other people would have embraced completely as a verification of their own worth—*achievement through association*, as it were—I was always happy to get home to my apartment.

More wonderfully, however, while I was riding the number 11 bus uptown on my way to see my mother one evening, I ran into my family's old friend Teddy Morgenbesser. I'd always wondered if he would be the sort to have read *The Mambo Kings*. If so, he might have recognized a bit of himself in the depiction of my character Bernardito

Mandelbaum, a Jewish guy gone *platanos*—or Cubanized—through his chumming around with one Cesar Castillo. If he had, it worried me that Teddy might have felt offended or lampooned. So what happened? I had been sitting in the back when he, getting off, saw me. Smiling, he summed up his feelings with a wink and a single sentence: "Oscar—I just loved that book. It was beautiful."

During that time, I had the strongest feeling of having pushed far off from the shore of who I had once been, though not a day passed when I did not have my share of memories and therefore my lingering depressions, no matter how wonderfully things were going for me professionally. I remember watching a version of *A Christmas Carol* that winter and feeling as if I were the ghost of myself destined to go through life dragging behind me my own apparently unshakeable memories, my life told in so many parts—illness, sheltered messed-up childhood, death of father, subsequent struggles with identity and just surviving, my sometime existence as a writer, etc. Until then, however, I really didn't think anyone could give a damn about me anyway—as a *cubano*, as a New Yorker, as a pensive, occasionally funny, melancholic man nearly forty years old tasting for the first time in his life a bit of success—though a loneliness-making one. As I pushed off from that shore, followed about by an image of myself as a sick child, or by my pop's very real and plaintive ghost, I hardly got through a week without being interviewed or photographed by someone—more and more often by foreign journalists, as *The Mambo Kings* sold all over Europe and the rest of the world (about thirty-six different foreign editions have been published to this day, discounting Britain and reissues).

Along the way, the attention I received led to some unexpected things. For one, the Cuban government's minister of culture, Abel Prieto, sent me a letter through PEN inviting me to visit Cuba. (Unfortunately, and something I now regret, it was simply unthinkable to me at the time. Visiting Havana, years later, I learned from my cousins that this minister often mentioned my book on Cuban radio.) At Hofstra, among my newly won frills, my schedule for the following semester became one of my own choosing—and I got to share an office with a professor who was never around, a jealousy-making triumph in a department where twenty-year veterans were sometimes crowded, as I recall, three and four to a room. Mr. Mascetti, who had gone to California, possibly to hide out from some people to whom he owed money, or to begin a new life (I really don't know), called me from Santa Monica after seeing some piece about me in the L.A. *Times*. With girls laughing wildly and music blaring happily in the background, he told me: "I'm so happy to heah that you're doing so fuckin' great, man!" My face eventually appeared in a very strange painting made for a calendar of "Famous Hispanics" sponsored by Budweiser beer: In it I, looking decades older, somewhat resemble, I am afraid to say, the former vice president Dick Cheney. I'd get invited to speak before public high school audiences as an example of a Latino who had come up without any advantages like them and made it, but the fact that I looked so white (or just like the enemy, in some of their eyes) confused the hell out of a lot of kids—I just didn't seem like them or their parents, and no amount of splainin', Lucy, about regressive familial genes or childhood illnesses or the kind of mixed neighborhood I had been raised in could make a difference. I would always accept such invitations, but I came to dread the actual moment when I would have to step onto an assembly stage at some rowdy school and hear, first thing, a rising murmur from the audience. If my schedule hadn't become so busy, I might have happily turned into a recluse. I recall that I felt so stressed-out about my public image that by the New Year of 1990, I had gotten back up to smoking two packs of Kools a day.

· · ·

On tour in England, during my spring break, where I smoked pack after pack of pungent Dunhills, I discovered that the promotional approach my publisher had taken for the book was one of supreme hipness: Hamish & Hamilton held the launch party at the jazz club Ronnie Scott's, and, as I recall, in addition to some straightforward news venues, I did countless interviews with print and radio music journalists, to the point that, talking constantly about the musical aspects of the book, I soon began to feel a little punchy. During one radio show for the BBC, my hostess, a very tall and aristocratic dame of the old school, made some comment about my height—at five feet eight—along the lines of, "Well, I hadn't realized that you Cubans were of such short stature," to which I answered, "Depends on whether you are speaking vertically or horizontally." (A long icy silence followed; then she cleared her throat and said, "Now, where were we?")

Later, I went to Belfast in the north to appear on the *Late Show* (Channel Four), broadcast live at eleven P.M. As it was the time of the troubles, as they say, it was the only program I have ever appeared on where I had to go through a metal detector and submit to a patting-down to get into the studio. There were also German shepherds being led through the place, sniffing around for bombs. The audience, of local townspeople, had to go through the same procedures: Once inside they could enjoy a large well-stocked horseshoe bar and were encouraged to drink to their hearts' content, as were the guests. I'd later learn that one of the in-jokes between our congenial Irish host, a fellow with a name like Mulligan, and the audience was that, sooner or later, he'd put on an act or do an interview with someone so far gone as to be completely amusing. In my instance, we had absolutely no discussion whatsoever of what he might ask me, though he did say it would be something really easy. In the meantime, I drank vodka and tonics and smoked—just about everyone in the audience did too—and no sooner would I put an empty glass down than would some assistant rush over with another from the bar. They actually had someone keeping their eyes on me just for that purpose.

When I finally went on camera, after a completely inebriated Irish punk band had performed, I was having trouble feeling my gums. Suddenly, my host sat down beside me, a beam of light blazed over our table, a camera rolled in, and smiling affably, with a deep brogue, he said: "Well, here I am sitting with my friend from America, Oscar Heeejewlloss, and he has written a new book and a very interesting one at that."

After a few congenial remarks he turned to me and said: "Now, may I ask you a simple question?"

"Sure."

"Would you explain to the people of Ireland how Cuban music relates to them, okay?"

I recall making some blithering idiot explanations of the northern Spanish and southern Irish being related, some business about how the bagpipe scales performed on a *gaeta* in Spain influenced the notion of a Cuban jam—"What is sometimes called '*una quemada*'"—and otherwise dancing around the question with a logic that might have made some sense if everyone else were drunk, that Cubans and the Irish, having Spanish blood in common, were really distant cousins just like Ricky and Lucy. I can't imagine what they made of seeing someone—who looked far more Irish than Cuban—explaining such things, but I suppose that even if I were Desi Arnaz himself, it would have been a difficult task anyway. In any event, how I answered didn't matter—I'd gotten a picture of the book jacket shown all over Northern Ireland and though I was fairly hammered during that live broadcast, my publishers in London told me that of all my appearances thus far it had been my more "relaxed."

· · ·

By the time I was done touring the States and UK, I had gotten so sick and tired of talking about *The Mambo Kings Play Songs of Love* that I found myself thinking that were I never to mention a word of that book again, it would be fine with me. And so, with a few days left before resuming my duties at Hofstra, I had taken up Francine Prose's generous offer to spend a weekend in her upstate home: I'd gone off one overcast morning with my girlfriend to prowl about the local antique shops and had come back with an iconic painting of the Holy Mother, which a Greek friend has since defined as a "black Madonna," when the phone rang. It could only have been my agent—no one else had that number. Excitedly, she told me: "Don't go anywhere—someone important is going to call you."

About ten minutes later, when the telephone rang again, I could hear the unmistakably raspy and lively voice of my publisher himself, Roger Straus Jr.

"My boy," he said. "You've done it!"

"Done what?"

"Why, you've been awarded the Pulitzer Prize for Fiction—that's what!"

"Say that again?" I recall asking him.

He did, and went on jovially: "I can't begin to tell you how proudly I—all of us—feel over your accomplishment. Well, well done, young man!"

What does one feel in such moments? A kind of disbelief, and in my case, a hokey sentimentality, over its significance. The first thing I thought, even as I lit a cigarette, was, of course, that a kind of miracle had taken place, that God (or whatever rules the world) had, for a change, decidedly looked out for me; that I had passed through a glorious door into a future that neither I nor my mother or father could have imagined when I was growing up; and yes, I felt a tremendous gratitude to whomever had been out there to make such a decision— for I had never really thought I would ever win anything (even the National Book Award nomination seemed a lark).

"Thank you, sir," I told him.

After some further niceties, Mr. Straus, explaining that there would be a great number of people waiting to speak to me, said good-bye. As he predicted, one reporter after the other, scheduled through my agent, called me from all over the country. Though I had a few breathers, I spent most of that afternoon and the next day talking about that which I had already been sick and tired of talking about—what else?—*The Mambo Kings* and myself, my destiny for the coming months, the coming years. In every conversation, these questions: Given my humble roots, how did I, as the son of Cuban immigrants, feel to be awarded a Pulitzer? And: Now that I had somehow scaled the Olympian heights of literature, how did I feel about becoming the *first Hispanic* to Win a Pulitzer Prize in Fiction?

The latter made me feel both proud and, at the same time, oddly singled out for the wrong reasons. Remember that back in 1990, my award had come on the heels of a period in America when the virtues of affirmative action were being debated: I couldn't help but feel, as I know others did, as if my prize had something to do with the afterglow of that benevolence. Later, I'd encounter a lot of folks who would all but voice the opinion that it was time for *some Hispanic* to finally win a prize like that, as if I happened to be the lucky one.

Indeed I was fortunate to have been in the right place, with the right house, at the right time, with the right book, and though *Mambo Kings*, under whatever circumstances, remains a unique creation, it could have easily slipped through the cracks. Just look at the record: Aside from myself and, nearly twenty years later, Junot Díaz, no other Latino has been given a Pulitzer in fiction. As for the National Book Award? Despite its fifty-plus-year history, a Latino novel has yet to win a single one. (And, if I may, more sadly, remark: Though an array of wonderful books by gifted authors like Sandra Cisneros, Cristina Garcia, Rosario Ferre, Virgil Suarez, Elena Castedo, and Patricia Engle, among others, has since been published, with a fair amount of attention paid to them, the balance in more recent years has tipped back to where it had once been, wherein the works of Latino authors are, so I have recently heard, considered old hat and of a category hardly deserving critical attention, as if Latino writing, once again, has fallen to the wayside in terms of critical appreciation as a form of authentically American literature.

In the weeks to follow, relatives I never even knew about suddenly came out of the woodwork, though, oddly enough, I never heard a word from my aunts Maya and Borja in Florida. (But at least I came into contact with my cousin Dalgis, my *tio* Oscar's daughter, whom I would later meet in California.) Mas Canosa's Cuban-American Freedom Foundation in Miami offered me a large sum of money to write an anti-Castro pamphlet on their behalf. (I refused, though not particularly for ideological reasons: I just didn't want to be selling myself to anyone, on the left or right.) I met people like Sting and Lou Reed and David Byrne, and many Latin musicians and personalities like Tito Puente and Celia Cruz and Graciela from the epoch I had written about. (My greatest honor? Playing the chords to "Guantana-mera" on the piano, while backing up Graciela as she sang at a party.) For at least a few years, I became one of the darlings of New York high society—at one dinner, I sat between Barbara Walters and Bill

Blass, at another with Lauren Hutton. At Bill Clinton's first formal dinner at the White House, shortly after he had come into office, I spent the night hanging out with the playwright August Wilson, an unrepentant chain-smoker, who remained my good friend until his recent death. A few years later, at a second White House dinner, a state affair in honor of the Colombian president Andrés Pastrana, I had the incredible thrill of meeting Gabriel García Márquez, who, finding out that I was the author of *Mambo Kings*, told me, "That's a book I wish I had written." (God bless you, maestro.) Around that time, I received an honorary doctorate from my alma mater, City College, a Literary Lion medal from the New York Public Library, and other awards that, quite frankly, I can't now recall, or that don't seem to have really mattered to the world in the long run, but that made me feel somewhat proud back when, as if I had done something good for my community—*los latinos*—by opening some doors, at least in terms of publishing, for suddenly, New York houses were actively seeking out such authors, a feeling that would most strongly come to me when I would meet a young aspiring Latino writer who, looking to me as, yes, a role model, wanted to one day duplicate my success, though I would hope without having to smoke all those cigarettes.

. . .

My mother, for what it's worth, would live off my Pulitzer distinction for years. Walking around the neighborhood like a grand dame, she took to wearing oversize sun hats with florid bands so that no one could miss her, and, as with my first book, carried the *New York Times* announcement of my prize tucked in a transparent plastic sleeve inside her purse, anxious to show it to anyone who expressed even the slightest interest. Calling out to shop-owner friends along Broadway, as we'd walk along, she'd say, "This is my boy, *el escritor!*" Then ask, laughing: "Have you something you'd like him to write for you?" (After all, I was her suddenly famous son, and as a result, we got along better after that, but the flip side? She could not look at me without suggesting that I buy myself a wig, the kind that true artists wear, like Liberace did.)

But to go back to the day when I first received the news, it wasn't until the later afternoon, with the gloom of that day finally lifting, that did I experience, while traipsing out into the emerging sunlight, a moment of true elation. I was in the front yard, relieved to be off the telephone, when I sensed in the shifting of light across the lawn my pop's presence. I will swear that as the light swelled, blinking, around me, he was there, standing just behind me and, I like to think, smiling, his spirit aglow with pride over my sudden accomplishment—not just because I would have my name and picture in the newspapers (though I would be proud of the fact that millions of people would see the rare surname *Hijuelos* in print) or because Tom Brokaw would nearly mispronounce my *apellido* over the air that next evening, but perhaps because I had taken so many disparate energies and hard emotions from *our* lives and turned them into something that so many people, across these United States and, as well, the world (I wonder what my pop would have made of seeing a Spanish-language edition of my book published in Madrid, in the windows of shops near the Prado, or in Japanese, sold off a Tokyo kiosk), might well enjoy and appreciate. I remember feeling that although he had not lived long enough for me to really know him, my novel, *The Mambo Kings*, was my way of doing just that, of holding a conversation with him, though he had long since been dead. His spirit, for better and for worse, in its kindness and gentleness, in its melancholy and, alternately, exuberance, his love of life, fear of death, his passions and vices—down to the thousands of drinks he had consumed and cigarettes he smoked—were all there, transformed, in that book. Or to put it differently, he was alive again, if only as a momentary illusion—and that, ladies and gents, felt absolutely superb.

Acknowledgments

. . .

I would like to thank my brother, José-Pascual, for his input about the chronology regarding my mother and father's lives in the 1940s, as well as for the rooftop photograph that graces the cover of this book. And to my cousin Natasha Bermudez, upon whose research I have largely based my references to the Hijuelos family line.

Thanks should also go to Lori Marie Carlson, for her translation of my mother's poem featured in this book, as well to the Free Press, in whose publication, *Burnt Sugar*, an anthology of Cuban poetry, "This Is My Book" first appeared. Further thanks go to the teachers who influenced my development as a writer: the late Susan Sontag and Donald Barthelme, and Frederic Tuten, who is, I am happy to say, still writing away. At Gotham, my thanks go out to William Shinker, who first encouraged this work, and to Lauren Marino and Cara Bedick. My gratitude also goes out to Jennifer Lyons, Karen Levinson, Lorna Owen and José Miguel Oviedo, whose inputs were invaluable. As for the others, from Richard Muller-Thym, a lifelong friend, to those who have always mattered to me, I also give thanks.

Finally, I thank all the wonderful Latinos—misunderstood as we may sometimes be—who have supported and shown me affection in the past.